'Elise Tipton's account of modern Japan is innovative, accessible and extremely useful. With her interest in Japan's minorities, her concern with developments since World War 2, and her sensitivity to contentious scholarly issues, she has managed to break new ground without ignoring any of the old, and certainly without sacrificing accuracy, coherence or readability.'

Professor Harold Bolitho, Edwin O. Reischauer Institute of Japanese Studies, *Harvard University*

'Elise Tipton has produced a lively and compelling synthesis, full of human interest and interpretative insight, of modern Japanese social and political history down to recent times. Her narrative of what Japan's modern trajectory has meant for women and minorities whose experience has been too-long neglected is especially unforgettable. This is an excellent book. I recommend it wholeheartedly.'

Stephen S. Large, Reader in Modern Japanese History, *University of Cambridge*

This comprehensive textbook provides a concise and fascinating introduction to the social, cultural and political history of modern Japan. Ranging from the Tokugawa period to the present day, *Modern Japan* charts the country's evolution into a modernized, economic and political world power.

The book widens the traditional approach to Japanese history to include social as well as political factors in the country's growth. Elise Tipton examines social groups and developments that have previously been neglected, such as gender issues, ethnic minorities, labour conditions, popular culture and daily life. Through this charting of a complex web of social and political interaction, her book represents a unique picture of the diversity of modern Japan and its people.

Highly accessible, this completely up-to-date textbook is an essential resource for students, teachers and scholars of Japanese Studies, History and Politics.

Elise K. Tipton is Associate Professor in Japanese Studies at the University of Sydney, Australia. She has published widely on modern Japanese history, including *The Japanese Police State: The Tokkō in Interwar Japan* (Allen and Unwin: 1990/1), *Society and the State in Interwar Japan* (Routledge: 1997), and co-edited *Being Modern in Japan: Culture and Society from the 1910s to the 1930s* (University of Hawaii Press: 2000).

The Nissan Institute/Routledge Japanese Studies Series

Editorial Board

J.A.A. Stockwin, Nissan Professor of Modern Japanese Studies, University of Oxford and Director, Nissan Institute of Japanese Studies; Teigo Yoshida, formerly Professor of the University of Tokyo; Frank Langdon, Professor, Institute of International Relations, University of British Columbia; Alan Rix, Executive Dean, Faculty of Arts, The University of Queensland; Junji Banno, formerly Professor of the University of Tokyo, now Professor, Chiba University; Leonard Schoppa, Associate Professor, Department of Government and Foreign Affairs, and Director of the East Asia Center, University of Virginia

Other titles in the series:

The Myth of Japanese Uniqueness
Peter Dale

The Emperor's Adviser: Saionji Kinmochi and pre-war Japanese politics
Lesley Connors

A History of Japanese Economic Thought
Tessa Morris-Suzuki

The Establishment of the Japanese Constitutional System
Junji Banno, translated by J.A.A. Stockwin

Industrial Relations in Japan: the peripheral workforce
Norma Chalmers

Banking Policy in Japan: American efforts at reform during the Occupation
William M. Tsutsui

Educational Reform in Japan
Leonard Schoppa

How the Japanese Learn to Work: second edition
Ronald P. Dore and Mari Sako

Japanese Economic Development: theory and practice: second edition
Penelope Francks

Japan and Protection: the growth of protectionist sentiment and the Japanese response
Syed Javed Maswood

The Soil, by Nagatsuka Takashi: a portrait of rural life in Meiji Japan
Translated and with an introduction by Ann Waswo

Biotechnology in Japan
Malcolm Brock

Britain's Educational Reform: a comparison with Japan
Michael Howarth

Language and the Modern State: the reform of written Japanese
Nanette Twine

Industrial Harmony in Modern Japan: the intervention of a tradition
W. Dean Kinzley

Japanese Science Fiction: a view of a changing society
Robert Matthew

The Japanese Numbers Game: the use and understanding of numbers in modern Japan
Thomas Crump

Modern Japan

A social and political history

Elise K. Tipton

London and New York

To Daisy L. Kurashige

First published 2002 by Routledge
11 New Fetter Lane, London EC4P 4EE

Simultaneously published in the USA and Canada
by Routledge
29 West 35th Street, New York, NY 10001

Routledge is an imprint of the Taylor & Francis Group

© 2002 Elise K. Tipton

Typeset in Times New Roman by Graphicraft Limited, Hong Kong
Printed and bound in Great Britain by TJ International Ltd,
Padstow, Cornwall

British Library Cataloguing in Publication Data
A catalogue record for this book is available from the British Library

Library of Congress Cataloging in Publication Data
A catalog record for this book has been requested

ISBN 0–415–18537–8 (hbk)
ISBN 0–415–18538–6 (pbk)

Contents

Illustrations

Series editor's preface

If there is an unforgettable date that marks the beginning of the twenty-first century, it is that of 11 September 2001. Whether and how far the terrible events of that day will have changed the history of the new century and set it on a course other than that it would otherwise have taken will be for future historians to say. The terrorist attacks on the United States led to a war that largely eliminated the Taliban and the Osama Bin Laden organization from Afghanistan. Its rationale was proclaimed to be that of an international struggle against terrorism. In February 2002, President Bush publicly described Iraq, Iran and North Korea as an 'axis of evil', in that they were dictatorial states sponsoring terrorist activities. Despite the great sympathy outside the United States for the Americans after the terrorist outrage, this speech met with widespread criticism on the grounds that it did not discriminate between three very different regimes, and that in any case terrorism was not the only 'enemy' that should be combated. The critics argued that more thought should be given to the causes of terrorism and to an understanding of why terrorists regarded US interests as a legitimate target. American 'unilateralism' and singlemindedness were becoming a deepening concern in Europe and elsewhere.

One effect of 11 September has been a revival of interest in the concept of 'civilization' and of 'the civilized world'. A manichaean vision of forces of civilization pitted against forces of darkness infuses much of the commentary to which the events of that day have given rise. In practice, however, 'civilisation' does not fit easily with those hundreds of millions of people who cannot escape from dire poverty, intolerance and exploitation. Unless these problems are tackled with determination and intelligence, it should surprise nobody that terror will be used to horrifying effect against the world deemed 'civilized'.

In all significant senses Japan today is part of our 'civilized world'. The average standard of living of the Japanese people is high. The GNP of Japan is second only to that of the United States, and is larger than the combined GNP of all the other countries of Asia. Even the economy of China, though attracting much attention for the rapidity of its growth and for its success in Japanese markets, is many times smaller than that of

Japan. The national interests of Japan, taking a hard-nosed view, lie with the interests of the so-called 'civilized' countries and their broad set of economic, political, social and moral values. Japan in most ways is an open democratic society. Since the early 1990s it has been suffering from severe economic and political mismanagement. In the widest of terms the problem is one of a painful transition from one form of political economy to another. The process of transition is far from over and mismanagement has cost the economy dearly. Japan is also faced by deeper structural problems, including that of a rapidly aging population. Nevertheless, the key point is that this is a gigantic economic power with enormous international weight.

The Japanese, being a proud people and heirs to an ancient civilization, have long been concerned to map out their own path in the world, and this creates a certain tension with the trends of globalization apparent in the world today. Nevertheless, Japan is slowly forging its own set of compromises whereby assimilation to essential global norms of behaviour is tempered by the maintenance of structures and practices based on its own cultural experiences. The next stage, however, in which Japanese expertise and commitment are desperately needed, is the long and painful task of reducing and eventually eliminating, not only the common terrorist enemy, but also the deepest causes of terrorism, namely global inequality, endemic poverty and squalor, exploitation and rejection. Japanese help is needed, not just in combating terrorism, but also in universalizing the conditions for civilization.

The Nissan Institute/Routledge Japanese Studies Series was begun in 1986 and has now passed well beyond its fiftieth volume. It seeks to foster an informed and balanced, but not uncritical, understanding of Japan. One aim of the series is to show the depth and variety of Japanese institutions, practices and ideas. Another is, by using comparisons, to see what lessons, positive or negative, can be drawn for other countries. The tendency in commentary on Japan to resort to out-dated, ill-informed or sensational stereotypes still remains, and needs to be combated.

In this book Elise Tipton provides an elegant and readable social and political history of modern Japan. She takes the story through from the early Tokugawa period in the seventeenth century to the beginning of the twenty-first century. While giving effective coverage of political, economic and military developments, she balances this with a deep concern for the lives of ordinary people and how they were affected by the actions of people and institutions that governed them.

She acknowledges, for instance, the success of Prime Minister Ikeda's 'income doubling' policies of the 1960s, and the social transformation that the economic miracle in that period created. But she is also at pains to show that the 'Japan Incorporated' metaphor popular at the time, whereby government officials claimed that they were the essential 'managers' of the economic 'miracle', was true only within very narrow limits. In addition, she demonstrates the deleterious environmental and other effects that ultra-rapid economic growth created.

The book is particularly strong on the part played by women in modern Japanese history, and the various subtle ways in which the system has continued to discriminate against them, despite their enormous contribution to national prosperity over many decades. Her final chapter is a sobering reflection on the 1990s, which has come to be called the 'lost decade'. This was the decade in which the stranglehold of vested interests combined with the spinelessness of political leaders in the face of gathering economic crisis, precluding the delivery of much-needed structural reform.

This is a critical history of how Japan has come to be where it is today, and is full of insight.

J.A.A. Stockwin

Preface

There have been many attempts to interpret the history of modern Japan. Until the last decade, that history was often written to explain Japan's success in achieving industrialization and modernization since the mid-nineteenth century. Considering Japan's uncertain recovery from a decade of economic stagnation, that history may have lost some of its rosy glow. Even before the collapse of the 'bubble' economy, however, historians had begun to question a narrow perspective focused on economic success led by Japan's governmental and business elites.

This book is an attempt to broaden the perspective on Japan's modern history by putting more emphasis on social groups and developments that have previously been neglected. In particular, I have given attention to women and minorities who contributed greatly to Japan's drive to modern economic growth and national power, but who still have not benefited equally with men and mainstream Japanese. In doing so, I have sought to reveal the diversity of Japanese society and the complexity of the modernization process in Japan. At the same time this is not solely a social history of Japan, nor a history of the marginalized or peripheral, but also an attempt to explore links between social and political developments of the various periods and to blur the boundaries between them. There is no denying the importance of politics and diplomacy, particularly the role of the state, in Japan's modern development, precisely because the state has sought to guide or more actively intervene in everyday life. Nevertheless, politics has not always taken command, and Japanese people have often been more concerned with issues closer to their individual interests than those of the government. Examining these interests as well as the opportunities and limitations on pursuing them is one aim of this book.

Readers should also notice the space allotted in this book to different periods in Japan's modern history and to varying perspectives on that history. It has been over fifty years since the Second World War ended, yet historians have only recently begun to treat those decades as history. We are reliant on much work done by sociologists, anthropologists and political scientists, but historians have somewhat different concerns from these social scientists. Here the objective is to contribute to the project of setting the period into the broader context of Japan's development during the past century and a half. As will become evident, the past is very much part of the present, but not necessarily because of the persistence of 'tradition'. Moreover, because the past is part of the present, it is constantly reshaped by concerns of the present. Consequently, the history of modern Japan, as is the case in other societies, is highly contested. I have offered my version of it here, but I have also introduced differing viewpoints and interpretations regarding a number of major events and other historical developments.

The opportunity for me to do this was provided by the editors at Routledge. First thanks must go to Victoria Smith, Asian Studies Editor, who encouraged me to undertake this project. Her successor, Craig Fowlie, has been equally supportive, as well as patient in awaiting its completion. Jennifer Lovel, Assistant Editor for Politics and Asian Studies, kindly arranged for the preparation of the two maps. The Research Institute for the Humanities and Social Sciences at the University of Sydney provided me with time off from teaching and administration in 1998 to make substantial progress on the first draft, and a study leave in 2000 enabled me to complete it. Although I have not been able to follow all their suggestions, five anonymous readers gave me many helpful comments for revisions, and corrected what would have been embarrassing errors of fact if left as is. My husband Ben took time from his vacation to read the initial draft, and as always, I have benefited from his constructive criticisms and ongoing support.

As is customary, I have followed Japanese name order for Japanese names, which is surname first, unless the person is writing in English and following Western name order. I have omitted macrons for major Japanese place names, such as Tokyo and Hokkaido, and for words that have come into common usage in English, such as shogun and zaibatsu.

Elise K. Tipton

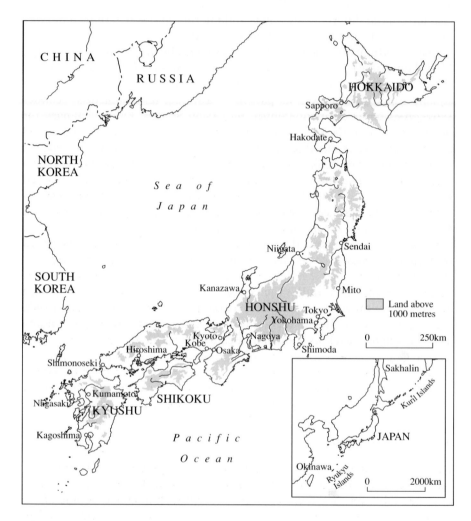

Map 1.1 Modern Japan

1   Tokugawa background
The ideal and the real

'Tokugawa Japan'. If the time and place suggests any picture at all, it is probably a Japan of samurai warriors, ninja, rice paddies and geisha. Asked to add a few political and social features to the picture, one might come up with a shogun, the country isolated from foreign contact, and a rigid feudal society of bowing samurai and commoners alike. What relevance does this picture of 'traditional' Japan have for a history of modern Japan except to present a stark contrast to the picture of present-day high-tech Japan, the second most powerful economy in the world?

Fifty years ago the answer might have been 'none'. Western histories of modern Japan started with 1853, the year that Commodore Perry 'opened' Japan to contact with the West, or with 1868, the year of the Meiji Restoration and the beginning of the government which consciously started Japan's modernization process. Today, however, no history of modern Japan would ignore the Tokugawa conditions which shaped that modernization process. The manner and extent of that influence remain a matter of debate which will be dealt with in a later chapter. The aim in this chapter is to provide an overview of the social changes that occurred during more than two and a half centuries of Tokugawa rule and that make comprehensible, though not inevitable, the great transformation of the late nineteenth century.

The Tokugawa order

Because the impetus for change derived from a growing gap between the official ideal of the socioeconomic and political order on the one hand, and the reality on the other, we need to begin with a simple outline of the Tokugawa social and political structure and the assumptions and objectives underlying it.

Perhaps the most fundamental attribute of the Tokugawa governing structure was its military character, the result of over a century and a half of civil war. Throughout the second half of the fifteenth century and the whole of the sixteenth century, Japan had been politically fragmented into 250 and sometimes considerably more territories dominated by military lords who constantly fought one another to expand their domains. In this situation

Japan displayed many similarities with the feudalism of contemporary Western Europe. Oda Nobunaga, the first of the 'Three Heroes' or 'Great Unifiers', began the process of military unification in the 1560s, and Toyotomi Hideyoshi completed it in 1591. Hideyoshi carried out highly significant administrative measures, notably a nationwide 'sword hunt' to disarm the peasants, and a land survey which separated samurai from peasants and demonstrated recognition by the other feudal lords of his pre-eminence as sole proprietary lord in the country. These policies contributed greatly to a fundamental revolution in Japanese political and social institutions. Hideyoshi also launched two invasions of Korea as part of an ambitious attempt to create a Japanese empire extending through China.

Besides failing to conquer Korea, however, Hideyoshi was not successful in passing on his power and authority to his 5-year-old son, as his generals soon began to vie with each other for pre-eminence after his death in 1598. Out of the intrigues and alliances, two large coalitions of feudal lords or *daimyō* emerged, bringing their armies of 80,000 each to confront each other at the battle of Sekigahara in 1600. After his victory, Tokugawa Ieyasu and his heirs constructed a system in the first half of the seventeenth century that was to remain stable enough to last for more than two and a half centuries; that is, until the Meiji Restoration of 1868. Ieyasu initially strived to legitimize his power with the help of imperial authority by becoming the emperor's highest military official – 'barbarian-quelling generalissimo' or shogun. In order to end the bloody civil wars and to ensure peace as well as lasting Tokugawa rule, Ieyasu and his successors had to create a political and social structure which would maintain control over the other *daimyō*. They forced the *daimyō* to swear loyalty and service to the Tokugawa shogun in a feudal manner and in return reinvested them with domains, now defined in terms of income calculated in measures of rice as well as territories. This included even former enemies at Sekigahara, the so-called 'outside' or *tozama daimyō*, who remained some of the wealthiest but held domains far from the political and economic centre of the country.

On a practical level the early Tokugawa shoguns also continued or extended many methods that *daimyō* had previously been utilizing to control their samurai retainers, such as rotation and confiscation of fiefs, strategic placement of *daimyō* allies, marriages and adoptions to cement political links, and bestowal of honours and material rewards for meritorious service and loyalty. Perhaps the most important of these in its long-term effects was the system of alternate attendance (*sankin kōtai*). This represented the culmination and institutionalization of the practice of hostage-taking by feudal lords to ensure the loyalty of samurai vassals in a time when treason and betrayal ran rife. The Tokugawa system required *daimyō* to be in attendance at shogunal headquarters in Edo (present-day Tokyo) so that the shogunate could keep them under close supervision. In alternate periods, usually every other year, when they were allowed to return to their domains, the shogunate forced them to leave their families in Edo as hostages. The system was also designed to drain the financial resources of the *daimyō* since it required not simply minimal maintenance of two residences, but residences and personnel of a number and level of luxury theoretically suitable for entertaining visits of the shogun.

In addition, the shogunate instituted restrictions on foreign trade to deprive *daimyō* of lucrative sources of revenue, and to reduce political threats associated with Spanish and Portuguese missionaries. The shogunate also utilized diplomatic relations to enhance the status of the shogun. These were the motives behind the so-called closing of the country in the 1630s which involved the suppression of Christianity and expulsion of all Europeans apart from the Protestant Dutch after they demonstrated that their interests were confined to trade and not religious proselytizing or politics. The shogunate confined the Dutch to a man-made island in Nagasaki harbour and maintained a monopoly control over foreign trade and its profits through that port. Notable exceptions, however, were permission for Tsushima's trade with Korea and Satsuma's with the Ryukyu Islands in the south. Korean embassies received by the shogun helped to legitimize the Tokugawa hegemony over the *daimyō*, since the shogunate treated them as tribute missions in a Japan-centred world order, even though from the Korean perspective Korea regarded the Japanese ruler as an equal rather than a superior. For the same reason, the shogunate refused to engage in official relations with China because this would have meant acknowledgement of a subordinate position in the Chinese world order and loss of status in the eyes of the *daimyō*, but it carried out a profitable trade with private Chinese merchants through Nagasaki. While limiting contact with Europe, Japan thus maintained active relations with other East Asian countries, so that the image of a closed country should not be overdrawn.

The various practical measures taken to ensure Tokugawa hegemony were necessary since the shogunate or *bakufu* governed and taxed areas only under direct Tokugawa control (amounting to about one-quarter of Japan) and possessed authority over the *daimyō* only in matters such as foreign policy which affected the country as a whole. It delegated administration of the rest of the country to the *daimyō*, who governed and obtained income from their domains known as *han* more or less as they pleased so long as they did not display disloyalty to the shogunate. Consequently, although the Tokugawa shogunate was the most centralized government Japan had had so far in its history, it did not exercise complete centralized authority. Hence, the term *bakuhan* in Japanese for the system representing a balance of power between the *bakufu* and *han*.

From a broader historical perspective, the consolidation of this balance between central authority and local autonomy differed from what was happening in Western Europe, where absolute monarchies were in the process of being established. In the past, the divergence from European developments led historians to view the Tokugawa system negatively. The reference by some historians to 'refeudalization' during the early 1600s suggests their view of the Tokugawa political order as a kind of arrested political develop-ment which could be blamed for Japan's subsequently missing out on the scientific and industrial revolutions, falling behind the West and therefore having to 'catch up' in the nineteenth and twentieth centuries. Focus on the limited contact with Europe reinforced this view of backwardness. Similarly, the once prevalent description of the system as 'centralized feudalism' high-lights the difference from Western political developments. It also implies a contradictory nature, since feudalism is characterized by decentralized political authority, and hence a rather negative judgement of it.

When historians' focus remained on Tokugawa feudalism, the establish-ment by the Tokugawas of a hierarchical, hereditary four-class system drew attention to the samurai as the most important actors in the history of the period as well as reinforcing the overall image of stagnation and oppression. This latter tendency was especially strong among Marxist Japanese scholars, for in Marxian use, 'feudal' refers to a society where farmers are bound to the land and denied political power, paying high taxes to a ruling class of military men. In post-Second World War Japanese usages, 'feudal' often referred to social and political traits going back to the Tokugawa period that had not yet been destroyed in the process of industrialization and modernization, such as hierarchical structures and relationships, loyalty and obedience to superiors, and vertical divisions in society. The term was there-fore often used in critiques of Japanese society and politics.

The important point in this discussion of debates over appropriate terms to describe the Tokugawa order is that views of the past are shaped by evaluations of the present. Consequently, in light of Japan's dramatic eco-nomic success since the Second World War, the image of Tokugawa Japan has gradually changed. Instead of depicting Tokugawa Japan as the feudal source of the authoritarianism and repression characteristic of politics until the end of the Second World War, many historians now emphasize the eco-nomic and social changes which occurred beneath the feudal facade and laid the foundations for modern developments. Should the Japanese economy collapse during the next few years, perhaps we will see a return to the image of backwardness and rigidity. At present, however, Conrad Totman's pre-ferred term of 'integral bureaucracy' indicates more positive evaluations of Japan's past. It suggests the early modern features of the Tokugawa period by shifting attention to the important role played by merchants as well as the samurai in Tokugawa society. Merchants had arisen as a new social group during the medieval period, but became prosperous and economically powerful during the Tokugawa period. 'Integral' reflects a complex relation-ship of cooperation between merchants and samurai. However, the term does not suggest the tension and conflict that also developed between them.

The social and political tensions inherent in the Tokugawa system, as between shogun and *daimyō* and between samurai and merchants, were kept in check for a long time. At first they were assuaged and later they were masked by the ideological rationalization of the Tokugawa order.

Neo-Confucianism from China, via Korea, developed as another method used in the process of legitimation and stabilization in the seventeenth century. Although historians such as Herman Ooms have revealed that NeoConfucianism was not the exclusive orthodoxy once presumed, it is still fair to say that it provided a philosophical foundation not only for the political order but the socioeconomic order as well. Rather than a religion, NeoConfucianism constituted an ethical code linking proper behaviour in social life to proper conduct of government. Since it posited that good government is a government ruled by ethical, cultured men and a benevolent paternalistic ruler, it could be used to help transform the samurai class into a civilian bureaucratic class in a time of peace.

In its assumption of a natural hierarchical order in society, it provided a justification for the class system which ranked the four main classes – samurai, peasants, artisans and merchants – in order of their presumed usefulness to society. Those employed in what were considered 'impure' occupations, most associated with killing animals and burying the dead, fell below and outside the four main classes and were known as *eta* (literally, 'great filth'). Criminals, prostitutes and actors were also categorized as outcasts, in their case *hinin* ('nonhuman'). Assumptions of female inferiority similarly relegated women to a subordinate status in society, though not subjected to systematic discrimination like *eta* and *hinin*. As Kaibara Ekken's *Onna daigaku* (*The Great Learning for Women*) of 1716 declared, 'seven or eight out of every ten women' suffered from the 'five infirmities' of indocility, discontent, jealousy, silliness and slander. The social order was further justified by the assertion that if everyone performed the duties and obligations of their place in society, there would be order, harmony and stability.

NeoConfucianism became the basis for samurai education, but it was not only a philosophy for the ruling class. It was popularized and diffused among both sexes and all classes and ages in Tokugawa society. For example, Kaibara's didactic writings helped to spread Confucian ethics among women and children of all classes. In his *Precepts for Children* (*Shogaku-kun*), he preached the primacy of filial piety and love of relatives as one with the obligation to serve nature, while his *Onna daigaku* emphasized women's duty to obey their husbands, in-laws and seniors and to practise frugality and modesty. Ishida Baigan also formulated a body of social and ethical teachings for townspeople known as Shingaku. He supported sumptuary regulations distinguishing proper clothing for the various classes as a means to maintain the social hierarchy from an ethical as well as an economical point of view: 'Lowly townsmen who are so ostentatious are criminals who violate moral principles.'[1] NeoConfucianism's popularization as well as maintenance as an officially approved school of thought helped to mask tensions that grew during the course of the Tokugawa period. In fact, its proclamation as the orthodox school of thought during the 1790s reveals the extent to which Tokugawa authorities saw tensions undermining acceptance of the existing system, leading to a perceived necessity to bolster its ideological rationale.

Urbanization, commercialization and the rise of the *chōnin* class

According to NeoConfucian theory, the Tokugawa polity should have been based on an agrarian economy, run by hard-working peasants growing rice and making the other necessities of life for themselves. The placement of peasants second to the ruling samurai class reflected the NeoConfucian view of peasants as more productive members of society than artisans or merchants. The reliance of the taxation system on a land tax paid in rice and other agricultural products indicates the dependence on (or exploitation of) the peasants for the governance of the country. These views of what was peasants' proper work and position in society remained officially unchanged throughout the Tokugawa period.

In reality, however, the socioeconomic basis of the political and social order underwent profound changes. Contrary to traditional views, the Tokugawa economy, society and culture did not stagnate, but rather developed in ways that economic historians agree laid foundations for industrialization and modern economic growth. Whether the changes made the Meiji Restoration inevitable is nevertheless still a matter of debate.

The Tokugawas' methods for controlling the *daimyō* and samurai ironically contributed to the economic and social changes which gradually undermined the feudal structure. Hideyoshi, the second of the 'Great Unifiers', had already separated samurai from peasants and prohibited their owning land. The four-class system simply made occupational status hereditary, but in doing so reinforced the movement of samurai into castle towns, which became the most important type of provincial town during the Tokugawa period. During the first two decades of the seventeenth century, Ieyasu ordered small castles destroyed and one large castle built as the capital of each *han*. All *han* samurai lived there, making up typically half of the population and giving castle towns a military character as well as the function of an administrative centre for the domain.

From the late seventeenth century, however, their military character gradually changed as their economic role increased. Castle towns with substantial populations, such as Kanazawa and Nagoya with almost 100,000 people, represented large markets, initially for basic living necessities but increasingly for other consumption items. Consequently, they attracted merchants and artisans to supply their wants and needs. Castle towns thus became regional economic centres as well as regional political-administrative centres.

Another political control method, namely the system of alternate attendance, contributed to the development of transportation and communication networks throughout the entire country which, in turn, fostered and facilitated establishment and growth of other smaller urban areas and expansion of a commercial economy and a national market. Major highways were constructed to meet the travelling requirements of the *daimyō* and their retinues. The Tōkaidō was the greatest, the coastal overland route linking Edo with Kyoto and Osaka made famous by Hiroshige's series of woodblock prints at the end of the Tokugawa period, the Fifty-three Stations of the Tōkaidō.[2] Travellers, mostly on foot, needed places to stop and eat, rest and spend the night, which led to the establishment of post towns and stations to provide inns, horses and porters. Crossing major rivers required boats since, for defensive purposes, the shogunate prohibited construction of large bridges. Hiroshige's print of Shimada, Station Number 24, shows one of many smaller rivers that had to be forded, whether in the relatively dry condition of a palanquin or piggy-backed depending on one's status and ability to pay. It suggests how large a *daimyō*'s procession could be, often filling up all the inns at a station. The *daimyō* of a large *han*, such as Okayama or Hiroshima, had approximately 1600 to more than 2000 men in his procession, and the *daimyō* of even the smallest domains had between fifty and several hundred people in their retinues.[3]

Of all the urban growth that resulted from the alternate attendance system, however, Edo's was the most sudden and rapid. Nothing but a marshy military outpost at the end of the sixteenth century, it flourished as the cultural and economic as well as political centre of Japan during the eighteenth century. With over one million inhabitants, Edo had surpassed London and other European capitals by the early 1700s. In spite of such growth, its origins as Ieyasu's castle town remained important for its layout and character as a city, remnants of which can be seen even in present-day Tokyo. By the time Edo castle was built after Ieyasu's victory at Sekigahara, however, there were no longer major military threats from outside, so the city was laid out for defensive purposes against potential internal threats. Rather than a wall enclosing the entire city, a wall was constructed only around the shogunal castle at the centre of the city.

The strict segregation of classes by residential area was intended to ensure security against internal threats from resident *daimyō* or commoners. Instead of the rectangular, geometrical layout which had characterized the earlier Chinese-style capitals of Nara and Heian (Kyoto) and Hideyoshi's plan for Osaka, these residential areas fanned out in a spiral or circular pattern from the castle, following the descent in the social ladder – the castle in the centre, then residences of the *daimyō* closest to the shogun, upper level retainers of the shogun, a central area for commoners at Nihonbashi, and out along the Tōkaidō to the south and west. Wide moats and canals rather than roads defined the sections and served as the primary means of transportation of goods as well as defence.

The defensive objective was also evident within residential areas. The commoner area followed a regular grid plan with barriers at every major intersection for close control. The samurai area also had frequent barriers and checkpoints, with most streets intersecting in 'T' shapes rather than crosses to prevent through access for rebellious forces. The predominance of T-intersections still characterizes Tokyo today. Furthermore, the shogunate prohibited virtually all wheeled vehicles, especially for personal transport, so that streets in Edo were narrow, designed for pedestrians rather than carriages.

Commoner sections were usually laid out in large blocks with the outer edge facing the main streets. Merchants and artisans lived in row houses with lots priced by the amount of frontage on the street, so they tended to be narrow, but deep. Business was carried out in the front section, living quarters occupied the middle section, followed by a small courtyard and storage in back. A dirt floor passage ran along one side for cooking and other household chores. In the centre of the blocks, criss-crossed by narrow lanes, lived the less fortunate, such as day labourers and the poor, in tenement-like one-storey apartment houses with shared water and toilet facilities. As Henry D. Smith II has suggested, these characteristics, especially of commoner areas, contributed to the development in Japan of the idea of the city as close, noisy, cluttered street life. Anyone visiting Japanese cities today would be struck with this same impression.

Streets in the samurai area were less cluttered, though. These were the early modern antecedents of suburbs, high whitewashed walls hiding mansion complexes with park-like gardens and barracks for lower samurai and servants as well as luxurious living areas for the *daimyō* and their families. The concept of a privatized residential area for the upper classes carried on into modern times in the idea of 'Yamanote' (towards the mountains), the hilly areas where Meiji officials and entrepreneurs lived.

In practice, the segregation of classes could not be strictly maintained. With no formal, coherent plan, the city tended to sprawl as it grew. The commoner area spilled over the Sumida River in the east with a rise in the conspicuous consumption demands not only of the upper ranking *daimyō*, but also a wealthy merchant class that emerged during the seventeenth century. With migrations, Edo gradually replaced Kyoto and Osaka as the economic and cultural centre of the country. Kyoto, the old imperial capital and home to the aristocracy, had reigned as the cultural centre for hundreds of years even though it had relinquished its political status to the rising samurai class. During the seventeenth century nearby Osaka had emerged as the commercial centre of the country when the shogunate made it the centre of its distribution control system. The *han* as well as the shogunate sent rice and other agricultural tax goods to Osaka to be sold, making the merchants who brokered the rice enormously rich.

Barred from participation in cultural activities designated for the samurai, such as Nō drama, these *nouveau riche* townspeople or '*chōnin*' patronized artists and writers catering to their tastes and thus helped create new forms of art and culture which we now associate with Japanese 'traditions', including kabuki, the puppet theatre and haiku. Woodblock prints (*ukiyoe*) and fiction known as *ukiyo zōshi* also reflected the lifestyles and values of the *chōnin* class. Courtesans and actors from the 'floating world' (*ukiyo*) of licensed brothel and theatre quarters defied their official outcast status when they featured as the main subjects of *ukiyoe*, and set fashion trends and standards not only for *chōnin* but also for samurai. The success of book publishing not only demonstrates the spread of literacy among commoners, but also stories and characters which appealed to *chōnin*. *Ukiyo zōshi* depicted city life with townspeople as main characters who pursued money, sex, pleasure and luxury, all contradictory to NeoConfucian values, but at the same time the stories emphasized frugality and family obligations.

The shogunate repeatedly passed sumptuary legislation to curb displays of wealth considered inappropriate to the *chōnin*'s place in the social order, but could not enforce the restrictions. As early as 1648 it warned *chōnin* to clothe their servants at most in silk pongee, not ordinary silk cloth, and forbade male servants to wear sashes or loincloths of velvet or silk. However, *chōnin* became very inventive in ways to circumvent the letter of the law, for example, using forbidden materials for kimono linings and undergarments to avoid detection. The frequent reissuing of sumptuary laws suggests that in fact they were not very effective, and reference to such laws as 'three-day laws' implies inconsistency of enforcement. Moreover, although the restrictions did influence *chōnin* fashion, they did not maintain the distinction between classes. For example, fashion in the eighteenth century leaned towards those colours unrestricted for *chōnin* to wear, namely browns, blues and greys, as *chōnin* tastes tended to infect those of classes higher in the social hierarchy, so that even though members of the samurai and nobility were not restricted in clothing colours, many wore commoner colours by the nineteenth century.

Nor could the shogunate keep *chōnin* and samurai culture completely separate. Although floating world art, literature and drama were created by and for *chōnin*, samurai also participated in it, though often incognito, and in Edo stimulated kabuki to create a distinctive regional style. *Daimyō* and Tokugawa retainers' fascination with kabuki actors particularly disturbed shogunal authorities, which tried in vain to check the increasing extravagance of theatres, adjoining teahouses, staging and costuming. One official writing in 1802 scorned samurai's imitating actors' speech and manners and *daimyō*'s putting on plays in their homes. Amateur productions by samurai and commoners were popular enough to warrant publication in 1774 of a book entitled *The Basic Book of Home Kabuki*, complete with references to specialty shops for stage props and make-up. Conversely, although Nō theatre was supposed to be confined to the samurai elite, rich merchants had Nō plays performed in their mansions. Edo kabuki actors created a 'rough style' to appeal to samurai audiences at the same time that they portrayed characters who defied samurai authority.

Samurai fascination with the licensed prostitutes of the cities similarly concerned government authorities. The shogunate had set up walled quarters, such as the Yoshiwara in Edo, in an attempt to confine prostitution, both male and female, to an area which could be supervised and controlled, another reminder of the shogunate's security consciousness. Unlicensed prostitutes became the object of police surveillance and crackdowns, but licensed prostitutes acquired a status in some cases equivalent to that of modern celebrity entertainers. A rigid hierarchy with distinct levels or classes of prostitutes developed within the quarters. At the top emerged a handful of elegant, highly accomplished and educated *tayū* able to pick and choose among patrons who were then invited for an 'audience'. A seventeenth-century treatise on the quarters, *The Great Mirror of the Way of Love*, noted that 'as for a guest who did not please [the *tayū*], no matter how high his standing, *daimyō* or otherwise, able to bribe handsomely or not, he could not meet the lady. Those known to have been refused were shamed irrevocably and fell into deep despair.'[4] The *tayū* of Edo in particular became known for their independent spirit and strong-mindedness, a female reflection of the samurai character of the city.

During the eighteenth century, however, the pleasure quarters suffered a decline as places of exquisite taste where expensive, high-class courtesans could be found. Paralleling changes in audiences for kabuki, clients changed to the less wealthy. A contemporary popular writer lamented in 1811:

> Yoshiwara has now fallen on hard times. Recently, for the first time in ages, I looked in a guidebook and noticed that there are only two *yobidashi* [replaced *tayū* and met customers at teahouses without any formalities]: Takigawa of the Ogiya House and Karauta of Chōjiya. . . . Tamaya has no *sancha* [mid-level courtesans]; all are the lowly *umecha*. . . . It seems to me that the courtesans are fewer and the number of famous ladies halved.[5]

While the change in customers may on the one hand indicate the development of a popular culture shared by aristocracy and commoner alike, this comment may on the other hand be a reminder that the majority of prostitutes did not fit the idealized image of the *tayū*. Most were neither cultivated nor living in luxury, but rather essentially slaves or indentured workers sold into prostitution by desperate parents. The term '*ukiyo*' derived from a Buddhist concept connoting sadness and melancholy, reflected in the popularity of plaintive songs of homesickness and fickle lovers in the licensed quarters. This mood also predominated in scenes of the quarters in drama, exemplified by Chikamatsu Monzaemon's plays which climaxed in double suicides of socially unsuitable lovers torn between love and family obligations. Moreover, although most *ukiyoe* depicted the highest class of courtesans in sumptuous clothes, a few also reveal the darker, unromantic side of the pleasure quarters.

Commercialization and peasant protests

The poverty which drove rural families to sell their daughters into prostitution might substantiate the traditional view of Tokugawa agriculture and village life as one of primitive subsistence farming and feudal oppression. Certainly from a late twentieth-century perspective, living conditions appear miserable. Most peasants lived in dark rectangular boxes with dirt floors and an open hearth which billowed smoke throughout the house but gave off little heat in cold winters. Although they paid their taxes in rice, it was regarded by authorities as a luxury food which peasants should not eat.

However, important developments must have been occurring in agriculture to make possible the remarkable urbanization and growth in population as a whole which occurred in the seventeenth century. Increases in agricultural productivity actually began during the period of civil war as a result of *daimyō* seeking to expand the economic basis of their political power. In addition to initiatives from ruling powers above, many innovations and technological improvements of the sixteenth and seventeenth centuries seem to have been products of commoners themselves. Urbanization during the seventeenth century and particularly the concentration of the upper samurai in Edo created a demand not only for basic necessities, but also luxury items and specialty products such as Tosa's famous dried bonito or enamelled Nabeshima ware. Peasants began to specialize in crops best suited to their areas, including mandarin oranges, indigo and cotton, or to manufacture goods to supply the growing demands of urban inhabitants. The demand for silk increased enormously, leading to some families' abandonment of old subsistence crops in favour of sericulture, the raising of silkworms.

The growth of regional markets and gradually a national market meant that peasants no longer had to produce everything they needed for everyday living. In addition, peddlers from towns plied consumers in the countryside with all sorts of goods, to the distress of NeoConfucian commentators. Even in economically poor regions, consumerism was emerging. The scholar Ro Tōzan, for example, complained in a 1726 memorial to his lord about the inappropriate lifestyle spreading among peasants:

> For some years merchants have come here from other places, but those who do the most business and bring the greatest distress are from Ōmi. They put together medicines, cosmetics, and cotton and silk cloth, which they distribute to agents who go everywhere in this area selling on credit. . . . In recent years buying on credit has become quite common, and there are places where debts amount to very large sums. . . . If, as in earlier times, such fellows did not come, then the peasants would make their own clothing, or even if they bought it they would save up the money first; but because these fellows come selling fine things on easy terms, the peasants go into debt to buy quite useless things.[6]

Evidence of commercialization of agriculture and economic growth in the countryside helps to explain Japan's later economic success in the late nineteenth and twentieth centuries, but what are the social and political implications of these economic developments? Who benefited from the increase in agricultural production? In the past historians assumed that the surplus was simply taken as increased taxes by the *han* and shogunal governments, but in fact the land tax did not increase substantially after the mid-1600s. No reassessments of land productivity, which was the basis for tax assessment, were carried out after 1700 or so, nor was there any large increase in the rate of the tax. Who, then, in the village got the surplus? This has been an important question to historians of modern Japan because Marxist historians have seen grinding poverty and oppression as fomenting popular dissatisfaction, which in turn underlay the fall of the Tokugawa shogunate. Marxist historians as well as the official NeoConfucian view of social classes have presented a picture of the Tokugawa peasantry as a homogeneous class.

However, studies both of village social developments and peasant protests and rebellions present a contrary view. Rather than homogeneous, the peasant class was stratified, even at the beginning of the Tokugawa period, and became increasingly differentiated as time passed. In addition, development of a commercial economy led to greater regional variations as rural areas near cities became more involved in the market than did remote areas such as Tōhoku in northern Honshu. Despite regional differences, by the eighteenth century village society comprised an economic, political and social pyramid with a stratum of very wealthy landowners and industrialists at the top, medium and small landholders in the middle, and landless tenant farmers, wage labourers and hereditary servants at the bottom. Out of the spread of commercial farming and rural industries, such as sake brewing, soy sauce manufacturing and handicraft production, had emerged a wealthy village elite who lived a luxurious lifestyle comparable to that of rich merchants in cities. They acquired education far beyond rudimentary reading and writing skills, employed private tutors to give them artistic and literary accomplishments, and purchased rare books and art objects to adorn their homes. They also possessed legal rights and could participate in village government.

Quite substantial expenditures on schooling of daughters in wealthy peasant families indicate that socioeconomic standing often became more important than sex in determining a girl's life experiences. Again, there was considerable regional variation, but by the early nineteenth century some wealthy families were sending their daughters as well as sons to temple schools (*terakoya*). Alternatively, their daughters became servants in upper samurai households in order to learn feminine deportment, or they sent their daughters on a pilgrimage to the Shinto shrine at Ise as a learning experience before marriage. All of these costly educational experiences for daughters seem to have been regarded as good investments to enhance the family's reputation and to improve her chances of achieving a good marriage.

The larger group of peasants at the bottom had no legal rights, much less wealth, and no power. Whether by bad luck or poor decision-making, many had lost their land and been forced to become tenants. In poor households women and men worked alongside each other in the fields, though women were paid less. Poor peasant women also added handicrafts to field work and domestic chores, and children had to help with household and farm work from as early as 4 or 5 years old. Most poor families had to send their daughters away to work as indentured servants, hoping that they would not be mistreated or sold into prostitution. Sons went to work as wage labourers on other people's farms or in rural enterprises. The availability of by-employments in rural industries as well as cities gave tenants a little economic independence from landlords, but at the same time they were less close socially than tenants had been in earlier times.

Commercialization had therefore led to increased stratification of village society and precarious dependence on the market, though it led to the promise of a better standard of living as well. As the peasant class became more differentiated, the close cooperation among village members that had contributed to the solidarity of early Tokugawa rural communities gradually declined. Not all cooperative aspects of village life disappeared, but they tended to become less important as a market economy penetrated more deeply into the countryside. In other words, traditions of cooperation survived longest in villages that remained more self-sufficient and isolated from the outside.

The increasing number of peasant uprisings and protests of violent as well as nonviolent types during the latter half of the Tokugawa period indicates the growth of social tension in the countryside which accompanied economic change. The total number of protests doubled between 1600 and 1750 and doubled again during the first half of the nineteenth century.[7] In addition, the predominant modes of protest changed from traditional nonviolent appeals to feudal authorities, such as petitions, or simple abandonment and flight from their land, to more violent acts including forceful demonstrations and destruction of property. The higher incidence of protests in commercialized areas and the targeting of property owned by the village elite reflect the social strains of changed class relations in rural areas, effects of economic growth and growth of a market economy rather than uniform misery and exploitation of the peasants. At the same time, however, the intravillage, localized nature of many protests suggests that they did not provide the motive force for a popular revolution against the Tokugawa shogunate, as some historians have previously argued.

The bureaucratization and impoverishment of the samurai class

The revolt against the shogunate came not from below, but from within the ruling class itself. The reasons for samurai disaffection may be found in the way the economic changes described above affected samurai and their superiors in the shogunal and various domain governments.

At the beginning of the Tokugawa period the samurai class had been a real warrior class emerging from the 150 years of civil war, but, after two centuries of peace and separation from the land, it had been transformed into a bureaucratic elite of civil administrators living in urban environs. The codification of *bushidō* or the Way of the Warrior had sought to keep warrior traditions alive while also stressing the pursuit of book-learning and other civil skills necessary for being state officials. However, with no actual battles to fight, the latter skills obviously became more important to cultivate for daily life and career advancement.

One of the first things to emphasize in order to understand the situation of samurai by the beginning of the nineteenth century is their total number. Senior nobles and *daimyō* totalled only a few hundred families, but the samurai class as a whole, including their families, made up 5 or 6 per cent of the total population of around thirty million, or about two million by the time of the Meiji Restoration. This was far larger than the English or any European aristocracy before or after the Industrial Revolution. Consequently, it is difficult to speak in generalizations about the samurai as a whole. In addition to many ranks or horizontal subdivisions within the class, there were great differences among *han*, regional differences which created vertical divisions within the class. A given rank in one large *han* would therefore carry a different stipend from the same rank in another, smaller *han*.

Another problem that arises in discussions of the social and economic conditions of samurai is that neither Tokugawa writers nor modern scholars have established an accepted usage in labels for the various strata within the class. Some writers speak of 'upper' and 'lower' samurai, some of 'upper', 'middle' and 'lower', but the dividing lines are not always clear. The existence of variations in usage is important to recognize because the Meiji Restoration is usually described as a movement led by 'lower samurai', which in turn implies socioeconomic and political dissatisfaction with the Tokugawa system as the motive for their actions. According to William G. Beasley's definitions in *The Meiji Restoration*, 'upper' samurai are the easiest to distinguish. They consisted of the *daimyō*, branches of *daimyō* houses, senior vassals and their counterparts in the shogunate. They possessed a near monopoly on senior administrative posts in most *han* and the shogunate even in the nineteenth century. 'Middle' samurai represented about half of all samurai. They had the right of audience with their lord and filled the middle range of offices in the various governments. However, since their stipends ranged from 20 to 200 or 300 *koku*,[8] their standard of material comfort varied extensively. 'Lower' samurai were the most diverse: footsoldiers, messengers, clerks, rear vassals of senior families, and so-called *gōshi*, nominal 'rural' samurai who may have been survivors of samurai-farmers of medieval times or originally commoners granted samurai rank as a reward for service to the *han*.

Social mobility within the class remained a possibility, but it was easier to move down than up the ranks. A samurai could advance by showing skill and efficiency in office and more quickly if he gained the personal favour of his lord – factional politics played a major role in the career fortunes or misfortunes of samurai. However, in Satsuma *han*, for example, it took three generations of personal promotion to secure a permanent rise in family rank, that is, before it became hereditary. Similarly, it was easier to become a merchant or farmer, though few wanted to, than to become a samurai. The latter was theoretically exceptional, and the fact that quite a large number of commoners were acquiring samurai status in the nineteenth century was seen as evidence that the country was teetering on the brink of chaos.

Bureaucratization of the samurai, combined with the broader economic changes in both the city and countryside described earlier, made it increasingly difficult by the nineteenth century to maintain either the traditional social or political structure. Transformation of the samurai into civilian administrators required the acquisition of literacy and formal education. Almost all *han* had established schools for samurai youth by the end of the Tokugawa period and numerous private schools also emerged, so that almost all samurai males were literate. The role of samurai women did not require such formal schooling, and education in the Chinese classics was regarded as inappropriate as well as unnecessary for women. Nevertheless, they received some education at home in reading and writing the Japanese syllabary, and needed training in order to manage servants, keep household inventories, design and sew the family's clothes, decorate the home and entertain guests. From about the age of 12, then, girls' education focused on learning how to cook, spin, sew and weave.

Differences of ability and discrepancies between ability and rank became visible both in schools and in performance of official duties. Such discrepancies were particularly irking to lower ranking samurai since differences in rank were so obviously reflected in the privileges accorded to one's rank. Rank, for example, determined the number of servants who could accompany a samurai boy to school – whether he would have one to hold his umbrella and another to mind his sandals. By the late Tokugawa period many middle samurai were showing dissatisfaction with the limitations of the hereditary rank system which blocked their access to high office. Reform writers began to urge appointment and promotion by merit, calling on the Confucian maxim of recruiting 'men of talent' as a solution to the country's ills without attacking the system of social hierarchy itself.

The system of hereditary rank had also changed the nature of loyalty and the lord–vassal relationship. Earlier samurai had chosen to follow a lord because of his demonstrated effectiveness as a leader, but since *daimyō* had become hereditary leaders, oaths of allegiance became unconditional and impersonal declarations of loyalty to the office, not the individual. Moreover, since the *daimyō* often resided in Edo, he became more a symbol of the *han* than a visible presence. In his classic study of Chōshū, Albert Craig described the development of a kind of '*han* nationalism' which prepared the way for modern Japanese nationalism. Loyalty had become impersonal and directed to a governmental unit, so when the foreign threat aroused consciousness of belonging to Japan, loyalty shifted quickly from *han* to nation.

Access to office was particularly important to samurai because it meant additional income. Stipends were fixed annual payments which went with rank; office brought a salary. Although governments expanded during the

Tokugawa period, there were not enough offices to go around. *An Oral Record of Mito History* illustrated the intensity of competition for government positions:

> One who became an official could eat grilled eel, but one who didn't had to turn to making the bamboo skewers used to grill the eel. To eat what had been on the skewers or to make them, therein lay the source of the factional struggles.[9]

In addition, with rising expectations as well as costs of living, many samurai suffered economic decline. Again, situations varied greatly. For some, increasing poverty was absolute as the shogunate and *han* governments tried to solve their financial difficulties by cutting stipends, but for others it was relative as their wants escalated, especially in view of the extravagant lifestyles of lower social classes. As early as the 1680s the originator of *ukiyo-zōshi* fiction, Ihara Saikaku, wrote disapprovingly about the ostentatiousness of commoners' clothes:

> In everything people have a liking for finery above their station. . . . Prostitutes make a daily display of beautiful clothes toward earning a living. But beautiful wives of commoners, when they are not blossom-viewing in spring or maple-viewing in autumn or going to weddings, should forego [*sic*] these many layers of conspicuous garments.[10]

Furthermore, he added that 'it is distressing to see a merchant wearing good silks. Pongee suits him better and looks better on him. But fine clothes are essential to a samurai's status.'[11]

Maintaining a certain number of personal retainers according to their rank was also essential, but the expense became a difficulty for samurai on fixed or reduced incomes. For example, a middle-ranking samurai in the Mito domain, with a stipend of between 100 and 500 *koku*, was expected to maintain two or three retainers, two maids and a horse. Even lower samurai always took an attendant with them when they went out. Women from samurai families, unlike commoner women, rarely left their houses, but when they did, always had to take a companion or attendant to uphold the family's respectability. Nineteenth-century commentators noted that samurai impoverishment was reflected in their keeping fewer and fewer hereditary retainers, instead employing retainers for fixed periods of time or hiring them only when ceremonial occasions required them.

The problem for both governments and individual samurai derived from continued reliance on the land tax as the primary source of revenue. Stipends as well as taxes were paid in rice, which meant that they had to be converted into cash to buy necessities. This made governments and samurai dependent on the price of rice and the merchants who brokered rice for them. By the mid-eighteenth century samurai increasingly fell into debt to merchant-moneylenders, and by the nineteenth century many were resorting to handicraft production or marriages and adoptions with wealthy merchant families to stave off poverty. In Mito, for example, 600 to 700 of the thousand-odd samurai retainers received stipends of less than 100 *koku*. Without a government position, it was impossible for them to manage their daily living without undertaking piece-work or other side jobs. Weaving was a standard side job for samurai wives and daughters, and women in lower samurai households had no servants to do the housework, cook or tend the vegetable garden. Since younger sons received no stipends, they became unmarried dependents of the household head if not adopted out as heir of another samurai house and had to engage in some kind of piece-work such as making umbrellas to earn a little income. No wonder historical dramas for both film and stage are full of ragged samurai heroes, exemplified by Mifune Toshiro in Kurosawa Akira's movies and reflecting the impoverishment of the class by the late Tokugawa period. The pride and arrogance of these samurai even in their state of destitution suggests the potential political effects resulting from the decline of the class. Frustration, resentment and criticism of wealthy merchants and farmers who acted like samurai became characteristic of commentaries on social problems of the day.

By the early nineteenth century, then, economic growth and social changes had created great tensions in the Tokugawa polity. The realities of the distribution of wealth no longer accorded with the traditional doctrine and the assumptions underlying the official social and economic structure. Samurai morale was deteriorating, criticism of the regime mounted, and unrest characterized both city and countryside.

2 The mid-century crisis

The tensions created by the gap between the real and ideal discussed in Chapter 1 were already reaching crisis level in the late 1830s, more than a decade before Commodore Perry's dramatic entry into Edo Bay threw the authorities into further turmoil. The Tempō crisis, referring to the name of the era from 1830 to 1843, may in fact encapsulate the cumulative problems facing the Tokugawa regime, and the failure of its response to the crisis in the form of the Tempō reforms is often seen as a background factor to the regime's collapse twenty-five-odd years later. This chapter will therefore begin with a close description and analysis of the internal crisis, and the responses of various individuals and groups in society.

However, historians remain divided over the emphasis they place on internal problems, as opposed to the Western threat represented by Perry's arrival, to explain the overthrow of the Tokugawa shogunate and beginning of the Meiji Restoration. Until the 1980s Marxian interpretations, which were more prevalent in Japan than in Western countries, focused on the oppressive character of the Tokugawa political and social system, especially for the peasantry. They viewed the growing number of peasant protests and rebellions in the second half of the Tokugawa period not only as evidence of this oppression but also of popular discontent with the feudal system which fuelled the revolutionary forces in society. These revolutionary forces came out of the ruling samurai class rather than the peasantry, but belonged to the lower ranks who chafed under the restrictions of the hereditary class system blocking their access to high office. Social and economic grievances in these views thus played a larger role in bringing about the end of the Tokugawa regime than political factors, although recent Marxian analyses have given more importance to the role of Western imperialism than in the past.

Most non-Marxian historians have also acknowledged festering domestic social and economic dissatisfaction, but their emphasis comes down harder on political factors, namely the emergence of nationalism. These views reject social grievances and, more specifically, class-consciousness as the motive for the 'lower samurai' leaders of the Meiji Restoration. More important was the sense of national identity and desire to save Japan from colonization that was galvanized by Perry's ultimatum to 'open' Japan. These interpretations attribute less importance to peasant rebellions as a destabilizing factor, for they stress the localized nature of peasant protests. In addition, although they point to socioeconomic problems in rural areas, they highlight the protests as reflections of intravillage conflict caused by economic growth rather than by stagnation. They do not see the majority of peasant protests as attacks on the feudal authorities outside the village, hence not on the feudal system as a whole.

In the last section of this chapter we will return to these interpretive problems, but the main foci will be an explication of, first, the domestic crisis, as exemplified by the Tempō crisis, and second, the foreign crisis. In addition, attention will be drawn to ways in which members of the major social classes discussed in Chapter 1 were affected by the crises and responded to them.

The internal crisis

The year 1830 began a new era auspiciously named Tempō or Heavenly Protection. The name expressed what was to be a vain hope for an improvement in the country's economic and social situation, for the year ushered in a decade of natural disasters, followed by famine, rural rebellion and urban uprisings, including one led by a former shogunal official. In fact, crop failures had been occurring frequently since 1824, but in 1833, brought about by exceptionally cold weather, they led to severe famine in northern Japan. The unusual weather continued, and by 1836 famine had spread nationwide, leading to reports of people eating leaves, weeds and even straw raincoats. Epidemics of smallpox, measles and influenza struck down those already weakened by hunger. The number of rural protests leapt into the hundreds, and now involved tens of thousands of peasants from whole regions rather than a few villages. Shogunal and domain governments opened relief stations, but starving peasants flooded the cities in search of menial work, often resorting to violence and attacking rice warehouses in frustration and desperation.

The most alarming of these urban disturbances was led by Ōshio Heihachirō in 1837. Ōshio had earned a reputation as a police official in Osaka for cleaning up corruption, but he had turned against the shogunate and attracted a group of followers with his mystical and iconoclastic ideas of revolution. Seeing the plight of the people in the midst of famine, he appealed to the Osaka city commissioners and rich merchants, such as the Mitsui and Kōnoike, to help. When these appeals failed, Ōshio called on the peasants of the four provinces surrounding Osaka to rise up and kill 'the heartless officials and luxury-living merchants who profited while the poor starved'.[1] The mass army failed to appear, and the shogunal forces quelled the revolt in a matter of days. Ōshio was forced to flee with a few dozen followers and took his life to avoid capture. Nevertheless, the attempt made a deep impression on Japanese throughout the country at both governmental levels and among the common people. It certainly became an important factor contributing to the enactment of reform policies in the early 1840s. Rural and urban disturbances did not end with Ōshio's failed uprising, and are indicative of the widespread economic hardships and social problems pervading the country during the early decades of the nineteenth century.

Popular anxiety was also reflected in other mass phenomena of these decades – pilgrimages to traditional religious centres and the emergence of a number of new religious movements with millenarian beliefs. Pilgrimages were common, but in 1830 an exceptionally large number of pilgrims (five million in just four months) converged upon the Grand Shrine of Ise, the sacred centre built for the Shinto Sun Goddess Amaterasu. The upsurge in pilgrimages to such traditional religious places in itself suggests a period of insecurity and instability, but the utopian visions of new religions reveal the acute need for a reintegrated community that many ordinary Japanese seemed to feel at this time. Among these, Tenrikyō is prototypical. Its founder, Nakayama Miki (1798–1887), promised salvation for the faithful who practised communal love, tolerance and humility and believed in the divine grace of Tenri Ōnomikoto, the 'supreme deity of heavenly reason', and Tenchi Kanenokami. In 1838 Nakayama founded a new religious centre at her home in central Honshū which attracted thousands of pilgrims made up of urban poor as well as peasants. As 'parent' for the faithful, she embodied the teachings of equality between the sexes and an emphasis on family life and personality development which conflicted with dominant Confucian mores and structures.

At the level of the ruling elite, this evidence of economic distress and dissatisfaction coincided with growing financial difficulties of the shogunal and *han* governments which were causing increased hardship for their samurai retainers. Suggestions for reform came forth from the samurai class. Some were radical. Honda Toshiaki, for example, argued for expansion northward in terms of both trade and colonization. Andō Shōeki called for abolition of the samurai class and a return to a completely agrarian economy, and Satō Nobuhiro wanted a centralized bureaucratic state to build national wealth and strength. Most, however, criticized the existing rulers on the basis of traditional values, not a new vision of society, and they represented isolated individuals rather than organized political groups. Few called for a restructuring of the political system, but rather a return to NeoConfucian moral standards and frugality through the recruitment of 'men of talent'.

Consequently, when the shogunate did respond to the crisis, it tried to cope with the situation using many of the same policies of past reform efforts, with the same dismal results. Following the earlier reform models of the Kyōhō (1716–35) and Kansei (1787–93) eras, the new senior councillor Mizuno Tadakuni began with measures to clamp down on unlicensed prostitution, gambling and other activities believed to have 'a bad effect on morals', in spite of his own notorious obsession with food and sex. As the attack on frivolity and immorality extended to more strict controls on publishers, theatres, actors and printmakers, a raft of sumptuary legislation tried to stem the tide of extravagance and spending inappropriate to one's station. There were also the conventional policies aimed at cutting government expenses and official corruption and increasing revenues. For example, for the third (and last) time the shogunate undertook the draining and reclaiming of Imbanuma swamp northeast of Edo to add 10,000 acres of potentially rich rice-growing land to the Tokugawa tax base. In an attempt to increase the number of taxpayers by halting the abandonment of farming, it tried the usual methods of prohibiting employment in rural manufacturing industry and discouraging mendicant religious sects. Merchants, as in the past, were blamed for erratic price fluctuations and the overall upward trend in rice prices, so the shogunate tried to control commerce more tightly, such as by lowering or freezing some commodity prices and limiting interest rates, pawnbroking charges and the level of shop rents.

All these initial reforms followed traditional patterns, but from late 1842 Mizuno's measures became more innovative – and also more threatening, not only to merchants, but to the shogunate's potential rivals, the *daimyō*. Instead of merely trying to control prices by conventional methods, the shogunate attacked the semi-official merchant monopoly associations, shipping syndicates known as *tokumi-donya*, by ordering their dissolution. Next it attempted to prohibit *han* monopolies as well. This represented a reassertion of the shogunate's right to control the *daimyō* domains, not merely to control prices. This was made clear by a series of other measures challenging the economic independence of domains over the next several months, but also by a seemingly ritualistic visit of the shogun to the tombs of his great ancestors in Nikkō in the spring of 1843. The visit represented more than an act of NeoConfucian filial piety. First, it placed a great financial burden on the *daimyō* who had to escort, house and protect the shogun and his retinue during the procession or provide guards and other ceremonial officials back in Edo during the shogun's absence. Second, it revived a symbolic ritual of Tokugawa supremacy after almost seventy years. Shortly after, the shogunate announced that the costs of the Imbanuma land reclamation project would be borne by five *daimyō*, and that fiefs in the vicinity of Edo would be rearranged (to the advantage of the shogunate's finances as well as security). While these measures all fell within the formal power of the shogunate, they had not been invoked for decades, so that the *daimyō* had come to believe that their subordination to the shogun was merely formalistic as well.

One month after the announcement of his ambitious rearrangement of fiefs, Mizuno was dismissed amidst accusations of 'dishonesty'. With his disgrace the shogunate's reforms ended, and the judgements of failure began. Most historians see the shogunate's failure to resolve the Tempō crisis as the beginning of a chain of events which ended in the Meiji Restoration, although beyond that they disagree on the relative importance of the social versus political consequences of the reforms. Some emphasize the significance for the future of the informal alliance forged between the lower samurai and rural elite during the Tempō years; others see greater significance in the contrast between the shogunate's failure in reform and the success of reforms in certain *han*, particularly Satsuma, that provided them with a sound financial base from which to face the crisis of future decades. According to Harold Bolitho, even the failure of some domainal reform efforts, as in Mito and Chōshū which later played key roles in the Meiji Restoration movement, left important impressions for the future. While awareness of economic weakness – hence power – created a sense of frustration and discontent, the Tempō crisis had also demonstrated the obsolescence of traditional power structures and political organization.[2]

The foreign crisis

The area where the inadequacy of existing political institutions became most evident was foreign policy. A threat from abroad had been the other instigator of the Tempō reforms, and whereas the return of good harvests temporarily assuaged anxiety about the internal crisis, the foreign problem did not go away. Again, as with the internal economic and social problems, the foreign threat was not new in the 1830s. Foreign ships had appeared with increasing frequency in Japanese waters since the 1790s: Russians in the north and British in the south. The shogunate had responded in 1825 with orders to the *daimyō* to drive away any and all such ships. Soon after the Tempō era began, clashes between Japanese and foreigners in far-away Ezo (Hokkaido) were reported, but in 1837 a clash occurred in Edo Bay, close to the very headquarters of the shogunate. The shogunate fired on the *Morrison*, a privately owned American ship attempting to return seven Japanese castaways and probably hoping to initiate commercial and evangelistic activities as well. Shogunal authorities were soon further disturbed by rumours of British plans to annex the Bonin Islands only a few hundred miles south of Japan and later by more reliable reports about China's humiliating defeat by Britain in the Opium War (1839–41). Critics and reformers not only focused on internal problems. Like Tokugawa Nariaki, the influential *daimyō* of Mito and head of one of the three senior Tokugawa branch houses, they often warned in good Chinese historical fashion that 'internal disorder invites external difficulties, while external problems provoke internal unrest'.[3] Many, such as Sakuma Shōzan, worried about the decrepit state of Japanese defence fortifications and recommended abolition of restrictions on building large, ocean-going ships.

   Worry about the foreign threat had therefore been a factor stimulating inauguration of the Tempō reforms, but when it came down to supporting domainal projects to improve the country's defences, the shogunate baulked. In 1843 Tokugawa Nariaki tried to persuade Mizuno that allowing *daimyō* and shipowners to build large ships would relieve the shogunate of the onerous expense. Mizuno countered, however, with the question, 'If we permit everyone to build warships, who can tell what evils may ensue? The *daimyō* of the west country and elsewhere may begin to conspire and build unorthodox vessels; this will have a significant impact on our administration of the law.'[4] This attitude, which manifested itself in various attempts to prevent the teaching or development of modern military techniques or armaments in the *han*, contributed to the atmosphere of suspicion and resentment being engendered by the Tempō reforms. It led many domains to build up their ships in secret and to smuggle in manuals and foreign arms.

The shogunate became exposed to more scathing criticism for its lack of military preparedness within a decade after its Tempō reforms ended so ignominiously. This was brought on by the dramatic entry of Commodore Matthew Perry's squadron of four American warships into Edo Bay in July 1853, the date which historians designate as the beginning of '*bakumatsu*' or 'the end of the Bakufu (shogunate)'. Japanese fishermen from Uraga, on first seeing the black smoke from their coal-powered steam engines on the horizon, called them the 'black ships', and described them as being as large as mountains and as swift as birds. For some years the shogunate had known from the Dutch that the Americans planned to seek trade relations, and only two years previously the *USS Preble* under Commander James Glynn had called at Nagasaki, demanding repatriation of a number of shipwrecked American sailors. American whaling ships, which had been operating in the western Pacific for more than a decade, and American traders, who were increasing their trade with China, needed a port for refuelling and food supplies. With the acquisition of California and the northwest territories at the end of the 1840s, the United States was also turning its eyes westward across the Pacific. As Secretary of the Treasury Robert Walker declared in 1848, 'Asia has suddenly become our neighbor with a placid, intervening ocean inviting our steamships upon the track of a commerce greater than all Europe combined'.[5] Although shogunal officials were aware of these developments, they had kept the information strictly confidential and made no significant preparations for an approach like Perry's to open relations. This is one reason for the surprise and confusion caused by Perry's appearance.

Moreover, Perry's mode of approach was no polite request conforming to Japanese diplomatic protocol. He rejected Japanese officials' attempts to send him to Nagasaki, demanding that President Filmore's letter be accepted by a high shogunal official at a ceremony in Uraga and hinting that a refusal would provoke his use of force. Prior discussions and study of Japan and earlier unsuccessful Western attempts to initiate contact had convinced him that to accomplish his mission he must 'adopt a course entirely contrary to that of all others who had hitherto visited Japan on a similar errand – to demand as a right, and not as a favor, those acts of courtesy which are due from one civilized nation to another'.[6] Perry prayed to God that his attempt 'to bring a singular and isolated people into the family of civilized nations' might succeed without bloodshed, but he concluded that since the Japanese were 'deceitful' and 'vindictive in character', the rules of diplomacy among civilized nations would not apply. While

Plate 2.1 A true portrait of Adams, Commodore Perry's second in command, 1853
Source: Courtesy of the Honolulu Academy of Arts, Gift of Mrs Walter F.
Dillingham, 1960 (2732.1)

shogunal authorities deliberated on an answer to his demand, Perry and his
ships carried out depth soundings and survey measurements in opposition
to Japanese requests to stop such activities.

Perry's arrival not only forced the shogunate and the domains in charge
of coastal defence into action, but stimulated activity among commoners in
the city of Edo and surrounding areas. City commissioners immediately issued
ordinances to try to ensure law and order as panicky commodity buying
and evacuation of women and children began in anticipation of hostilities.
Long pacified samurai rushed around trying to find arms and armour. While
some people followed ward officers' orders to stay indoors, other brave and
curious souls set out in small boats to take a look at the foreigners. With the
Dutch confined to Deshima in Nagasaki harbour, apart from an annual visit
to Edo during the past 200 years, few Japanese had ever seen a Westerner,
and popular images depicted them as hairy, big-nosed, red-eyed demonic
beings.

Once the shogunate received Filmore's letter – it really had no choice
given the squadron's overwhelming superiority of military force – the crisis
receded, but only temporarily, since Perry promised to return the following
spring for an answer to the American demands. Some commoners responded
with comic verses and stories mocking the shogunal authorities' helplessness:
Only four cups of tea [the word for 'tea' sounds like 'steam ships'] and a
peaceful night's sleep is impossible [the word for 'night' sounds like 'world'].[7]
Others laughed at the unpreparedness (and indebtedness) of the samurai
class more generally:

At a time when helpless warriors are more troubled by high pawnbrokers' costs than the price of military equipment One would rather have a monetary allowance than a leg guard.[8]

However, they also shared the shogunate's dilemma, and many offered suggestions for dealing with the foreigners. Most proved impractical, but showed a common desire to repel the foreigners at the same time as seeing an opportunity to make a profit.

These proposals came in response to the shogunate's unprecedented request for opinions from all the *daimyō* and shogunal retainers, rather than only high shogunal officials, and, beyond them, even from ordinary townspeople. If it was a consensus that the shogunate was seeking to support what would be an inevitable capitulation to American demands, this was not what it gained. Anti-foreign feeling was widespread, but beyond that *daimyō* and other samurai solutions varied greatly. At one end of the spectrum were those who vociferously called for maintaining the seclusion policy, expelling the barbarians (*jōi*) by all means. The vocal Mito *daimyō*, Tokugawa Nariaki, represented this view. He had been addressing memorials to the shogunate, criticizing its domestic and foreign policies since the 1820s and proposing reforms based on the ideas of his retainer Aizawa Seishisai. Mito had become the centre of a reform-minded NeoConfucian school of learning in the eighteenth century. In the 1840s its writers had been concerned with defence problems as well as internal economic problems, but aimed at reforms which would rebuild the domain without threatening the shogunate. In the 1850s and 1860s they became increasingly critical of shogunal leadership, notably its handling of the foreigners, and turned to advocating direct action to restore imperial authority and destroy the shogunate.

At the other end of the spectrum of *daimyō* responses were those who favoured opening up the country (*kaikoku*), not only because Japan had no choice, but because it would enable adoption of Western techniques to advance the country. Sakuma Shōzan, military adviser to the *daimyō* of Matsushiro, represented this view. Charged with the practical problem of coastal defence and cannon casting, Sakuma had begun Western studies in the 1840s. His encounter with the new knowledge led him to advise not only knowing the enemy, but also 'combining their learning with ours'. The lesson he derived from China's experience with the West was that morality alone was an inadequate defence against colonization; Japan must use new technologies from the West to defend itself. China's defeat in the Opium War resulted from its failure to abandon the view of Westerners as mere barbarians. Consequently, Sakuma's recognition of Western knowledge as the source of the West's power led him to advocate foreign trade and other contact with the West.

The shogunate's view fell somewhere between these two extremes. Because of their greater knowledge of the West, shogunal officials knew that expulsion was impossible. However, they were not as positive as some *kaikoku* advocates about the advantages of opening the country to full trade. The shogunate's answer to Perry was actually a foregone conclusion, but, in asking the *daimyō* for their opinions, it had given up its exclusive right to decide matters of foreign policy and opened the door to debate and criticism which was not confined to matters of external relations.

The unequal treaties

Perry's return in 1854, with eight ships instead of four, resulted in the Treaty of Kanagawa's opening the ports of Shimoda and Hakodate to American ships for fuel and supplies, though not trade, and allowing consular representation at Shimoda (see Map 1.1). Since this fell short of full commercial relations and the two ports were minor, the shogunate viewed this compromise as a modest achievement. However, the new American consul Townsend Harris immediately set about negotiating another treaty which would open up Japan completely. He argued with some accuracy that the Japanese would fare better with their American friend and mentor than with the British, who were at that very time defeating the Chinese once again in the Arrow War and were planning next to send warships to Japan. Harris had to rely on persuasion and persistence mainly because he did not have a naval force to back him up, and he noted in his journal that 'the absence of a man-of-war tends to weaken my influence with the Japanese. They have yielded nothing except from fear.'[9] Though often frustrated by Japanese officials' delaying tactics and 'interminable discourses', Harris eventually succeeded in 1858.

Although spared from war and military defeat, the Harris Treaty imposed the same humiliating conditions upon Japan as China: low import duties fixed by treaty; opening of ports such as Yokohama to foreign residence and trade; and extraterritoriality whereby foreigners accused of committing crimes were tried in consular courts (in other words, subject to the laws of their own country rather than Japan). Treaties with Britain, France, Russia and the Netherlands followed quickly. These 'unequal treaties' included provisions similar to those in the Harris Treaty, with the addition of a most-favoured-nation clause that automatically gave all the Western powers any privileges which might be conferred on any one of them in the future.

Although Harris had succeeded in persuading the shogunate's key decision-makers to accept a treaty far exceeding what they had previously considered a reasonable concession, shogunal leaders now had to win support for its ratification. Although most political leaders, even Tokugawa Nariaki, had come to realize since Perry's arrival that some trade agreement could no longer be avoided, opinions within the shogunate as well as among *daimyō* remained deeply divided over opening Japan to full trade, and to the foreign missionaries who would surely accompany the traders. Hotta Masayoshi, who had become chief councillor in late 1855, hoped to save the shogunate's face by obtaining the approval of the imperial court, but even his personal visit to Kyoto and strong arguments for the treaty as a necessary condition for avoiding war failed dismally.

Part of the reason for the failure was the court's anti-foreign sentiment, which exclusionists like Tokugawa Nariaki were fortifying. In addition, however, there was its lack of political experience. For centuries the court had been removed from all but the rituals of politics, so it hesitated to take sides on such a controversial matter. Complicating the situation was controversy over a successor to the Tokugawa Shogun Iesada. *Daimyō* favouring reform, many from *han* previously excluded from shogunate offices such as Shimazu Nariakira of Satsuma, supported Tokugawa Yoshinobu,[10] the promising young *daimyō* of Hitotsubashi, while supporters of the status quo in Edo were pushing the very young Tokugawa Iemochi. The emperor in expressing disapproval of the treaty recommended further consultation with the *daimyō*, but also indicated support for Yoshinobu, a hitherto unprecedented interference in a purely Tokugawa matter.

Hotta's failure triggered his replacement, this time by Ii Naosuke, who had backing among the traditional *daimyō* supporters of the Tokugawas. While acknowledged to be a strong and intelligent person, Ii faced difficulties in his attempt to reassert the shogunate's leadership when he went ahead with signing the Harris Treaty without imperial approval, thereby offending *jōi* adherents and turning the court into a rallying point for anti-foreign elements. He then alienated reform *daimyō* by declaring Iemochi the shogunal heir and purging Yoshinobu's supporters by forcing their retirement and arresting their retainers.

Opening up the country

While political leaders, now drawn from a wider pool, became increasingly involved with national foreign policy issues, commoners were also being affected by the opening up of the country to Western contact in both direct and indirect ways.

As an example of immediate consequences, shogunal projects to construct batteries at strategic points around Edo Bay beginning soon after Perry's first visit affected commoners in many ways. The shogunate originally planned to build twelve batteries, and pressured Edo and Osaka merchants and wealthy farmers in Tokugawa lands to contribute towards the costs. But wealthy commoners were not the only ones affected. Construction on the battery at Shinagawa required over 5000 labourers and stone carvers from the Edo area. Houses had to be torn down and the course of the Meguro River changed to make way for the earth-moving project. As many as 2000 freight boats and pleasure boats from all over the Kantō region were turned into earth-moving barges.

Perry's first visit had thrown the city of Edo into economic as well as social turmoil, and even after his second visit when fears of hostilities declined, the economic situation in the city remained unstable. To this was added a natural disaster in the form of an earthquake in October 1855. The quake of an estimated 6.3 magnitude killed about 4000 people and destroyed 14,000 houses, although one account listed over 130,000 killed. Fortunately, the quake occurred fairly late at night, so that fewer fires were burning. While some carpenters and tradesmen benefited from the reconstruction work after the earthquake, many more poor people suffered, especially because their areas of the city suffered the most damage.

Many people linked the earthquake to the Black Ships, a sign that Japan should keep out the foreigners, and more natural disasters and epidemics during the following years added to the turmoil of the Bakumatsu years. Less than a year after the Edo earthquake, freak winds and rains hit the city, causing even more damage by some reports than the earthquake. Then a series of epidemics occurred: influenza in 1857; measles and two outbreaks of cholera in 1858; measles and influenza in 1860; smallpox in 1861; measles and dysentery in 1862; and influenza in 1867. The worst was the cholera epidemic of 1858 which rumour blamed on American ships arriving in Nagasaki.

In the newly opened port cities Japanese came into direct contact with Westerners for the first time, and the cultural differences became immediately evident. Brawls erupted frequently between sailors and local Japanese. One American officer boasted in his memoirs of turning on samurai and kicking them when he was unable to stop their staring. This related to foreigners' common complaints about being spied upon and restricted. While some American sailors in Hakodate demanded rum and women or else they would seize the port, other Westerners expressed shock at mixed public baths, public display of phallic symbols, and Japanese people's open interest in sex, which were all seen as evidence of Japanese immorality and reinforced Western attitudes of cultural and racial superiority.

Outside the treaty ports, ordinary Japanese farmers felt the impact of the opening up of the country more indirectly, but perhaps more severely. Although the Japanese market remained small for many Western-style consumer goods, cheaper machine-made textiles and other manufactured goods began to flow into Japan, and domestic producers were unable to compete with them. The loss of the right to control imports or levy tariffs meant that the shogunate could do nothing to protect these domestic industries. At the same time, foreign buyers began to purchase Japanese-produced raw silk and cotton, which benefited some Japanese but also pushed up price levels so that domestic spinners and weavers could not compete with foreign imports. This not only created a balance of payments problem for the country, but deprived many farm households of the cash income they had come to earn from by-employments in rural industries. Peasant families often depended on this supplemental cash income to buy fertilizers and other commercial inputs as well as daily necessities which they were no longer producing themselves.

The large number of peasant and urban disturbances of the Bakumatsu years as well as the growth of new religions mentioned earlier reflected the severe economic and social problems afflicting Japan in the middle of the nineteenth century. The number of peasant uprisings, many with millenarian overtones, rose sharply in the decade before the Meiji Restoration, reaching a peak in 1866 with the outbreak of at least 106 disturbances.[11] Most of these were destructive rather than constructive, reflecting the frustration triggering them. Judging from demands made by the protestors and their targeting of rich peasants, however, commoners tended to blame sources closer to home rather than the foreigners or even higher feudal authorities for their problems. Small landholders, more than landless peasants, dominated the movements and were more concerned with protecting their status as independent cultivators than with rebelling against government authorities. Consequently, while the increasing violence in the cities and countryside created anxiety, perhaps even fear, among shogunal and *han* officials, historians agree that commoners did not come to play a direct role in the end of the Tokugawa regime.

'Men of spirit' and the years of terror

Most Japanese remained preoccupied with matters connected with daily living and the local region, but some members of the samurai class became increasingly interested in national issues and actively involved in seeking solutions to problems facing the country as a whole. The number of activists still remained small (perhaps around 1000[12]), but came from lower ranks of the samurai class than in the past. Most conspicuous among the activists and having an impact disproportionate to their numbers were the *shishi* or 'men of spirit' who formed the so-called loyalist movement and terrorized the imperial capital of Kyoto during the late 1850s and early 1860s under the banner of *'sonnō jōi'* (revere the emperor, expel the barbarians).

The unequal treaties had made foreign policy the core issue of what was now 'public' discussion. They aroused strong emotions which led men to see beyond their regional boundaries and feudal loyalties, and opened up opportunities in political life for people who previously had had no voice in decision-making. Foreign policy soon became inextricably linked with proposals for domestic change, although until the mid-1860s most proposals for change, including those put forth by *shishi*, did not aim at the kind of wholesale destruction of the feudal system that was to eventuate under the Meiji government.

The actions of the *shishi*, however, were certainly radical. Gathering in Kyoto around certain court nobles, they terrorized the city and other parts of Japan with their attacks on foreigners, shogunal officials and others seen as responsible for giving in to the foreigners. Notable among their successful assassination attempts was Ii Naosuke outside Edo castle in 1860. Ii had not only signed the unequal treaties, but purged the reforming *daimyō* who supported Tokugawa Yoshinobu in the succession dispute. Ii's 'crimes' indicate the complexity of motives for the *shishi*, which in turn accounts for the division of opinion among historians about the nature of the Meiji Restoration and the forces that lay behind it. To some historians, and Japanese nationalists in the later nineteenth and twentieth centuries, the *shishi* were true imperial loyalists reflecting a ground swell of sentiment focusing on the emperor and aiming at repositioning his role in national political life from being the 'principle' to the 'principal'.[13] Others link the *shishi* to the shift from a feudal to a bourgeois stage of historical development, emphasizing their low rank backgrounds in the samurai class and their connections with an emergent merchant class or 'modern' landlords. Still others relate the *shishi* to popular, revolutionary protest, or alternatively to a shared feeling of social grievance.

Part of the problem of ascribing motives to the *shishi* is that they did not make up a single organized movement with a manifesto of stated goals. Although most came from the domains of Satsuma, Chōshū, Mito and Tosa, they acted as individuals or in small groups. Western historians such as Marius Jansen and William G. Beasley have noted certain commonalties of young age (early thirties and even younger), lower or pseudo-samurai rank, ambition, and a temperament characterized by idealism and adventurousness, but they have found inconsistencies too, and not all loyalists became terrorists. Beasley concludes that loyalists who eschewed radical action in favour of manipulating *han* politics usually came from the middle ranks of the samurai class, but had connections with a few upper samurai to give them access to those who monopolized high levels of decision-making and also with a few lower samurai to provide a link with the extremists. Prime examples would be Kido Takayoshi (Kōin) of Chōshū and Ōkubo Toshimichi and Saigō Takamori of Satsuma, all of whom became leading figures in the Meiji Restoration. In contrast, the radical activists tended to be loyalists on the fringes of the samurai class (sons of village headmen or rich merchants), samurai whose rank precluded them from participation in *han* politics or others who considered legal methods to be ineffective or inadequate.[14] Sakamoto Ryōma of Tosa, a *gōshi* or rural samurai, exemplifies this type, as do many followers of Chōshū's Yoshida Shōin.

Yoshida is the most famous of the *shishi*, though he died in 1859 when the loyalist movement was just beginning. In fact, his teachings and death provided a model and inspiration for the *shishi*, and more than half of his students followed him in meeting early and often violent deaths, although a few surviving ones, including Kido Takayoshi, Itō Hirobumi and Yamagata Aritomo, went on to become leaders during the Meiji period. Yoshida's own education was eclectic, though like all samurai having a base in Neo-Confucianism. As a very young man he studied in Edo under Sakuma Shōzan, the Western military expert who favoured opening up the country, but later studied with the Mito exclusionist Aizawa Seishisai. The latter visit to Mito was not authorized by his *han*, costing him the loss of his samurai rank and the stipend going with it, which foreshadows the rebellious actions he later became famous for. When Perry arrived in 1853, he went to see the ceremonial landing and, with Sakuma's encouragement, tried to persuade the Americans to take him with them so that he could pursue his Western studies. Although finding him 'courteous and highly refined' the Americans refused, and Yoshida was imprisoned, first in Edo, then in his castle town in Chōshū.

Yoshida remained under house arrest from the beginning of 1856, but was able to start a school which nurtured many of the *shishi* of the Bakumatsu period. His teachings initially recommended reforms, but the 1858 treaties and purges radicalized him. Abandoning hope in the shogun, *daimyō* and *han* officials, he called for 'humble heroes' to demonstrate their sincere concern for the national interest by a rising in the name of the emperor. Yoshida himself planned the assassination of Ii Naosuke's emissary *en route* to Kyoto to obtain the emperor's support for the Harris Treaty, but his plot was discovered, and he was arrested and executed in late 1859. Although some of his students, including Kido, proved reluctant to abandon their domain and to take up direct action, a number of other young samurai from Chōshū and other *han* took up his call to armed action.

The next several years witnessed the peak of anti-foreign activities with nearly seventy incidents of political assassination from the beginning of 1862 to the middle of 1864.[15] Consequently, the conventional depiction of the Meiji Restoration as a relatively bloodless coup overlooks the violence that preceded it during the years of *shishi* terror, not to mention the background of peasant protests and urban riots.

From '*jōi*' to '*fukoku kyōhei*'

While *shishi* activists carried out their anti-foreign attacks or manoeuvred for influence among court nobles, more pragmatic loyalists and leaders in Chōshū and Satsuma took initiatives to give their domain a larger role in national affairs. The shogunate's weakness in the foreign crisis had opened up the possibility for *daimyō* as well as the imperial court to increase their say in national politics, especially after Ii Naosuke's death. In September 1862 Satsuma proposed a rearrangement of political structures under the rubric of the 'unity of Court and Bakufu'. Hoping to use the court's prestige to bolster its own, the shogunate accepted, but the plan involved concessions which further weakened its authority over the *daimyō* and enhanced the position of the court as a counterweight to the shogunate. For example, a relaxation of alternate attendance requirements in October 1862 freed *daimyō* families from their hostage status and led to a great exodus of samurai from Edo, while the announcement of a shogunal visit to Kyoto for the following year symbolized the political centrality of the emperor because it would be the first time that a shogun had visited Kyoto since the seventeenth century.

Conrad Totman therefore dates the beginning of the Tokugawa shogunate's 'time of troubles' to 1862, but the overthrow of the shogunate was not yet imminent. Although Kyoto had become a hive of activity and intrigue, and Chōshū and Satsuma were making bids for national political roles, they saw each other as rivals rather than allies, and their proposed reforms did not envisage fundamental changes in the political system. Factional politics between 'conservatives' and 'loyalists' within the *han* were contentious, and the future leaders of the Meiji Restoration did not yet occupy high positions in their *han* governments. In fact, the loyalists in *han* governments had trouble keeping the more impatient radicals under control as Japan entered the peak of *shishi* terrorist activity. *Shishi* threatened moderate or pro-shogunate court nobles by sending them the ears or heads of murdered retainers with explicit warning notes. More and more samurai from Chōshū gathered in Kyoto, and in March 1863 Chōshū came out openly in support of the *sonnō jōi* extremists. In such a climate senior court officials found it difficult to resist loyalist pressure to make demands on the shogunate to expel the foreigners, and the shogunate, not wanting to provoke a head-on clash with the extremists, agreed to set a date for expulsion: 25 June 1863.

The consequences of Chōshū's solitary attempt to expel the Westerners on the appointed date may be seen as an important step in the shift from *jōi* to *fukoku kyōhei* (enrich the country, strengthen the army). The *han* cannon fired on American, French and British ships in the Shimonoseki Straits and closed the straits to foreign ships, but the Western powers retaliated in August 1864 with a squadron of seventeen ships which bombarded Chōshū's coastal defences and destroyed its batteries. This demonstration of Western military might proved the impracticability of *jōi* more effectively than the words of any *kaikoku* advocate. Assessing the situation in September 1865, Ōkubo Toshimichi of Satsuma wrote,

> since the Chōshū fighting, the so-called irrational extremists have for the most part had their eyes opened, so that they have come to argue the impossibility of expulsion and even recommend the opening of the country; while the more enlightened domains – Hizen, Echizen, Tosa, Uwajima, and so on – are definitely inclining toward arrangements for trade.[16]

This reinforced the lesson of a similar demonstration of Western military power in Satsuma a year before when Britain retaliated for the murder of a British merchant, Charles Richardson, by Satsuma samurai. Satsuma's refusal to produce the murderers to face punishment resulted in a military engagement which ended with large parts of the castle town of Kagoshima destroyed.

Although hotheads did not disappear completely and neither did anti-foreignism, the attitude among leaders of the subsequent anti-Tokugawa movement changed towards a greater willingness to use Western methods, especially Western weapons and science, for strengthening Japan against the West. Military reforms involved formation of rifle companies. In Chōshū these were made up of both commoners and samurai and played a key role in the fighting which followed during the remaining years of the shogunate. Although the commoners came from various occupations (fishermen, townsmen, hunters), many were sons of village headmen. The samurai included *rōnin* (masterless samurai) from other *han*, *shishi* who flocked to Chōshū as it became the centre for *sonnō jōi* extremism. Recognition of the need for foreign trade and military reform also encouraged increased study and direct contact with the West, including *han*-sponsored student groups in Europe, and brought middle samurai loyalists to power in Satsuma and Chōshū, the future leaders of the Meiji Restoration.

Towards the Meiji Restoration

The last phase of the Bakumatsu period was characterized by Western-oriented reform efforts in the leading *han* which reflected the victory of reformers over both conservatives and extremists and was paralleled by the decline of terrorism. It also saw the shogunate inviting French advisers to help in its own reform efforts and attempting to reassert its authority. However, although Satsuma supported the shogunate in the summer of 1864 in restoring order in Kyoto and punishing Chōshū for an attempted coup d'état, it gradually turned towards cooperation, then an alliance with Chōshū when it perceived 'selfish' Tokugawa attempts to subordinate the *han* once again. Ironically, the first punitive expedition against Chōshū set off a civil war in the domain which brought reformers to power there and made its policies similar to Satsuma's. A second expedition against Chōshū in the summer of 1866 consequently failed because of Satsuma's lack of support, since Chōshū and Satsuma had created a secret alliance in March to overthrow the Tokugawas when a new shogun's reorganization and modernization efforts threatened them with a Tokugawa resurgence. Nevertheless, as evident in detailed histories of the Bakumatsu period, traditional rivalries between *han* and differences in policies among groups even within Satsuma and Chōshū themselves as well as in the court and other domains meant that the unity and success of the Restoration movement was not ensured even when the Satsuma–Chōshū forces, joined at the last moment by Tosa and Hizen, staged their palace coup, 'restoring imperial rule' (*ōsei fukko*) on 3 January 1868.

Although many traditional accounts of the overthrow of the Tokugawa shogunate end here, in fact this was the beginning of a civil war which continued until May 1869 when the last Tokugawa holdouts in northeastern Honshū surrendered. In the most fierce campaign of the war, Tokugawa supporters in Aizu lost nearly 3000 samurai and the castle was burned. A family history of samurai life in Mito reveals how the violence extended to women and children of samurai families caught up in the factional struggles within and between domains during the last years of the Tokugawa shogunate.[17] Not only were *shishi* and, during the civil war, Tokugawa supporters hunted down, but their families were also frequently executed.

The response of Japanese commoners and foreign residents to the events of late 1867 and early 1868 also does not indicate that in the eyes of contemporaries Japan had reached a major watershed in its history. Although not directly involved in the intrigues, people in the capital of Kyoto had for years been kept up to date on political developments through posters and placards displayed throughout the city by *shishi*. One samurai observer noted that 'people [in the capital] showed no surprise . . . and seemed generally to doubt whether the new administration would last'.[18] The British diplomat Sir Harry Parkes sent a dispatch to London reassuring his government that the situation in Japan did not possess 'an alarming nature as regards ourselves'.

At the same time, although the number of rural disturbances dropped dramatically in 1867 after a peak the previous year, another kind of mass disturbance broke out in cities, towns and villages throughout the country known by the crowds' chant, *'ee ja nai ka'* ('Isn't that good?' or 'What the hell!').[19] Inspired by the mysterious falling of thousands of paper talismans from the skies, people everywhere took to frenzied dancing and singing in the streets, men and women, young and old trading styles of dress and always ending their songs with the refrain, *'ee ja nai ka'*. Some contemporaries as well as historians have seen nothing political in these hysterical revels except as an epiphenomenal reflection of an age of disorder, but others have argued that they contributed to that disorder and set the stage for the Meiji Restoration. George Wilson views *ee ja nai ka* in the same category of public disturbances as the pilgrimages to the Grand Shrine of Ise or the new religions like Tenrikyō, 'the last of these deviant (or defiant) behaviours' and a form of protest against the old order.[20]

The Meiji Restoration in historical perspective

The differences among historians' assessments of the political significance of *ee ja nai ka* comprise only one issue among many in the historical debate over explaining the end of the Tokugawa order and the beginning of the Meiji Restoration. Underlying the *ee ja nai ka* debate are different evaluations about the impact of popular protest and the role of commoners in the Restoration movement's success. While all historians acknowledge samurai leadership of the Restoration movement, some would argue that the widespread popular disturbances of the late Tokugawa years undermined the regime and made possible fundamental change.

Examining the motives of the samurai leaders themselves, historians differ in their attribution of social versus nationalist consciousness. Albert Craig's now classic study of Chōshū, for example, rejected the then dominant view of Japanese historians emphasizing the 'lower' samurai background of the Meiji leaders as the reason for their revolutionary actions. Craig argued that samurai identified themselves with a particular *han* rather than a social class; they acted as members of 'hierarchically ordered groups bound by ties that were both vertical and particular' rather than as members of horizontal classes. 'Han nationalism', loyalty easily transferred to the nation when Japan as a whole was threatened by the West, led to 'a change carried out in the name of old values' rather than a revolution in the name of new values.[21] Thomas Huber, in contrast, concluded from his study of Yoshida Shōin's students that the lower samurai background of Meiji leaders did matter, that they acted in common out of a sense of grievances against their social group as a 'service intelligentsia'.[22]

This controversy is related to the more general split among historians between those emphasizing the domestic crisis and those emphasizing the foreign crisis as the motive force for the Restoration, although in recent studies the split is based on a matter of emphasis rather than complete disregard of other factors. Was the Meiji Restoration a social revolution or a nationalist revolution? And why does such a question matter? It matters because the determination of 'causes' of the overthrow of the Tokugawa shogunate is directly linked to one's interpretation of the nature and objective of the changes later initiated by the Meiji government. This, in turn, is linked to one's interpretation of the direction taken in Japan's modernization process and to evaluation of its effects. While many historians now reject linear, teleological views of history which see historical processes moving towards a given end, others, including both influential Japanese political leaders and 'progressive' critics, trace characteristics of present-day Japan in a direct line back to the Meiji Restoration.

To celebrants and critics alike, the Meiji Restoration was 'the departure point of modern Japan', but as we shall see in the next chapter, the new leaders of Japan in early 1868, only somewhat less than ordinary Japanese, were far from certain or agreed as to the shape of the future.

3　The early Meiji Revolution

The Meiji Restoration has aroused immense controversy among both Japanese and Western historians during the twentieth century: controversy over the objectives of the Meiji leaders, the degree of 'success' or 'failure', and the nature and degree of changes initiated by the Meiji government. No disagreement exists, however, that the Meiji Restoration is the key to our understanding of modern Japanese history. Conversely, historians' personal views of contemporary Japanese society and politics shape their interpretations of the Meiji Restoration. Historians either blame or credit Meiji government policies and institutions depending on their evaluations of twentieth-century history. But the Meiji Restoration is not only significant for historians; it is also part of Japan's national history and public memory, and as such has been highly contested terrain. Among both conservatives and critics, there is a narrative of 'the long modern' which sees the work of modernization that Meiji began completed only in the post-1945 period, and whether for good or bad depends on their ideological or political leanings.

At the beginning of the century a very positive view dominated, but met with a competing view from the 1920s onwards. The establishment view pictured the Meiji leaders as a united group of enlightened, far-sighted statesmen who accomplished their goals with remarkable speed and at little cost or conflict. Such interpretations emphasized political change, namely the overthrow of the shogunate and restoration of imperial rule. During the 1920s this view continued, but a new one also emerged as Marxism gained popularity among intellectuals and academics after the Russian Revolution of 1917. The Marxist view emphasized socioeconomic factors as the motive forces for the overthrow of the shogunate and the nature of Meiji reforms. It highlighted the conservatism of the Meiji leaders rather than their reforming zeal, the limitations of the changes rather than their extent. It traced the conservatism to the socioeconomic background of the Meiji leaders and their supporters; that is, their membership in the old samurai elite with the support of wealthy landlords and the newly emerging bourgeoisie.

Considering the continued strength of these 'feudal remnants' in the Meiji order, Marxists became divided over the strength of bourgeois elements in the Meiji Restoration process. During the 1920s a fierce debate arose between the so-called 'Kōzaha' (Lectures faction) and 'Rōnōha' (Labour–Farmer faction), which had practical implications for Japanese Communist Party strategy. In simple terms, the Kōzaha considered the feudal remnants still too strong to make the Meiji Restoration a complete bourgeois revolution, which, according to Marx's theory of historical stages, meant that in the 1920s and 1930s communists had to work towards achieving a socialist revolution in two stages. The more impatient, or optimistic Rōnōha saw the bourgeoisie as having become stronger since 1868 so that Japan had reached the stage of finance monopoly capitalism, the final stage of capitalism. Only a one-stage revolution was therefore required to reach socialism. After the Second World War the lines between the two schools blurred since the bourgeoisie was clearly in the ascendant, but traces of the two interpretations lingered for decades.

Since the 1980s orthodox Marxism declined as in the West, yet the overall image of the Tokugawa and Meiji periods remained much the same for various types of so-called progressive historians, and still pervades popular literature and the press. All condemned the Tokugawa period as feudal, hence oppressive. Most continued to judge the Meiji period negatively because feudal remnants remained strong and impeded Japan's historical development towards socialism and thence the communist utopia. Many remained concerned to find the roots of the policies and governmental system that took Japan into a disastrous war and occupation and found them in Meiji 'absolutism' or the 'emperor system' (*tennōsei*).

Postwar conservative politicians and historians in Japan, however, maintained a positive view of the Meiji Restoration, tracing Japan's economic successes to that period. Seeking continuity with the past, prime ministers such as Yoshida Shigeru in 1952 could extol 'the extraordinary progress made within a half century after the Meiji Restoration'. Celebration of the Meiji centennial in 1968 sounded like the happy ending to Japan's story of modernization and industrialization. The increasingly nationalistic climate of the 1980s and parallel decline of orthodox Marxism reinvigorated the view of the Restoration as the beginning of Japan's modern success story.

In contrast, in Western scholarship there have emerged some less favourable, if not critical views of the Meiji Restoration since the 1970s. These began with the Vietnam War and 'New Left' revisionist views of modern Japanese history. The revisionists criticized past American work dominated by so-called 'modernization theory' for seeing the modernization process as a positive and linear progression based on Western industrialized societies' experiences. They stimulated a rethinking of Japanese history which led to the decline of modernization theory. At the same time, increasing awareness of social and environmental problems that Japan was facing in the 1970s despite, or because of, its 'economic miracle', led to more critical evaluations of the Meiji period and to investigation of the social as well as political costs of industrialization and modernization along with the gains. This has gradually put an end to the image of harmony, unity and consensus that previously dominated both positive and negative interpretations of the Meiji Restoration.

As we begin to focus on 'the departure point for Japan's modern history' in this chapter, keep in mind these points of contention. And while we will give prominent attention to the policies of the Meiji leaders and their object-ives, whatever their intentions, Japanese society and politics did not develop exactly as they hoped and tried to ensure.

The Meiji leaders

This cautionary note said, the Meiji leaders were undeniably a group of talented individuals who historians would probably agree made a difference to Japanese history. The government was characterized by a collective leader-ship, or oligarchy, with the decision-makers numbering no more than two dozen or so. While representing a diverse range of political opinions and ideologies, they shared common *han* origins and a NeoConfucian education, and, although young, had experience in government administration and the military and contact with the West or Western studies. During the early years three emerged at the top: Ōkubo Toshimichi, Kido Takayoshi and Saigō Takamori. Besides giving them faces or personalities, a profile of these three will provide a better picture of the Tokugawa society from which they emerged and the role they played as Meiji leaders.

We will start with Ōkubo and Kido, the two most powerful and creative of the early Meiji leaders. Ōkubo was born in 1830 some distance from the Satsuma castle town of Kagoshima, the only son in a family of middle-ranking samurai. Since samurai made up 40 per cent of Satsuma's popula-tion and most were *gōshi* (rural samurai) and rear vassals, this put Ōkubo's family in quite a high stratum – significantly, high enough for him to be eligible for *han* offices. His grandfather was a Dutch-style doctor, while his father studied the action-oriented Wang Yang-ming school of Confucianism and Zen Buddhism. Ōkubo went to the *han* academy and formed important friendships in the district youth organization, notably with Saigō Takamori, another future leader of the Restoration. After entering the *han* bureaucracy at the age of 17 or 18, his career followed the ups and downs of *daimyō* clique politics. By 1858 he held a fairly responsible middle-grade position, but was dismissed when his *daimyō* benefactor, Shimazu Nariakira, died. Ōkubo then became leader of the moderate wing of a *sonnō jōi* group, perhaps as a means to regain his lost position. Hisamitsu, father of the young, new *daimyō*, attempted to forestall the group's action, which provided the opportunity for Ōkubo to gain an audience with him and thereafter reappointment to the bureaucracy. From 1861 Ōkubo acted as a member of the top circle of *han* policy-makers.

As a Meiji leader, Ōkubo continued this pattern of a career bureaucrat, presenting an image of a single-minded, highly integrated personality, a totally political person dedicated to the Meiji state. The force of his character and will was recognized by all his contemporaries and is revealed in his tough and forceful, but colourless letters and diary. According to the court noble Iwakura Tomomi, 'Ōkubo has no talent and no learning; his virtue is that he is firm and unmoving'.[1] Another official wrote that coming together with Ōkubo was 'like meeting an iceberg in the Arctic Ocean'. The contrast with Kido in their effect on associates is evident in an observation of the First Assembly of Local Offices held in 1875: 'When Kido was in charge, the meeting was in an uproar. But when Ōkubo entered the hall, it became quiet like dust settling when water is scattered. Ōkubo gave a few words of explanation and even those that did not understand pretended that they did'.[2] An austere personal life paralleled this public image. Unlike most Meiji government leaders, including Kido, Ōkubo rarely drank and did not frequent geisha houses, and favoured Western dress, diet and personal habits.

The policies he favoured, like his personality, were marked by a practical, down-to-earth quality, caution and moderation. In the early years he was concerned most with consolidation of the central government, not necessarily Westernization *per se*. In late 1871, however, he embarked with other top officials on a diplomatic mission and study tour of the West led by Iwakura Tomomi. Although the mission failed to achieve its diplomatic goal of revising the unequal treaties, the firsthand observation of Western societies and industrial strengths made a tremendous impact on Ōkubo and other participants. Ōkubo returned from the Iwakura Mission in 1873 with a new vision of social and economic change. Consequently, he opposed his old friend Saigō on a plan to provoke a crisis in Korea which could be used to justify a military invasion. Up to this point Ōkubo had been important in preventing Saigō and potential opponents in Satsuma from turning against the new government. This time, however, differences in temperament and goals could no longer be bridged.

Soon after Saigō withdrew angrily from the government over the Korean issue, Kido did also, due to an illness from which he died in 1877. This left Ōkubo the dominant figure in the government until his assassination by samurai dissidents in 1878. Some Japanese historians describe this period as that of the 'Ōkubo dictatorship', and, despite his great power and dedication to the government, Ōkubo is not remembered warmly in Japanese history books. Because of his personality, he was admired and feared, but never loved.

Kido Takayoshi, in contrast, has been described by Albert Craig as irresolute and subject to mercurial emotional fluctuations, yet it was this more emotional, expressive character which made him easier to get along with and therefore effective as a clique leader. His socioeconomic background was not dissimilar to Ōkubo's, though. Kido was born into a Chōshū samurai family of similar rank to Ōkubo's, but having a larger income. His father, like Ōkubo's grandfather, studied Dutch medicine. At the age of 8, however, he was adopted out as heir to the neighbouring and slightly higher ranking Katsura house, a not uncommon practice during the Tokugawa period and even earlier. After this comfortable childhood he reached a turning point when he became one of Yoshida Shōin's first students, and another when in 1852 he received permission from the *han* government to study swordsmanship in Edo. There he learned Western military techniques as well as fencing, which led him to propose recruitment of peasants as soldiers after Perry's arrival. He later studied Western shipbuilding in Nagasaki, and his memorial to the *han* resulted in Chōshū's attempt to build a Western-style schooner in 1856.

Like Ōkubo, Kido owed his rise to a top position in his *han* to his influence in two key groups: the regular *han* bureaucracy and the *sonnō jōi* clique. Although a leader of the *sonnō* clique, Kido, again like Ōkubo, was not impractical in his policies. He disagreed with the radical activism of his teacher Yoshida, counselled caution when Satsuma and Aizu opposed Chōshū in 1863, but joined Chōshū's coup attempt in Kyoto in 1864. After Chōshū's civil war he rose to the top of the *han* government. As a Meiji leader he was more excitable, as well as exciting, than Ōkubo, but more open to new ideas and able to hold together the precarious Satsuma–Chōshū coalition. Neither impractical nor imprudent, he consistently supported Ōkubo against Saigō's Korean expedition plan in 1873.

If Kido appears to later generations in a warmer light than the more powerful Ōkubo, the same must be said, but to an even greater extent, of Saigō Takamori. Saigō became a 'traitor' to the Meiji government, but in the twentieth century became the most popular of Restoration leaders and the ideal hero in modern Japanese history. Even his opponents admired his honesty and courage and were moved by the force of his personality. His physical attibutes reflected his larger-than-life personality and charisma – almost six feet tall, weighing 109 kg, and with a 49.5 cm neck. Even as a boy in Satsuma he exhibited leadership qualities as leader of the samurai youth organization. Though from a somewhat poorer family than either Ōkubo or Kido, Saigō's rank was also high enough to qualify him for *han* office. *Han* factional politics affected his early career as it did Ōkubo's, and his leadership of the *sonnō* group led to a five-year banishment from the *han* until Ōkubo and others got him pardoned. After this he advanced rapidly in the *han* government along with Ōkubo and led the Restoration armies in 1868.

Saigō retained a rural samurai ethos even after becoming a Meiji government leader. He differed from most in his dislike of luxury and ostentation, and he loathed the new emphasis on commerce and business. Still dressed in simple country clothes, disdaining the Western frock-coats and top hats that his colleagues usually wore, he even visited the Imperial Palace in sandals or clogs. It is no wonder, then, that he eventually parted company with the government. He was particularly disturbed by the conscription law and other legal and economic blows to the samurai class, and his 1873 plan for a military expedition to Korea aimed to provide employment for samurai. Saigō never visited the West, nor expressed interest in doing so. Consequently, his cultural orientation remained Japanese and, unlike other Meiji leaders, he never had any experience with the West that might have changed it.

After his Korean plan was blocked, Saigō departed in outrage from the government and became the central rallying point for discontented samurai. This culminated in leadership of the Satsuma Rebellion in 1877. While pointing out his mistakes as a general, a staunch pro-government newspaper expressed its admiration:

> What sort of man was Saigō Takamori? In his house there was neither wealth nor a retinue of servants. But he was able to so secure the confidence of the people that he could lead a great army into rebellion against the Imperial forces, and though only three provinces joined him in revolt, by successive battles and retreats he held out against the government for more than half a year. Finally . . . when surrounded by Imperial troops, he cut his way out and escaped to his native place in Kagoshima, and there he was killed in battle. If we carefully consider his course, we see that he fully sustained his fame until the last. He died without shame and closed his eyes in peace.[3]

In fact, Saigō took his life in the samurai tradition of ritual suicide (*seppuku*), and was all the more admired for that. By 1890, when the government was looking for symbols of national identity and unity, it rehabilitated Saigō and so began the Saigō legends. He became the last true hero of Japan, the epitome of sincerity and devotion to a cause which are the ultimate qualities of a Japanese hero. Nationalists of the twentieth century glorified him as a superpatriot, but at the same time liberals and progressives admired him as a symbol of freedom and resistance to an unjust government.

Centralization, institutional borrowing and social restructuring

Saigō's leadership of the Satsuma Rebellion and Ōkubo's death in 1878 at the hands of an assassin are indications of the violence and struggle involved in establishing the new Meiji government – it was not entirely a bloodless revolution from above as is often depicted. Ōkubo and Kido were bureaucrats, but Saigō's military background replicated the character of other Meiji leaders, all important military commanders in the civil war.

During the first decade of the Meiji period government leaders focused on centralizing and stabilizing their power and authority, not only for securing their personal positions, but also for preventing foreign intervention. While domestic factors were always extremely important shapers of policymaking, Japan no longer tried to operate as a closed country, isolated from Western influence. In the name of the emperor in 1868, the new government proclaimed its general principles for the future in the Charter Oath, including 'knowledge shall be sought throughout the world'. The proclaimed goal of 'a rich country, strong army' also highlights the changed world view and nationalist motives of the Meiji leaders. The abandonment of '*jōi*' had not meant abandonment of the desire to get rid of the foreigners. Rather, the new goal of 'a rich country, strong army' signalled the desire to eliminate the unequal treaties by becoming the equal of the Western imperialist powers. To do this, the Meiji government initiated a period of foreign borrowing matched only by its own previous experience of borrowing from China in the seventh and eighth centuries.

This involved dismantling the old Tokugawa *bakuhan* structure and destroying the *daimyō*–samurai class that had dominated it. The former, in particular the 1871 abolition of the *han* and establishment of a prefectural system of local government, is often referred to as 'the second Restoration', while the latter constituted a social revolution from above. The result was ultimately a radical departure from the Tokugawa system of political authority and administration, but, while expanding the base of political participation, the new system did not satisfy everyone. Historians now point out that few of the leaders had expected, much less planned, the abolition of the shogunate or samurai class in 1868, though the foreign threat during the Bakumatsu years had exposed the weaknesses of the decentralized *bakuhan* system. The changes towards a strong centralized government were therefore gradual, and resulted from a lot of vigorous debate, experimentation and trial and error, as reflected in the numerous changes in government department name changes during the first few years. Eighth-century Nara court ranks and titles were restored for a little while since that was a period when some emperors ruled as well as reigned, and the emperor himself was sent on national tours of the country to give visible evidence of imperial sanctioning of the new government. The abolition of the *han* in 1871 finally completed centralization by creating a single pyramidal administrative structure which stretched down and around the entire country. At the top stood the oligarchs, the handful of decision-makers primarily from Satsuma, Chōshū, Tosa and Hizen with authoritarian powers. They headed ministries staffed by samurai. Below followed prefectures (*ken*) headed by appointed governors, then came districts and villages in rural areas, or cities and wards in urban areas.

Lack of resistance to abolition of the *han* may be explained by the preponderant military strength of the central government, the financial crises being faced by *han*, and the fear of foreign intervention if national unity were not achieved. In addition, appointments as prefectural governors served to coopt the *daimyō*, who might have become rallying points for disgruntled samurai. Creation of a modern Western-style military had obviously assumed top priority among the new government's goals. Initially it was necessary to protect Japan against Western intervention, but as this became unlikely in the 1870s, it continued to be required to reach the larger goal of equality with the major Western powers. In view of the remaining threat of samurai opposition and peasant protests, a strong national army was also essential for maintaining internal order.

Changes in military institutions provide an excellent example of the Western institutional borrowing characterizing the Meiji modernization drive. They were the first areas of major structural change, the first to adopt Western organizational patterns, and the first to hire foreign advisers. They became the largest scale organizations in Japanese society and models of modernization for other areas, stimulating the development of other fields such as shipping, mining and munitions. The Meiji government did not start from scratch, however, since the *han*, especially Chōshū and Satsuma, as well as the shogunate, had undertaken military reforms from the early 1860s. Satsuma had employed British advisers to build a navy after the Kagoshima bombardment, and the Meiji government continued to follow the British model. The navy introduced Western-style uniforms and structures before the army did.

The army, however, developed more rapidly and extensively than the navy until the late Meiji period, perhaps because the internal threats loomed larger than the foreign threats by the early 1870s, and purchasing warships from abroad was costly. After some disagreement over whether to adopt the French or German model, the government formally adopted the French model, even though Prussia defeated France at Sedan only one month after the decision. A government statement defending the decision reveals the sensitivity of Japanese leaders to foreign opinion:

> After deciding to adopt the French system, if we changed our mind only because France was defeated, this would give a wrong impression to other countries that the Japanese Empire has no backbone and [is] unreliable, and eventually [it would] become a laughing stock among the nations.[4]

In 1872 French military officers arrived to become the core of teachers in the new military academy.

Debate over recruitment of the new army's soldiers proved to be even more contentious than choice of a Western model, and led to the assassination of at least one advocate of universal conscription. Since there were close to half a million unemployed samurai, the government need not have widened the base of recruitment. However, those favouring universal conscription, including the 'father of the Japanese army' Yamagata Aritomo of Chōshū, prevailed with arguments ranging from the historical and political to the economic. Remember that mixed commoner–samurai units in Chōshū's army had played a significant role in the battles against Tokugawa forces. The Conscription Edict of 1873 is seen as a landmark decision representing the government's commitment to building a modern nation-state on the Western model. Like its French counterpart, it included categories of exemptions and the possibility of purchasing exemptions, but it nevertheless broke the centuries-long samurai monopoly over a military role in Japanese society and opened up an avenue of upward mobility for commoners.

Not all the social consequences of universal conscription were intended by Yamagata, who became known for his social and political conservatism, but other measures introduced by the Meiji government intentionally

destroyed the old Tokugawa social order. Central among these was abolition of the hereditary four-class system. In 1872 upper strata of the samurai
class became part of a new aristocracy (*shizoku*), but the majority of samurai
joined peasants, artisans and merchants as commoners (*heimin*). Outcasts
(*eta* and *hinin*) were elevated to the status of 'new commoners' (*shinheimin*),
but later became more commonly referred to as 'Burakumin'. The next few
years saw the gradual elimination of all samurai privileges and economic
support. All Japanese were now allowed to pursue whatever occupation they
chose, to travel freely and ride on horseback, and to take surnames, while it
became 'optional' for samurai to wear their distinctive topknot and to carry
two swords. Because samurai stipends cost the debt-ridden government too
much money and their military services became obtainable from others after
the Conscription Edict, in 1876 commutation of all stipends became compulsory and samurai were forbidden to wear their two swords. The former
daimyō ended up with substantial capital in government bonds, but most
samurai were reduced to mere subsistence if not financial ruin.

The financial problems of the new government also led to heavier economic
burdens for much of the peasant class. Elimination of samurai stipends did
not provide a long-term solution to creating a stable source of revenue. This
began in 1873 with the introduction of a uniform land tax to be collected
in money rather than rice and based on the value of the land rather than
size of the harvest. This did not allow for any variation in the tax if there
was a bad harvest, though peasants might benefit if the harvest was good.
Peasants did benefit by receiving title to their land and freedom to do with
it as they desired, but the greatest beneficiaries were the already well-to-do
landowners. Although there is some dispute among economic historians, it
seems that further financial reforms in the 1880s led by Matsukata Masayoshi
hurt poorer peasants greatly, forcing many into tenantry and wage labour.

'Civilization and enlightenment'

Although adopting an approach to Western borrowing based on 'Japanese
spirit, Western techniques', the Meiji government did not confine its use
of Western models and advisers to political institutions and organizational
methods. The complaints and condescending attitude of Westerners evident
in treaty port cultural clashes had indicated early during the Bakumatsu
years that Japan would have to change more than its political system to
revise the unequal treaties and win acceptance as an equal to the West. The
1868 Charter Oath's principle of abandoning 'evil customs of the past' foreshadowed social and cultural changes. Consequently, Meiji leaders both
outside and inside government encouraged the adoption of Western social
customs and cultural styles to reach the goal of 'civilization and enlightenment'
(*bunmei kaika*), with no doubt that 'civilization' meant Western civilization.

At the state level, pursuing 'civilization and enlightenment' led to the
establishment of a national fine arts school, employing the Italian painter

Antonio Fontanesi to teach Japanese artists to paint in Western styles. The school aimed to become the equal of the best art academies in the West by training artists in Western realism. Takahashi Yuichi, one of Fontanesi's students, became a leading representative of early Meiji Western-style painters. He was attracted to Western painting because it was 'so astonishingly life-like and attractive'. Ironically, Claude Monet, a leader of the European Impressionist painters, was saying almost the same thing, but of Japanese art: 'Look at that flower with its petals turned back by the wind, is that not truth itself?'[5] Monet and other Impressionists were influenced by Japanese woodblock prints (*ukiyoe*) to break away from established academy styles of composition, colour and light.

The government also hired foreign architects to design new public buildings, including schools and government offices, and to teach Japanese how to construct Western-style buildings. As in all fields, the government did not want Japan to be dependent on foreigners for long. Influential political leaders, such as Inoue Kaoru, wanted to give the new capital of Tokyo a modern – meaning European – appearance in order to help eliminate the unequal treaties. Consequently, when a fire wiped out large parts of the downtown commercial area in 1872, the governor of the city decided that the Ginza district should be rebuilt in brick to the designs of the English architect Thomas Waters. Gaslights flared all along the main street northward to Kyōbashi and westward towards the palace. The new bright Ginza 'Bricktown' became a star attraction for sightseers as a symbol of 'civilization and enlightenment'.

Westernization of outward appearances also included aspects of daily life such as dress and diet. Japanese leaders had learned from Western advice, such as Townsend Harris's, the importance of appearance in judgements of other cultures. Explaining the Western system of salutes, Harris had told a Japanese official: 'I told him that I was anxious that the Japanese should take their place among the civilized nations of the world, and that all the small things were so many steps in that direction'.[6] Aside from the introduction of Western-style military uniforms, the government passed an ordinance in 1872 requiring Western dress for government officials at formal occasions. The empress took the lead for women by giving up the custom of blackening her teeth and shaving her eyebrows and by adopting Victorian dress. The playwright Hasegawa Shigure recalled her return home one day to find her mother transformed:

> She performed the usual maternal functions without the smallest change, but she had a different face. Her eyebrows had always been shaved, so that only a faint blue-black sheen was where they might have been. Her teeth had been cleanly black. The mother I now saw before me had the stubbly beginnings of eyebrows, and her teeth were a startling, gleaming white. It was the more disturbing because something else was new. The new face was all smiles, as the old one had not been.[7]

Her mother's new look also included a pompadour hairdo, but apparently she returned to a traditional coiffure when neighbours harshly criticized it.

To encourage social interaction between the Japanese and Western elites, the government commissioned Josiah Conder to build the Rokumeikan, a Renaissance-style hall, for Western-style dancing, eating, card-playing and other innovative events like charity bazaars. The Rokumeikan gave its name to the height of the civilization and enlightenment era in the mid-1880s. Fancy-dress balls became all the rage among government officials, culminating in Prime Minister Itō Hirobumi's ball in 1887 where Itō appeared as a Venetian nobleman and his wife as a Spanish lady in a mantilla. Itō's wife Umeko led women of the elite in learning the new etiquette and conversational skills of socializing in Western manner by establishing 'improvement' groups for ladies. Although 'improvement' did not include new social roles other than those dictated by their husbands, it did lend respectability to new ideas of men and women socializing together in relative equality and of women expressing themselves in public.

While the Rokumeikan symbolized civilized and enlightened leisure for the Meiji elite, the Ryōunkaku in Asakusa, known more popularly as Twelve Stories, symbolized new Western entertainments for ordinary Tokyoites. It was built from red brick with the advice of an Englishman, but by a Japanese architect. The tallest building in the city, it also boasted the country's first elevator. It contained shops selling exotic wares from all over the world and galleries for art exhibitions. The top floor was fitted out with telescopes for observation, and the entire building was a tower of light, another emblem of civilization and enlightenment.

A strong desire to gain Western approval and avoid its ridicule is revealed in measures seeking conformity to Western standards of public decency. A newspaper article explaining an ordinance against public nakedness directed towards rickshaw men and day labourers declared, 'you must not be laughed at by foreigners'. Similarly, the headline 'Do not be laughed at by foreigners' preceded an article about another ordinance requiring public bath-owners to place screens at the entrance and to separate men and women. Officials issued warnings against obscene plays and tried to ban pornographic art.

To what extent urban dwellers followed these orders and instructions is unclear, but Western dress and styles did become a craze in the cities during the 1870s and 1880s. Western rings, watches and black umbrellas (nicknamed 'batwings') were especially popular as well as Western haircuts for men. Because imported Western items were still very expensive, however, people could not always afford a complete outfit, so some odd combinations of Western and Japanese dress resulted. Contrary to the Buddhist proscription against eating hoofed animals, beef-eating became a fad, as satirized in Kanagaki Robun's short story 'The Beefeater',[8] while beer quickly gained popularity equal to that of traditional sake.

However, while Western dress and social customs came to be seen as correct and up-to-date, at home even government officials typically reverted to

Plate 3.1 An early 1870s print depicting an 'unenlightened' man, a 'half-enlightened man' and an 'enlightened man'
Source: Kanagaki Robun, *Seiyō dōchū hizakurige*, vol. 2, revised edn by Kobayashi Chikahira, Tokyo: Iwanami Shoten, 1958, p. 94

kimonos, sitting on tatami floors and eating Japanese food. Most homes continued to be built and furnished in traditional Japanese style, making Western dress and shoes inconvenient and uncomfortable. Moreover, although a number of woodblock prints depict Japanese women in Western dress, in practice the majority of Japanese women continued to wear kimonos, even in the Western fashion centre of the Ginza, until the 1920s. In the countryside Western styles were also yet to come.

Nevertheless, although farming techniques and rural daily living continued largely unchanged, 'civilization and enlightenment' did affect villagers as well as city inhabitants in some ways. Houses gradually became lighter and cleaner with modern materials of paper and glass for windows, and with wood or tatami for floors. In its long-term consequences, however, the introduction of compulsory education in 1872, initially for sixteen months and extended to four years in 1886, proved most important. Ahead of many European countries, this not only gave access to education and new career prospects for children of all classes, but it also provided new opportunities and ideas for girls as well as boys. The government regarded education for girls as important for training future mothers. This was the reason for sending five young girls with the Iwakura Mission to the West. They included 7-year-old Tsuda Umeko, who later returned to found a school for girls that developed into what is now Tsuda College in Tokyo.

Foreign advisers, especially from the United States, helped to shape the new educational system, but intellectuals and educators outside government, such as members of the Meirokusha, also played a major role in advancing this aspect of the drive towards 'civilization and enlightenment'. Foremost among these was Fukuzawa Yukichi, whose picture appears today on the 10,000 yen note. He was one of the first Japanese to travel to the West, accompanying the shogunate's mission to the USA to ratify the Harris Treaty. On his return, he popularized knowledge about Western countries through best-selling books as well as the private academy (later Keiō University) which he founded. His *Conditions in the West* (*Seiyō jijō*), for example, sold 150,000 copies in its first edition. Fukuzawa represents the quintessential Meiji liberal – strong advocate of a spirit of personal independence, but for the purpose of defending the country against the foreigners and raising Japan to a higher form of civilization as much as for gaining individual prosperity and happiness. While often critical of the Meiji government and refusing offers to join it, Fukuzawa nevertheless remained a staunch nationalist and was as full of praise for Japan's victory over China in 1895 as was any government official.

Other Japanese intellectuals, many from the old samurai class, found Christianity to be the spirit of Western civilization and the source of Western success. Missionary schools gave them access to Western knowledge, and nurtured their hopes and ambitions to be leaders of Japanese society. A number of Christians, such as Niijima Jō, the founder of Dōshisha University in Kyoto, went on to establish influential educational institutions of their own. These schools not only produced clergymen to spread the Christian message, but also leading social critics and reformers of the early twentieth century. In addition, missionary schools and other private schools provided the only opportunities for higher education to girls. The government did not establish girls' high schools until 1899, and women remained barred from universities until after the Second World War. On the whole, however, Christianity appealed to only a minority of Japanese, although their influence was disproportionate to their actual numbers.

The beginning of industrialization

If Christianity appeared to a minority of Japanese to be the basis of Western superiority, economic power and industrial strength appeared to many more Meiji leaders to be essential in Japan's struggle for equality. This was an important lesson learned by Ōkubo and other government officials during the Iwakura Mission's study of Western societies. Through direct observation and study, their eyes were opened to the diversity of the 'West' as well as to its material and technological superiority.

Recognition of Japan's need to industrialize rather than to embark on expansionary foreign ventures led to Ōkubo's opposition to Saigō's plan to provoke a war with Korea in 1873. The government then stepped up its efforts to encourage private industrialists, such as providing low interest loans and direct subsidies, and enabling the establishment of banks and joint stock companies. It also built model factories to bring in expensive foreign technicians and technology to get industries started, not only those directly related to military needs, but also industries manufacturing goods to reduce reliance on imports or to earn foreign exchange through exports, notably cotton and silk. The importance of these government enterprises for Japanese industrialization remains questionable, since most failed to be profitable until they were taken over by private entrepreneurs in the 1880s, but economic historians agree on the importance of the government's investments in infrastructure such as railways and communication facilities.

Although it was also sold to a private company in the 1890s, the Tomioka silk-reeling mill provides a good example of such government enterprises, especially as it led the development of Japan's first successful export industry. Opened in 1873, it provided a model for workforce management as well as the most up-to-date equipment and the best foreign technical advisers. Government recruiters tried to appeal to patriotic sentiments and status when they called for 'student workers' among daughters of samurai and well-to-do rural families, but few volunteers came forth for fear of working under foreign male supervisors so far from home. Since Europeans drank red wine and cooked with lard, it was also widely believed that they drank human blood and cooked with human fat. It was not until government officials offered their own daughters that many regarded the mill as a 'safe' place for young women. Nevertheless, while Wada Ei's father told her 'not to fail for the honour of the country and the family', her mother warned her that her 'body was most important, and [she] should be especially careful with so many men around . . . nor to do anything to disgrace either [her] father or mother'.[9]

Working conditions at Tomioka were better than those at private mills, but set the basic pattern for conditions in the textile industry for the next seventy years. Work and leisure hours were highly regulated, and the work was physically demanding. Both the French and Japanese supervisors enforced strict discipline and expected speed as well as accuracy in the girls' work. The French supervisors seemed to get results with shouts of 'Japan has a lot of lazy daughters!', but physical punishment became a more common reaction to slow work or mistakes in later mills.

As demand for workers increased during the 1880s, mill recruiters turned to poor farm families, promising free room and board, frequent days off and classes to teach their daughters skills which would enhance their marriage propects when they returned home at the end of their contracts. The payment in advance in fact proved to be a loan which bound their daughters to the mill until paid off. There they found themselves confined to prison-like dormitories where they shared a tatami mat for sleeping with another girl in alternating shifts, and found the hours long (twelve- to fourteen-hour shifts), the treatment harsh and their bodies too tired at the end of a shift to get much benefit from classes. Distressingly high numbers contracted tuberculosis or other illnesses and were sent home to die. Despite the tight security, many ran away. As a saying in silk-producing districts put it: 'The day may come when the cock ceases to crow but never the day when factory girls stop running away'.[10] Still others despaired so greatly that they resorted to suicide. While no statistics exist, suicides were sufficiently common for silk workers around Lake Suwa to claim that the water level changed because of frequent suicides.

Cotton became the other industry to lead economic growth. As with silk, the government set up model factories and subsidized private ventures, but in this case to replace the foreign imports which had hurt domestic spinners and weavers as well as creating a trade imbalance. Modern cotton mills, however, required more expensive and complicated technology than silk, so these and early private mills ran into many problems. It was not until Shibusawa Eiichi's highly capitalized Osaka Cotton Spinning Mill became profitable in the mid-1880s that the industry took off. Its twenty-four-hour operations, under dangerous kerosene lamps before electricity was introduced, and its wage-grade classification system became characteristic of the cotton-spinning industry. Other entrepreneurs followed Shibusawa's lead to make cotton, along with silk, Japan's dominant exports by the end of the Meiji period. Japan became the world's largest producer of cotton and silk in the 1910s and 1920s.

Although the cotton industry initially employed more male than female workers for operating the mule spinner, the introduction of ring spinners requiring less physical strength led to the employment of more women. By the end of the 1890s female workers dominated the cotton industry workforce as they did the silk industry. Since females were paid less than males in all classifications, this helped to increase profits. Working conditions in cotton mills were similar to those in silk-reeling factories, and they deteriorated further in the 1890s. Companies were nevertheless still able to recruit young women from poor rural families as the number of landless had grown with the deflationary policies of the 1880s.

Impact and responses

As should now be clear, the government itself initiated or encouraged change along Western lines in all sorts of areas, largely for domestic political and foreign policy reasons but also to resolve many of the social and economic problems which had accumulated during the centuries of Tokugawa rule. Some of the social, technological and cultural changes were greeted with wonder and enthusiasm, especially in the cities, but others created discontent and dislocation, as revealed by samurai and peasant rebellions and the emergence of a political opposition movement in the 1870s and 1880s.

Saigō's Satsuma Rebellion represented the peak of samurai discontent with the loss of their privileged status and the most threatening armed challenge to the new government. Its suppression also meant it was the last. Why were there not more samurai uprisings and why were they unsuccessful? To begin with, the samurai lacked a landed base and their leaders, the *daimyō*, were coopted by the new regime. Their potential supporters in the countryside, wealthy landlords, were also given a role to play in the new order by being drawn into new prefectural assemblies. The government probably also benefited from the general fear that disorder would invite foreign intervention and from the legitimacy bestowed by the imperial symbol. Moreover, the samurai class was a large one which had been divided both horizontally by numerous ranks and vertically by regions, and its members were not uniformly affected by the new policies, but became scattered in many different fields. Although unsurprisingly they dominated the military, police and bureaucracy, the proportion of commoners in these institutions had risen greatly by the end of the Meiji period. These institutions also did not provide enough positions for the majority of samurai, but with their high levels of literacy many took advantage of increased opportunities in education, art, literature and the new field of journalism. Despite government encouragement, traditional anti-mercantile attitudes worked against many going into business, so that, contrary to early studies which believed that samurai entrepreneurs dominated Meiji industrialization efforts, entrepreneurs came from diverse social backgrounds.

Many samurai did, however, become critics of Meiji policies, including leaders of the People's Rights Movement. The People's Rights Movement became the main form of organized opposition to the government after the failure of the Satsuma Rebellion. It has been associated with Western ideas of liberalism and democracy, and its suppression is seen by Marxian historians as part of the establishment of the absolutist emperor system. At the top level of leadership, however, the personal ambitions of the movement's leaders appear to have been more important than ideological or philosophical motivations. The two main leaders, Itagaki Taisuke and Ōkuma Shigenobu, left the government at different times. Itagaki left over rejection of the Korean expedition in 1873; Ōkuma was dismissed in 1881 after demanding immediate establishment of a national representative assembly, criticizing government officials for selling Hokkaidō assets cheaply to friends, and favouring a financial programme based on foreign loans. Although circumstances for leaving the government differed, they both involved *han*-based factional politics, Ōkuma's dismissal leaving Satsuma and Chōshū monopolizing all important posts. Although they founded Japan's first political parties based on progressive Western political concepts and probably accelerated the government's announcement of plans for a parliamentary system, their party programmes favoured the interests of former samurai as well as national expansion.

One must look beneath the level of leadership to find participants in the People's Rights Movement with true commitment to democratic values. Investigating the Chichibu uprising of 1884, Irokawa Daikichi, founder of the 'people's history' school, discovered a draft constitution written by middle-level farmers and other rural participants in the movement in an old farm storehouse. Besides Irokawa's grassroots participants, there was one other group in the movement which raised new, progressive ideas. These were women who promoted women's rights as well as popular rights more generally. Twenty-year-old Kishida Toshiko was one of the most prominent and effective, whose speeches drew standing-room-only crowds and national attention. However, just as women were beginning to organize and discuss women's issues, Itagaki's Liberal Party was dissolved in 1884. It had been weakened after Itagaki was stabbed in an attempted assassination and thereafter left for Europe, apparently with funds from the Mitsui industrial conglomerate funnelled through the Meiji government. Upon his return he showed no interest in supporting peasant members' demands and opposition to the government. With the dissolution of the party, women organizers were also left with little means of expression besides newspapers and women's magazines. Tighter censorship as well as other restrictions on political activities proved effective along with cooptation to undermine the movement.

Repression and their internal character also explain the failure of peasant protests and rebellions. The large number of peasant uprisings during the 1870s reflects dissatisfaction with changes under the new government and growing inequalities in rural communities. The Meiji reforms abolished legal class distinctions and theoretically opened up new opportunities, but they were not immediately welcomed nor did they ensure greater income equality. By the end of the Tokugawa period the village had already been transformed into a community with diverse interests and varying degrees of wealth and poverty. With the Meiji reforms this diversification increased. As in the Tokugawa period, those closest to urban commercialized centres were affected the most. As these areas were drawn into the growing national market, cities offered opportunities for work to younger sons and women. For poor families this provided a way to relieve economic distress, but others migrated for more positive reasons.

Similarly, the reforms varied in their impact on people in different socio-economic strata who therefore responded to them in divergent ways. The changes in the land tax and recognition of private property enhanced the position and authority of the village elite of large landowners and owners of commercial and industrial enterprises, such as sake brewing and soy sauce manufacture. Although Marxist historians characterized them as 'parasitic', recent research has shown that they introduced new techniques and adapted to the more market-oriented economy, especially as restrictions on land use were abolished. Among rural groups, they embraced 'civilization and enlightenment' most enthusiastically, sending their children to the new public schools and organizing study groups and cultural activities. Middle-level landowners also responded positively to urban demand and the opportunities of the growing national market, as they had already been doing during the Tokugawa period.

It was small landowners and tenant farmers who suffered most from the rural reforms. They lost some rights (for example, to common land) that had customarily been recognized. Rent burdens for tenants remained high, while the land tax became fixed. Placed in precarious dependence on the market, many fell into debt and lost their land. Complaints against the land tax and land assessments were the most common, but not the only causes of protests. In fact, the most violent rural disturbances were protests against conscription. An uprising in Misaka soon after issuance of the law in 1873 exemplifies this and other features of rural protests. The edict referred to Westerners calling conscription a blood tax, meaning that soldiers should be prepared to die for their country, but many villagers believed that the army drained the blood of conscripts for sale to foreign countries. Participants in the uprising also objected to the cost of compulsory education, which was not free until the end of the century and took children away from farm work, to the raising of outcasts to equality with them as commoners, to the slaughtering of cows and to new hairstyles. As the uprising spread throughout the prefecture, crowds attacked schools, slaughterhouses, outcast communities and government buildings. Their uprising was not simply based on ignorance or prejudice against modernization, however, for when they marched to protest to the district magistrate, they attacked the homes and shops of wealthy farmers, moneylenders and merchants, who could buy exemptions for their sons, and went on to demand tax reductions.

Nevertheless, nearly half of the rural protests and disturbances in the 1870s remained local conflicts, often tenants against landlords and grounded in concerns of daily life, not with demands for far-reaching or fundamental reform nor threatening to the central government. The Meiji government's reforms further undermined village solidarity so that rural protests were not broadly based and therefore could not be sustained. In particular, the protesters often targeted the village elite, who benefited most from the reforms and were protected by the new legal system and policing at the local level.

As pointed out in the previous section, businessmen and industrialists also received support and encouragement from the new government. Wealthy *chōnin* were freed from the restrictions they had faced under the Tokugawa shogunate, but at the same time they faced new competition from samurai, rural merchants and industrialists, and foreigners. Not all wealthy urban merchant families adapted to the new circumstances, but the house of Mitsui stands out as one which succeeded, becoming one of the emerging zaibatsu of the twentieth century. It ran a very successful dry goods store in Edo which became Mitsukoshi Department Store during the Meiji period. Mitsukoshi led the way in advertising and the transformation of mercantile outlets using traditional Edo methods and selling specialized goods into those making mass sales of a variety of commodities. These innovations came at the end of the Meiji period, however, and will be described in more detail in a later chapter.

By the end of the 1880s Mitsui and new private entrepreneurial types were leading Japanese society into a new stage of industrialization and modern economic growth, supported by the Meiji government. The Meiji government leaders had also promulgated radical changes in all areas of Japanese life while managing to maintain, and indeed entrench, their power. Samurai and peasant resistance was no longer a major threat to internal order and stability, and the waves of government-led institutional change would soon be coming to an end with the establishment of a constitution in 1889. While the political, social and cultural revolution may in hindsight be seen as winding down, it probably did not look that way to contemporaries. True, modernization was most visible in the cities, but as we have seen, rural areas were affected as well. Many of the most revolutionary changes were only barely beginning to be seen and not necessarily intended by the government leaders. These will be the subject of the next chapter.

4   The 1880s and 1890s

Defining a Japanese national identity

Contrast the following passages:

> Evil practices of the past shall be discarded and [all our actions] shall follow the just way of the world. Knowledge shall be sought throughout the world so as to broaden and strengthen the foundations of imperial rule.[1]

> The way here set forth is indeed the teaching bequeathed by Our Imperial Ancestors, to be observed alike by Their Descendants and the subjects, infallible for all ages and true in all places.[2]

The first extract appeared as Articles Four and Five of the Imperial Charter Oath, the statement of progressive principles issued by the new Meiji leaders in 1868. The second formed part of the conclusion to the Imperial Rescript on Education of 1890 whose reinforcement of Confucian values and indigenous Shinto myths of divine imperial origins is seen by many historians as signalling the end of the Meiji revolution.

The Imperial Rescript on Education exemplifies the nationalistic reaction to Westernization that began in the late 1880s, a reaction against what was seen by many contemporary critics as indiscriminate borrowing. The shift in domestic atmosphere occurred at the same time as the government's drive towards treaty revision reached a climax and Japan emerged as an imperialist power with its defeat of China in 1895. However, these developments should not be seen as a simple reversion to anti-foreignism and the end of Westernization. Rather, the late 1880s and 1890s represented a period when the Meiji leaders continued to use Western institutions and practices as models, but, even more deliberately and selectively than earlier, adapted rather than merely copied them to suit Japan's particular conditions and needs as they perceived them. A shift to Western models, often German, and considered to be more suitable to Japan, reveals a growing understanding that the West was not an undifferentiated West. Moreover, these developments obviously did not mean a return to Tokugawa isolationism since Japan joined the Western powers in expansion on the continent.

The shift in Western models and slowdown in institutional borrowing is not really surprising if we recall the superficiality of Westernization in daily life and customs and its limited influence beyond urban areas. Yet it was the very frivolity and indiscriminate borrowing of outward Western habits that prompted the search for a peculiar cultural and national identity which could be called Japanese. By the late 1880s there existed a widespread feeling that if Japan continued to Westernize as it had done in the previous two decades, it would lose all its special qualities, part of a growing realization that the distinction between 'Western techniques' and 'Japanese spirit' might not be so easy to maintain. It is an indication that modernization, which in non-Western countries means cultural borrowing, is a complicated and disruptive process, and one which even a strong, centralized state may not be able to keep under control. As we will see in Chapter 5, by the late Meiji period the tremendous optimism and faith in progress of the early Meiji leaders began to give way to disillusionment and insecurity.

Japanese-style constitutional government

The 1890s was therefore a period when government leaders and also non-government leaders and intellectuals attempted to redefine Japan and Japaneseness in domestic affairs. The promulgation of a constitution in 1889 and establishment of parliamentary institutions were not only intended to hasten elimination of the unequal treaties, but also to make the imperial institution a symbol of national identity and the Diet a means for achieving national unity.

In Chapter 3 we saw that the People's Rights Movement put heavy pressure on the government to establish a national representative assembly during the second half of the 1870s and the 1880s. The government responded by expanding political control mechanisms and institutions, such as the police, and increasing central control over political activities and organizations. These repressive measures no doubt weakened the movement, but in addition to repression, the government undermined the opposition by inaugurating constitutional government in 1890. The new constitutional framework not only coopted opposition leaders by providing an avenue for achieving their personal ambitions, but was also compatible with their political principles and beliefs.

In a number of fundamental ways government leaders' views on constitutional government did not differ from those of opposition leaders. Like Itagaki and Ōkuma, Ōkubo and later Itō Hirobumi, the leader most responsible for the Meiji Constitution, viewed the aim of the Meiji Restoration as Japan's overtaking the West. Constitutional government was seen by both sides as essential to achieving treaty revision by giving credence to the assertion that Japan was a civilized country with up-to-date political practices. Both sides also saw a national assembly as a way to mobilize Japanese loyalties and evoke national identity with the Meiji government. Even Itagaki, who favoured more radical French concepts, did not see political parties as interest groups and wanted a representative assembly in order to create unity between the government and the people. Government leaders expected the assembly to provide a means of transmitting the government's wishes and goals to the people and to act as a safety-valve for social discontent. As Yamagata Aritomo argued, 'If we gradually establish a popular assembly and firmly establish a constitution, the things I have enumerated above – popular enmity towards the government, failure to follow government orders, and suspicion of the government – these three evils will be cured in the future'.[3]

Given the concern with preserving the government, as well as their positions in it, and with achieving national unity, it was decided that Japan should adopt a Prussian-style constitution. Itō Hirobumi departed on a study mission to Europe, and upon his return the government hired two German legal specialists to give advice on drafting the constitution. Since the Second World War the Meiji Constitution has been heavily criticized for its authoritarian aspects, but at the time of promulgation in 1889 it was greeted with almost unanimous acclaim, including praise from leaders of the People's Rights Movement and liberals such as Fukuzawa Yukichi.

The emperor emerged not simply as the central symbol of the political structure but the locus of sovereignty. The first clause declared him 'sacred and inviolable', being the descendant of a dynasty that has 'reigned in an unbroken line for ages past'. The constitution was presented as a 'gift' from him to his people. Similarly, civil liberties listed as protected by the Constitution, such as the right of association and publication, were considered to be privileges granted by the emperor rather than natural and inalienable. They were protected within the limits of the law, and might therefore also be restricted by laws. In theory, the emperor possessed all the powers of governance, including executive authority as well as supreme command over the armed forces. As in Germany, military personnel swore an oath of allegiance directly to the emperor. This placed them outside the authority of the army and navy ministries.

A legislative role was partially given to the Diet or parliament which consisted of two houses: the Lower House of Representatives and the Upper House of Peers. The House of Representatives was to be elected by all males paying taxes of 15 yen or more. This meant that only about 5 per cent of the male population at the time became eligible to vote. Despite the limited enfranchisement, the House of Peers, comprising the imperial family, the new nobility and imperial appointees, was intended to serve as a conservative check on the lower elected house. Moreover, since the emperor possessed legislative authority, delegated to his officials in the bureaucracy, the Diet did not act as initiator of legislation, although its approval was required for all new laws. Anticipating the possibility of an uncooperative Diet, the drafters provided the government with a loophole – if the Diet did not approve a budget, the previous year's budget would continue. In addition, the emperor had the right to suspend the Diet temporarily, to dissolve the lower house and to issue ordinances when the Diet was not in session. Only he had the power to initiate amendments to the Constitution. Other institutions and groups which were more central to policy-making than the Diet were not even mentioned in the Constitution, namely the oligarchs (known as the elder statesmen or *genrō*), the Cabinet and the Privy Council. This is indicative of the continuing exercise of power and decision-making by the original leaders of the Restoration and their protégés in practice.

The Constitution thus embodied the view of the national assembly as a means of achieving national unity. It was based on a concept of state sovereignty, not popular sovereignty. Nevertheless, as indicated above, this principle was shared by leaders of the People's Rights Movement as well as Meiji government leaders. Like government leaders, they accepted the centrality of the imperial institution – their opposition largely represented a challenge to Satsuma and Chōshū's monopoly of the right to speak for the emperor. Virtually all elites also regarded Japan's emperor as the unique, distinctive feature of Japan's constitution.

But since constitutional government was seen as a means of achieving national unity, not just the cooperation of the elites, the occasion of promulgation of the Constitution was utilized as an event for drawing in ordinary Japanese people to participate in the new national community. The promulgation ceremonies and associated festive activities became a model for later imperial ceremonial events. According to Takashi Fujitani, it was Japan's first modern national ceremony.[4] The ceremonies began with rites emphasizing the divine aspect of the emperor and making the promulgation sacred. The emperor conducted the rites, wearing priestly robes, in the private Palace Sanctuary, but newspapers reported on them in great detail, and imperial messengers were dispatched to shrines and mausoleums of the Restoration heroes, such as Ōkubo Toshimichi, to report on the establishment of the Constitution. The emperor then changed from his priestly robes into his military uniform to perform the visible ceremony of handing the constitution to Prime Minister Kuroda, highlighting the granting of the Constitution as his gift to the people. The witnesses included not only Japanese nobility, high officials and foreign dignitaries, but also newspaper reporters, including five from provincial newspapers and three from English-language papers.

In the afternoon the ceremonies became even more inclusive when the emperor processed with this entourage to make an inspection at the Aoyama Military Parade Field. Five thousand carefully instructed schoolchildren lined the route shouting '*banzai*' and singing the unofficial national anthem, 'Kimi ga Yo'. The empress rode with the emperor, signalling her emerging prominence in fashioning a new public image for the imperial family as one centred on a modern, monogamous couple. Their English carriage, drawn by six perfectly matched bays and attended by grooms in full livery, signified the modernity and international prestige of the Japanese monarch, but was also topped by a golden phoenix as used in ancient times on imperial palanquins.

The following day the emperor and empress again processed through the city to cheering crowds. At key points along the eight-kilometre course private companies and local organizations had built huge arches decorated with lanterns, electric lights, streamers and national flags. Throughout the city enormous crowds celebrated with all sorts of floats and festive eating, dressing and dancing. Foreign and Japanese contemporaries, as well as most scholars, have scoffed at the people's celebrations as meaningless, since they could not understand the Constitution's significance. 'There are many who simply get excited thinking that it is one festival or another', complained a *Jiji shinpo* journalist. However, Fujitani argues:

> the forms of the familiar community festival facilitated mass participation in new celebrations of the emerging national community. New national symbols – such as national flags, portraits of imperial family members, the 'Kimi ga Yo' anthem, and Rising Sun lanterns – began to combine with customary festival objects and music. In time, people would begin to forget the newness of most of these symbols and ceremonials and they would come to think of them as an unproblematic part of received Tradition.[5]

Education for the nation

As suggested by the mobilization of thousands of schoolchildren to celebrate the promulgation of the Constitution, the government viewed education as a primary means of developing a sense of nation. The government's attempt to define Japan and Japaneseness with the imperial institution at its core may be seen in the shift in education policy which took place in the late 1880s. Moral education based on a combination of traditional cultural values and modern nationalism became the core of the primary school curriculum.

The school system introduced with compulsory education in 1872 had followed a centralized French model, but in practice considerable diversity had remained in the content of education, including a mixture of Western, Japanese nationalist and Confucian values in ethics and language texts. Because of the costs of schooling, attendance rates rose only slowly, especially attendance of girls for whom education was thought to be a waste of time and expense.

The reforms of the late 1880s followed intense debate over philosophies of education as well as structures, and resulted not only in a more uniform and centralized system, but also one designed to serve state purposes. Standardization and centralization helped to reduce inequalities among schools based on region and class and widened access to education. Attendance by girls as well as boys at primary schools rose rapidly and strikingly to nearly 100 per cent within a decade after fees were abolished in 1899, and the proportion of commoners in middle schools and universities increased to over 50 per cent. Similarly, the establishment of normal schools raised the level of teacher training and made teaching a new occupation open to women, but teacher training also became more standardized. Apart from normal schools, girls did not have access to education beyond the compulsory four years until 1899, when the Education Ministry ordered each prefecture to establish at least one girls' higher school. Universities remained accessible only to boys. Introduction of a civil service examination in the 1890s contributed to recruitment of government officials by merit, but graduates of private universities continued to be disadvantaged because private universities did not have the resources that the imperial universities possessed. Nevertheless, although the path to upward social and economic mobility remained narrow, the reforms did open the way for expansion in the twentieth century.

It was in the primary schools that the government focused its ideological efforts. Promulgation of the Imperial Rescript on Education in October 1890 epitomized these efforts and encapsulated the values forming the core of the curriculum. Here is what schoolchildren recited first thing every morning until the end of the Second World War:

> Know ye, Our subjects:
> Our Imperial Ancestors have founded Our Empire on a basis broad and everlasting and have deeply and firmly implanted virtue; Our subjects ever united in loyalty and filial piety have from generation to generation illustrated the beauty thereof. This is the glory of the fundamental character of Our Empire, and herein also lies the source of Our education.
> Ye, Our subjects, be filial to your parents, affectionate to your brothers and sisters; as husbands and wives be harmonious, as friends true; bear yourselves in modesty and moderation; extend your benevolence to all; pursue learning and cultivate arts, and thereby develop intellectual faculties and perfect moral powers; furthermore advance public good and promote common interests; always respect the Constitution and observe the laws; should emergency arise, offer yourselves courageously to the State; and thus guard and maintain the prosperity of Our Imperial Throne coeval with heaven and earth. So shall ye not only be Our good and faithful subjects, but render illustrious the best traditions of your forefathers.
> The Way here set forth is indeed the teaching bequeathed by Our Imperial Ancestors, to be observed alike by Their Descendants and the subjects, infallible for all ages and true in all places. It is Our wish to lay it to heart in all reverence, in common with you, Our subjects, that we may all attain to the same virtue.[6]

This greeting clearly defined the Japanese people as subjects of an absolute monarch rather than citizens in a democratic state, and references to 'Imperial Ancestors' called upon indigenous Shinto myths to legitimize this autocratic power. The Rescript declared Confucian values of loyalty, filial piety, moderation and benevolence for the sake of communal welfare to be the values of the nation, but besides the traditional emphasis on morality and learning there was added a modern emphasis on upholding the Constitution and the law, and on being willing to sacrifice oneself for the nation-state.

These educational reform efforts did not take immediate effect, however. For example, not all texts produced in the 1890s were of high quality, nor did they all follow the official line of interpretation of the Rescript. Much criticism emerged in the House of Representatives against privately produced texts of all types. Consequently, in 1897 both houses of the Diet ruled that ethics texts, being of such crucial importance to the morale of the nation, should be produced by the government. The first government-produced texts still did not materialize until 1903, and even these were criticized by some as lacking an emphasis on national values.

Gendering the nation

The state's nation-building efforts of the 1890s did not exclude women. In fact, the decade witnessed heightened attention by the state to defining women's role in service to the nation. The educational system played a key part in articulating and disseminating the state's policy on women's role, but was also supported by the mobilizing efforts of Home Ministry organizations and restrictions imposed by legislation. The admonition in the Imperial Rescript on Education to wives being in harmony with their husbands points to the Meiji emphasis on women as wives more than as mothers, even though the Ministry of Education popularized the twin ideals of 'good wife, wise mother (*ryōsai kenbo*)' from the 1890s onward. After the Meiji period these twin ideals were extended to all Japanese women, but during the Meiji period they were meant only for middle-class women – the labour of women of the urban and rural lower classes was required for the industrializing economy.

In fact, what distinguishes the Meiji state's ideal of womanhood from that in contemporary Britain and the United States is the development of what Sharon Nolte and Sally Hastings have described as a 'cult of productivity' rather than a 'cult of domesticity'.[7] As in the USA and Britain, Japanese bureaucrats defined womanly virtues as those of modesty, frugality and purity, and situated women's primary activities in the home and their responsibilities to the family. A law of 1890 prohibited all women from attending political meetings or joining political organizations. However, unlike in the USA and Britain, the Japanese state claimed the home and family to be a public, not private sphere. According to the Ministry of Education-sponsored *The Meiji Greater Learning for Women*, 'the home is a public place where private feelings should be forgotten'.[8] Exclusion from political activities may have been partly a response to the appearance of women activists in the People's Rights Movement, but was also justified because of the important social role women played in management of the home and education of children.

In order to perform this family-oriented role well, girls as well as boys needed to be educated. This thinking lay behind the decision to make four (later six) years of primary education compulsory for both girls and boys. However, only boys needed to go beyond the primary level, and even after the establishment of higher schools for middle-class girls, these schools did not offer the same curriculum as middle schools for boys, or lead to university. Their aim was to produce young women of refined taste and gentle and modest character. Girls at both primary and higher school level therefore studied less science, history, geography or other more academically rigorous subjects than boys, and learned sewing rather than attending exercise and military drill classes. This type of education was considered suitable for women of all classes who would form the backbone of their families. However, the state's policy also enjoined women of the lower classes to go on to work in the farms and factories of the nation, and encouraged women of the middle and upper classes to utilize their womanly qualities to benefit society through charity and other volunteer activities.

Although the 1890 prohibition on political activities rendered impossible public appearances of the type that Kishida Toshiko had made so successfully in the People's Rights Movement, not all women confined their activities outside the home to paid work or charities. Some educated women, represented by Yajima Kajiko of the Tokyo Women's Reform Society, turned their energies to social reform. Though acting in a ladylike manner acceptable to conservative times, they attacked the concubine system and prostitution, including the 'national shame' of overseas prostitution. Behind this was a deeper challenge to male privilege and patriarchal institutions. The Reform Society achieved some success in mobilizing public opinion through newspaper publicity and lecture tours, and through petitions and memorials in pushing local governments to pass regulations dealing with prostitution.

However, the political potential of the Society was never realized as the 1890s came to an end and a new civil code issued in 1898 reinforced women's lowly status in the family. The civil code strengthened the concept of the *ie* (household) and tied it to a patriarchal emperor system. It recognized only men as legal persons, classifying women in the same category as the 'deformed and the mentally incompetent', and gave the patriarchal head of the *ie* absolute authority over all members of the household. Married women therefore had no economic independence or right to take independent legal action. Only wives could be punished for adultery. Not only were they 'borrowed wombs' as in Tokugawa times to produce sons for the family, but also for the Empire. The 'good wife, wise mother'-based curriculum of the girls' higher schools to be established in the following year aimed to socialize and train women for this role.

Homogenizing the nation

Education was also a major tool for incorporating minority groups into a new racialized definition of Japan during the 1890s. The focus here will be on the Ainu and Okinawans who inhabited territories which were fully incorporated into Japan only during the Meiji period. Until recently, few serious studies had been carried out about either group, largely due to the pervasive image of Japan as a homogeneous society. Official government policy did not recognize the Ainu as a minority, regarding them as completely assimilated, and educated elites in both communities had often seen assimilation as the best route to ending discrimination and poverty. Attention and pressure from the outside during the 1980s and 1990s (for example, the United Nations' Year of Indigenous People) and heightened consciousness and organized activity within the minority groups themselves has led to increased scholarly attention to the history and contemporary situation of the Ainus and Okinawans.

Histories, especially at the popular level, have been mainly stories portraying Ainus and Okinawans as victims of Japanese 'internal colonization' and 'racial' discrimination. While confirming the narrative of exploitation and seeing similarities in the history of the two groups, Richard Siddle also sees some differences, and has questioned certain key assumptions. Moreover, he has documented diversity in attitudes among Okinawans and Ainus themselves towards incorporation into the new Japanese state. The complexity of their histories needs to be kept in mind even as we highlight the state's policies towards these groups in the context of its efforts to create a sense of nation at the end of the nineteenth century. Siddle's findings also point to the role played by scholars, intellectuals and local leaders in creating that sense of nation and the position of Ainus and Okinawans in it.

Okinawa became a prefecture in 1879, but the central government treated it differently from other prefectures in its administration, economy and society because of the 'low level of civil society', as the Home Minister explained to Prime Minister Katsura Tarō in 1904.[9] Okinawa's anomalous treatment derived from its past existence as the Kingdom of Ryukyu, which had had tributary relations with China while at the same time under the *de facto* control of Satsuma. The pro-Chinese Ryukyuan gentry and China rejected incorporation into Japan, an issue that was not settled until China's defeat by Japan in 1895. Thereafter a policy of Japanization replaced a conciliatory attitude towards local customs, such as Ryukyuan dress and hairstyles. A language and education policy was introduced to eradicate the Okinawan dialect and impose the cultural ideals of the 'mainland'. Mainland Japanese, predominantly from Kyushu, continued to dominate the top positions in the prefectural government as well as the economy, while ordinary Okinawans suffered from disproportionately heavy taxes. Okinawan attempts to gain political representation, such as a People's Rights Movement led by Jahana Noboru and a petition from the islanders of Miyako in 1893, were suppressed or ignored until the end of the Meiji period. Achievement of representation came even later than in Hokkaido.

Such Japanization policies were supported by new scientific theories about race coming from the West that stimulated various inquiries and debates among mainland Japanese scholars about the origins of the 'Japanese race' and the relation of peripheral Others such as the Okinawans and Ainus to the 'Japanese'. The debates resulted in the placement of Okinawans on the evolutionary ladder of becoming 'Japanese' while the Ainus were completely excluded. Local Okinawan intellectuals starting with Iha Fuyū tried to establish an Okinawan identity by emphasizing the uniqueness of Okinawan history and culture, but at the same time he concluded from his studies of folk customs and 'racial' comparisons that Okinawans were descended from the Japanese as a 'branch race'. During the 1890s Basil Chamberlain came to the same conclusion from his comparison of the Ryukyuan language with mainland Japanese dialects. What ordinary Japanese believed is less clear since the messages they received were somewhat contradictory. For example, a 1901 primary school textbook represented both Okinawans and Ainus as 'natives', but Okinawans were generally not displayed like Ainus at colonial expositions. In any case, prejudice and discrimination persisted in daily living based on perceptions of Okinawan inferiority.

If the racial identity of Okinawans remained ambiguous into the twentieth century, that of the Ainus did not. During the Tokugawa period Japanese had established a trading post system in the Matsumae domain which was clearly delineated from Ainu territory both politically and culturally. The Japanese there referred to themselves as humans in contrast to the Ainu 'barbarians'. In addition to this legacy of images, Japanese academics during the late nineteenth century received the influence of Western scholars and travellers who disseminated theories of scientific racism. They in turn advised the Ministry of Education in writing textbooks which described Ainus as people who did not bathe or style their hair, or read, write or count. Expositions both at home and abroad displayed Ainus as 'primitives'.

This racial ideology justified the economic, social and cultural policies which the Meiji government imposed and from which private Japanese settlers benefited. In contrast to Okinawa, Hokkaido became an internal colony rather than a prefecture until 1882. The colonial administration appropriated Ainu land, relocating Ainu communities to less rich lands where it could also keep them under control. A humanitarian movement to prevent the extermination of this 'dying race' resulted in the Protection Act of 1899, but this only institutionalized Ainu inferiority. The Act explicitly referred to the Ainu as an inferior race whose poverty reflected the 'law of survival of the fittest'. It tried to transform them from a savage wandering people into civilized farmers by giving them small plots of land (but without full ownership rights), and to assimilate them through a special system of Schools for Former Natives. With this, the central government discharged its responsibility to the 'emperor's children'.

An emperor for the nation

The image of the emperor as the patriarch of the Japanese family-state became a prominent characteristic of the national identity being constructed during the late Meiji period. Certain other changes were also made to his image. Since the beginning of the Meiji period the government had used the imperial institution to legitimize its policies. Because the emperor had been almost invisible during the Tokugawa centuries, it initially tried to bring him down from 'above the clouds', emphasizing direct contact with the people by sending him on several extensive tours throughout the country.

When the emperor was placed at the centre of the new Constitution and the upsurge of national identity-making efforts of the 1890s, however, his image underwent a change. He was again gradually removed from direct contact with the people and raised above politics, as reflected in a decline in the number of his national tours. During the Sino-Japanese War the emperor performed his role as commander-in-chief of the army by going to Hiroshima and living austerely in the Fifth Division compound, but ten years later during the war with Russia he stayed in Tokyo, appearing as a statesman rather than a commanding officer. Instead of his person, the emperor's photograph was placed before the public, though in many more places than he could ever have personally visited. This was fitting since the public itself was enlarged to encompass all the people, including marginal Others such as the Ainus, Okinawans, and the *shinheimin*, former outcasts known as Burakumin. Moreover, despite the premodern references in the Constitution and the Imperial Rescript on Education to divine ancestors, the emperor was presented as a modern monarch symbolizing national progress and national unity of a patriotic and civic kind rather than political and legal. Consequently, despite an increasing emphasis on moral and religious attributes of the imperial institution towards the end of the Meiji period, the emperor became less the repository of Japanese traditions than the embodiment of modernity.

The public ceremonies and festivities accompanying the promulgation of the Constitution which have been described earlier were only the beginning of a new style of imperial ceremonial events which were aimed at fashioning a modern monarch for the nation and involving the people in the national community. For example, borrowing the practice of Western royalty, the people helped to celebrate the twenty-fifth wedding anniversary of the emperor and empress in 1894, cheering them in packed crowds along the processional route from the palace to the parade field as for the Constitution's promulgation. Many had come from provincial areas, not just the city, as was evident from their travelling clothes. Newspapers reported on the emperor and empress entering the banqueting hall arm in arm, along with the other guests in husband–wife couples, demonstrating a modern and civilized conjugal relationship. People who did not travel to Tokyo to participate in the celebrations could thus receive reports through the media. They also participated in coinciding local festivities supported and organized by businessmen, priests, landowners, teachers and other local private leaders as well as government officials. On this and other national occasions, officials declared holidays from work and encouraged the people to put out national flags, hold local observances and celebrate with other festivities. In the case of one town's celebration of the emperor's twenty-fifth wedding anniversary, over a thousand students, officials and other citizens attended the main ceremony in the Imari Primary School grounds where they worshipped the pictures of the imperial couple. More than four hundred attended a banquet held later, which, however, was interrupted by 'drifters' and 'rowdy dancers'.

This interruption indicates that people did not always celebrate in the disciplined way that government officials considered appropriate to the modern, civilized nation, or with the proper respect. Japanese journalists as well as foreigners and government officials complained that some people came to see the emperor naked or dressed as transvestites. At other times they broke into wild, frenzied and often farcical dancing reminiscent of '*ee ja nai ka*', or did not behave in a serious, respectful way when visiting shrines or monuments to war dead after the Sino-Japanese or Russo-Japanese wars. More seriously, Miyatake Gaikotsu and Adachi Ginkō lampooned the promulgation ceremony in their *Journal of the Society of Ready Wit*, including a print with a skeleton on the dais where the emperor should have been to hand the Constitution to Prime Minister Kuroda. This landed them in prison for *lèse-majesté*.

While expansion of the print media and transportation helped to diffuse national consciousness, construction of Tokyo Station, the Central Station in Tokyo, during the first decade of the twentieth century also demonstrated the association of modern technological achievement with the Meiji state headed by the emperor. Although not completed until 1914, design of the building began in 1898, and the story of that process reveals the political purposes that the government intended for the building. As William Coaldrake has shown, Tokyo Station became 'no less than a temple to progress and a monument to empire'.[10] The building was conceived during a period when railways and capital city stations were being constructed throughout the world as expressions of national confidence, state power and technological mastery – for example, Grand Central Station in New York, St Pancras Station in London and Union Station in Washington, DC. Railways symbolized the machine age of revolutionary speed and power, and central railway stations represented gateways to the world as well as to the centres of political and economic power for people of all classes. Tokyo Station was part of a comprehensive plan to create a unified national railway system from southernmost Kyushu to the northernmost part of Honshu. More specifically, it would complete the Tokyo urban rail system which lacked a link between Shinagawa in the south and Ueno in the north. It possessed symbolic political significance because it was the station from which the emperor embarked on state visits. At the same time its location in the heart of the new business as well as the administrative centre of the city emphasized the relationship between the Imperial Palace and the emergence of Japan as a commercial, industrial nation.

As in the case of many other major construction projects, Western advisers were hired by the Meiji government to devise plans. A Prussian railway engineer carried out surveys in the late 1880s, and another German, Franz Baltzer, arrived in 1898 to draw up the first detailed plans. His design, however, was rejected, and the Japanese architect Tatsuno Kingo ended up making the final design which won approval. The committee rejected Baltzer's design because it was too Japanese! The Meiji government wanted to represent Japan as a modern, Westernized nation, but Baltzer's design consisted of a series of structures similar to the architecture of mansions of the former *daimyō*, and included an elegant cusped gable (*karahafu*) reminiscent of Momoyama and Edo styles over the entrance to the imperial chambers. The committee then employed Tatsuno to design a station in red brick and Western style.

The red brick and steel frame construction marked Tokyo Station as definitely Western as well as attesting to Japanese mastery of the latest construction technologies. In addition, ribbed domes crowning the north and south wings enhanced its visual impact and symbolic political importance, distinguishing the station from other red brick buildings facing it in the new Marunouchi business district. The main entrance, used exclusively by the imperial family, faced the Imperial Palace, and the imperial waiting room and reception chambers formed the heart of the complex. The station stood at one end of a wide boulevard suitable for orchestrating the emperor and his entourage's grand processions when departing and returning from state visits.

A 'National Teaching' for the nation

Upon taking power, the new Meiji leaders believed that Shinto rituals and symbols could be useful tools for legitimizing their rule and uniting the people with a common creed. The government had therefore raised the status of Shinto and called for its complete separation from Buddhism. It attempted to create a unified national religion out of Shinto, which until the Meiji period had no comprehensive organizational structure or doctrines, by establishing a Department of Divinity to conduct rites of state, organizing all shrines into a hierarchy under the Ise Shrines, unifying all rites and replacing Buddhist temple registration of all subjects with shrine registration. The demotion of Buddhism relative to Shinto, in combination with the desire to appear 'progressive', meaning Western, led to neglect of traditional Buddhist buildings such as the Daibutsuden, the principal building in the Tōdaiji temple in Nara. Support for the preservation and restoration of Buddhist temples, Shinto shrines and other historically significant art and architecture emerged only in the late 1880s, not primarily as a result of the anti-Western policies of conservatives in the bureaucracy, but due to pressure of foreigners such as art patron Ernest Fenollosa and German architects' repeated use of traditional architectural features in their commissions. Moreover, in the case of the Daibutsuden, sufficient financial support for restoration came only after ten years of persistent lobbying by the chief abbot, emphasizing the unique historical significance of the building and past patronage by eminent political figures.

Neglect of a Buddhist temple during the early Meiji period may not be too surprising, but more surprising is the decline of state support for Shinto shrines from the late 1880s through the first years of the twentieth century when many other efforts at national identity-making were being made. In 1887 the government decided not to provide support for all shrines and to reduce financial support even for those designated Imperial and National Shrines. It also dismantled the Department of Divinity. These decisions may be partly explained by financial considerations, and also by understanding the pressure being exerted by foreign diplomats to provide for freedom of religion in the constitution being drafted. Article 28 of the Meiji Constitution did eventually provide for religious freedom, but 'within limits not prejudicial to peace and order, and not antagonistic to their duties as subjects'.[11] The effect in later years when the state again wanted a closer alignment with Shinto was to make observance of Shinto rites appear as part of each Japanese subject's obligation to the state rather than part of their religious life.

As in the case of the Daibutsuden's restoration, an interest group, again the priesthood, played an important role in regaining support from the state. Thus, although we have highlighted government efforts to define and disseminate a distinctive Japanese national identity at the end of the nineteenth century, ideology-making was not a consistent, unified effort, nor were government leaders and bureaucrats the sole makers. Like the lobbying efforts of the chief abbot of Tōdaiji, Shinto shrine administrators had to wage a long campaign to obtain state support. To do so they tried to present Shinto as 'the nation's rites and creed', a 'National Teaching' superior to a religion and therefore distinct from Christianity and Buddhism. A memorial calling for the re-establishment of the Department of Divinity illustrates their line of argument:

> National Teaching (*kokkyō*) is teaching the codes of national government to the people without error. Japan is called the divine land because it is ruled by the heavenly deities' descendants, who consolidate the work of the deities. The Way of such consolidation and rule by divine descendants is called *Shintō* . . . the National Teaching of the imperial house is not a religion, because religions are the theories of their founders. The National Teaching consists of the traditions of the imperial house, beginning in the age of the gods and continuing throughout history. . . . The National Teaching is Shintō . . . and Shintō is nothing other than the National Teaching.[12]

Ironically, the campaign initially did more to unite the previously diverse Shinto priesthood and shrines, eventually into a single, national organization, than to win substantial state support. It was not until after the Russo-Japanese War that political leaders or the public paid much attention to the question of shrine support, although when they did, the priesthood's efforts to align Shinto with civic duty and patriotism proved successful.

Defining Japan to the world

Much of this chapter has focused on efforts to define a national identity for the Japanese themselves, although in some cases such as Tokyo Station the targeted audience was a foreign one as well. In the final section of this chapter the focus will be more sharply on the image of Japan that Japanese people projected abroad, which will then direct attention to issues and events in foreign affairs in Chapter 5. Images of Japan came to the West through a rather limited range of sources even after the Meiji Restoration. Individuals, for example, on diplomatic missions like the early Iwakura Mission or as students studying privately or on government scholarships, gave Americans and Europeans some impressions of Japan. A few foreign residents and travellers, the most influential being Basil Chamberlain and Lafcadio Hearn, wrote books about Japan. Gilbert and Sullivan's *Mikado* contributed to an exotic image of Japan among audiences in the West, and Japanese woodblock prints (*ukiyoe*) and paintings influenced Impressionist artists. But the largest number of Westerners gained their image of Japan from international fairs and expositions.

International expositions stand out as a hallmark of nineteenth-century civilization, considered by many contemporaries to symbolize the peaceful progress being made by Christianity and technology throughout the world. The Crystal Palace Exposition in 1851 marked the first international fair, and many followed its lead in both Europe and the United States throughout the rest of the century. The huge numbers of people exposed to such exhibitions is indicated by the close to fifty million attendants at the 1900 Paris world's fair. Japan had first been represented at the Paris fair of 1867 and under the new Meiji government at the Vienna fair of 1873, but its first full-scale exhibition appeared at the American centennial exhibition in Philadelphia in 1876.

The Japanese exhibition stood out among the more than thirty other nations represented not only because of its large size and obvious costliness, but for its novelty. Americans had never seen anything like the Japanese art wares on display. Even as the pavilion was being constructed, the carpenters with their 'almond eyes' and strange building methods (for example, using posts rather than masonry foundations) attracted crowds. Their quietness, neatness and precision contrasted with that of the Chinese, the only Asians familiar to Americans. The exhibition's concentration on porcelains, bronzes, silks, embroideries, lacquered wares and other art objects reinforced these impressions of careful, patient and accomplished craftsmanship. One newspaper complained that it told little about the country's modernization efforts or its people, but most observers enjoyed and praised it.

After the Philadelphia centennial, Japan presented similar exhibitions in European expositions and also in smaller American ones, but its exhibition at the enormous World's Columbian Exposition held in Chicago in 1893 changed its focus and the image it wanted to project to the world. The costly and elaborate art objects were still there, and continued to attract the most attention, but there were also displays of manufacturing and other aspects of Japanese economic and social life: seventy-two exhibits of rice, 215 exhibits of tea and tobacco, photographs of railways and telegraphs, textbooks, crime statistics, toys and numerous other products like those found in Western countries. The government succeeded to a great extent in impressing Americans (almost thirty million of whom visited the exposition) with Japan's achievements in industry and modernization as well as traditional art and crafts. Writers about the fair acknowledged Japan's progress and efforts to bring the country into alignment with the West. Denton Snider, for example, wrote approvingly:

> The Japanese are plainly the vanguard in the Occidental movement toward the Orient. . . . It allies itself with the nations of the West, especially does it appeal to the United States. . . . One cannot help noticing here the care with which the Japanese man explains that he is not a Chinaman.[13]

Exhibiting in Chicago made an impact at home as well. The national organizing commission, although headed by the minister of agriculture and commerce, had an advisory council which included manufacturers and other businessmen, and appointed local commissions in every prefecture to select and advise potential exhibitors. The response to the call for exhibitors had been tremendous: 7000 tons of material, seven times what had been expected, which was finally cut down to 1750 tons. Advertising for the fair had been so widespread that one American visitor to Japan in the 1890s declared, 'Everyone knows about it'. Another met priests at Izumo in western Japan who proudly showed him a ticket on the arm of a statue of the Sun Goddess giving notice of the prize that the temple had won for its exhibit at Chicago.

The exposition at Chicago therefore had meaning for Japanese as well as Americans, and for ordinary Japanese, not just government officials trying to impress Westerners. It had involved a nationwide effort at the local as well as central level to project a modern image of Japan to the world. In this respect, it is another reminder that the identity-making of the 1890s was not exclusively a government endeavour, and, because it did involve many individuals and groups at different levels of society and in different places in the country, the resulting ideology was neither monolithic nor unproblematic.

We will see in the next chapter that the government's success at Chicago in demonstrating to Westerners that Japan was a modern, civilized nation helped the diplomatic efforts going on concurrently to eliminate the unequal treaties. During the final two decades of the Meiji period the government achieved its goals in foreign policy, bringing Japan into the company of the major Western powers. At the same time, despite continued and even stepped-up attempts to rally the Japanese people in support of the nation, there emerged a number of disturbing signs of both present and future discontent and instability.

5   Late Meiji

An end and a beginning

In 1911 the quintessential Meiji novelist Natsume Sōseki observed that Japanese no longer resorted to 'such foolishness as saying to foreigners, "My country has Mt Fuji". But since the [Russo-Japanese] war one hears boasting everywhere that we have become a first-class country.'[1] At almost the same time, Sōseki was writing his novel *Kokoro* in which the protagonist Sensei commits suicide, along with the Russo-Japanese war hero General Nogi, following the death of the Meiji emperor. The pessimistic mood at the end of *Kokoro* contrasts starkly with the attitude of national self-confidence in Sōseki's observation. But such contradictions emerge as characteristic of the final two decades of the Meiji period.

The foreign policy successes achieved through diplomacy and war during these decades contributed to the building of the sense of nation that was focused upon in Chapter 4. As the leading journalist Tokutomi Sohō commented during the Sino-Japanese War, 'Before we did not know ourselves, and the world did not yet know us. But now that we have tested our strength, we know ourselves and we are known by the world.'[2] Defeat of China and later Russia gave Japanese a new sense of self as well as self-confidence and self-respect. Moreover, in the international arena not only did Japan gain independence and equality by revising the humiliating unequal treaties, it also achieved foreign recognition and parity with the Western powers by acquiring colonies through the two wars. Japan's new status was symbolized by an alliance formed in 1902 with Britain, then the most powerful nation in the world.

However, as with late nineteenth-century Western imperialism, Japanese imperialism emerged very much as an expression of uncertainty and insecurity, and in turn created new uncertainties and insecurities. Pride in national power may in some cases have provided a way of overcoming cultural alienation for many Japanese intellectuals like Tokutomi who had favoured Westernization and modernization, but it did not always compensate for new hardships faced by the poor rural and urban families who provided the soldiers and coolies for the wars. The Russo-Japanese War produced the first anti-war movement, but as shown by a recent study, even the earlier Sino-Japanese War did not have the unanimous support of the Japanese people as was previously depicted.

Meanwhile, the processes of modernization and industrialization begun by early Meiji policies were starting to have social and political consequences which government officials regarded with both concern and hostility. Modernization and industrialization did not affect Japanese uniformly in their economic benefits, and in fact created new social groups whose needs and desires led to political as well as social and economic demands. Nor were cultural areas unaffected, as represented by the new gritty realism of the naturalist writers.

Building the nation through war

Two diplomatic issues dominated Japanese foreign policy during the Meiji period. Revising the unequal treaties, namely regaining tariff autonomy and abolishing extraterritoriality, had dominated Japanese relations with the West since the late 1850s, and settling the status of Korea stood at the centre of Japanese military strategy. The two were interrelated, and their resolution during the final two decades of the Meiji period would contribute to the ambiguity of Japan's position in the world in the twentieth century.

The Sino-Japanese War proved that Japan's efforts to build 'a strong army' had been successful. Victory assured the recovery of its independence and sovereignty, and ushered in Japan's entry to the club of imperialist powers. The pragmatic objective, however, was control of the Korean peninsula, or at least its neutralization. Korea had been important historically to Japan since prehistoric times as its link to the more advanced civilization of China, but in the nineteenth-century struggle for power involving economic concessions and conquest of territories, Korea had become strategically important as well. Military strategists regarded it as a 'dagger' pointing at the heart of Japan.

Remember that a plan for invasion of Korea had been the issue setting off the governmental crisis of 1873, resulting in Saigō Takamori's and Itagaki Taisuke's withdrawal from the government. In 1876 Japan had 'opened' Korea by carefully adopting Perry's tactics of gunboat diplomacy, parading its forces in an imposing manner and with much pageantry. Foreign advisers, including an American hired by the Foreign Ministry, had encouraged such behaviour. Through the Treaty of Kangwha, Japan imposed an unequal treaty system on Korea similar to the one Japan itself was trying to dismantle in its negotiations with the Western powers.

Since Korea remained a vassal state of China under the old tribute system, however, the 1880s saw increasing competition between China and Japan for influence in the Korean government as a faction favouring Meiji-style reforms and modernization opposed a pro-Chinese conservative faction. In 1885 China and Japan tried to prevent further escalation of their rivalry. Both agreed to withdraw their troops from Korea and in the future to give each other prior notice if circumstances required dispatch of troops. While Chinese domination of Korea remained a concern, Russian ambitions in the peninsula posed a growing threat to Japanese perceptions of national security.

Japanese leaders feared that construction of the Trans-Siberian Railway, which began in 1891, would enable Russian expansion into north China, then into Korea and perhaps even Japan itself.

Not all Japanese at either elite or popular level clamoured for war, however; in fact, the war may be seen as aimed at uniting the nation and regenerating Japanese society. At the level of national politics the years between 1890 and 1893 were tumultuous. Although the creation of the Diet had brought in the opposition leaders from the People's Rights Movement, the government continued to be run by the oligarchs from Satsuma and Chōshū because cabinets were not required to be formed by the majority party in the Diet. The parties in the Diet, made up mostly of wealthy men from rural areas, continued to attack the government for failing to achieve treaty revision and insisted on a hard line against China over Korea. At the same time, however, they pressed for a reduction of military expenditures in order to ease the tax burden on the people. The people themselves showed no eagerness to join the army. As a local newspaper observed in June 1894 when war appeared imminent, 'The martial spirit has greatly declined in our country of late and there are even those who would wish to miss out on the lottery or escape conscription!'[3]

Nevertheless, a rebellion of the anti-Western Tonghak religious movement led to the Korean king's request for Chinese assistance, a violation of the 1885 agreement which provided the occasion for Japanese intervention. At the outset of war China was still regarded as a powerful country despite its defeats to Western powers, and its larger navy led most Westerners to anticipate a Chinese victory, although they hoped for a Japanese one. As an American foreign service official wrote in the *North American Review*:

> the success of Japan in Korea means reform and progress – government, social and commercial – in that unhappy country. . . . The success of the Chinese means the forcing back of the Koreans to Oriental sluggishness, superstition, ignorance, and anti-foreign sentiment. It is a conflict between modern civilization, as represented by Japan, and barbarism, or a hopelessly antiquated civilization, by China.[4]

Standard histories note unanimous enthusiasm among Japanese for the war, including Fukuzawa Yukichi who depicted the war as a 'battle for the sake of world culture'. Soldiers, though perhaps reluctant conscripts, returned home to be treated as local heroes and able to recount their new experiences in a foreign country with exotic customs and landscapes. As Japan scored victories, the foreign press enthused as well:

> The enthusiasm in Japan continues, and the spectacle of this Eastern nation fighting and maneuvering and organizing with a verve and intelligence worthy of a first-class European war has sent a thrill of admiring wonder through the military world.[5]

The war inspired many war songs and a militarization of society evident in children's games and toys, as well as the expansion of physical training and military-style exercise in school life. Education authorities used the war as an opportunity to explain history, geography and morals, and to emphasize the wisdom and concern of the emperor for his people. War heroes featured in primary school textbooks were ordinary privates to demonstrate the loyalty and courage of the modern conscript army, and mock battles conducted by schools involved girls as nurses to strengthen the idea of the whole nation's involvement in the war. Theatres produced war plays, the most popular being those in the new Western style. Similarly, the war gave impetus to new-style poetry and other literature.

In art the war stimulated a boom in one traditional medium, namely woodblock prints, before they were superseded by photographs. These prints reveal a significant shift in attitude towards China and in a broader sense towards the rest of Asia. Not surprisingly, they depicted Japanese heroism, but the differences in representation of Japanese and Chinese soldiers indicate the spread of Western racial theories to Japan and Japanese attempts to distance themselves from other Asians. The prints not only depicted the Chinese as abject cowards running from battle, but, dressed in garish colours and drawn with jutting cheekbones, broad noses, gaping mouths, slanting eyes and pigtails, they represented primitive taste and barbarism in contrast to the dignified Japanese with their military moustaches and trim Western-style haircuts, standing tall with European facial features. Soldiers' diaries and letters suggest that ordinary Japanese began to sense differences as well, for they replicate the prints' portrayals of Chinese and Koreans as uncivilized, disorderly and foolish. Sergeant Hamamoto, a teacher in civilian life, gave this description of Koreans upon first landing:

> Though we belong to the same East Asian race, the only thing in common is our yellow faces. Not a single custom or habit is the same. . . . Their character is very mild but they are lazy and have no spirit for progress.[6]

Although Japanese press support for the war was almost universal and popular enthusiasm great, Stewart Lone has shown that the war did not exclusively preoccupy the attentions of ordinary Japanese and that even this short war created hardships. Articles about domestic political and business matters and local events continued to appear in the newspapers, and as soon as hostilities began, prices of daily food items sky-rocketed while wages showed little improvement, even in Hiroshima which was the departure point for all Japanese troops. Hardest hit were families, mostly in rural areas, who provided the soldiers and sailors for the war. Since the government provided little relief, more women were forced into wage labour.

While government support for military families proved meagre, it utilized funerals for war dead and fostered a cult of war dead to promote nation-building. Burials of soldiers became public affairs attended by county and local officials, schoolteachers, schoolchildren and other ordinary towns-people. Prefectural governments assisted with funeral expenses and the estab-lishment of imposing stone grave markers instead of the usual wooden tablets. Shinto shrines, especially those designated as Special Shrines, benefited from the war's enhancing their national character. Among Special Shrines which enshrined those who had loyally served the emperor, Yasukuni Shrine in Tokyo acquired the greatest respect because the emperor himself paid trib-ute to the souls of the war dead enshrined there. Although Yasukuni Shrine's status was exceptional, surpassed only by the Ise Grand Shrines, shrines at all levels began to be associated with national and patriotic affairs in the minds of Japanese people. People often gathered at the local shrine to pray for victory or to give thanks following news of victories, and the national flag flew over the village shrine. Attempting to regain state support at this time, the priesthood expressed no reservations about shrines being used to glorify death in battle.

The Sino-Japanese and Russo-Japanese wars stimulated the government to support Shinto as a means to bolster national unity. It was the beginning of what has been called State Shinto, referring broadly to government support of Shinto shrines and rites and encompassing education in Shinto mythology and persecution of other religious groups considered to be disrespectful of Shinto ideology. Although state support was to reach its peak during the 1930s and 1940s, Helen Hardacre has emphasized that political support and public funding developed by 'fits, starts, advances and retreats' rather than by following 'a single blueprint'.[7]

The Treaty of Shimonoseki of 1895 rewarded Japan with the spoils of war: territories (Formosa/Taiwan, the Pescadores Islands, Liaodong/Kwantung Peninsula), Chinese recognition of Korean independence, a big indemnity, opening of more ports and the promise of a new commercial treaty. By the following year Japan had acquired all the privileges in China that the West-ern powers possessed, and beyond the immediate gains lay the psychological significance of defeating Japan's object of emulation for the past thousand years. While Japanese might still feel cultural indebtedness to China, China could no longer claim superiority. However, despite the praise and open admiration for Japan's victories from Westerners, the Russian, German and French governments were disturbed by Japanese ambitions on the conti-nent and forced Japan to abandon its claim to the Liaodong Peninsula in southern Manchuria. The Triple Intervention reflects the significance of the war in bringing Japan into Western consciousness – Japan as an *Asian* imperialist. For Japanese, although government leaders had been forewarned of the intervention, it was a blow to their national pride and left a feeling of bitterness and resentment about not being treated as an equal.

Historians of Japanese imperialism still debate the motives and intentions of Meiji government and business leaders and the extent of their expan-sionary visions at the beginning of the war, but many would agree that the outcome contributed to the beginning of the perception that a pre-eminent position in Korea and northeast China was necessary for national security and autonomy. This perception lay behind the outbreak of war with Russia less than a decade later.

The Russo-Japanese War: a turning point in Japanese history?

The scramble for railway and mining concessions and 'dividing the melon' which was China into 'spheres of influence' among the imperialist powers formed the context which shaped the foreign policies of Japanese leaders at the turn of the century. Russia posed the main threat to Japan's position in Korea, since it took over most of Manchuria following the Western powers' intervention in China to put down the Boxer Rebellion in 1900. Britain, which also opposed any further Russian advance, agreed to an alliance with Japan in 1902. Among the treaty's provisions was Britain's recognition of Japan's interests in Korea 'in a peculiar degree politically as well as commercially and industrially'. In response to such pressure Russia agreed to a gradual withdrawal of its forces from Manchuria, but an unexplained delay in the second stage of withdrawal led to the onset of hostilities.

The Japanese military could claim successes in the taking of Port Arthur in January 1905 and the decisive victory over the Russian fleet in the Tsushima Straits in May,[8] but by mid-year both sides were ready to welcome the American President Theodore Roosevelt's offer to mediate an end to the war. Russia was facing a revolution at home, and Japan could not sustain the level of costs in human casualties or material involved with a likely military stalemate. Japan emerged from the negotiations with Russian recognition of Japan's pre-eminence in Korea, cession of the southern half of Sakhalin Island (Karafuto), and railway rights and concessions in southern Manchuria. There was no indemnity to pay for the expenses of war, but the peace settlement and international agreements that followed substantially altered Japan's position in East Asia as the victory over China had not. They secured a sphere of influence in Korea and south Manchuria whose preservation and enhancement became the primary goal of Japanese foreign policy during the subsequent four decades. Peter Duus has argued that in this sense the Russo-Japanese War rather than the Sino-Japanese War marked the take-off point of Japanese imperialism.

In other respects, the defeat of Russia heightened Western fears of the emergence of an Asian or 'Oriental' imperialist power. The Triple Intervention had manifested these fears after the Sino-Japanese War, but the racial and cultural overtones became even more marked after Japan's defeat of a white nation. Immigration of Japanese to the United States had begun to increase after American annexation of Hawaii, but it accelerated after the Russo-Japanese War, giving rise to alarmist thinking about a Japanese invasion. According to Archibald Cary Coolidge's *The United States as a World Power,* the Japanese victory over Russia may have given a rude blow to the complacent assumption of the peoples of Europe and America that they were called upon to rule the world; but this has not altered a whit the determination of the Californian or the Australian to keep his land, at any cost, 'a white man's country'.[9]

He saw Japanese immigrants as 'the vanguard of an army of hundreds of millions, who, far from retreating before the white man, thrive and multiply in competition with him'.[10] Sensationalist writings about the 'yellow peril' appeared more frequently in the press, and popular novels in both the USA and Japan depicted future war between the two nations, heavily laden with racial overtones.

In foreign relations many historians therefore view the Russo-Japanese War as a turning point. The Japanese victory brought Japan into the consciousness of Westerners in a new way – for its military power and modernization achievements, not just its exoticism. But the Western attitude was full of ambivalence and contradictions. There was praise for achievements, but also anxiety or hostility towards a new threat. The Japanese reacted to this in a similarly ambivalent way, taking pride in the praise for their nation's achievements and therefore resentful towards lack of equal treatment by the West.

The ambivalence in Japan about foreign relations reflected ambivalence towards a broad range of issues during the final decade of the Meiji period. There was widespread discussion of a lack of national purpose and a search for new national goals since the early Meiji goals had now been achieved. This was paralleled by a decline of consensus which many commentators noted and lamented. This was perhaps a nostalgic, idealized view of the early Meiji period, but nevertheless significant for shaping the climate of opinion at this time. Despite many disagreements among early Meiji leaders, it is true that there was no longer a visible threat such as Western imperialism to galvanize energies in pursuit of national goals. The decline of consensus is also notable in the sense that new social and political forces had emerged by the late Meiji period which were beginning to express their dissatisfaction with existing conditions and claiming a new role in society and politics. Again, early Meiji leaders had their differences and disagreements, but with suppression of the Satsuma Rebellion and, as we saw through examining the aims and ideologies of People's Rights Movement leaders, their ultimate goals were not so far apart, and their samurai and *han* background provided a source of cohesion.

By the late Meiji period, the very institutions of education and recruitment that the early Meiji leaders had created had produced a different generation of leaders who were less bound by personal ties of loyalty and background. Moreover, establishment of constitutional government, while resulting in a stable form of political system, also made way for the growth of political parties despite the oligarchs' dislike of them. By the late Meiji period, they had become a new force in politics. Clashes between the Diet and oligarchs characterized the 1890s and hampered the conduct of administration. By the beginning of the new century the oligarchs recognized this and were forced to cooperate with the parties in the Diet. They eventually established the Seiyūkai and Kenseikai, which became the two major parties of the following three decades. At lower levels of society there also emerged new forces: labour, socialism, youth and women. The last two were not yet 'forces' in an active social or political sense, but the subject of concern.

Most of these different strands may be seen reflected in the Hibiya riot of 1905, notably the intertwining of foreign and domestic issues. The flood of popular criticism of the peace treaty, which culminated in riots and martial law in Tokyo, suggests that the nation-building efforts surrounding the Sino-Japanese War and the 1890s more generally had succeeded in generating a popular nationalism. Flush with Japanese victories, many ordinary Japanese as well as right-wing nationalist groups saw the treaty as a 'humiliation' because it provided for no reparations and little territory. They organized a rally to oppose ratification of the treaty by appealing to the emperor.

However, while the occasion for the rally shows the nationalistic and traditional chauvinistic sentiments of the crowd, the transformation of the rally participants into rioters suggests a broader dissatisfaction with socioeconomic conditions. Victories in foreign wars were not sufficient to compensate for hardships at home created by war. Military families suffered extra hardships during the Sino-Japanese War, but this had not given rise to public expression of antiwar feelings or organization of an antiwar movement as emerged during the Russo-Japanese War. Casualties were heavier during the Russo-Japanese War, and dying for the nation was not always glorious, as portrayed in a new school of realistic naturalist writings such as Tayama Katai's 'One Soldier'[11] or poignantly expressed in Yosano Akiko's pacifist poetry. Those at home felt the burden of increased taxes and 'voluntary contributions', so the lack of an indemnity in the Portsmouth Treaty set off the public furore against ratification which became three days of riots in Hibiya Park. Martial law was declared, but by the time heavy rain finally dowsed the rioters' fury, more than 350 buildings had been smashed or burned and casualties ran to more than 1000, including seventeen dead.

Many see the riots as the first manifestation of mass politics in Japan, although historians differ on the ideological motivations of the rioters. Since police were the main targets of the crowd, Marxist historians have viewed the riots as evidence of the 'people's struggle against despotic ruling powers'. Certainly Japanese citizens held long-standing grievances against police arrogance and repressive actions, and the crowd was angry at police intervention in banning the rally. Okamoto Shumpei, however, points out that the crowd did not oppose all government powers, displaying loyalty to the emperor in their appeals. While a simple class-struggle interpretation does not hold up, a less deterministic explanation pointing to socioeconomic conditions in the cities is suggestive. City life had become extremely unstable by the beginning of the century, and urban slums had sprung up as many day labourers flooded the cities. The Russo-Japanese War had exacerbated conditions with conscription, increased taxes and price rises. Consequently, while neither ideologically motivated nor well organized, the Hibiya Riot indicates the emergence of mass movements as a new factor in Japanese politics. It set a precedent for mass mobilizations of the next decade, culminating with the rice riots of 1918, and is therefore seen by some historians as the starting point for 'Taishō democracy'.

'The social question'

The economic and social welfare concerns of rioters in 1905 and subsequent years reflect social problems associated with the beginnings of industrialization and the consequences of the Meiji government's modernization policies which became evident in the decade between the two wars. The industrial sector of the economy still remained proportionately small. In 1904 those gainfully employed in agriculture still made up 65.3 per cent of the workforce.[12] Nevertheless, the number of industrial workers had reached approximately half a million by that time, and more than half of these were females. The majority were employed in the textile industry (silk and cotton) where female workers made up an even larger percentage of the workforce (83 per cent of cotton factory workers in 1909).[13] As we saw in Chapter 3, working conditions in textile factories were horrible. Workers in chemical, machinery, match, glass and other factories as well as mines and shipyards suffered in brutal conditions too, except that skilled workers in these industries had the option of leaving, which female textile workers did not because they were housed in prison-like dormitories. As early as the late 1880s, textile workers had engaged in strikes to protest against management practices and to improve treatment and working conditions as well as demand wage increases. The number of strikes among factory workers increased during the 1890s, thirty-two occurring during the last six months of 1897 and forty-three during 1898, the same time that a labour movement emerged.[14] The coincidence between the upsurge in strikes and beginnings of labour unionism raised concern among both government officials and social commentators about 'the labour question' and the larger 'social question'.

   Christian intellectuals and social reformers formed groups to study socialism in the late 1890s and began the small movement to organize workers into unions. However, they were acting in a hostile environment, with Law 270 of the Civil Code and later Article 17 of the Public Peace Police Law of 1900 in effect forbidding labour organization and strike activity as threats to the public peace. The legal obstacles turned labour activists to politics, but the government's animosity to socialism was obvious in its banning of the first Social Democratic Party within hours of its inauguration in 1901, despite the moderate nature of its platform. In fact, the party aimed more at democracy than at socialism, seeking abolition of the House of Peers, for example. It also claimed to work for the prosperity of the nation as a whole rather than just the interests of the poor. Nevertheless, such demands were attacked as 'seditious', even by former leaders of the People's Rights Movement.

Since government repression made even moderate reformist activities impossible, socialists were limited to educational and propaganda work. Socialist thought became a minor intellectual fad around 1902 to 1903, but socialists lost contact with workers in their preoccupation with abstract theorizing, and divided among themselves over different theories and tactics. This was to become a characteristic of the socialist movement throughout the twentieth century. Opposition to the Russo-Japanese War and concern about its impact on poor people brought together Christian and secular socialists, but their influence did not reach beyond intellectuals to workers, and instead provoked more restrictive government measures on publishing and meetings.

Meanwhile, workers responded to deteriorating working and living conditions with spontaneous strikes. More workers participated in strikes in 1907 than ever before, especially in the growing heavy industrial sector that had been stimulated by the war. Besides difficulties caused by postwar inflation, workers in heavy industry objected to companies' efforts to phase out the system of semi-independent labour contractors and impose more direct control over their employees. Such efforts were largely designed to reduce the high turnover rates of employees, especially skilled workers.

Contrary to the present-day popular image of Japanese workers as hardworking, reliable and loyal to their companies, Japanese workers in Meiji times displayed no such devotion or industriousness, coming and going without regard to hours, rules or holidays. One factory director of the Shibaura Engineering Works complained in a series of magazine articles in 1908 that young, educated workers were rude, and quit if not promoted quickly, but that older, uneducated workers would not learn new ways – 'teaching them anything is like trying to teach a cat to chant the *nembutsu*'.[15] He further criticized Japanese workers for their lack of diligence, failure to follow instructions promptly and spendthrift habits. Ironically, he held up the American worker as a model. Despite feeling some sympathy for management's frustration with their workers' unreliable habits and attitudes, it must be pointed out that employers did not demonstrate benevolent paternalism except in their rhetoric.

The frustration of constant defeat in workers' disputes with employers turned some socialists to the anarcho-syndicalism being advocated by Kōtoku Shūsui after his conversion to radicalism during a stay in the United States in 1906. Anarcho-syndicalism rejected the state-oriented political approach of both reformist parliamentarism and the contemporary 'orthodox' Marxism of German socialists in favour of an emphasis on direct action and direct negotiation with employers. Two violent disputes involving thousands of miners occurred in the Ashio and Besshi copper mines. At Ashio a Christian socialist organization had been important in arousing a new consciousness among workers against their living and working conditions, but the dispute broke out spontaneously, and the workers did not confine their protests to peaceful negotiation. Using explosives and fire, 3600 miners virtually levelled a large part of the mine complex in what has been described as 'three days of uninterrupted mayhem'. Both disputes were ended only after the intervention of military troops.

The Cabinet under Katsura Tarō from 1908 to 1911 imposed even harsher repression on labour and socialist activists, both those favouring legal means and those supporting 'direct action'. Repression culminated in the arrest and execution of Kōtoku and eleven other anarchists, and life sentences for another twelve in 1910 to 1911 for plotting to kill the emperor. According to Kanno Suga, the sole woman executed, only a handful were actually involved in the conspiracy, but the government's response displayed a strong sense of the danger posed by socialism and radical anarchism. The executions ending the 'Great Treason Incident' and the arrests of organizers of the Tokyo municipal streetcar strike in 1912 mark the end of the Meiji labour and socialist movements. The establishment of Special Higher Police (Tokkō) sections in Tokyo and Osaka aimed to hamper their resuscitation.

Although repression characterized much of the Meiji government's attitude and policies towards labour unionism and socialism, it did not make up the whole of Japanese thinking about 'the social question', including the thinking of government officials. Both government officials and social critics saw the social, economic and political problems which Western industrialized countries had experienced earlier in the nineteenth century and hoped that Japan might be able to avoid them, leading to a new interest in social policy at the end of the 1890s. Tokyo Imperial University economists formed the Japanese Social Policy Association in 1897 to campaign for protective factory legislation, based on German models, and soon extended membership to include respected higher civil servants and businessmen. Stimulated by exposés of poverty, particularly Yokoyama Gennosuke's 1899 study of the 'lower strata of society', and study of German social policies, government officials in the Home Ministry conducted their own surveys which convinced them of the necessity of factory legislation not only to end exploitation of young women and children, but also to improve the health and productivity of the nation as a whole.

Employers strongly resisted the legislation, arguing that industrial harmony derived from Japan's 'beautiful custom of master–servant relations' would be destroyed by legally sanctioning workers' interests. After the wave of strikes following the Russo-Japanese War, however, government officials believed that 'beautiful customs' alone would be insufficient to prevent social conflict and ensure industrial development, and finally passed the Factory Law in 1911. Among its provisions, the law set minimum health and safety standards, a minimum age of 12 for employment, and a twelve-hour day for women and youths under the age of 15, but the big firms had succeeded in watering down the prohibition of night work for women and children by obtaining a fifteen-year delay in enforcement.

The controversy over labour legislation marked a change in the pattern of business–government relations. Although cooperation between them remained close throughout the twentieth century, during the debate over social policy business leaders emerged as a more independent elite whose perceived interests would not always coincide with those of bureaucrats. They hoped to maintain control over industrial relations primarily through their own company practices, whereas a new generation of bureaucrats favoured state intervention and coordination of social development. Behind the split between bureaucrats and business leaders was the bureaucrats' fear that if businessmen were left to manage workers themselves, they would undermine social and political order not only in factories, but society at large. A high-ranking Finance Ministry official argued:

> We cannot find security in the fact that our nation's people are rich in compassion. If the state does not take some slight role in employer–employee relations there will be no way to protect the interests of the employed, and as a result there will be increasing cases of social illness, disturbance, and struggle.[16]

Bureaucrats were concerned for the wider social order because it was not only the minority of industrial workers who were displaying dissatisfaction with existing conditions. The younger generation, especially well-educated youth who would be future leaders, were exhibiting a change in values which government officials did not welcome. During the 1870s and 1880s influential educators and liberal intellectuals like Fukuzawa Yukichi had promoted individual independence and success of a kind associated with national prosperity and social progress. These were not incompatible with the Confucian samurai tradition or the political aims of the Meiji government. In those days young, upwardly mobile males could be optimistic about their chances for success through education. As one declared, 'If we carry through the hard work of being a student, bear up under the load, study and work like a lion, it will not be the least difficult to be a great man.'[17] And by 'great man' he meant prime minister. During the 1880s the People's Rights Movement had also stimulated a conception of advancement as study for wealth and honour through government service.

However, by the late 1880s and early 1890s, social and political change had slowed down, and opportunities for rapid advancement among educated youth also declined. An editorial in the most important youth-oriented publication *Shōnen'en* (*Garden for Young People*) stressed that times had changed:

> Around the time of the Restoration or the opening of the ports, by some kind of good fortune, or by the patronage of some famous person, or by entering the gate of some dignitary, it was possible to go to the United States or Europe without a bit of one's own capital and, before half a year had passed, make a great amount of money. Although there

were not a few who did this, things are completely different today. Because the social order is being stabilized, this kind of good fortune is hard to find even in dreams. If you do not tread the proper path when you come to Tokyo, you will not be able to do or know even a single thing.[18]

The proper path meant systematic advancement by entering the right schools. The educational reforms of the late 1880s had established a system of higher-middle schools (*kōtō chūgakkō*) which became the basic route into Tokyo Imperial University, the training ground for government officials. The magazine gave practical information on how to prepare for the entrance examination to enter these schools.

During the early 1890s success was still associated with a bureaucratic career, but the Sino-Japanese War stimulated an expansion of the economy and a shift to youth dreaming of money instead of politics, despite the nationalistic fervour generally aroused by the war. The Christian critic Uchimura Kanzō sarcastically noted the change:

Get money; get it by all means, for it alone is power in this generation. Wish you to be patriotic? Then get money, for you cannot better serve your country than by getting money for you and it. Be loyal? Then get money, and add wealth to your Master's land. Be filial to your father and mother? You cannot be so without getting money. The strength of your nation, the fear of your name – all come from money. Morality ever for the sake of money. Honesty is the best *policy* for – getting money.[19]

It was also reflected in the rush for places in business schools after the war, whereas many had remained empty before the war.

By the beginning of the twentieth century much of the writing on success focused on money and the 'secrets' of acquiring wealth comparable to that of the American Andrew Carnegie. Critics of this infatuation with American multimillionaires complained that Japan's moral base was being eroded by American values and argued for a modified *bushidō* (Way of the warrior) to halt the tide of materialism, ignoring Japan's own tradition of ostentatious consumption among both samurai and *chōnin*. At the same time, encouragement of success associated with wealth came in 1897 when the entrepreneur industrialist Shibusawa Eiichi was made a peer, giving recognition to the possibility of honour and rank coming from wealth.

However, not all late Meiji youth were dedicated to the pursuit of personal advancement and wealth. Social commentators gave attention to 'anguished youth' and 'decadent youth' as well as 'success youth'. This was triggered by a series of suicides emulating the suicide of a student at the First Higher School in Tokyo (the top feeder school to Tokyo Imperial University), who carved his suicide note into a tree trunk before leaping into Kegon Falls at

Nikko. A civil service examination system had begun in the 1890s because there were more Tokyo Imperial University graduates than jobs in the government. Consequently, by the end of the Meiji period competition among educated youth became so severe that success in terms of traditional wealth, honour and bureaucratic affiliation was not assured even for graduates of elite institutions. Even those who succeeded in gaining government positions often became no more than low-paid clerical flunkies.

The emergence of 'anguished youth' was also reflected in the new vernacular literature. The character Bunzō in Japan's first modern novel *Ukigumo* (*Drifting Cloud*) is an example of a well-educated young man who is seemingly on the road to success after having obtained a position in the government, but he loses his job for not toadying enough to his boss. Throughout the novel he wallows in indecisiveness or 'anguish' which threatens loss of not only a career, but also a desirable prospective wife to his sycophantic rival Noboru (whose name means 'to climb'). Even more anguish emerges from the pages of Ishikawa Takuboku's *Rōmaji Diary*, kept by the poet in 1909 and freely baring his contradictory thoughts and emotions. Takuboku left his parents, wife and daughter in the countryside to come to Tokyo to write, but took an office job to pay his living expenses. Like Bunzō, he seems incapable of making any decision or doing anything, including reading and writing, although he feels 'haunted' by a compulsion to do 'something'.

> Then, what am I seeking? Fame? No, it's not that. Achievement? No, not that either. Love? No. Knowledge? No. Then, money perhaps. Yes, money. Not as an end, but as a means. What I am searching for with all my heart is peace of mind. Yes, that is it.[20]

After the Russo-Japanese War there was heightened consciousness of changing values among youth. There was a change in the meaning of success to one of individual success, rather than the family's success or success in one's home town, and to mean success in terms of money rather than government position. Even Takuboku wanted money. One commentator exclaimed in 1910: 'never since the dawn of world history has the growth of the individual been so respected and material happiness so sought after as in present day Japan.'[21] While obviously exaggerated, this is suggestive of the degree of change perceived at the time.

A revision of school ethics textbooks and issuance of the Boshin Imperial Rescript in 1908 revealed authorities' concern and anxiety about these changes in social values and behaviour. The Rescript read:

> Only a short while has passed since the war, and governmental administration is increasingly in need of new vigor and discipline.
>
> We desire that all classes should be united in mind and spirit, devoted to their callings, diligent and frugal in their work, faithful, and dutiful. They should cultivate courtesy and warmheartedness, avoid ostentation

and adhere to simple realities, guard against laxity and self-indulgence while undertaking arduous toil.

The heritage of our divine ancestors and the illustrious history of our nation shine like the sun and stars. If our subjects cleave to that tradition and sincerely strive for its perfection, the foundation for national development will largely have been secured.[22]

We can see officials' worry about materialism, hedonism, extravagance and sensual dissipation, blamed on selfish individualism which was undermining loyalty to the state and nation as well as the family.

Changes in primary school textbooks tried to halt these disturbing trends among youth for the next generation. The first series of government-written ethics texts introduced in 1904 reflected the attitude prevalent before the appearance of anguished youth. They still presented self-advancement as something good to be encouraged. The second series which began to appear in 1907 placed less emphasis on self-advancement and changed the framework in which it was to occur. The change was exemplified in lessons on Toyotomi Hideyoshi, the second of the great unifiers of the country at the end of the sixteenth century. The first series had portrayed Hideyoshi as a model of self-advancement, a poor boy who from childhood wanted to become famous and acted to realize his goal. In contrast, the second series laid more emphasis on his alleged contributions to the prosperity of the imperial household than on his individual achievements. More passive verbs were used to describe his rise to wealth and power, such as 'was pulled up' instead of 'rose in the world' to give the impression that rank and fame were rewards for loyal service rather than the result of military or power struggles. A story about Hideyoshi warming his lord Oda Nobunaga's sandals with his body suggested not just the virtue of diligence and loyalty, but perhaps also the effectiveness of currying the favour of one's boss, like Noboru in *Ukigumo*.

Officials and commentators on the anguished youth phenomenon feared youth would turn to socialism or decadence if not suicide. A few did, but more did not. While anguished youth displayed individuated behaviour, their individualism remained limited and self-destructive. Business ideologues such as Shibusawa as well as government authorities rejected socialism, and the poor employment situation for educated youth was not conducive to deviancy, but rather put pressure on them to conform. The harsh repressive measures against socialists referred to earlier also militated against the spread of radical social and political activism.

In the aftermath of the Great Treason Incident, fear of new social and political forces was still in the air when Emperor Meiji died in July 1912. The Japanese people at all levels responded with a great outpouring of grief. Hundreds of thousands lined the streets for the funeral procession. On the one hand, his death symbolized the end of an era of great accomplishments, putting Japan well on the way to 'a rich country, strong army'. Japan was now recognized as a major power in East Asia with an empire consisting of Taiwan, the Pescadores Islands, Karafuto and Korea (annexed in 1910). In addition, its economy had entered a second phase of modern economic growth after the Russo-Japanese War as heavy industry expanded. On the other hand, his death marked the beginning of a new era whose goals were not clearly defined. The question of whither the nation now hung heavily over the people in mourning. Not only was a vigorous emperor dead, but also most of the vigorous leaders of the Restoration. Government by oligarchy was ending. Many welcomed this, but not the decline of consensus and broad vision. New social and political forces were surfacing, not just the small labour and socialist movements, but the conservative political parties in the Diet and the military as separate and more influential elite groups. But the first two years in the new emperor's reign remained relatively quiet. It was the ripples of a far-away war that were to be the stimulus for the new period of rapid social and political changes, to be discussed in the following chapter.

6   An emerging mass society

Demands for equity and the dilemmas of choice

In Japanese tradition the naming of each new emperor's reign is meant to signal political leaders' hopes and expectations for the future. While the designation 'Meiji' had foreshadowed the radical innovations to accompany the 'Enlightenment' drive of the 1870s and 1880s, naming the new era beginning in 1912 'Taishō' announced a period of rectification and stabilization. Although individual emperors exercised no significant decision-making power, the vigorous Meiji emperor and the mentally and physically weak Taishō emperor have become symbolic of their two reigns. Much ambivalence continues in evaluations of the Taishō period (1912 to 1926), and except for domestic political developments, the 1910s and 1920s have not attracted as much scholarly or popular attention as the years of war which followed. Perhaps this relative neglect reflects past historians' chief interests in politics and foreign affairs. Japan's involvement in the First World War fades in importance compared to the Second World War, and during the 1920s Japan's international relations were calm as it pursued policies of cooperation and peace.

In politics this is the period of 'Taishō Democracy' when the political parties in the Diet came to dominate the cabinets. In light of their loss of influence to the military in the 1930s, however, this period of party domination appears brief and ephemeral, and the depth and extent of democratization during the 1920s have consequently been a bone of contention among historians for many years. Much of the discussion of political developments in this chapter will revolve around this issue.

However, if we focus on developments in society and culture as well as politics, the picture is full of dynamic changes and conflict. The concept of Taishō Democracy can refer more broadly than to party rule, to demands for more social justice and equality advanced by the 'social movements' of the period, such as socialist and labour movements, a student movement, women's movements, a Burakumin liberation movement, and a tenant farmers' movement. Foreign developments, such as the Russian Revolution of 1917, the 1918 German revolution, the rise to power of the Labour Party in Britain and the growth of the American Federation of Labour, stimulated demands for social and political reform and revolution. They also provided models for organization and tactics. At the same time, the movements were outcomes associated with the processes of modernization, urbanization and industrialization that were accelerated by the First World War and the influx of new foreign ideas. Discussion of patterns of demographic change will focus on Tokyo as the prime example of urbanization, suburbanization and other developments, but will also look at concern about population problems and the emergence of a large Korean minority suffering poverty and discrimination, a development having political as well as social significance.

Other forces stimulating the social ferment and cultural dynamism of the 1920s were the Kantō earthquake of 1923 and the expansion of a new white-collar middle class pursuing a new lifestyle and culture concerned with personal autonomy and enjoyment, and influenced by Western ideas and social practices introduced through the burgeoning mass media. A final section of the chapter will follow discussion of these trends with an examination of intellectual and other cultural developments. Although proletarian literature and avant-garde art represented critiques of the dominant political and social structures, a dichotomizing between politics and culture characterized the 1920s, which may help to explain the lack of opposition to aggressive foreign policies among intellectuals in the subsequent decade of the 1930s.

Peaceful internationalism

The domestic social, cultural and political changes of the 1920s took place in an international context of peaceful cooperation with the major Western powers. Due to its alliance with Britain, Japan ended up on the winning side at the end of the First World War. The war did not create the psychological trauma that it did for Europeans because relatively few Japanese soldiers engaged in combat and none in the trenches of Western Europe. Instead, the withdrawal of the Western European countries from Asian markets opened up opportunities for growth by Japanese manufacturers especially in China. The Japanese government was able to take advantage of European preoccupation with the war to expand its economic privileges and influence over Chinese policy-making. The so-called Twenty-One Demands issued to the Chinese government represented an ultimatum which, if accepted, would not only have consolidated Japan's position in China, but installed Japanese as military, financial and political advisers in the Chinese government, extended Japanese concessions to new areas, and privileged Japanese firms in commercial dealings. The Chinese managed to stave off the worst demands, using Western protest as support, but Japanese ambitions had been exposed and Chinese hostility engendered. Japan had also occupied German territories in China and the western Pacific at the start of the war, and expected to receive these as spoils of war. Japanese leaders therefore participated in the Versailles Peace Conference as representatives of one of the victors, retaining prewar notions and expectations of empire. At the same time Japanese were caught up by the wartime democratic rhetoric expounded by the American President Woodrow Wilson.

The Japanese delegation achieved mixed gains. On the one hand, Japan became a council member of the new League of Nations established after the conference to promote peace through collective security. On the other hand, American, British and Australian opposition defeated the Japanese proposal for inclusion of a racial equality clause in the League charter, and, although maintaining control of the former German Mariana Islands, it was through a League mandate rather than outright ownership. Japan was able to keep the Shandong territories and other rights in China secured during the war, but this provoked the outraged protests known as the May Fourth Movement in China in 1919.

Despite these setbacks, Japanese diplomatic leaders led by Shidehara Kijūrō adopted a foreign policy of accommodationism during the 1920s in the belief that Japan's interests would be best served through diplomacy and multilateral international agreements rather than belligerency. The business community also supported peaceful expansion of overseas markets in both China and the West. Japan's acceptance of agreements made at the Washington Conference of 1921 to 1922 reflected this commitment to peaceful internationalism. The conference reaffirmed the territorial integrity of China and foreshadowed a gradual end to the unequal treaty system. To demonstrate its good intentions, Japan returned its Shandong territories to China, although retaining economic rights there. Japan also accepted the inferior ratio of a naval arms limitations treaty establishing a 5:5:3:1.75:1.75 ratio of capital ship tonnage for Britain, the United States, Japan, France and Italy. To compensate for the inferior ratio, Britain and the USA gave Japan the promise of no new fortifications in the Pacific.

Scaled-down military budgets and further participation in international arms limitation conferences characterized Japan's foreign policy through most of the 1920s. Even primary school textbooks reflected the climate of peaceful coexistence in China and cooperation with the Anglo-American powers, downplaying stories of military heroes while emphasizing the Meiji and Taishō emperors' accomplishments in 'international amity and world peace'. They also encouraged participation in the League of Nations and freely acknowledged Japan's cultural debts to foreign countries. Military leaders resented the budget cutbacks and diplomatic concessions, but for the time being Japanese were left to pursue their diverse lives without major distractions or demands related to foreign military expansionism.

Party rule and democratization

The policies of peaceful internationalism were conducted by the party-dominated governments of the 1920s. Since the end of the Second World War, many historians have criticized Taishō democrats for betraying their liberal principles during the 1930s, and for giving in to the military and its policies of aggressive foreign expansion. Other historians, however, have regarded the party rule of this period as providing a sound foundation for the rapid revival of parliamentary politics after 1945. The debate has led to questions as to why Taishō democrats 'failed', to how liberal and democratic they were, and even to whether or not Taishō democracy existed. As we will see, the posing of such questions and their answers reveal as much about historians' concerns and judgements about the present as about the past. I will return to issues of interpretation at the end of this section, but an overview of the parties and their rise to power will provide some answers to questions as to the nature of Taishō democracy and its relation to Japanese historical developments both before and after. It will also indicate the kinds of changes that were occurring in Japanese society and the problems facing the nation after the Meiji period.

The common assumption is that the 'established parties' of the 1920s were a direct outgrowth of the parties of the Meiji period, namely those formed during the 1870s and 1880s and making up the People's Rights Movement. However, they differed greatly both in membership and goals. The parties of the People's Rights Movement were not real parties in the sense that they were not devoted to the pursuit of power, but represented instead a general protest against the Meiji government and particularly its being dominated by the *han* clique of Satsuma and Chōshū. Their activities therefore concentrated on education and agitation. It was only after the Diet was established that disciplined organization began.

During the first two decades after the Diet opened, so-called 'transcendental cabinets' ruled the nation. Composed of the oligarchs and their protégés, they were meant to operate 'above' the divisive conflicts of partisan politics. But political conflict soon erupted as the parties criticized the government for *han* clique favouritism and failure to achieve revision of the unequal treaties. Even after this foreign policy issue died down in the mid-1890s, cooperation with the Diet became necessary for the smooth running of the government, notably for obtaining Diet approval of budgets. Itō Hirobumi was the first oligarch to recognize this and formed the Seiyūkai to coopt certain Diet leaders. After the Russo-Japanese War anti-Seiyūkai groups merged to form a second party, the Dōshikai, under another oligarch, Yamagata Aritomo's protégé Katsura Tarō.

The period from 1913 to 1918 was characterized by 'covert party government', as described by Peter Duus. Politics was getting more complex as a three-way struggle among the oligarchs (known as the *genrō* or elder statesmen), the Seiyūkai and the Dōshikai (later Kenseikai) ensued. Yamagata Aritomo stubbornly stuck to the 'transcendental cabinet' ideal and was still influential enough to block appointment of a cabinet headed by a party leader. But the parties held *de facto* power because all governments needed Diet support. A new style of election campaigning in 1915 also foreshadowed the future of party politics as the parties conducted an American-style whistle-stop campaign at train stations around the country and other direct appeals to the public. In addition, party influence in policy-making was revealed when the Dōshikai's Katō Kōmei (Takaaki) as foreign minister insulted the *genrō* by not consulting or even informing them about the government's 'Twenty-One Demands' to China in 1915. These demands attempted to enlarge Japan's economic role in China in a manner which Yamagata presciently criticized for creating Chinese hostility, a danger for the future.

In 1918 the leader of the Seiyūkai Hara Kei (Takashi) became 'the first commoner' prime minister in Japanese history, meaning the first member of the House of Representatives rather than the House of Peers. All Cabinet members, except the military, belonged to the majority party in the Diet. This coincided with the emergence of a new atmosphere in public opinion which raised demands for widespread political, social and economic reform. Moreover, in August 1918 riots protesting inflated rice prices, and also more general social grievances, had spread from a remote rural area to towns and cities throughout the country. Soldiers had to be mobilized to put down the riots, leading to the resignation of Prime Minister Terauchi Masatake. The nationwide scale of the rice riots points to further development in the role of the masses in politics. Nevertheless, Hara's appointment did not yet represent a new commitment to participatory democracy. When the Cabinet was formed, Yamagata had still not been converted to the principle of party government, but none of the protégés was willing to serve as prime minister, and the parties were threatening organized resistance in the Diet if a party prime minister, was not appointed. Consequently, the Hara cabinet did not represent the beginning of party government viewed as 'normal constitutional government' or the start of party-led participatory democracy.

If we look at Hara's background and personality, we can understand the policies of his government. He came from an upper samurai family in one of the few *han* that supported the Tokugawa shogunate and was therefore an outsider to the Meiji government. It was not until he gained the notice of one of the oligarchs, Inoue Kaoru, in the early 1880s that he entered the bureaucracy, a reminder of the necessity of personal connections and patronage for government positions.

Even as a bureaucrat, Hara showed an interest in party politics of the 1890s, so it is not surprising that he helped to form the Seiyūkai, working with Itō Hirobumi, and then actively sought election to the House of Representatives. He then worked tirelessly to make himself into the party's key leader, to make his party the majority party in the Diet, and to increase party power and influence – a shift in goals from early Meiji parties. He became a political boss *par excellence* who worked to weave a fabric of personal ties and friendships within his party, with rank-and-file members as well as leaders, and used generous donations to create personal loyalty. He also cultivated relations with Yamagata to reduce Yamagata's mistrust of him.

As Tetsuo Najita has shown, Hara was extremely successful in the 'politics of compromise', using tactics of compromise, flexibility and pragmatism. His party had not been organized on the basis of policy or ideological aims, and his government reflected the party's bases of power and methods of success. Consequently, it did not introduce any programme of legislative reform, and when the opposition party responded to a popular movement for universal suffrage, his government's proposal was more limited – just a reduction of the tax qualification to 3 yen. Instead, Hara worked to cultivate further the party's bases of power. Using pork barrel legislation, he sought votes among local, rural elites and money among business leaders to finance escalating election expenses. To increase influence over the multiple decision-making institutions, he worked to 'partisanize' the bureaucracy, the House of Peers and the Privy Council.

Hara's rival Katō headed a Kenseikai government a few years later which tried to introduce a programme of moderate reform, including universal male suffrage. He seems to have been more committed than Hara to social reform and the principle of parliamentary government, but the Kenseikai was not substantially different from the Seiyūkai in its tactics or its bases of power. Even though it sponsored universal male suffrage, it was not a mass party with a grassroots base. Contemporaries criticized both the Kenseikai (replaced by the Minseitō in 1927) and Seiyūkai as 'established parties' or 'entrenched parties' due to their connections with business and rural leaders. Corruption scandals reminiscent of those of recent times frequently made headlines. The parties' reluctance to institute more rapid social and political reform also alienated intellectuals, leftist reformers and urban socioeconomic groups. Peter Duus suggests that perhaps it was precisely because the tactics of compromise were so successful that the parties did not attempt any structural reform of the policy-making system which would have institutionalized party rule. Moreover, in the late 1920s rule by the two main parties did appear to be 'entrenched'. In the first general election after the passage of universal male suffrage, proletarian parties won only about 10 per cent of the vote.

What would have happened if there had not been a foreign crisis in the 1930s? Was it external factors such as the international crisis created by Japan's invasion of Manchuria or internal deficiencies such as the lack of truly liberal ideals which explain the decline of party government in the 1930s? As mentioned at the beginning of this section, such questions have occupied much attention among historians since the Second World War. Most historians now seem to agree that the parties' liberal character 'has been exaggerated', as Henry D. Smith II put it, and if by 'democracy' we mean wide participation in social and political structures, we may conclude from the previous overview that the democratic aspects of the dominant Taishō parties were in fact quite limited. Most Western historians are also agreed that Taishō party politicians were loyal to the emperor and the existing constitutional structure, accepting the theoretical or legal sovereignty of the emperor.

This also applied to prominent liberal intellectuals and scholars, such as the Tokyo Imperial University professors Yoshino Sakuzō and Minobe

Tatsukichi. Yoshino is known for translating and conceptualizing the English term 'democracy' as '*minponshugi*', literally 'people-as-the-base-ism'. Rejecting a Japanese Marxist translation that implied class struggle and an Anglo-American style term that meant popular sovereignty, Yoshino opted for an interpretation of democracy that aimed at the people's welfare without destroying imperial sovereignty. Similarly, Minobe's interpretation of the Meiji Constitution maintained the emperor, although viewing him as an 'organ' of the state, a constitutional monarch rather than one with absolute powers.

However, while historians generally agree on the limited liberal character of the parties and Taishō intellectuals from a late twentieth- or twenty-first-century perspective, they do not agree on whether to condemn the parties and intellectuals for this, nor on whether this made the events and policies of the 1930s and 1940s inevitable. Some, such as Stephen Large, have criticized the Taishō liberals for the shallowness of their liberalism; this is why the potentials of Taishō democracy were so short-lived. However, others, such as Smith, argue that the limited nature of Taishō liberalism did not make the 1930s inevitable, since Taishō political life was 'complex, contradictory, and multivalent'.

Demands for equity

Smith's conclusion needs emphasizing, for we need to look beyond the established parties to gain a sense of the political, social and intellectual ferment of the late 1910s and 1920s. Historians' past focus on the established parties led to a narrow political definition of Taishō democracy and to a neglect of important new developments in society and culture which formed the beginnings of the mass consumer society of the present. Before we turn to these social developments, however, we will examine sociopolitical movements which claimed to represent the interests of disadvantaged groups in Japanese society, including women, minorities and industrial workers. Tenant farmers also organized to advance their interests, but will be discussed in Chapter 7.

Founding of the New Women's Association (Shin Fujin Kyōkai) in 1920 signalled the organization of a feminist movement seeking equal rights for women in politics, the home and the workplace, but discussion of 'the woman question' had been taking place in mainstream journals for several years since Hiratsuka Raichō announced in the 1911 inaugural issue of *Seitō* (*Bluestocking*):

> In the beginning, woman was the sun. An authentic person.
>   Today, she is the moon. Living through others. Reflecting the brilliance of others.
>   And now, *Bluestocking*, a journal created for the first time with the brains and hands of today's Japanese women, raises its voice.[1]

The members of the Bluestocking Society had not initially intended their literary journal to be a vehicle for advocating the economic and political emancipation of women, but hostile criticisms of their writings and private lives soon raised their feminist consciousness and led to social and political activism. The press portrayed 'new women' like Raichō as selfish and irresponsible young women who used their overdeveloped sexuality to undermine the 'good wife, wise mother' ideal. Raichō, in a special issue of *Chūō kōron*, tried to counter such images and emphasize the oppression of Japanese women by men:

> The new woman does not merely destroy the old morality and laws constructed out of male selfishness, but day by day attempts to create a new kingdom, where a new religion, a new morality, and new laws are carried out, based on the spiritual values and surpassing brilliance of the sun. . . . The new woman is not simply covetous of power for its own sake. . . . The new woman today seeks neither beauty nor virtue. She is simply crying out for strength, the strength to create this still unknown kingdom, the strength to fulfill her own hallowed mission.[2]

The changing emphasis in *Seitō* from literary to social and political issues lost some support from women contributors and prompted government moves to counteract perceived dangers raised by organization of a women's movement. The Home Ministry banned a number of women's magazines, and police censors scrutinized each issue of *Seitō* for 'dangerous thoughts', especially after Itō Noe took over editorship and published debates on abortion, prostitution and motherhood. Lacking financial support and exhausted from stresses in her relationship with the anarchist Ōsugi Sakae, Itō closed the journal in 1916, but by then the Bluestockings had introduced new ideas and demands regarding Japanese women's condition.

Public discussion of women's issues continued, and women's organizations such as the New Women's Association in the 1920s campaigned for rights of political participation and suffrage, and worked to revise the civil code in order to give women equal legal rights in matters such as marriage, divorce and property ownership. They were partially successful when in 1922 women were permitted to participate in political meetings, and in 1930 the House of Representatives of the Diet approved a bill extending the voting franchise to women. The conservative House of Peers, however, rejected the women's suffrage bill. Meanwhile, Christian women pushed for abolition of licensed prostitution and concubinage, while socialist feminists formed the Red Wave Society (Sekirankai) in 1921 and sought to organize women workers and achieve more radical restructuring of the entire social and economic system.

Socialist feminists made some gains among women textile workers, as suggested by the intensity of the struggle in the Tōyō Muslin Factory strike in 1930. In that strike the textile workers clashed in the streets with gangs hired by the factory owners and even halted trains in the area. Two years

later Nakamoto Takako dramatized in a serialized novel the changing consciousness of the women workers. Through scenes tracing secret meetings
among female workers and later with male workers, she demonstrated the
development of a sense of class-consciousness and militant resistance under
the guidance of a Marxist labour organizer, a dormitory supervisor named
Ushiyama Chie. Although women textile workers were not the passive victims portrayed in most histories of the labour movement until the late 1980s,
their activism took place outside the union movement. Only 1 per cent were
unionized. However, this was due less to women's lack of consciousness as
workers than to the structures and attitudes of the male-dominated unions.

The labour movement's lack of attention to women workers' issues is one
reason that the socialist and more radical communist movements as a whole
remained weak throughout the 1920s and early 1930s. Moderate socialists
were assimilated into the existing political system, and radical socialism and
communism never made substantial headway as a political force. As George
Beckmann noted in his history of the movement, communists were 'only dissidents on the fringes of society; they never became a mass force'.[3] In fact,
the history of the Japan Communist Party (JCP) in the 1920s and 1930s was
characterized by one defeat after another. The party was formed three times
during that period beginning in 1922, but was completely destroyed in 1932
and not re-established until after the war.

Why, then, have historians, as well as the Japanese governments of the
period, given the communist and other left-wing movements attention disproportionate to their strength? Because the JCP presented a fundamental
challenge to the emperor-centred ideology and governmental structures
of post-Meiji Japan. Moreover, despite defections in the 1930s, communists
numbered among the few Japanese who openly opposed the authoritarian
and imperialist policies of the prewar and wartime state. Answering the question of why the communists failed is therefore linked to the larger question
of why there was so little opposition to government policies in the 1930s and
1940s, and to the earlier question of the nature of Taishō Democracy and
the reasons for its decline.

Why did the communist movement fail? In Marxist-Leninist terms, the
'objective' conditions were not at all favourable for the existence, much less
success, of a communist movement. The industrial workforce or proletariat
was small and lacked a strong, unified union movement. Workers in manufacturing numbered about 1.5 million in the 1920s, but over half were young
women confined in closely supervised company dormitories in the textile
industry. Peasants still made up more than half of the labour force in 1920,
but the majority were hostile to socialist ideas.

Furthermore, the dominant ideology of post-Meiji Japan promoted a col-
lectivist ethic opposed to open clashes and social conflict, which in turn justified repressive measures. The Meiji Constitution and Imperial Rescript on
Education had established the sanctity of the *kokutai* (the national essence
or polity) with the emperor at its centre. Worried by the nationwide scale of

the rice riots in 1918 and the influx of revolutionary ideas and models from Europe, police authorities tightened their surveillance and harassment of anarchists and other radical socialists. Discovery of the organization of a communist party in 1922 quickly led to arrests. In the aftermath of the 1923 Kantō earthquake civil and military police rounded up leftists who allegedly were using the chaos to foment revolution. These included the anarchists Ōsugi Sakae and Itō Noe who were murdered by military police, and ten labour activists who were killed at the Kameido police station.

In 1925 passage of a new political control law, the Peace Preservation Law, made attempts to organize an association aimed at destroying the *kokutai* or denying the private property system punishable by imprisonment. There was much debate both inside and outside the Diet over the bill, but critics did not oppose the principle of protecting the *kokutai* – 'no one in Japan would want to destroy the *kokutai*'.[4] A 1928 revision of the law made crimes against the *kokutai* punishable by the death penalty, more important even than protection of the private property system.

Government hostility and repression escalated to systematic suppression beginning with mass arrests in 1928 following proletarian parties' garnering almost half a million votes in the first general election under universal male suffrage, even though this amounted to only 10 per cent of the votes. Marxist academics and students were no longer safe from police repression even if they confined their activities to university campuses and to research. The Special Higher Police (Tokkō) in charge of controlling 'thought' expanded nationwide, and new 'thought procurators' were appointed in the Justice Ministry.

If objective conditions were unfavourable to a communist movement, so were 'subjective' conditions. The party faced problems of strategy and tactics because Japan did not fit the European pattern of industrialized societies upon which Marx had based his theory of historical development. Neither did Japan fit the pattern of development of Asian agricultural, colonial societies. Japanese communists became divided among themselves and isolated from potential allies as well as most ordinary Japanese when the Soviet Union-dominated Communist International (Comintern) dictated policies which pitted the JCP against the imperial institution, ignored women workers in light industry and the peasant majority, and opposed cooperation with moderate socialists. The large number of conversions (*tenkō*) from Marxism among arrested communists during the 1930s and active support of many converts for the war indicates the strength of the emperor-centred ideology and nationalism during the 1930s.

While communism and other radical leftist ideologies made little headway among mainstream Japanese, they were more influential among marginalized social groups such as Burakumin and Koreans. Despite being raised to equal legal status as commoners in 1871, the Burakumin descendants of Tokugawa outcasts continued to suffer discrimination in education, employment, marriage and other social matters. Most lived in segregated rural hamlets (*buraku*) while those in cities were forced into slum ghettos located near rubbish dumps, crematoriums, slaughterhouses or other undesirable places. As one man in Hiroshima prefecture described the prejudice against Burakumin,

> They called the bridge at the entrance to our section the 'Bridge of Hell.' Parents told their children, 'Don't go across the bridge or you'll get into terrible trouble. . . . The people who live there kill oxen and dogs and eat the meat. . . . Don't cross the bridge to the other side of the river. You can't tell what they'll do to you.'[5]

Stimulated by democratic rhetoric during the First World War and revolutionary ideas from Europe, Burakumin activists organized the Suiheisha (Levellers Society) to combat discrimination. Their main tactic, which has been employed up to the present, was denunciation of individual cases of overt prejudice. For example, in a case of school segregation, the association demanded a public apology from the principal or some other token of sincere repentance. Demands did not always remain verbal, however, and some violent incidents erupted. Communist and anarchist influence on the movement increased during the 1920s, and it became closely associated with the proletarian movement, but at the same time Buddhist influence was also important. Some of the movement's efforts to eliminate discrimination were effective, but it made little progress towards ending Burakumin poverty.

Communism and other radical ideologies also had some appeal among the Korean students and workers who made up the expanding immigrant population of the 1920s. Korean students turned to radical ideologies, especially after the Western powers failed to support the First of March Movement for Korean independence in 1919. Anarchists emphasized terrorist activities, while communists focused on organizing workers. Both sought the goal of Korean independence, though. The Korean labour movement emphasized elimination of discriminatory treatment and agitation for improved working conditions, but also included Korean national liberation among its primary goals. Many Korean labour activists played important roles in the JCP. They were even less successful than their Japanese counterparts in organizing Korean workers into unions, however. Besides facing harassment by governmental authorities, they faced difficulties in the very nature of Korean workers themselves. Korean immigrants were mostly unskilled peasants made landless by Japanese colonial policies and lured by promises of a better life by Japanese companies seeking cheap labour. Textile and mining companies were the most active recruiters of Korean workers, but firms in construction, glass manufacturing and machinery also sought workers from Korea.

However, upon arrival in Japan, Koreans landed at the bottom of a discriminatory labour market; they always received wages which were lower than those of their Japanese counterparts. Meagre wages and social discrimination led to extreme poverty among Koreans. Authors of a 1924 government report on Korean living conditions in Osaka were shocked at Koreans' poor diets: 'with their diet, it is impossible to ingest the nutrition necessary for survival.' Japanese landlords often refused to rent housing to Koreans, claiming that Koreans were often in arrears with the rent, did not maintain the conditions of the house, and shared the house with too many other Koreans. Korean tenants countered such complaints, pointing out that Japanese owners charged Koreans a higher rent than Japanese.

Prejudice against Koreans manifested itself violently in massacres of Koreans after the Kantō earthquake in 1923. The chaos in the earthquake's aftermath not only brought out the anti-leftist attitudes of government authorities, but allowed them to play on anti-Korean prejudices among the Japanese people. Police and other government authorities helped to spread rumours that Koreans were poisoning wells and attempting an armed insurrection, which led to ordinary Japanese forming vigilante groups who murdered hundreds, if not thousands, of innocent Koreans. Police and soldiers also joined the hunt for suspected Korean agitators. But despite such violent treatment and impoverished living conditions, the number of Korean immigrants to Japan continued to grow during the 1920s. In 1926 there were more that 148,000 Koreans in Japan.[6]

Urbanization and social diversification

A major weakness of the communist and other radical leftist movements was lack of mass support, particularly among heavy industrial workers whom the movements targeted to lead the socialist revolution. This group of workers remained small throughout the 1920s and early 1930s. Although this was the period when Japan was becoming an urban industrial society, it was also a period of economic stagnation and depression which contributed to social and political problems and conflict. The inability of party governments to solve these problems is another reason for their loss of power in the 1930s.

Both the industrial and agricultural sectors of the economy suffered during the 1920s, although the First World War had been good for Japan. With European countries preoccupied with supplying wartime needs, demand for Japanese manufactured goods had increased. Companies had also sought out more workers, especially skilled workers, as they introduced the latest advanced technology. These conditions stimulated revival of a labour movement, beginning with the establishment of a mutual aid society known as the Yūaikai. Strikes broke out when wages did not keep up with inflation. The end of the war brought more difficulties for workers when European industry returned to prewar markets and demand for Japanese goods collapsed.

Recession set in in 1920, and no real recovery occurred before the world depression at the end of the decade affected Japan as well. Unemployment became a problem for the first time, mainly for young males seeking either manufacturing jobs or white-collar work. A large proportion of the increasing urban population had to turn to employment in low productivity retail shops and services. These economic conditions aroused government officials'

concern about resources to supply Japan's ever-increasing population, especially after the possibility of emigration to the United States ended with the
passage of the Immigration Act of 1924. While Meiji governments had
encouraged a large population because it was equated with national strength,
Japanese governments of the 1920s, like others throughout the world, began
to worry about 'overpopulation' leading to war as well as poverty.

Financial difficulties for families also pushed more women into the paid
workforce. Poor women from both the countryside and cities continued to
enter the textile industry, which remained larger than heavy industry until the
1930s. The new phenomenon was middle-class women's entrance into the
workforce as new occupations, such as schoolteaching, nursing, journalism,
department store sales and clerical work, opened up for them. Higher levels
of education both stimulated and enabled workforce participation, but women
surveyed cited 'helping the family budget' as the main reason for working.
While work in teaching and journalism provided relatively high job satisfaction and social status as well as pay, it also produced much stress as women
tried to juggle home and work responsibilities. As is still true today, married
women shouldered primary responsibility for childcare and housework even
if they worked.

Despite these difficulties of managing dual responsibilities, the increasingly diverse opportunities for work attracted young women to the cities.
Similarly, younger sons who could not inherit the family farm were drawn
to urban areas where educational as well as employment opportunities were
greater. This accounts for the rapid urbanization which occurred during the
1920s despite the sluggish state of the economy as a whole. Tokyo in particular grew rapidly. Its population doubled between 1895 and 1923, when it
reached almost four million, and a drop after the 1923 earthquake proved
only temporary. Moreover, the urban populations of the country as a whole
also grew significantly, so that by the outbreak of war in the late 1930s, only
about half of the population lived in communities of less than 10,000.

As mentioned earlier, many of the migrants to urban areas ended up
in the tertiary sector, or in women's cases textiles, rather than better paid
manufacturing or white-collar jobs, but skilled and middle-school educated
young men were sought out by large industrial enterprises, the only ones
which did not go into a slump. Because such workers were in short supply,
large companies introduced Western labour-management methods and incentives to keep them. These included not only higher wages, but wages and
promotions based on seniority, quarterly bonuses, welfare facilities and lifetime employment. Here we can see the origins of the so-called Japanese employment system which many credit with Japan's postwar economic success,
but begun by employers more from pragmatic considerations than from
sentiments of benevolent paternalism.

The favourable treatment accorded to permanent full-time workers in
large enterprises contributed to increasing differentiation and stratification
of the industrial working class. Differentials between workers in large factories and workers in small factories increased, not only in incomes, working

conditions and security of employment, but also consumption patterns. Workers in large enterprises gradually spent more of their food expenses on milk, eggs and meat, though vegetables and fish continued to be their main non-staple food items. They also began to drink beer rather than sake. Shorter hours and more holidays gave them more time for leisure activities, such as reading newspapers and popular novels and going to the cinema, the theatre or dining halls with the family, whereas traditional artisan-type workers and others in medium and small factories spent their fewer leisure hours and income mainly on drinking sake and gambling.

Despite their relatively better treatment, it was heavy industry workers in large factories who participated most actively in the labour unions and strikes of the 1920s and 1930s. Although union membership never made up more than 8 per cent of the industrial workforce, industrial disputes numbered in the hundreds annually throughout the two decades (with a high of 940 in 1931) and involved tens of thousands of workers.[7] Historians differ somewhat over whether workers' demands derived from heightened class consciousness under the influence of Western ideas of workers' rights or from traditional expectations of employer's benevolence.[8] However, they agree that besides the usual demands for better wages, shorter hours and the right to organize, Japanese blue-collar workers also expressed a strong desire for

Plate 6.1 Ikeda Eiji, 'Same faces again for the year' in *Tokyo Puck*, 1930
Source: Courtesy of the Kawasaki City Museum

better 'treatment' as human beings and benefits similar to those of white-collar workers. They resented their lack of status manifested, for example, in having to enter the factory via separate doors and to eat in separate dining rooms from white-collar employees.

These white-collar workers in private business made up another new social group which emerged in the early decades of the twentieth century. Along with white-collar employees in government and the professions, they represented a new urban middle class distinguished from the old middle class of small businesspeople by their higher level of education and taste for a Western lifestyle. These were the precursors of the post-Second World War 'salaryman' of corporate Japan. But despite blue-collar workers' aspirations to achieve white-collar workers' status, in reality many members of the new middle class struggled financially during the 1920s when white-collar jobs did not increase. They were often no more than 'poor people dressed in Western clothes', the lifestyle portrayed for them by the mass media and advertisements remaining as elusive for them as for most Japanese.

Beginnings of a mass consumer society

However elusive, the affluent lifestyle associated with the new urban middle class nevertheless became the ideal for most Japanese during the 1920s. 'Culture' (*bunka*) replaced 'civilization' (*bunmei*) as the watchword of the early 1920s, spawning 'culture houses', 'culture pots', 'culture knives' and other 'culture' things to make up 'cultured living', and modern and modernism ('*modan*' and '*modanizumu*') took over in the later part of the decade as the leading trend in urban society and culture. While many people became active participants, or at least spectators, in the new 'modern life' of the cities, modernity was regarded ambivalently by social commentators as well as by conservative government officials.

The Kantō earthquake of 1923 proved to be a major stimulus to the new developments. It struck just before noon on 1 September, setting off fires which raged through Tokyo for two days. The disaster destroyed almost all of the 'Low City' which had been the centre of commercial activity and Edo culture, thus creating the conditions for a new phase in the history of Japanese modernity as well as the history of Tokyo. Martial law brought back order after days of violence and chaos, and the city's inhabitants turned their attention to reconstruction. Temporary barracks were thrown up to house people, and businesses quickly responded to supply their needs, not only for food and clothing but entertainment. Temporary cinemas, for example, appeared almost immediately. By 1930 the Tokyo city government declared reconstruction complete.

Reconstruction provided opportunities for new directions in all sorts of areas. The latest advanced technology was installed in rebuilt factories and film studios, for example. But perhaps even more significant for living and working patterns was the accelerated growth of suburbs west and south of the central business district. In the wake of the earthquake, business managers and entrepreneurs moved their offices westward from Nihonbashi to the less damaged Marunouchi district, and, along with their salaryman employees, moved their homes westward towards the suburbs. Private railway companies extended their lines, and built culture house developments and shopping centres to attract people to live in the new suburbs. Railway transfer points to city lines, such as Shinjuku, became surrounded by even larger shopping and entertainment areas for commuters, filled with department stores, theatres for films and live performances, dance halls, cafés, bars and restaurants.

Nihonbashi also began losing out to Ginza as a retail district, and in fact, the decade after the earthquake may be called the 'Ginza era'. Although associated with the modern from the 1870s when it was reconstructed in brick, it was not until after the earthquake that Ginza became a symbol of Tokyo and modernity for all Japanese. Modern department stores catering to ordinary Japanese drew in crowds during the day. Mitsukoshi and Shirokiya had pioneered new, Western methods of retailing during the last decade of the Meiji period, such as glass display cases which permitted customers to browse instead of having to ask a salesperson to bring out goods from a storage area. With the earthquake, department stores began offering goods for everyday living rather than only expensive specialty or imported items. They also introduced an innovation which brought in the masses – customers did not have to take off their shoes. Ginza department store dining rooms with Western tables and chairs also eliminated the necessity of sitting on tatami floors to eat and made it respectable to keep one's coat on. Women, notably the growing number of middle-class working women, for the first time felt comfortable eating out in public. Ginza continued to exude class and elegance, however, so many members of the crowds, who were mostly young, could only afford to 'window shop'. This became a typical way for 'modern boys' (*modan boi* or *mobo* for short) and 'modern girls' (*modan gâru* or *moga*) to 'pass the time in Ginza' during the day.

At night they passed the time in cafés and bars which sprouted up 'like bamboo shoots after rain' after the earthquake. Cafés offering Western cocktails, Western food and a Western ambience had existed since the late Meiji period, but they had been gathering places for intellectuals and artistic types. The patrons of the post-earthquake cafés came mainly from the new middle class and were attracted to the increasingly American style of modern entertainment that they offered, characterized by bright neon lights and jazz music. They also went for the romantic atmosphere or 'love feeling' provided by the café waitresses. Representative of the modern girl, her potential for financial independence and sexual liberation appeared threatening to the 'good wife, wise mother' ideal which had come to dominate official ideology since the 1890s. The Tokyo Puck drawing of a modern girl contrasts with the image of a Yumeji girl that symbolized the pre-earthquake Taishō look. Takehisa Yumeji's women, while appearing more Western than Meiji images of women, are wan and weary-looking. Late 1920s *moga*, however, appear more comfortable, confident and energetic in their Western dress and permed hair, striding briskly along the streets of Ginza.

This liberated woman was one aspect of modernity which social commentators as well as government officials regarded with anxiety if not hostility. For all the glamour associated with the café waitress, however, in reality most came from the lower classes and took such jobs to add to the family income. Many became involved with prostitution after hours because their income from tips was low. This brought them to the attention of social welfare and police authorities, and led to restrictions on cafés and dance halls, bans on students in such places, and arrests of students and café waitresses beginning in the late 1920s.

The extent to which modern girls actually existed is debatable. It seems that the modern girl was largely a construct of the media, which points to another important aspect in the development of a mass consumer society. Newspapers and magazines, which during the Meiji period had generally been outlets for the political and social views of their editors, became mass circulation publications. In the 1920s three daily newspapers had national circulations, winning thousands of readers by introducing new features such as advice columns, sports coverage and cartoon strips. Popular magazines with commercial objectives also proliferated, notably women's magazines such as *Shufu no tomo* (*The Housewife's Companion*) which carried articles on practical matters like household management and on social topics like birth control and working outside the home as well as on food and fashion. In 1925 radio began broadcasting, and by 1941 more than 45 per cent of households throughout the country owned a radio set. Unlike other forms of media, radio did not become commercialized until the 1950s, but remained under the monopoly of the state-owned NHK (Nihon Hōsō Kyōkai).

The cinema stood out as the most popular media and entertainment form, although Western-style musical revues and other live performances, including Western opera, also thrived during the interwar period. A Japanese film industry grew up, especially when new studios were built after the earthquake, but many American movies were imported and influenced Japanese film-makers. Charlie Chaplin amused Japanese filmgoers, while Rudolph Valentino, Clara Bow and Greta Garbo became models for *mobo* and *moga*. And it was not only young people of the middle class who flocked to the cinemas, for these were located in entertainment districts throughout the city. The Asakusa Sixth District had fourteen cinemas in 1930 and drew crowds of all classes and ages from all over the city. Even people in the countryside had access to this modern form of entertainment, since films were screened regularly in villages.

Culture without politics

The attraction of millions of Japanese to such mass entertainment during the 1920s was paralleled at the elite level by the replacement of 'civilization' (*bunmei*) by the concept of 'culture' (*bunka*), as was mentioned at the beginning of the previous section. '*Bunmei*' reflected the Meiji faith in progress and the universalism of an advanced civilization, and was associated with self-sacrifice and nationalism. '*Bunka*', in contrast, evoked individualism, consumerism and cosmopolitanism. Instead of public service and national goals, it stressed personal self-cultivation and subordination of public considerations to private choice. As H.D. Harootunian pointed out, the identification between individualism and culture led to apoliticality, which became the distinguishing characteristic of intellectuals and writers of the Taishō era. Substituting culture for politics also raised the status of culture and aesthetics, and thereby created a distance between middle-class intellectuals and the rest of society who engaged in the consumption of 'mass culture'. Exceptions were the proletarian writers, but they formed a small minority who enjoyed only a few years of prominence at the end of the 1920s.

In Chapter 5 we saw the beginnings of these changes in the discussion of late Meiji youth who either avidly pursued wealth for themselves personally or displayed no ambition whatsoever and sought an end in suicide or dissipation. The Boshin Rescript of 1908 had the objective of reinstilling values of frugality and loyalty and service to the state. Nevertheless, in 1916 Tokutomi Sohō, a former advocate of Westernization and reform, lamented that 'the greatest single illness of our times is the loss of state ideals and national purpose'.[9]

The same lack of interest in national issues is evident in the literature of the 1910s and 1920s. This was the period when the 'I-novel' (*watakushi shōsetsu*) became the dominant genre. These were inward-looking novels concerned almost exclusively with the author's personal psychological state. They included the writings of some of the greatest writers of the twentieth century even beyond the Taishō period, such as Shiga Naoya, Akutagawa Ryūnosuke, Tanizaki Jun'ichirō and Kawabata Yasunari. While these major writers did not always write in a strictly autobiographical manner, they clearly did not write anything that might be related to public issues. Akutagawa wrote some satirical works, such as *Kappa* (1927), but these focused more on the human condition in general rather than a critique of contemporary Japanese society. The same may be said of the Shirakaba (White Birch) writers, led by Shiga Naoya, who are regarded as 'quintessential Taishō writers'. Consequently, in the aftermath of the Second World War, Taishō writers, like Taishō democrats, were often severely censured for their 'narcissistic' retreat into aestheticism.[10]

Roy Starrs suggests that Taishō writers' 'navel-gazing and insouciance toward public issues' should not seem so surprising in light of the enormous changes that had taken place in Japan since the beginning of the Meiji period. By the early Taishō period nation-building goals had been achieved, and while further importations of Western culture still had some faddish aspects, Japanese writers of this generation had more of an education in Western literatures than in the traditional Sino-Japanese classics. Although some of these writers turned away from Western styles of writing in the 1930s, they did not necessarily abandon what they had learned from Western modernism. Kawabata, for example, 'never lost his taste for surrealistic imagery and stream-of-consciousness narrative'.[11]

Starrs also points out the deep impact on the literary world made by the Great Treason Incident at the end of the Meiji period, when Kōtoku Shūsui and other anarchists were executed. Nagai Kafū, a leading writer who is noted for his elegaic works on fading Edo culture, expressed his shame at the lack of opposition from Japanese writers, including himself, to the incident.

> Of all the public incidents I had witnessed or heard of, none had filled me with such loathing. I could not, as a man of letters, remain silent in this matter of principle. Had not the novelist Zola, pleading the truth in the Dreyfus Case, had to flee his country? But I, along with the other writers of my land, said nothing. The pangs of conscience that resulted were scarcely endurable. I felt intensely ashamed of myself as a writer.[12]

Passage of the Peace Preservation Law in 1925 and the persistent suppression of left-wing sympathizers and liberal critics of government policies during the 1930s no doubt later deterred many writers from speaking out. This is assuming, however, that they themselves did not share the state's plans for expanding the empire.

The one group of writers who did dare to speak out through their writings were the proletarian writers. In fact they attacked 'establishment literature' for its lack of a political or social conscience and conceived of their writings as a vehicle for advancing their socialist cause. Kobayashi Takiji stood out as the best writer in the proletarian literary movement and as someone who constantly strove to explore new themes and methods to promote the socialist revolution. His best-known work, the novella entitled *Kani kōsen* (*The Crab Cannery Boat*) (1929), powerfully depicts the exploitation and brutal treatment of workers on the ship. Living below decks in 'a shit pot', they are eaten alive by fleas, lice and bedbugs, while the supervisor and other representatives of the capitalist management feast above them in the ship's saloon. As the novel progresses, the workers unite, become aware that the capitalists are their enemy, and finally rise up in a strike. However, the supervisor calls in the navy to suppress the strike, thus revealing that the military is a tool of capitalism.

Kobayashi's obsequious acceptance of criticisms from Soviet-dominated leaders of the Japan Proletarian Writers' League and the manner of his death mirror the history of the communist movement as a whole. Like the JCP, the proletarian literary movement was strongly influenced by pronouncements from the Soviet Union, and, like the party, was weakened by organizational splits and realignments stimulated by outside events, often over political rather than artistic differences. Heightened police suppression during the early 1930s resulted in a drift, then a flood of numbers away from the movement. Internal dissension also grew as certain members objected to the extreme politicization of the literary movement. Kobayashi's death as a result of police torture in February 1933 presaged the collapse of the movement. Having lost most of its leading figures, the Writers' League decided to dissolve itself a year later.

Looking at the social and cultural as well as political history of the 1920s does therefore present a 'complex, contradictory and multivalent' picture of Japan. Meiji social and political leaders and intellectuals certainly had many disagreements, but shared a concern for national or public issues. By the beginning of the Taishō era this consensus had disappeared as new social groups emerged to challenge the domination of politics and the economy by the former samurai, wealthy landlords and businessmen. Ordinary Japanese of all classes increasingly pursued their individualist goals as the range of choices expanded not only for their working lives, but also for their leisure time. Industrialization and urbanization were responsible for this expansion of choice, but so also were new ideas and social practices from the West disseminated widely by new mass media. National political issues consequently did not dominate everyday life or individual aspirations. However, during the following decade of the 1930s, national political issues came to the foreground again as crises in foreign affairs led Japan to set itself against the Western powers. These developments will be the subject of the next chapter.

7　Contesting the modern in the 1930s

As we examine more closely the developments of the 1930s in this chapter, we will gradually enter that 'dark valley' by which Japanese designate the period of domestic repression and foreign expansion preceding and encompassing the Second World War. Indeed, the decade began in the depths of economic depression and a constitutional crisis which foreshadowed the precipitous independent actions taken by the field army in Manchuria in 1931. The expanding political role of the military and increasing prominence of foreign affairs will receive a great deal of attention in this chapter, but it is important to understand that these developments were linked to a sense of domestic crisis on the part of social reformers and commentators as well as civil and military leaders. At the same time, although Japanese historians refer to the 1930 to 1945 years as 'The Fifteen Year War', attention to cultural and social developments suggests that the everyday lives of Japanese people did not change immediately or dramatically after the Manchurian Incident, nor did Japanese quickly abandon their leisure pursuits or other, more individualistic concerns to direct their energies towards the national goals of the state.

The chapter will begin with an examination of these social developments in urban areas, looking particularly at how leisure and entertainment changed from the 1920s. The emergence of '*ero-guro nansensu*' (erotic, grotesque nonsense) indicates a turn to frivolous, glitzy and perhaps sordid escapism against a background of economic depression. If this was modernity, many Japanese commentators rejected it. Associating it with the decadent West and the city, many turned to the Japanese past and the rural countryside to redefine a more acceptable Japanese modernity. But the Japanese countryside was itself experiencing social strife as well as severe economic decline by the early 1930s. In the second and third sections we will examine the efforts of villagers to solve these problems as well as the solutions offered by theorists of the right and the left, by military leaders and government officials.

The debates over domestic problems no longer took place in a context of international peace, however. Consequently, in the fourth section we will see that the domestic crisis became linked to an international crisis created by the field army in Manchuria in 1931, but erupted soon after in violent incidents at home in Japan as well. The rise of the military in politics, paralleled by the decline of the parties, will be traced as foreign matters gradually assumed more importance in national politics. The intertwining of domestic and foreign problems may be seen in the debates over modernity that became widespread among intellectuals during the 1930s. These are introduced in the final section of the chapter to give a sense of the diverse ways in which Japanese tried to find a Japanese form of modernity which would prevent Japan from becoming a mere carbon copy of Western societies.

'*Ero-guro nansensu*'

In histories of the 1930s and 1940s the dark shadows and bitter memories of the Second World War colour the images of the social and cultural as well as political developments of the period. In particular, the 'erotic, grotesque nonsense' fad of the early 1930s seems to represent the 'dark valley' into which Japan was descending. On the one hand, the flashy, sexy, garish stage shows and neon-lit cafés epitomizing '*ero-guro nansensu*' indicate a crass materialism and the commodification of eroticism which many contemporary as well as later commentators deplored. On the other hand, they offered an outlet from dreary, depression-era lives and, however hedonistic, suggest the attraction of 'modern' entertainments and the new desire among urban Japanese for social and cultural commodities to enhance their lifestyles. The depression at the end of the 1920s severely hurt urban dwellers, both white-collar and blue-collar workers, yet crowds continued to flock in their tens of thousands to the entertainment districts of the cities.

Changes in cafés during the late 1920s and early 1930s exemplify the emergence of a mass consumer society and reveal Japanese conceptions of a 'modern lifestyle'. Cafés represented 'mass' culture in two senses: first, as products of advanced technology and beneficiaries of mass media and advertising; second, as producing and responding to desires and tastes of the masses, i.e. large numbers, of ordinary Japanese. In contrast to earlier cafés, the cafés of the late 1920s and early 1930s attracted new middle-class salaried workers rather than mainly intellectuals, artists and writers. In sheer numbers they expanded to mass levels – 37,065 cafés and bars throughout the country in 1934.[1] In addition, many large-scale cafés appeared on the main street of Ginza in Tokyo and in the Dōtonbori district of Osaka, employing over a hundred waitresses each. These competed fiercely with each other, trying to outdo others with lavishly decorated interiors sparkling with light-reflective materials and exteriors emblazoned with red and blue neon lights. They devised new advertising gimmicks to attract publicity, such as the Bijinza Café's flying in thirty waitresses from Osaka by plane, a rarity in 1930. Owners also encouraged or pressured their waitresses to treat patrons in a more friendly and seductive manner, and when the depression reduced patronage, they tried to attract more customers by hiring more waitresses. Smaller cafés relied more and more on selling erotic services, such as the

Plate 7.1 Ginza Palace, 1933
Source: Hatsuda Tohru, *Kafē to kissaten*, INAX Album 18, Tokyo: INAX
          Shuppan, 1993, p. 35

'organ service' where a waitress lay across the laps of her male customers
and sang different notes depending on which part of her body they touched.

Many social commentators as well as middle-class Christian moral
reformers and government officials criticized these 'perverse tastes' and eroti-
cization of café waitresses as indicative of the emptiness of 'modern life',
which was preoccupied with nothing other than consumption and the pursuit of pleasure. Marxist critics saw cafés' and café waitresses' association
with erotic, grotesque nonsense as symptomatic of the final stage of capitalism, although at the opposite end of the ideological spectrum, government
authorities tried to halt the moral rot by imposing restrictions on cafés, and
banning students from cafés and dance halls. Arrests of café waitresses and
students mentioned in Chapter 6 continued into the 1930s.

The café therefore symbolized a modernity which was urban, industrialized
and affluent. To some observers this was liberating and egalitarian, allowing
women as well as men to express their sexuality and to pursue pleasure. To
others, however, modernity meant a selfish preoccupation with individual
materialistic goals. In a word, decadence.

The plight of the countryside

While all these changes were taking place in the cities and formed the beginnings of postwar Japanese society, it is important to remember that until about 1930, the majority of the labour force still worked in agriculture and fisheries. It was not only urban intellectuals, social reformers and conservative government officials who looked at 'modern life' with disfavour. Most Japanese in rural areas also rejected the modernity represented by the city and resented the affluence upon which it was based. As the Agriculturalists' Self-Rule Society proclaimed in 1928, 'The cities grow more luxurious day by day . . . while the villagers have to live on moldy salted fish and wear shopworn clothes . . . the cities are living off the sweat of the farmers'.[2] Most tenant farmers never ate the white rice they produced except perhaps on New Year's Day. Nevertheless, traditional portrayals of Japanese farmers passively if not enthusiastically supporting government policies of imperialist expansion prove to be simplistic. Rural as well as urban society became more diversified during the early decades of the twentieth century, as reflected in the tenant farmer disputes of the 1920s and 1930s, and rural support for war did not emerge automatically.

Although farming methods did not change significantly until after the Second World War, this does not mean that Japanese villagers were isolated or ignorant of changes in the wider world. Universal primary education provided basic literacy for both girls and boys. Conscription took young men away from their villages, gave them new experiences and exposed them to new ideas. As indicated in Chapter 6, so did expanding opportunities for work in towns and cities for both young women and men. Leaving the village for the army or work did not involve cutting all ties. Besides continuing links with family and friends through letter-writing and holiday visiting, people often returned home when employment in urban areas became difficult. Returnees and relatives in the city made those in the countryside aware of new developments, and in some cases prodded them to become more up-to-date – like the daughter who sent her parents condoms, telling them to use them because they had too many children. Urban experiences and media images raised lifestyle expectations and made young people dissatisfied with the harder work and longer hours of farming.

The development of mass media in the late 1910s and 1920s meant increased opportunities for exposure to new ideas and knowledge about what was going on beyond local areas. National daily newspapers and popular commercial magazines, such as the women's magazine *Shufu no tomo* (*The Housewife's Companion*), as well as the government-sponsored monthly magazine *Ie no hikari* (*Light of the Home*) reached the countryside. Both imported and Japanese-made films were screened regularly in rural areas, and radio, though government controlled, provided a means of nationwide communication.

The images of the 'modern life' of the cities coming from these varied sources remained unattainable in reality to most farmers, however, for the

1920s and early 1930s were difficult economic years. Rice prices declined, especially with bumper crops during the late 1920s. Exacerbating the situation was the collapse of American demand for silk when synthetics such as rayon were invented. By this time the majority of Japanese farm households depended on sericulture to supplement their income. The collapse of the international economy in 1929 further worsened conditions in the Japanese countryside, but the government's decision to remain on the gold standard, while other countries were devaluing their currencies, made Japanese yen relatively more expensive, which created even more difficulties for farmers to export their silk.

Poor rural families continued the late Meiji pattern of supplying girls for the urban brothels and textile factories, a practice they resorted to more frequently after a famine devastated six prefectures in northern Honshu in 1934. Reports showed that more than 6500 girls were sent to brothels and geisha houses from the six prefectures in 1934, and over 17,000 went to urban mills and factories.[3] But fewer of the girls now returned to the countryside when their contracts ended. More stayed on in the city, moving to other textile factories or increasingly into heavy industry as jobs for women expanded there. Or, as suggested earlier, the pretty ones might become café waitresses, which did not require years of training as did becoming a geisha.

Farmers did not accept their situation without complaint. Taking labour union activities during the First World War as a model, tenant farmers organized themselves into unions to bargain collectively against landlords. In contrast to most earlier peasant protest movements, tenant unions of the 1920s were formal organizations, presenting a united front conceived of as an effective instrument of power. When they pressured landlords or the government for improvements to their members' economic and social status, they based their demands on an assumption of their entitlement to equity, not paternalistic benevolence. As one tenant union leader passionately wrote,

> 'Beg for three days and the taste will last three years'. By relying on the benevolence of their landlords as if they were dogs or cats, tenant farmers have led a beggar's existence for a long time. . . . The only way to change this – to free tenants from the opiate of benevolence and paternalism that oppresses them in everything they do and reduces them to groveling for favours like dogs and cats, the only way to elevate them from the demeaning status of beggars to the dignity of human beings – is by means of tenant farmer unions.[4]

Between 1917 and 1931 there were nearly 25,000 tenancy disputes in the country, and from 1932 to 1941 the number increased to 47,695.[5] Contrary to early postwar studies of tenant farmer disputes, recent studies have found that disputes during the first period were more numerous in commercially advanced areas in central and southwestern Japan rather than the poor regions of northern Japan, such as the Tōhoku. Moreover, during the 1920s the most common immediate cause for disputes was crop failure or a poor harvest rather than high rents. Several prefectures with the lowest number of disputes had rents exceeding the national average of 50.9 per cent of the crop. In fact, according to Ann Waswo, disputes were generally more numerous where tenants were best nourished, most adequately housed and most prosperous. How can we explain this?

One reason was the increased urban job opportunities in these areas which had been stimulated by industrial expansion during the First World War. This led to less competition for land among tenants who became less interested or dependant on farming. Unable to replace dissatisfied tenants easily, landlords were more likely to give in to demands for rent reductions. The recession of the early 1920s resulting in lay-offs and declining wages forced some people back to the farms. Even if not generally worse off than before the war, their expectations had risen and their experience as urban workers with lighter work and shorter hours made them less willing to tolerate the hard physical labour and less profitable rewards of tenant farming.

Another reason for the high incidence of disputes in central and south-western Japan was the type of landlord in those areas. A higher proportion were absentee landlords than in northern Japan. Although common depictions of absentee landlords as villains charging exhorbitant rents might explain the high frequency of disputes, in fact the opposite was the case. Because they usually had other sources of income, absentee landlords were less dependent on tenant rents, and, lacking intimate knowledge of local conditions, often charged lower rents than resident landlords. But while tenancy conditions were not worse under absentee landlords, absentee landlords performed fewer traditional social functions than resident landlords. Tenants complained of absentee landlords' lack of interest in local affairs and the lack of traditional personal, semi-familial relations with their landlord. Consequently, economic growth and the disruption of traditional social relations lay behind the tenant unrest of the 1920s.

Besides organizing unions and conducting disputes collectively, villagers used local newspapers to discuss local problems and air opinions on ways to solve them. The government paper *Ie no hikari* promoted state solutions, but as Sandra Wilson has shown, the newspapers of young men's associations in the rural heartland of Nagano prefecture reveal ideologies of both the left and the right competing for favour as the best solution to rural problems. These newspapers paint a picture of villagers preoccupied with effects of the depression in their local area, but far from indifferent to political and social issues, and sometimes harshly critical of existing capitalist structures and political processes. Criticism was applied not only to government handling of rural economic problems, but also to foreign policy matters.

Contrary to most descriptions of strong public support and enthusiasm for the army's actions in Manchuria in 1931, the young men's association newspapers made comparatively little comment about Manchuria, and those that did expressed a wide variety of views: some lukewarm or ambivalent, some openly critical and others supportive. So while one contributor argued that Manchuria and Mongolia would become Japan's 'new paradise', another declared that 'the only role allotted to us over there [Manchuria] is to spend our blood and sweat in toil. Dreams of success without that hardship should be left to people like party politicians and the zaibatsu.'[6] The diversity of responses reflects the strains and tensions in rural areas that had developed along with increasing social stratification, generational differences and the influence of Western ideas.

Villagers therefore did not all obediently or automatically fall in behind government and army policies, but during the early 1930s voices of support won out over voices of dissent. Government repression through heightened censorship and arrests of left-wing radicals and tenant farmer union leaders weakened opposition movements and discouraged dissent in general. This paralleled the nationwide destruction of the radical left, centred on the Communist Party, during the early 1930s. However, repression was not the only means employed by the government to quell dissent. At the same time it initiated the rural rehabilitation movement to counter the depression, promoting agricultural cooperatives with youth leagues to rival the young men's associations. Besides offering practical solutions to rural economic problems and expanding structures to encourage identification with the state, the movement drew upon and fostered long-held notions of community solidarity, harmony and cooperation to defuse class conflict and overcome generational differences.

During the 1930s the government also turned to mass emigration as a solution to the rural crisis. Starting in 1932 with experimental settlements in Manchuria, the policy expanded in 1936 into the 'Millions to Manchuria' programme. Farmers had not responded in large numbers to the early attempts to recruit colonists, especially on hearing reports about Chinese 'bandit attacks' and other hardships. But the government put substantial funds into the campaign and turned the dangers and privations faced by colonists into the elements of a story of Japanese empire-building with Japanese settlers as the heroes. The Ministry of Agriculture and Forestry even encouraged film companies, playhouses, record companies and publishers to visit the model village of Ōhinata to dramatize and popularize the Village Colonization Movement. Wada Tsutō's classic novel, *Ōhinata mura*, resulted from one of these ministry-subsidized tours.

The programme was so successful that by the early 1940s it had mobilized over 320,000 emigrants to Manchuria. A disproportionate number came from Nagano, Yamagata and nearby prefectures, all in east central and northeast Japan. These had been hardest hit by the agricultural crisis and where tenancy disputes (many concerning eviction) were most prevalent in the 1930s. In contrast to the Japanese community in Shanghai which remained a separate foreign enclave, Japanese in Manchuria were real settlers who adapted to what they regarded as their new permanent home. Japanese in Harbin integrated into the community, mingling with Chinese and White Russians, so that the end of the war brought psychological traumas of reintegration into Japanese society in addition to the physical hardships and dangers of evacuation from the lost colony.

Rise of the right wing, the military and 'ultranationalism'

The government felt pressure from many groups to solve the problems of the countryside. Criticism from what is usually referred to as the right wing intensified during the 1930s, and in some cases linked with violent terrorism. The right wing represented very disparate ideas and social groups with different, in some cases contradictory objectives, but were similarly inspired by the plight of the countryside. Many right-wing reformers and revolutionaries extolled agrarianism, and military leaders used the plight of the countryside to support their self-projection as saviours of the nation. Moreover, like most rural inhabitants, these groups were alarmed by the spread of 'degenerative habits' and 'dangerous ideas' in the cities, especially the hedonistic doctrine of individualism and divisive ideas of class struggle.

In this respect, both left- and right-wing movements of the 1920s and 1930s can be seen as the result of dissatisfaction with industrialization and its sociopolitical consequences. Both represented attempts to solve social and economic problems arising at the end of the First World War which were seen to be the consequence of modernization and the development of capitalism. Both viewed the Meiji Restoration as incomplete; for Marxists, in the creation of a bourgeois democratic revolution; for rightists, in the realization of a popular nationalism based on a distinctive Japanese spiritual legacy. Both remained movements of elites despite claims to represent interests of ordinary Japanese, employing methods and pursuing objectives considered radical and extreme by the majority of Japanese both in and out of government.

Despite these similarities, there were at the same time significant differences. Leftists held a universalistic view of history in contrast with the rightists' particularistic view of history. Marxists criticized the Meiji Restoration for not advancing Japan completely into the stage of bourgeois democracy, which they considered a necessary stage of historical development on the way to achieving the ideal communist society. Implicit in this analysis of the Meiji Restoration in terms of universal world development lay a desire for Japan to follow the course of Western development. Rightists, in contrast, viewed Japan's current conditions and problems in terms of Japan's peculiar historical traditions, and consequently were critical of bureaucrats and other political leaders since the mid-Meiji period for abandoning or obstructing the spirit of the Meiji Restoration. They opposed the 'Europocentric' view of the modern world and the 'excessive' influx of Western ideas and practices during the 1920s. Instead they defended Japan's unique historical development and advocated revival and retention of Japan's distinctive spiritual and cultural legacy.

Leftists' and rightists' views of the nature of the Meiji Restoration and the causes of historical development therefore differed greatly. To Marxists, the Restoration represented the forging of an alliance of the remnants of feudalism (samurai and landlords) with a weak bourgeoisie for the creation of an absolutist emperor system (*tennōsei*). Historical change was thus seen as the result of the working out of socioeconomic forces – i.e., class conflict. Rightists, however, possessed a romanticized view of the Restoration, so when they called for a 'Shōwa Restoration', they meant that Japanese should find spiritual inspiration in the Meiji Restoration. Although historically inaccurate, they generally saw the Meiji Restoration as a popular upheaval embodying anti-feudal ideals of legal equality, mobility and political justice for all. In their view, the Restoration had been carried out by decisive acts of extraordinary individuals, epitomized by Saigō Takamori. Saigō alone remained true to the spirit of the Meiji Restoration, while other leaders like Iwakura Tomomi and Ōkubo Toshimichi used bureaucratic techniques to check rapid change and failed to understand the popular ideal for which the imperial institution stood. While it is again historically inaccurate to attribute democratic beliefs to Saigō, interwar rightists were attracted by his absolute opposition to conservative bureaucratism. To them, he symbolized the extraordinary individual who could make history, in the tradition of the '*sonnō jōi*'extremists of the Bakumatsu period who remained committed to selfless acts of loyalty.

In the first half of the 1930s this type of individualism became evident in terrorism and attempted *coups d'état* by young military officers which culminated in a nearly successful rebellion in 1936 known as the February 26th Incident. Political violence became so constant that one foreign journalist referred to Japanese politics as 'government by assassination'. Young Officer groups succeeded in assassinating two prime ministers, several cabinet ministers and business leaders too. The murder of Prime Minister Inukai Tsuyoshi in 1932 proved to be the end of party rule. After that, Japan was governed by cabinets made up of bureaucrats and military leaders, although the military never took power outright and the Meiji constitutional order remained intact.

The Young Officers were inspired by, though not always directly connected with, the ideas of civilians with varied reform programmes. Inukai's assassins, for example, were linked with Tachibana Kosaburō, an advocate of agrarianism who blamed big government, big business and imitation of Western societies for villagers' poverty and the loss of communal values. As Tachibana cynically observed, 'According to a common expression, Tokyo is the hub of the world. But I regret to say that Tokyo appears to me nothing but a branch shop of London.'[7] And echoing Tachibana's concern for rural poverty, one officer on trial declared, 'In utter disregard of poverty-stricken farmers the enormously rich zaibatsu pursue their private profit.'[8] Another reformer, Gondō Seikyō, also blamed the expansion of cities at the expense of villages for rural economic distress and the decline of agrarian life, which he regarded as 'the foundation of the country and the source of habits and customs'.[9]

But other right-wing theorists, notably Kita Ikki, advocated a radical restructuring of Japanese society and politics far different from the primitive agrarian utopias of Gondō or Tachibana. Criticizing the selfishness of the zaibatsu and the corruptness of politicians, Kita advocated nationalization of major industries and assets, an eight-hour day for workers, and land reform. While paying homage to the emperor as 'representative of the people and as pillar of the nation', he argued for a sweeping reform of the imperial court, abolition of the peerage system and House of Peers, dismissal of existing members of the Privy Council and establishment of a new Consultative Council to assist the emperor. The Diet would be maintained and all men over the age of 25 would have the right to vote, but women would still be excluded from participation in politics. According to Kita's plan, the new government instead would institutionalize protection of women's right to be 'mother of the nation and wife of the nation', echoing the existing state's ideal of 'good wife, wise mother'. Making references to 'the stupid talkativeness of Western women or the piercing quarrels among Chinese women', Kita used advocacy of women's suffrage as an example of the 'ugliness of direct and uncritical borrowing' from the West.[10]

Kita's book outlining his plan for the reorganization of Japan called for a *coup d'état* to create the conditions of martial law required for implementation of the radical changes that he proposed. This provided ideological support for the Young Officers responsible for the wave of coup attempts during the 1930s. Nevertheless, the Young Officers did not generally have any concrete plans for the society once they had destroyed the existing one. *Coup* participants usually expected that their violent actions would bring about a martial law situation in which higher military leaders would emerge to take charge of constructing a new society. Since they saw the established political parties and bureaucrats as corrupt, supported by the zaibatsu, incompetent and unsympathetic to the people, they gave the military the leading role in reform.

Historians have often blamed the insubordination and violence of the Young Officers for pushing weak superiors and cabinet officials towards the increasingly nationalist and expansionary foreign policies of the 1930s, but the Young Officers were not a completely isolated strata, and their rebellion in 1936 nearly succeeded because they had support among high army officers. In fact, they represented one contender among several army factions which competed for domination of army leadership and policy during the first half of the 1930s. While rivalries were complex, two major factions emerged: the Imperial Way Faction (Kōdōha) and Control Faction (Tōseiha). War Minister Araki Sadao led the Imperial Way Faction, appealing to the radical Young Officers with his emphasis on the efficacy of Japanese spirit in solving the country's ills. Araki favoured 'spiritual mobilization' as preparation for war that was sure to come. The Control Faction, led by a coalition of elements in the General Staff, opposed Araki's lenient attitude towards the young radicals, disliked his right-wing rhetoric, and felt that he was a weak advocate of army, as opposed to navy, interests in the cabinet. This group disliked Araki's belligerent anti-Soviet attitudes and feared that he and other Imperial Way generals lacked a sufficient understanding of modern military theory. Consequently, they favoured long-term economic planning and national mobilization rather than simply 'spiritual mobilization'.

These factional rivalries and the Young Officers movement reached a peak with the February 1936 mutiny. First Division elements led by Young Officers took over key government offices in Tokyo and attempted to assassinate top officials, including Prime Minister Okada, key cabinet ministers, important court bureaucrats and army leaders, and even the *genrō* Saionji Kinmochi. The rebels held Tokyo for three days, waiting for Kōdōha generals to come forward to take command. The insurrection finally collapsed when the emperor expressed his personal dismay at this breach in army discipline, whereupon the navy moved warships into Tokyo Bay and the army high command ordered the rebels to surrender. Thirteen of the rebels were subsequently tried and executed, along with Kita Ikki and three other civilians. Araki was placed on reserve, which blocked his further participation in politics when a rule requiring the War Minister to be an officer on the active list was revived. Other Young Officers not directly involved in the mutiny were posted to the provinces or overseas.

Suppression of the 1936 rebellion thus resulted in victory for the Control Faction. This meant the end of terrorism by military officers, but not the end of preparations for war, since the Control Faction was no less concerned with 'national defence' than the Imperial Way Faction. What the group objected to was the Young Officers' violent, extremist methods and the Imperial Way Faction's prioritization of spiritual mobilization over modernization of military structures and equipment. The end of factional rivalries and restoration of army discipline now cleared the way for a more concerted effort led by military leaders to mobilize national economic and social resources for war, although the advocacy of spiritual mobilization by no means disappeared. Some years later the chief opponents of Tōjō Hideki's rise to power were right-wing nationalists whose devotion to a spirit of uncompromising individualism pitted them against Tōjō as a representative of rational, bureaucratic authority. The Young Officers therefore may be seen as indicative of the contradiction between an indigenous Japanese tradition of individualism and modern bureaucratic organization. However, it was due to this belief in individual resistance to authority that they were unable to develop a popular movement.

International crisis and the road to war

The near-success of the 1936 rebellion shows how prominent the military and military leaders had become in Japanese politics by the mid-1930s. If we now look at foreign developments, we can see how they contributed to this shift in the balance of power among governing elites away from the parties and in favour of the military, for although the military came to prominence partly because of the ineptitude of civilian party governments in solving domestic socioeconomic problems, the military also became more important politically because the international situation changed from the early 1920s and became a crisis from 1931. War came to be seen as a necessary resort for Japan's national security and autonomy.

From the Second World War viewpoint of Americans, the attack on Pearl Harbor on 7 December 1941 was a symbol of the 'duplicity' of the Japanese, 'the end of isolation' and 'the folly of unpreparedness'. It justified the mission to 'destroy' Japanese militarism once and for all. But from the Japanese standpoint, the attack was not an infamous deed, but a blow against the efforts of the Western powers to strangle Japan and to perpetuate their colonial and semicolonial rule in Asia. This viewpoint and the ultimate decision to go to war against the United States was based on the following:

- a belief that resort to force was part of a rational strategy;
- a definition of national security and autonomy requiring a paramount position in Northeast Asia;
- discontent aroused by specific events of the 1920s and 1930s, beginning with the Versailles Conference.

Pearl Harbor (that is, war with the United States) was not 'inevitable' from the beginning of the twentieth century, much less the result of a ruthless, systematic and calculated plot begun by the Japanese from the Sino-Japanese War of 1894 to 1895, but it *was* a by-product of Asian nationalism, which in turn was stimulated by nineteenth-century Western imperialism. In this way the Second World War may be seen as a conflict between Asian nationalism and Western nationalism.

Until the 1930s Japan had adjusted its diplomacy according to the dictates of the Western powers when they united against its continental policy, for example, acquiescing to the Triple Intervention after the Sino-Japanese War, giving up an indemnity after the Russo-Japanese War, and modifying its Twenty-one Demands on China during the First World War. During the 1920s party governments had also gone along with the major Western powers in the climate of anti-militarism accompanying disillusionment with war which the horrors of the First World War had created. This climate of opinion was the context for Japan's joining the League of Nations and participating in the international arms limitation conferences held during the 1920s. Led by Foreign Minister Shidehara Kijūrō, Japan also refrained from overt aggression and militaristic expansion in China.

However, discontent from the Versailles Conference and the Washington and London naval treaties, in conjunction with domestic economic and social problems and the belief that hegemony in East Asia was necessary for national security and autonomy, formed the background for the decision to go it alone against the wishes of the Western powers after the Manchurian Incident of 1931. At the Versailles Peace Conference, the Western powers projected a new international norm based on American President Woodrow Wilson's Fourteen Points, which touted democracy, tenets of arms control, a League of Nations for collective security, peaceful solution of disputes and the principle of national self-determination. However, the principles were neither applied throughout Asia nor to all countries. In China the principle of national self-determination was applied only to Japan's wartime acquisition of Shandong. When Wilson opposed Japanese territorial claims, Japan saw the American stance as hypocritical and discriminatory since the USA did not give up its colonies or Chinese concessions, and European countries were acquiring ex-German colonies elsewhere. As mentioned in Chapter 6, the Western powers also opposed recognition of the principle of racial equality in the League of Nations covenant. Wilsonianism was therefore seen as a means of checking the growth of imperial Japan and protecting the semi-colonial rights of the Western powers in China. This was further evidence of the Anglo-Saxon nations' unwillingness to recognize Japan as an equal. Then, despite the League being Wilson's idea, the US Congress voted against joining the new international body.

Despite the disappointments at Versailles, Japan joined in the arms control settlement arrived at during the Washington Conference in 1922. It accepted a 5:5:3 ratio for Britain, the USA and Japan in the building of capital warships. Though kept to a lower level of shipbuilding compared to Britain and the USA, France and Italy were even further restricted, and the USA agreed not to fortify the western Pacific, which ensured Japan's absolute superiority there. Moreover, Japan was able to continue a buildup of ships in unrestricted areas such as cruisers. Nevertheless, the inferior ratio, accompanied by policies of retrenchment and cuts in the armed forces, created resentment in military circles.

Simmering resentment erupted in open criticism of the government after conclusion of the London Naval Treaty in 1930. At the conference the Japanese government indicated a willingness to accept an additional limitation on shipbuilding, i.e. a 10:7 ratio in heavy cruisers, as long as the principle of naval supremacy in the western Pacific was not compromised, but the United States, supported by Britain, pressed for a 10:6 ratio. Japan gave in to this pressure. The USA agreed not to build its full allotment of cruisers until 1936, giving a *de facto* 10:7 ratio until the next conference, but the treaty aroused huge domestic opposition from the navy general staff, the opposition Seiyūkai party and patriotic organizations. Naval officials caused a constitutional crisis by accusing the government of violating the emperor's right of supreme command. Although the Cabinet prevailed in ratification of the treaty, the agreement resulted in much popular dissatisfaction with the Minseitō party, and raising the issue of supreme command represented the first step in increasing military authority in political decision-making.

Meanwhile, important developments were taking place in China. After the Manchu dynasty was overthrown in 1911, China had fragmented into regions dominated by military warlords. Nevertheless, Chinese nationalism had been born and during the 1910s and 1920s took on an increasingly anti-Japanese character. During the late 1920s when the Nationalist Party, led by Chiang Kai-Shek, began the reunification of China, many Japanese viewed this as a threat to Japanese interests. The increasing power of the Soviet Union also put Japanese interests in northern China and Manchuria in a vulnerable position. Prime Minister Tanaka Giichi's 1927 proclamation of a new 'positive policy' towards China reflected Japanese leaders' desire to keep Manchuria with its vast natural resources separate from a unified China. In 1928 certain young officers in Manchuria, not satisfied with these diplomatic measures, assassinated the Manchurian warlord Zhang Zuo-lin in the hope of precipitating a Japanese takeover of the region. However, neither Tokyo military headquarters nor the Tanaka Cabinet supported their actions.

Convinced that Japan's position on the Continent was being seriously undermined by both world economic depression and the new Manchurian warlord's leanings towards the Nationalists, field army officers in Manchuria again took matters into their own hands in September 1931. Without orders from Tokyo General Staff headquarters, they provoked a clash with Chinese soldiers on the South Manchurian Railway as a prelude to full-scale invasion. This 'Manchurian Incident' is usually viewed by historians as the pivotal event setting Japan on the road to war. Indeed, Japanese historians usually refer to 'the Fifteen Year War', but war was still not inevitable nor was there unanimity on foreign policy. The Manchurian invasion marked the beginning of Sino-Japanese conflict, but the idea of organizing an economically self-sufficient and militarily impregnable empire in Asia was still only dimly foreshadowed. At the time, the Wakatsuki Cabinet with Shidehara as Foreign Minister tried to restrain the army, while the League of Nations and the USA insisted on a peaceful settlement. Domestic pressure for the takeover of Manchuria forced the Wakatsuki Cabinet to resign, and the succeeding Cabinet sanctioned the move of the Kwantung Army into northern Manchuria. Japan set up the puppet state of Manchukuo which the Western powers refused to recognize, and when in 1933 the League's Lytton Commission named Japan an aggressor, Japan withdrew from the League. Japan was now censured and isolated from the West.

Domestic political turmoil over the next few years was connected to the rise of nationalist sentiment and the military's role in politics, including the terrorist activities of the Young Officers. Military expenditures increased, and military activities in north China were stepped up. Nevertheless, the military did not make all the decisions – war did not result simply from weak high command and civilian officials being dragged along by field staff, a common view in the early postwar period. When full-scale war did finally break out, it was not field armies which instigated it as in 1931. Rather, it was a minor skirmish at the Marco Polo Bridge outside Beijing in 1937 which escalated into war.

This so-called China Incident quickly evolved into a *de facto*, though undeclared Sino-Japanese war. After occupying Beijing and Tianjin, fighting spread to Shanghai and up the Yangtze River. In taking Chiang's capital of Nanjing in December, the Japanese committed atrocities on the Chinese civilian population as well as military personnel on a scale ranging from tens of thousands in apologist Japanese estimates up to 300,000 in Chinese estimates. Meanwhile, Chiang moved his capital inland to Chongqing, and refused to surrender even after Japan captured Guangzhou in the south, extended a blockade of the coastline and set up a puppet regime under Wang Jing-wei. Although the outbreak of war in Europe in September 1939 prevented the European powers from giving Chiang much support, Nationalist armies continued to fight the Japanese in the south while communist guerrillas dominated rural areas in the north, creating a costly stalemate for the Japanese.

Even after the war with China began, however, Japanese leaders did not anticipate or prepare for a Pacific war with the United States. Japanese army leaders instead looked upon the Soviet Union as the potential enemy and therefore concluded the Anti-Comintern Pact with Germany and Italy, only to be humiliated when Germany and the Soviet Union subsequently signed a non-aggression pact. In Japanese leaders' calculations, the USA did not have enough interests in China to go to war over, but they did not perceive that America's Asia policy was not a regional one, but part of a global one. Neither did Japanese leaders properly estimate the importance of moral elements in American foreign policy and the strength of the China lobby in American politics.

American policy did gradually move from the purely moral to a 'get tough' policy of economic sanctions after the outbreak of the Sino-Japanese War. Congress and the majority of Americans still wanted to avoid war, but public opinion became more and more sympathetic to China, especially with pro-Chinese mass media views such as the film version of Pearl Buck's novel *The Good Earth* which was seen by twenty-three million Americans in 1936. Aid to China increased, and expansion of the navy accelerated. An increasingly active group favouring economic pressure on Japan included influential advisers to President Franklin Delano Roosevelt. According to Secretary of War Henry Stimson, 'the only way to treat Japan is not to give her anything'.[11] Reminiscent of Perry's attitudes in the 1850s, Stimson concluded that Japan has 'historically shown that when the U.S. indicates by clear language and bold actions that she intends to carry out a clear and affirmative policy in the Far East, Japan will yield to that policy even though it conflicts with her own Asian policy and conceived interest'.[12]

After Japan signed the Tripartite Pact forming the Rome–Berlin–Tokyo Axis alliance in September 1940 and started troop movements in IndoChina, the United States imposed an embargo on iron and steel scrap headed for

Japan. By the end of 1940 licensing stopped the flow of all war materials to Japan other than oil. The freezing of Japanese assets and an oil embargo beginning in July 1941 forged the final link in Japanese perceptions of encirclement and strangulation.

'Overcoming modernity'

This summary of events leading up to full-scale war has had to over-simplify the complexities of military rivalries as well as the confused relationships among officers, bureaucrats and politicians. What may be highlighted by way of concluding this chapter is the view of Japanese nationalists, both civilian and military, towards confrontation with the Western powers. Some Western historians and many Japanese at the time and since have described Japanese foreign policies in the 1930s as a quest for 'autonomy'; that is, a search for freedom of action in East Asia from an international order dominated by the United States and Britain. From the Japanese point of view, the war was a conflict between the 'have' and 'have-not' nations. Japan was aiming to create a Japan-dominated international order in East Asia to replace the one that the West had constructed in the nineteenth century for its own advantage and in which it refused to let Japan have an equal share. Expanding the empire to assure Japan's place in the world represented achievement of the modernity project begun by the Meiji leaders.

Historians in the 1930s supported this project by reconstructing Japan's past to make war a legitimate means for achieving national goals. Histories were rewritten to ignore the costs of Japan's past wars, notably the Russo-Japanese War, turning them into glorious victories. Revised texts also provided justification for Japan's claim to Manchuria by making that region the object of conflict with Russia in 1904 and 1905, when in fact control of Korea had been the central concern. By extolling the aeroplane and other technology associated with modern warfare, Japanese writers made going to war 'a *modern* thing to do', or an attribute of modernity.[13]

But the Second World War represented as much a cultural as an economic or political conflict between Asia and the West, an attempt to define a Japanese as distinct from a Western modernity. This was reflected in the traditionalist vocabulary of the Young Officers and right-wing civilian reformers of the 1930s, and particularly the widespread commitment to the imperial institution and Japan's unique *kokutai*. It was also clear in the discourse among writers and intellectuals who took up the poet Hagiwara Sakutarō's call to 'return to Japan', culminating in the 1942 symposium on 'overcoming modernity'. In the 1920s Hagiwara had stood out as Japan's leading modern poet. His collection *Howling at the Moon* (*Tsuki ni hoeru*) showed the influence of Edgar Allen Poe and other Western poets. But in the 1930s both his poetry and essays expressed a sense of cultural loss under the impact of Western technology, symbolized by the city. His 1937 poem 'Return to Japan' encapsulated the crisis of modernity felt by many

intellectuals during the 1930s. None of the participants in the 1942 symposium wanted to return to a preindustrial era, but sought ways to preserve
the cultural elements which made Japan distinctive.

The symposium failed to reach a consensus on ways to solve the problems
of modernity, but the ethnologist Yanagita Kunio was more successful in
providing both an explanation and a solution to the uncertainties created by
rapid social and economic change. Yanagita established a new discipline of
minzokugaku (folklore studies) and advanced a 'new nativism' which aimed
at restoring archaic religious beliefs and practices to the centre of national
life. This, he believed, would solve the problem of unevenness between city
and countryside that resulted from modernization. He constructed an imagin-
ary Japanese folk, 'complete, coherent and unchanging', based on tales and
materials collected during travels to Japan's peripheries, especially Okinawa,
areas least changed by modernization and Westernization. Yanagita offered
a comforting image of Japan at a time when class divisions were growing
and modern girls were challenging gender roles. This countered the threats
of Marxism and rural class conflict which could tear society apart. H.D.
Harootunian concludes that

> by the end of the 1930s folkic Japan had become the basis for a larger,
> more encompassing identity called the East Asia folk, providing ideo-
> logical support to a variety of imperial and colonial policies that were
> demanding regional integration and incorporation.[14]

These policies and their impact on Japanese people and society are the
subject of the next chapter.

8   The dark valley

The year 1937 is often regarded as another critical point like 1931 on the road to total war. However, as Thomas Havens pointed out in his social history of the Second World War, civilians back home paid little attention to the clash at the Marco Polo Bridge, thinking it was just the latest in the series of skirmishes between Japanese and Chinese troops that had been taking place in north China since the late 1920s. After all, it was being reported simply as the 'China *incident*'. The difference between 1931 and 1937 is that the 1937 confrontation was not perpetrated by the military, nor was it meant to be the first step in an attempted takeover of all China. Certainly it was not expected to escalate into a war that would eventually cost Japanese themselves nearly three million lives.

For everyone who lived through the war, it left a lasting memory. Even more than five decades after its end it continues to haunt Japanese domestic politics and foreign relations. Yet the generations born since the war have learned little about it in their school books and, having lived prosperously in the years since the 'economic miracle', can have little understanding of the deprivations their parents or grandparents went through as total war made its impact.

This does not mean that Japanese were immediately engulfed by the demands of war after the Marco Polo Bridge incident. As in the case of German history, the wartime and postwar view of Japan as a fascist totalitarian state has been revised in recent decades. Despite the efforts of the government to mobilize the spiritual and economic resources of the country for total war, Japanese people and even business leaders responded half-heartedly in the early years. Attempts to organize everyone into centrally controlled national associations similar to those in Nazi Germany and Fascist Italy also failed to live up to expectations. The military did not become monolithic as army–navy rivalry continued; nor did it establish uncontested domination as the bureaucracy maintained and extended its administrative control throughout the country. Even party politicians did not disappear. Nevertheless, after the attack on Pearl Harbor brought the United States into the war, few Japanese families remained unaffected, and peoples in the older colonies as well as the newly occupied areas of Southeast Asia felt the brutal consequences of Japan's empire-building.

This chapter will trace the widening impact of war on the Japanese people and society, and, as the empire expanded, the war's effects in colonial areas. Section one will focus on domestic mobilization policies from 1937 to 1940 aimed at drumming up psychological support, while section two will assess the efforts to organize the Japanese people and restructure politics, the economy and society for waging total war, efforts which culminated in the New Order Movement of 1940. Looking outward in the third section, we will examine the reorientation of thinking about Asia during the late 1930s as Japan became more and more embroiled in the war with China, and explore developments in the Greater East Asia Co-prosperity Sphere after Japan drove out the European colonial powers from Southeast Asia. For the Japanese at home, total war came with Pearl Harbor, and its effects will be traced in section four. The chapter will end with the atomic bombings of Hiroshima and Nagasaki and their legacy for post-1945 Japan.

This legacy suggests that the defeat and destruction did not put a complete end to a significant period in Japanese history. It has been a common view among liberal and 'progressive' (leftist) historians in both Japan and Western countries that the highly authoritarian, expansionist system of wartime Japan was an aberration in Japan's modern development, and that defeat and postwar occupation reforms steered Japan back to the democratization process begun during the Taishō period. Since the 1980s, however, some historians have been whittling away at the view of a great wartime–postwar divide, arguing that in many important ways mobilization for total war laid the foundation for the postwar democratic system which is characterized by rationalization, mobilization and high levels of social integration and control. Such arguments provide the basis for a critique of not only the postwar Japanese system, but all 'advanced' capitalist societies.

Meanwhile, conservative Japanese historians as well as conservative politicians since the 1970s have been attempting another kind of revision of history textbooks, one which resembles the arguments put forward by Japanese military leaders during the 1930s. These historians do not want school history textbooks to depict Japan as the aggressor and brutal perpetrator of atrocities or sexual slavery, but rather to portray Japan's resort to war as little different from the Western powers' wartime actions as they attempted to cling to their empires. These diverse points of view raise major questions about continuity and discontinuity between the prewar and wartime periods and between the wartime and postwar periods. In addition, they raise questions about the peculiarities of Japan's modern development which have implications for understanding world history as well as Japanese history. Was Japanese expansionism and wartime authoritarianism due to pathological factors peculiar to Japan, in particular residues of premodern irrationality? Or were they the result of tendencies common to all modern, capitalist nations?

Mobilizing spirit for total war

The first national spiritual mobilization convention on 10 September 1937 kicked off the government's mobilization measures, and the government continued to work hard to generate spiritual support for the war in China for the next three years. As the previous chapter has demonstrated and as Thomas Havens reiterates,

> the war at home began with ideological standardization because in the 1930s it was so notably absent within society as a whole. . . . Not only were people preoccupied with internal matters, but they also knew that there had been no real provocation and that Japan's more likely enemies were to be found elsewhere. The lack of exhilaration among the public helps explain why the government labored so hard at spiritual mobilization and why the movement, from start to finish, had such a humorless mien.[1]

Sober slogans admonished the Japanese people to 'work, work for the sake of the country' and to 'respect imperial rescripts'. The phrases remained empty and abstract throughout the campaign, but succeeded in focusing attention on the far-away war and, by using local subcommittees, laid the groundwork for organizing the people into community and neighbourhood associations. Soon people were being led on pilgrimages to shrines and imperial tombs, seeing men off to the front or home with their wounds, singing old Russo-Japanese war songs, and practising traditional martial arts like judo and kendo.

From early in 1938 the Finance Ministry also used the movement to launch a savings campaign, warning that 'extravagance is the enemy'. The government tried to persuade citizens to forgo entertainment in favour of worshipping at shrines and volunteering their time for public service. Prohibiting neon signs saved on electricity and also presaged the closing of theatres and other entertainments. From 1939 spiritual mobilization leaders and frugality campaigners targeted dresses and kimonos, as well as cosmetics and permanent waves, as unnecessary luxuries, and mobilized women and children to stand on street corners in Ginza and other shopping areas to reprimand stylishly dressed or coiffed women. A Tokyo survey conducted the following year found that these efforts had been largely ineffectual, so that it was only when the war economy tightened textile supplies further that women finally gave up their dresses and kimonos and adopted the officially approved *monpe* pantaloons worn by peasant women.

Until Pearl Harbor, mobilization through propaganda in the mass media was poorly coordinated, so that censorship and news manipulation were more characteristic. Formation of a single news agency ensured that there was only one source for international news, and, using paper conservation as the excuse, the government reduced the number of newspapers and magazines allowed to publish. Both new and old press control laws restricted what people read as the police censors continued their vigilance against 'dangerous thoughts'. Being already state-controlled, radio quite easily became a means for raising civic-mindedness in addition to limiting dissemination of news to what the government wanted people to hear. Recognizing radio's potential as a propaganda vehicle, the government waived the monthly subscriber fee for large families and those with men at the front, and even gave away radios to poor rural villagers.

Despite their popularity, films initially escaped much attention from censors. The outbreak of the China war also saw little immediate change in films because the industry had no history of making war films. Tasaka Tomotaka's *Five Scouts* (*Gonin no sekkohei*) in 1939 set the pattern for the first war films. In stark contrast to the wartime films of Germany, Russia, the United States or Britain, it did not display the ultranationalism of the militarists' propaganda. Instead, continuing the trend towards realism in films since the beginning of the decade, it carefully examined the personality of the soldiers and portrayed them as ordinary people rather than as heroes.

However, in 1939 the government introduced new film laws, modelled after those written by Josef Goebbels in Germany, which set out positive guidelines for producing propaganda as well as negative controls on film production and distribution. The following year pre-production censorship of scripts began and restrictions became more specific: for example, no stories about the rich, no scenes of women smoking or drinking in cafés, no foreign words. Film-makers in all genres were encouraged and, after 1941, were required to develop 'national policy' themes centred on the 'spirit of sacrifice'. Besides eliminating individualistic and class attitudes, films were supposed to provide models for proper social behaviour – men dutifully going to war, women staying at home and looking after the family.

However, not all film-makers complied and a few, such as Gosho Heinosuke, even directly opposed national policy. Gosho did this by turning military scripts submitted to him into simple love stories. The military rejected the stories but did not punish him because his health was poor. Meanwhile, some makers of period dramas turned to producing films about the Meiji era to avoid the restrictions of national policy.

In education, the spiritual mobilization movement made more systematic use of radio broadcasts to schools, and other changes brought the war closer to home. The Education Ministry had already introduced new ethics textbooks in 1936 emphasizing Japan's uniqueness, but with the spiritual mobilization movement the China war was worked into all subject areas, and more physical training and marching became part of the school day. Judo and kendo gradually displaced baseball in sports. Furthermore, class hours were reduced so that students could perform labour service in the community, such as street cleaning and gathering charcoal. Nevertheless, the Education Ministry did not take up all of the spiritual mobilization movement's policies, notably its campaign against the use of English. While radio baseball commentators had to replace *sutoraiku* (strike) with *honkyū* and *bōru* (ball) with *gaikyū*, schools were not forced to eliminate English from the curriculum, although later in the war many local authorities dropped it when demands for student labour service and military training increased.

Organizing for total war

Just as the results of the spiritual mobilization movement fell short of expectations, especially when the anticipated quick victory over China did not materialize, reformists' attempts to carry out a drastic restructuring of politics and the economy during the late 1930s failed to create a tightly controlled national defence state. The suppression of the February 1936 rebellion had ended violent factionalism in the army, but had not led to complete domination of political decision-making by the military, nor even to an end to disagreements within the military itself. The plural elite structure of politics institutionalized by the Meiji Constitution remained an obstacle to the establishment of a military dictatorship. Moreover, although the outbreak of full-scale war with China raised national defence to the nation's top priority among both civilian and military leaders, there continued to be conflict between reformists advocating radical changes and conservatives preferring to work within the status quo.

After the quelling of the 1936 uprising and resignation of the Cabinet, reformist bureaucrats, particularly in the army, seized the opportunity to propose sweeping political, economic and administrative reforms in order to create a 'national defence state'. For example, these reforms would have amalgamated several ministries, centralized national administration, and greatly expanded government regulation of trade, electricity, fuel and the aircraft industry. Despite having lost their leverage as inter-elite mediators since 1932, party politicians in the Diet found supporters among conservatives in the bureaucracy, business and local elites in their opposition to the proposals and their massive budget of ¥3.13 billion. The confrontation over the reform proposals forced the Hirota Kōki Cabinet to resign, but failed attempts to assemble reformist cabinets finally persuaded General Hayashi Senjūrō to pursue more moderate changes and to work in cooperation with business. This compromise approach worked for a little while during which military buildup made some progress, but the parties retained some vigour and Diet support proved to be still necessary for accomplishing reform, as Hayashi learned to his regret.

Hayashi's successor as prime minister was Prince Konoe Fumimaro, who by this time had become established as a prominent behind-the-scenes mediator of conflicts among the elites. A supporter of the moderate reform consensus that was emerging among the non-party elites, but also popular with party politicians, Konoe was considered to be the leader most likely to succeed in getting reform legislation through the Diet. While Konoe's government was drafting legislation for a five-year industrial development plan, the unexpected war with China broke out. This generated patriotism among Diet members so that they passed many of the measures proposed by the government in 1938.

The core of the legislative package was the National General Mobilization Law (Kokka Sōdōin Hō). This gave the government widespread powers over the economy, including controls of wages, prices, profits, working hours, labour allocation, and installation of new equipment even in private firms. The second important piece of legislation established state management over electric power generation and transmission facilities, but Diet support was gained only after providing generous compensation to company owners and giving them an advisory role in setting policy on the new mobilization council. Business thus joined military and civilian bureaucrats in the economic management of the nation.

The struggle between reformists and conservatives did not end, however, since the reformists considered these new government controls over business too limited and pushed for creation of a new reformist party to take over the lower house of the Diet. Meanwhile, the war in China dragged on, draining resources and undermining achievement of the five-year industrial development plan's goals. As Gordon Berger observed, 'Japan's involvement in the China war ultimately exacerbated political conflict among the nation's elite groups, rather than promoting the establishment of rigid totalitarian political controls.'[2] Consequently, Konoe and his successors in 1939, the traditional right-wing 'Japanist' Hiranuma Kiichirō and General Abe Nobuyuki, countered pressures for further reforms in an attempt to ease the conflicts.

Conservatives in business, the bureaucracy, the navy, the imperial court and the parties succeeded in getting Admiral Yonai Mitsumasa appointed prime minister in January 1940, but the volatile international situation reinforced the importance of military preparedness, increased military influence in policy-making and intensified reformist demands for more structural change. The war in Europe had begun in 1939, and Japanese involvement in the China war took on long-term prospects when Chiang Kai-shek continued to fight after moving the capital to Chongqing. Now that the possibility of a total American embargo on strategic materials loomed close, Japan was tempted to seize the resource-rich Southeast Asian colonies of the European nations while they were preoccupied with the Nazi invasion of Poland, occupation of Denmark and Norway, and defeat of the Netherlands, Belgium and France.

According to Gordon Berger, this changed international environment seems to have turned Konoe into a supporter of reform by the time he began his second term as prime minister in the middle of 1940 and launched the formation of a new political order at the same time that Japan moved into northern Indo-China and concluded an alliance with Germany and Italy. But the new order ended up being, in Peter Duus's words, 'a far cry from the fascist one-party dictatorships of Europe'.[3] During the summer all the political parties dissolved themselves as a prelude to creation in October of the Imperial Rule Assistance Association (IRAA or Taisei Yokusankai). This institutional embodiment of the new order was intended to be a national organization for integrating and mobilizing the population into the state. However, even Konoe's popularity proved insufficient to win over conservatives in the bureaucracy, such as Hiranuma, and in the lower house of the Diet which continued to function. They remained opposed to creation of the 'high-degree national defence state' desired by the military because it would infringe upon their vested interests and power. Consideration of contending elite viewpoints in the context of a delicate international environment led to compromises from the start. By March 1941 all reformist leaders had been purged from official positions in the IRAA, and it had become part of the Home Ministry. In short, the IRAA was absorbed into the state's existing administrative structure. Plans for a new economic order under tight state control similarly met with frustration. When opponents charged that the plans to nationalize industrial management and production violated private property rights and equated with communism, the Cabinet backed away, dropping state control over private enterprise from the new economic policy adopted in December.

General Tōjō Hideki became prime minister after Konoe resigned in October 1941. He had been army minister since 1940. Although Allied images during the war depicted him as the dictatorial Japanese counterpart of Hitler and Mussolini, Tōjō faced the same problems as his predecessors of making a stable coalition from the ministries, business and the Diet. He took over multiple posts as the war wore on, but this indicated attempts to bolster his power as it in fact waned. Competition between the army and navy continued, as did competition among civilian ministries to obtain a greater share of the budget and raw materials.

Although the IRAA never became the mass organization for political integration as was intended, the incorporation of huge numbers of people into its suborganizations brought the war to the Japanese people much more systematically than before. Virtually everyone belonged to one of its suborganizations, such as the Greater Japan Youth Association, the Greater Japan Women's Association and the Greater Japan Patriotic Industrial Association. These national organizations brought together associations which already existed at local levels, but although it seems that centralization remained mainly nominal, reorientation of their activities and ideology towards identification with the state may have had a significance even beyond the war years.

The Greater Japan Women's Association, for example, absorbed all women's organizations, both autonomous and official. Many well-known women leaders, including the leading suffragette Ichikawa Fusae, accepted high positions in the association and actively engaged in government efforts to enlist women's services to support the war. Some postwar feminists have criticized these women for their wartime collaboration, but Ichikawa justified it, seeing the war as opening up opportunities for women to expand their public roles. Moreover, being a feminist did not preclude being a patriot. Being invited to aid the nation in its 'Holy War' was regarded as an honour as well as official acknowledgement that women had a role outside the home. As Kōra Tomi declared:

> I greatly appreciate the honour bestowed upon women by the invitation [as family members] to this historically significant family council [National Cooperation Council, also known as the Family Council]. I am grateful for the emperor's mercy in permitting women who have been insignificant and useless to attend the council meeting to present their views of women and children.[4]

By leading campaigns to economize or buy war bonds, to mobilize women for factory work, to act as guardians of public morality or to improve hygiene, such women leaders hoped to demonstrate women's capabilities. At the same time, however, in using the state's interests to further their goals, they were tied to the state and remained constrained by the state's conception of women's role. In addition, the close relationship between organized women and the state that developed during wartime was to persist in the postwar period, as will be discussed in a later chapter.

Similarly, the Greater Japan Patriotic Industrial Association did not achieve its goals as a mass organization to integrate both workers and employers in support of national objectives. Employers resented government intervention in their relations with workers, while workers viewed local units as places where 'they just listen to the sermons of the boss'. Nevertheless, Saguchi Kazurō has argued that the state's wartime work ideology provided 'significant motivating energy for the postwar labor movement' by recognizing the honourable nature of 'work' as service to the state.[5] This in a sense answered the demands for 'recognizing the workers' humanity' that had characterized labour disputes since the First World War. Saguchi also views the postwar labour movement's efforts to abolish discrimination between white- and blue-collar workers as based on the wartime assumption that all workers were active subjects contributing to national production, and therefore all equal.

The new order movement also gave a boost to other organizations at local levels, namely neighbourhood associations and community councils, expanding their functions and involving more and more people in cooperative activities as the war wore on. The top best-seller of 1940 to 1941, *A Reader for Neighbourhood Associations*, signalled their increasing importance as institutions of local administration:

> Up to now, the main purpose of neighbourhood associations has been social, and there is nothing wrong with that. But as neighbourhood associations are steadily solidified, they will be obliged to cooperate more for daily living and have some connection with distributing commodities.[6]

According to IRAA figures, there were over 1,300,000 neighbourhood associations in Japan by 1942 as a result of authorities' efforts to mobilize everyone into units of ten or fifteen households. Their activities extended over sanitation, air and fire defence, counter-espionage, crime prevention, encouraging savings, honouring soldiers and their families, and labour service as well as distributing rations. Although not everyone liked being forced into neighbourhood work, the associations and the national crisis more generally helped to break down differences between classes and gender roles. In particular, they brought women out of their homes into more public activities, for although men generally ran neighbourhood associations and clearly dominated community councils, women carried out most routine duties. By 1944 when most eligible men had been drafted for military or labour service, women took on more and more association responsibilities. The *Asahi shinbun* observed: 'there are days when the wives of [association] captains are entirely absorbed by work "on behalf of the neighbourhood association". It is said that a certain captain's wife had only sixty days out of the entire year for her own life.'[7]

War and the expanding empire

While the spiritual mobilization movement tried to drum up psychological support for the war and the elites clashed over how and to what degree the political and economic system should be restructured to prepare for total war, Japan was deepening its involvement in China, and consequently becoming increasingly estranged from the United States and Western European powers. In this section we will look first at some intellectual developments which supported these foreign policies, then move on to tracing the expansion of the empire and its effects in Asia as Japan occupied most of Southeast Asia.

As discussed in Chapter 7, the intellectual debates over modernity during the late 1930s and early 1940s amounted to a rejection of Western modernity which some historians view as ideological support for the state's break with the Western imperialist nations. Even more directly supportive of expansionary policies were Pan-Asianist ideas developed by members of the Shōwa Kenkyūkai (Shōwa Research Association) under Konoe's patronage. Pan-Asianism had been a current since the beginning of the century but now gained new vigour as the idea of Japan's obligation, as the first successful non-European modernizer, to assist the uplifting of less fortunate Asian peoples became the justification for Japan's 'Holy War' for the 'liberation' of Asia. Japanese expansionism, according to Japanese Pan-Asianists, differed from Western imperialism because it sought to free Asia from the West, whereas Western imperialism was self-seeking tyranny.

The idea of the Japanese being the leading race because of its 'bright and strong' moral superiority and purity was not confined to intellectuals. As John Dower found, popular songs indicated the depth and breadth of its penetration among Japanese people. In contrast to American songs during the Second World War, Japanese songs rarely denigrated the enemy or even mentioned the enemy by name; rather, they concentrated on aspirations for transcendence and purity in association with colour images of red and white. A popular song of 1938, for example, described four 'Flowers of Patriotism': 'cherry blossoms on the slopes of "pure white" Mount Fuji, red plum blossoms in winter, crimson camellias, and "sparkling" chrysanthemums.'[8]

Such ideas and rhetoric supported the drive to create Japan's own economic and strategic bloc to survive in a world believed to be moving towards economically self-contained and politically autonomous supranational regional blocs. In 1938 Konoe called for a 'New Order in East Asia' promising economic cooperation, common defence and friendship, particularly to China. But Japanese actions in China belied the promises of cooperation and friendship. The 'Rape of Nanking' in December 1937 had left a middle-range estimate of 200,000 Chinese killed after heavy shelling and six weeks of authorized rape, executions and random murder.[9] There was also no doubt that Japan would lead and benefit most in the new order. For example, Japan was to have special rights to exploit raw materials in Mongolia and North China. These same contradictions characterized the 'Greater East Asia Co-prosperity Sphere' which Foreign Minister Matsuoka Yōsuke announced in August 1940 was the aim of Japanese policy.

In the old colonies, especially Korea, concepts of a Japan-led new order, combined with remilitarization, led to a movement for the 'imperialization' of Japan's dependent races. This meant that the gradualist, somewhat accommodative policy of assimilation of the 1920s gave way to a coercive policy aimed at destroying manifestations of Korean, Taiwanese or other cultural or national identity and emphasizing colonial peoples' obligations as Japanese subjects. Koreans, for example, were forced to change their names to Japanese ones, and Japanization of outward appearance, customs and lifestyles accelerated. Assimilation policies became most severe in Korea because demands for national independence had been most strident and persistent there even after suppression of the First of March 1919 rebellion.

As preparations for war stepped up in the mid-1930s, the colonies all took on more importance for creating a self-sufficient economic bloc. Like European imperialism, Japanese colonial policy had always viewed its colonies as territories serving the strategic and economic interests of Japan. Economic policies aimed at making Taiwan and Korea producers of foodstuffs for the home islands – Taiwan mainly for sugar, Korea for rice. As discussed in Chapter 6, land policies in Korea had driven many Korean farmers out of agriculture and into emigrating to Japan during the 1910s and 1920s. During the 1930s economic priorities shifted from agricultural production to major industrialization programmes to provide the raw materials for Japanese heavy industry, such as petrochemicals, ores and metals. After outbreak of the war in China, Korea became not only a logistical base for military operations, but a supplier for Japan's armies in China while continuing to send rice to

the home islands. Geared as they were to Japanese military needs, these programmes provided little benefit to Taiwanese and Korean consumers and,
since Japanese dominated ownership of business and industry, profits went
to only a small minority of indigenous entrepreneurs.

In fact, as labour shortages increased during the war, Taiwanese, Chinese
and especially Koreans were conscripted for work in Japan. This began as
part of a general mobilization of 1.1 million workers in 1939, of which
85,000 (7.5 per cent) were to be Koreans. Until the end of 1941 achievement
of labour quotas relied as in the past on voluntary recruitment, and Koreans
continued to go primarily into coal and metal mining and the construction
industry. However, recruitment had fallen short of quotas and domestic
manpower resources were shrinking as more and more Japanese men went
to the front. Consequently, when the two-year contracts of the first cohort
of Korean workers were about to expire, the Welfare Ministry arbitrarily
extended them. The range of industries employing Korean workers subsequently expanded, and recruitment became progressively more coercive until
'forced migration' or 'forced labour' was instituted in 1944. Even though not
officially forced, there are numerous recollections of unsuspecting Koreans
being kidnapped or forcibly taken from their homes and sent to Japan.

Forcible conscription affected Asian women and girls too, but to provide
'comfort' for Japanese soldiers. The Japanese government tried to deny
official sponsorship after former Korean comfort women exposed the practice
and filed a class action suit for compensation in late 1991, but documents
with the seal of the Imperial High Command have confirmed the existence of officially established military brothels. The military set up comfort
stations, beginning in the early 1930s as the Japanese armies encroached on
China and occupied Manchuria, but later throughout Asia and the Pacific
islands wherever it was fighting. Often lured by false promises of employment, many other women were forcibly abducted or coerced into recruitment.
The terrible conditions suffered by the women amounted to what many
label 'sexual slavery'. Accounts vary, but the women often had to service
twenty or thirty soldiers a day without any direct payments. Although regulations banned violence against the women, most women felt they were not
treated as human beings and still bear the marks of physical abuse. Moreover, although military authorities ordered soldiers to use condoms and
generally carried out regular medical check-ups for venereal disease, venereal infections still occurred, and the women suffered from all sorts of other
diseases such as malaria, jaundice and vaginal swelling.

Precipitating war with the United States not only placed heavier burdens
on people in the old colonies, but also meant that Japan would need to find
other suppliers of material resources for the military. This led to the offensive
in Southeast Asia and sudden expansion of the empire soon after the attack
on Pearl Harbor. Because of Japan's involvement in total war, the Greater
East Asia Co-prosperity Sphere never amounted to more than a rhetorical
ideal, but nevertheless, the slogans that went with it – 'Asia for the Asians',

'Eight Corners of the World Under One Roof' – stimulated movements throughout Asia which lasted beyond Japan's own defeat. The speed and extent of Japanese successes in Southeast Asia during early 1942 were like a match lighting the fires of Asian nationalism. Japan conquered the peninsula of Malaya in seventy days, and Singapore, supposedly impregnable and the symbol of British supremacy in Asia, fell in just seven. Within a few more months Japan drove out the Western colonialist powers from the entire region.

Many of the 150 million new subjects of the Japanese empire 'rejoiced' over the Japanese victories. According to Mohan Singh, first leader of the Indian National Army, Japan at least professed the goal of Asian freedom while the British promised nothing. And an Indian member of the Malayan civil service declared that although his 'reason utterly rebelled against it', his sympathies 'instinctively ranged themselves with the Japanese in their fight against Anglo-America'.[10] The collapse of the British defence of Singapore, the hasty retreat from Burma and the easy Japanese victory over the Dutch made the Western powers look like they had run away. Moreover, in their discriminatory evacuation of Penang, the British revealed their racism. Wrote one Chinese after the war, 'the memory of that unseemly stampeding from Penang still had its sting, of launches cleared of Asiatic women at the point of the bayonet.'[11]

The unexpected speed and size of the victories caught the Japanese unprepared. They were short of trained colonial administrators and had no plans ready for governance of the new empire. Consequently, in most places the Japanese used local people to staff the colonial governments and turned to nationalist leaders to head them: Aung San and Ba Maw in Burma, Sukarno in Indonesia, Jorge Vargas and José Laurel in the Philippines. Most of these people did not regard themselves as collaborators with an enemy, nor were they viewed as collaborators by fellow Southeast Asians after the war.

Because the Japanese government lacked concrete plans for Southeast Asia, policies in the occupied areas varied depending on the views and actions of Japanese field commanders and bureaucrats on the spot. Some, like Colonial Suzuki Keiji in Burma and Fujiwara Iwaichi in Malaya, sincerely believed in Japan's 'mission' to liberate Asia. They established independence armies which played key roles in nationalist revolutions after 1945. Suzuki was a swashbuckling, eccentric character trained in intelligence work and sent to encourage and organize a nationalist group in Burma considerably before the Japanese military takeover. He became very close and even loved by his Burmese protégés – 'we feared him from our youth, and we also loved him'.[12] But Suzuki's and Fujiwara's genuine commitment to Asian independence was not always shared by Tokyo headquarters or by army field commanders and successive colonial administrators.

So within months of the Japanese takeover, the goodwill which had greeted the Japanese turned to fear, dislike and hostility. The Chinese in Singapore were early victims of Japanese brutality. The Japanese government later admitted to killing 5000 Chinese in the so-called 'Operation Clean-Up', looking for 'anti-Nippon' elements. Overseas Chinese were very supportive of their homeland of China, so the Japanese targeted them. Some Japanese officers and most military police (Kenpeitai) swaggered around arrogantly, and Kenpeitai officers in particular became dreaded for arbitrary brutality and ruthlessness.

Other Japanese policies also made clear that European imperialism was simply being replaced by Japanese imperialism – Tokyo time, the Japanese calendar, Japanese occupation money and the Japanese flag had to be used. American music and films were banned, the press censored, and only Japanese-controlled radio stations could be listened to. Schoolchildren had to learn Japanese, though in practice English often had to be the language of communication. 'Superior' Japanese modes of thought and behaviour were promoted, and newspapers published lessons on Japanese customs. All public meetings began with a collective bow towards Tokyo and the emperor, and many people remember being slapped for not bowing or bowing improperly to Japanese officers. This practice of slapping as a disciplinary measure became a widespread grievance among military trainees. While common in the Japanese Army, it went against local religious and social concepts. This ignorance of Southeast Asian customs created dislike, and contributed to the change in attitude towards the Japanese.

Moreover, while the Japanese government lacked in-depth plans for Southeast Asia, it soon became clear that its overall aim was really 'Asia for the Japanese', not 'Asia for the Asians'. The region's rich natural resources, especially oil, were exploited for the war effort. Up to 30 per cent of food crops were requisitioned for the Japanese Army and home islands. Zaibatsu, such as Mitsui and Mitsubishi, moved in quickly and monopolized business and trade. Black markets in rice flourished, pushing rice prices sky-high and forcing most farmers to eat tapioca and corn. As the American stranglehold on Japanese shipping tightened after mid-1943, supplies of other foodstuffs, medical supplies and other goods shrank and prices spiralled. For example, sugar averaged US$1.40 a pound in late 1943 Manila when it had earlier sold for five cents a pound, and it took a bagful of Japanese currency to buy a single banana. A great famine in northern Vietnam in 1944 to 1945 claimed 400,000 lives according to the French, two million according to the Vietnamese. Eyewitnesses accused the French and Japanese of hoarding rice for their own soldiers. Forced labour was the greatest hardship, though. Japanese authorities rounded up able-bodied men and women in Indonesia, Malaya and Burma and sent them to various places in their countries to work, or worse, to work on the notorious Thai–Burma railway. Thousands never returned.

In 1943 Japan declared Burma and the Philippines 'independent' to compensate for the slackening of military victories, but independence was obviously only a façade, and Southeast Asian leaders knew it. Aung San declared at the first anniversary ceremony, 'our independence exists only on paper and the peoples have yet to enjoy its benefits.'[13] By the end of 1944 Japan's military weakness was undeniable, and unrest reached explosive proportions which burst into revolts in Indonesia and Burma in 1945. In Java the revolt broke out in Blitar, stronghold of the Indonesian Communist Party, home to many nationalist leaders, including Sukarno, and a base for Peta (the Japanese-trained independence army). The Blitar soldiers commiserated with forced labour conscripts, resented Japanese condescension, and were ired by reports of Indonesian girls being taken away by Japanese troops. While a combination of conciliation and force ended this revolt, the one in Burma spread to almost the entire Burmese National Army.

Assessments of Japan's brief occupation of Southeast Asia are mixed. On the one hand, memories of harsh treatment and exploitation created hostility to postwar Japanese 'economic imperialism' and any signs of remilitarization which has lasted to the present. On the other hand, postwar Southeast Asian leaders as well as historians have concluded that the occupation changed the politics of the area irrevocably. A British official returning to Burma observed, 'in the trite phrase, things could never be the same again'. Despite the self-interested, propagandistic intent of their slogans, the Japanese had unleashed powerful nationalist sentiments which they could not keep under control. Besides politicizing Southeast Asians, they gave them administrative and military training, including many high-ranking generals in the postwar revolutionary armies such as Suharto and P.H. Djatikusumo of Indonesia. According to Djatikusumo,

> The Dutch were better in theory, but the Japanese were more practical. . . . What we learned from the Japanese was more important: how to create an army from scratch and lead it. We learned how to fight at company level, how to recruit soldiers, and how to devote yourself to your country.[14]

The Japanese also introduced guerrilla training. But perhaps most important, Japan's own collapse exposed colonial omnipotence of both white and non-white as a myth. Southeast Asians were left with the confidence that they would never again submit to foreign rule and with the means to ensure that they never would.

Life on the home front

As indicated in previous sections, the government had to work hard, and without complete success, at mobilizing the people and material resources for total war during the first three years of the China war. Ordinary Japanese were still too preoccupied with leading their individual lives, and deprivations in their daily lives were not yet too great. Leisure entertainment still thrived, though with reduced hours, and even dance halls remained open until Halloween 1940. Rice rations did not begin until Christmas Day 1940.

But in 1941 the problems of economic production and supply which were to become acute during the final year of the war began to be evident. New Year 1941 began with no delivery of New Year cards and few rice cakes. Formal rationing followed in April in the six largest cities, and by Pearl Harbor a network of distribution centres covered the whole country. Neighbourhood associations organized scrap metal drives, collecting lamp-posts, railings, and even temple bells and gongs for melting down and recasting as guns. Clothes made of bark and wood pulp began to appear. Men were already wearing the officially approved civilian uniform, but now women finally began wearing *monpe*. Government efforts to recruit more labour for war industries became more systematic. Officials tried some incentives like higher pay and extra sake rations, but also began conscription in November. All men between the ages of 16 and 40 and women between 16 and 25 had to register for possible service. The number of recruited or conscripted Korean workers also jumped substantially – from just over 67,000 in 1941 to almost 120,000 in 1942.[15]

Total war came with the surprise attack on Pearl Harbor, but at first the announcement of the 'death-defying air-raid upon the American fleet' and the string of victories in the first half of 1942 helped compensate for the growing material deprivation and regimentation. High school student Saitō Mutsuo remembers arguing with his unusually pessimistic father: 'Didn't you hear what they said on the radio? We've wiped out the American fleet. The whole Pacific is open to us now. Of course we're going to win.'[16] Despite his father's doubts about defeating a country as rich and powerful as the United States, Mutsuo's family followed the fashion of those first months of Japan's incredible military victories throughout Asia, recording each conquest on a large wall map of the Pacific with a tiny rising-sun flag and each enemy vessel sunk with a little crossed-out picture of a warship. Students like Mutsuo continued their studies relatively untroubled by the political events, except for the requirement of several hours of military training each week. Despite rationing, there were still some amusements, including baseball games, sumo wrestling and movies, though now with titles like *Spirit Warriors of the Skies*. And for children, even later in the war, war was the material for play. Satō Hideo recalled, 'I was born in war. It was always around. But war is fun. Boys like war. . . . All our games were war games, except ones with cards. . . . I loved playing at war.'[17]

The battle of Midway in June 1942 ended the Japanese Navy's offensive and marked a military turning point. Although the Japanese people were not told of the defeat, Mutsuo noted something odd about that report: 'it was the first time that the loss of a Japanese warship had been officially announced.'[18] As the struggle for Guadalcanal began, students were sent off on a week-long military training camp, which then became a regular feature of their lives.

By early 1943 material austerities worsened considerably. The hardships of war showed in the outward appearance of Tokyo: crowded streets by day, but people wearing ragged and faded clothes; sparse vehicular traffic

Map 8.1 The Japanese Empire

because of the fuel scarcity; grubby buildings and parks since no one was available to tend them; many luxury stores closed for lack of stock; and dark at night with blackouts in force for fear of 'B-san', B-29 bombing raids. Rationing became more strict in Tokyo than elsewhere in Japan or in the overseas empire as the government prepared people for prolonged resistance. Every necessity except vegetables was tightly limited. Even soap was rationed, and the government could not keep up the allocation. The daily rice ration consisted of half a pound per person, about half the normal pre-war consumption. By 1945 rice became virtually unobtainable by ordinary Japanese, and pumpkin became the staple. Every scrap of arable land was cultivated, including the stadium constructed for the aborted 1940 Olympics and the land alongside railway tracks. Authorities imposed travel restrictions because of the fuel shortage, and some railway companies introduced passenger trains without seats to save raw materials.

By mid-1943 normal student life ended as students joined everyone else remaining in Japan, except married women, in compulsory labour service in factories or on farms. The government lowered the age of deferment from military service for students to 20. In October 70,000 teachers, parents and younger students gathered in Meiji Garden Stadium in Tokyo to bid fare-well to 25,000 mobilized students. The following year, despite drafting men from the colonies, the labour shortage was so severe that the government began conscripting women for war work too. Nevertheless, the home-centred conception of women's role inhibited full mobilization of women's labour. By the end of the war more women held jobs than ever before and made up 42 per cent of the civilian workforce, but they remained less sys-tematically recruited than any other social group in Japan or compared to women in other countries.

The outbreak of war with China had stimulated various government efforts to bolster motherhood. Worried about a decline in the birth rate since the early 1930s, government authorities began to oppose birth control more openly, detaining birth control leaders and closing down clinics. Pronatalism became official policy in 1940 with the passage of the National Eugenics Law (Kokumin Yūsei Hō). Based on the Nazi law, it banned contraceptives and encouraged sterilization of parents with mental illness or hereditary defects. Under the slogan 'Give birth and multiply' (*ume yo fuyase yo*), the state promoted large families with awards, worked to lower the average age of marriage and established marriage counselling offices. It enacted a Mother-Child Protection Law in 1937 to assist impoverished single mothers and their children, and established health clinics for mothers and children. Magazine editors felt pressured to run articles promoting motherhood and motherly qualities, and films supported this image by portraying women as upholders of the family. Consequently, when the government finally applied labour conscription to women, it drafted only young single women and widows.

The terrors as well as hardships of war arrived with the B-29 planes carry-ing incendiary bombs from late November 1944. Less tonnage was dropped on Japan than on Germany, but the bombs were almost as destructive due to the wooden construction of most buildings. One of the worst raids occurred in Tokyo in March 1945 when winds turned the fires into fire storms, leav-ing 75,000 to 200,000 people dead. This would be about three times as many as would be killed at Hiroshima. By the end of the war almost all large and medium-sized cities had been bombed. Forty per cent of Osaka was destroyed and 50 per cent of Tokyo and Nagoya. Millions of people fled from the cities during the last months of the war, and disruption of Japanese society became constant. Aside from the daily struggle for food and survival, people waited for the end of the war. Many expected a ferocious struggle with invad-ing American forces as took place in Okinawa in June 1945. Volunteer corps were organized and trained with bamboo spears to make the final resistance.

Criticism of the government increased, even at grassroots level. Tōjō had been forced to resign in July 1944 after the fall of Saipan, and a peace group worked among advisers to the emperor. Still, the Cabinet could not come to a decision to surrender. Leaders were divided because the Potsdam

Declaration issued by the Allied powers in late July 1945 called for unconditional surrender, leaving the fate of the emperor and imperial institution
unknown. The bombings of Hiroshima and Nagasaki on 7 and 10 August
(Japan time) with 'a new kind of bomb' and the entrance of the Soviet
Union into the war finally persuaded the emperor to break the deadlock.

On 15 August the emperor, speaking for the first time directly to his subjects, made his historic announcement on the radio. In a high, squeaky voice
through poor transmission facilities and using the formal, unfamiliar language of the court, he called on the people to 'endure the unendurable' of
defeat and surrender. Saitō Mutsuo was training near Kumagaya Air Base
that morning. Although responses to the broadcast were diverse, his seems
to have been representative of many Japanese. He felt full of regret and
bitterness for all those who had died, but at the same time relieved: 'perhaps
I am going to survive. Perhaps this thing they call peace is going to come.'[19]
Like Mutsuo, most Japanese were war-weary but resigned to fight to the
end. It is not at all clear that many opposed the war their government had
led them into. Certainly it was only a few hundred communists who had
continued to criticize government policies openly, and they had suffered in
prison for their criticism.

In addition, the atomic bomb experience may have contributed to the
lack of a sense of war responsibility. It ironically made Japanese feel that
they, not their colonial subjects or their enemies, were victims of the war –
'guinea-pigs' in a racial war. While contributing to the 'nuclear allergy' that
has characterized post-1945 foreign policy, the atomic bombings have not
always been connected with the fact that they culminated a war that Japan
had some responsibility for getting itself into in the first place. And while, as
a result of the atomic bombings, many Japanese in the postwar period have
viewed their nation as the victimized, the actual victims of the bombs have
suffered from special problems and the stigma of being *hibakusha* (atomic
bomb victims), which is different from the situation facing survivors of other
bombs. Not only were they victims of the immediate effects of a new, colos-
sally destructive weapon, but they continued to suffer from deadly after-
effects from radiation, including leukemia and cancer. In addition, even if
not scarred, they faced social discrimination in finding jobs and marriage
partners which may have reinforced a common sense of guilt for having
survived. This guilt underlay many survivors' ambivalence towards the establishment of the Peace Dome in Hiroshima, towards the peace movement,
and towards Hiroshima's rebuilding and prosperity.

The terrifying atomic bombings and the shattering announcement of surrender thus marked in many senses the end of an era, but not one that could
simply be forgotten despite attempts to do so. Moreover, Saitō Mutsuo's
typical relief at hearing that the war had ended did not mean the end of
suffering and deprivation or a return to stability for the majority of Japanese
people. As will be clear in the next chapter, the defeat was as much a beginning as an end.

9 'Enduring the unendurable' and starting over in the 'new' Japan

The defeat in 1945 was not just the loss of one war, but represented defeat of the foreign policy goals which had been pursued since the mid-nineteenth century. By that I do not mean specific territorial goals, but the broad goal of achieving great power status and equality with the Western powers. It is still debatable as to how planned or inevitable the war was, but historians agree that until 1945 war had been seen by most Japanese as a legitimate means of pursuing national interests. With defeat and occupation this assumption was destroyed.

The emperor's unprecedented and difficult to understand speech on 15 August symbolized the confusion of contradictory emotions that characterized Japan's condition in 1945. Few Japanese still felt confident of victory, but most expected to fight to the end. They were horrified and sad at this first defeat in Japan's 1400-year history. Unlike the *kamikaze* (divine wind) which had saved Japan from a Mongol invasion in the thirteenth century, the suicide missions of the young *kamikaze* pilots had failed to save Japan. Many people now believed that the long years of sacrificing had been in vain and that the country stood on the verge of annihilation, with almost three million Japanese dead, ninety cities bombed and two-and-a-half million dwellings wholly or partly destroyed. Tokyo's population of 6,700,000 in 1940 was down to 2,800,000, and the city looked like a wasteland. Perhaps the physical evidence of war and the desperateness of the economic situation helps to explain the Japanese response to the Occupation, for although very preoccupied with daily struggles for survival, Japanese people on the whole responded enthusiastically, not just passively to the great experiment in democratization that the Occupation undertook.

The Occupation reforms of the late 1940s have been regarded as the second great turning point in modern Japanese history after the Meiji Restoration. During the Occupation and after it ended in 1952 the reforms were considered to be a great success. Since the 1980s some new research and reinterpretation has downplayed the epochal nature of the Occupation, placing more emphasis on the 'reverse course' which supported the return and rise to hegemony of conservative elites in the economic and sociocultural realms as well as politics. These reinterpretations have criticized both the

Occupation and present-day Japanese politics and society, seeing the change in Occupation policy as a betrayal of the democratic promise and principles of the early Occupation. John Dower has been one of these critics, but his 1999 history of the Occupation nevertheless begins with defining 1945 as 'a watershed moment' dividing 'militarist Japan and a new democratic nation'.[1] The legacy of the Occupation will no doubt remain a matter of debate and reinterpretation, but historians agree that in the areas of foreign relations and the Constitution, the Occupation's effects were lasting. A close, though sometimes friction-filled relationship with the United States continues to the present, as does the American-imposed Constitution with no amendments.

This chapter will trace the course of the numerous reforms introduced by Occupation authorities and examine their consequences, but first we need to have a picture of the harsh economic and social conditions which demanded the attention of most Japanese after the war's end, especially in the cities.

The struggle for survival

Everyone who lived through the postwar years remembers the hunger. At the end of the war an ordinary adult living in one of the six largest cities received a daily ration of only 350 grams of a staple food such as rice or barley and averaged 1200 calories per day, down from 2160 in prewar years. Although nominally the mainstay of Japanese diets, rice was eaten by many families only in the form of a thin, watery gruel. Food became an obsession, as reflected in the popularity of 'bread-eating races' in school athletic contests. Women's magazines featured many articles on how to cultivate home vegetable gardens and how to cook new foods like acorns and grasshoppers.

Farmers and other suppliers of the black market prospered, selling their products in this time of scarcity, even though black market prices far exceeded official prices of food and other commodities. Even in 1948, for example, black-market rice sold for about seven-and-a-half times rice distributed through the official rationing system. City people regularly descended on rural areas in search of food. Living a 'bamboo-shoot existence' (*takenoko seikatsu*), they peeled off their clothes like the layers of a bamboo shoot and traded them and other valued possessions for food. Absentee rates rose as workers took time off to search for food, and even the Tokyo metropolitan police gave their employees monthly 'food holidays'. Pretending to hold a black market was reported to be one of the three most popular games among children in early 1946. Another was pretending to leave home to search for food, even in 1949.

In another popular children's game called 'repatriate train' children put on their school bags, jammed together on the teacher's platform at the front of the classroom, shook and trembled, and got off at 'Osaka'. This represented the struggles of the six-and-a-half million Japanese spread throughout Asia and the Pacific at war's end. More than half were soldiers and sailors, but about three million were civilians, including many women and children who had become settlers in the empire. While defeat meant loss of the empire for the nation, for such individuals it meant loss of all possessions and being driven into refugee status. In Manchuria and northern China many refugees were also driven into leaving their youngest children with Chinese families because the dangers of returning to Japan were so great. Returnees who managed to survive threats of disease, starvation and violent reprisals from former colonials then faced difficulties of finding a place to go in Japan.

Repatriation of military personnel was not necessarily faster or safer. The United States and European powers retained many prisoners of war as labourers, while the Nationalist Chinese government delayed repatriation of more than 50,000 Japanese for their technical skills. Japanese soldiers who fell into Soviet hands suffered most, with more than 300,000 never returned or accounted for. Upon repatriation and demobilization ex-servicemen often faced reproach not just for losing the war, but for committing the war crimes which were being reported in the newspapers. Veterans suffering from battle shock were commonly shunned, as were those with physical disabilities, like the survivors of Hiroshima and Nagasaki. Homeless people, including war widows and orphans as well as other abandoned or outcast people, filled public places such as railway stations even in the 1950s.

Adding to the confusion of millions of Japanese returning to Japan was the movement of hundreds of thousands of Koreans and smaller numbers of other colonial peoples who had emigrated voluntarily or involuntarily. More than 1,300,000 Koreans were repatriated to Korea. Perhaps half had been more or less forcibly conscripted for labour service during the war. Yet many of those repatriated later came back to Japan, probably because of the uncertain political and economic conditions in now divided and occupied Korea.

A sense of moral annihilation in the midst of economic chaos and social confusion was reflected in postwar novels such as Dazai Osamu's *The Setting Sun*. Although *The Setting Sun* told the story of a declining aristocratic family, it may have been symbolic of postwar Japan which may explain why it was so popular. The main character's decision to struggle on was also what the Japanese people decided to do rather than give in to pessimism, though Dazai himself resorted to suicide.

The 'democratic revolution from above'

The arrival of the American Occupation forces and first impressions of General Douglas MacArthur, Supreme Commander of the Allied Powers, reinforced the sense of defeat, but also raised a glimmer of hope for the Japanese. Never having been occupied by a foreign power and encouraged by wartime propaganda to expect the worst treatment by their American enemies, most Japanese expected to be punished. However, when MacArthur landed in Japan on 28 August 1945 he appeared without guards, unarmed, smoking a corn-cob pipe, and although in uniform, wearing no tie or medals in contrast to Japanese military officers' dress on formal occasions. While this was

MacArthur's well-cultivated personal image, it was also indicative of both the style and objectives of the Occupation. The lack of an armed guard exuded the confidence of the absolute victor, the casual attire signalled the end of war and beginning of a non-military relationship between Japan and its former enemy, and the corn-cob pipe symbolized the Occupation's democratic goals. The carefully calculated first impression succeeded in giving great relief to Japanese fears and apprehension and provided an early contribution to Japanese admiration of MacArthur as a great statesman.

As in MacArthur's manner of arrival, there were no indications of an intention to use American military power, but there was evidence of it everywhere. There was no doubt as to who was the victor and who the defeated. Units of gum-chewing American soldiers in strange vehicles called Jeeps were initially sent all over the country. They were instructed to act respectfully, but their presence impressed Japanese with American power and authority at the same time that sighting Americans in the flesh allayed fears. Many Japanese recall their conclusion that the United States must truly be rich and powerful upon seeing the tall, well-fed, well-clothed and superbly equipped American soldiers cheerfully giving away chocolates and cigarettes.

A Japanese journalist, Kawachi Uichirō, recalled a similar first impression of American superiority, portentious of the great changes to come. The first Americans he encountered were a group of American reporters, not soldiers, arriving in Jeeps at the Diet building. They greeted Japanese journalists whom they had known before the war like old friends. They then proceeded to mount the dais and took turns having themselves photographed in the very chair occupied by the emperor when he opened sessions of the Diet or issued proclamations. Kawachi could not get over his shock at this casual lack of reverence for the emperor's chair.[2]

The surrender ceremony on 2 September on the deck of the huge battleship *Missouri* in Tokyo Bay was also heavily laden with symbolism. The ship had an association with President Truman, having been named after his home state and christened by his daughter in 1944 when Truman was still the senator from Missouri. On the day of the surrender ceremony it flew the same American flag that had flown over the White House on the day Pearl Harbor was attacked, but also the flag that had been used by Commodore Matthew Perry on his flagship when he had sailed into Tokyo Bay with his 'black ships' in 1853. Two officials, one representing the military forces and one representing the imperial government, signed the surrender documents for the Japanese side, while representatives of the nine Allied powers signed for the Allies. Exempting the emperor and even a court representative from the proceedings suggested to the Japanese that the victors would not hold the emperor responsible for the war.

MacArthur's eloquent speech expressed the hope that 'a better world shall emerge out of the blood and carnage of the past – a world founded upon faith and understanding – a world dedicated to the dignity of man and the fulfillment of his most cherished wish – for freedom, tolerance and

Plate 9.1 The Emperor visiting General MacArthur, 1947
Source: Courtesy of the General Douglas MacArthur Memorial

justice'.[3] His radio broadcast to the American people following the ceremony stated a commitment 'to see that the Japanese people are liberated from this condition of slavery'.[4] Such statesmanlike words offered some hope and comfort to Japanese leaders, but a thunderous fly-past of 400 B-29 bombers and 1500 Navy fighter planes during the ceremony also brought home the reality of defeat and demonstrated American material strength and affluence.

Japan's, and at this time the emperor's vulnerability were captured in a photograph of the first meeting between the emperor and MacArthur on 27 September. This photograph, which appeared in both Japanese and American newspapers, became the most famous visual image of the entire occupation period. Standing side by side in the Supreme Commander's office, MacArthur towers above Emperor Hirohito. In contrast to the emperor posing stiffly in formal morning dress, MacArthur stands casually, wearing an open-necked khaki uniform and no medals. The Home Ministry was appalled at the ways in which the photo visually represented the emperor's inferiority and tried unsuccessfully to ban its publication in the newspapers. The censors were right in that many people have said that the photo marked the moment when most Japanese faced the reality of being defeated and under American rule.

Perhaps the impact of a visual image was most telling, but at a press conference nine days after the surrender ceremony MacArthur had already made

Japan's weakness and vulnerability explicit with an observation that Japan had now become a 'fourth-rate nation'. To be relegated to such a status after striving since the Meiji Restoration to become a 'first-rate nation' evoked great emotional trauma. Sensitivity to this decline in status was clear, as the term 'fourth-rate country' immediately became a catchphrase. Such statements displayed American ethnocentrism and a self-righteousness sense of justice, the paternalistic arrogance of a country at the peak of its power and influence in the world.

This arrogance and condescension indicates some of the inconsistencies in Occupation policies. On the one hand, everything was now to become 'democracy'. However, Japan remained under military rule, though now American instead of Japanese. Although technically an Allied Occupation and some Commonwealth military forces participated, the Occupation was dominated by the US military. There was no division into zones as in Germany, and on-the-spot administration and policy-making was given to the control of a single Supreme Command of Allied Powers (SCAP), headed by the Supreme Commander Douglas MacArthur who took orders directly and solely from the US Joint Chiefs of Staff. Even American civilian agency representatives could visit or operate in Japan only with SCAP approval and only through SCAP's communication systems. Due to practical considerations, namely language, the Japanese government implemented SCAP policies, but there was no equality in the relationship, since the surrender terms specified unconditional surrender. And although democracy was the goal, SCAP exercised wide-ranging censorship of films, literature, popular songs and theatre as well as radio and all forms of publication. The existence of censorship itself was a taboo subject, as were criticisms of SCAP and its commander, the nation's 'second emperor'. Despite the inconsistencies, many Japanese people welcomed the heralded 'democratic revolution from above'.

Disarmament and demobilization characterized policies of the first few months, but the rhetoric of democracy soon turned into concrete policies. Early in October MacArthur issued a civil liberties directive abrogating the Peace Preservation Law of 1925 and other laws which had restricted political expression and organization. It also abolished the Special Higher Police or 'thought police' and what was regarded as the all too powerful Home Ministry, purged leaders in the Home Ministry and national police, and ordered the release of political prisoners from jail, including Tokuda Kyūichi and others who would become leaders of the Communist Party. More purges followed in 1946, amounting eventually to removal or exclusion from office of about 200,000 people in the military, extreme nationalist societies, the IRAA, and overseas financial and development organizations or others who were 'active exponents of militant nationalism and aggression'.

Suspected war criminals were arrested, starting with General Tōjō Hideki whose Cabinet had declared war in December 1941, but not including the emperor. On 29 April the following year the International Military Tribunal for the Far East (IMTFE) indicted 28 Class A suspects. Most were senior army and navy officers, others senior government officials, but none were industrialists or bureaucrats. Trials of these suspects and those charged with lesser war crimes continued until late 1948. Eventually, seven of the Class A defendants received death sentences, including Tōjō who until the end justified Japan's resort to war as an exercise of the 'right to initiate wars of self-defence'. Some historians have criticized the war crimes trials as 'victor's justice', and even at the time the convictions were not unanimous. Although not read out in court, four of the judges' opinions were critical of the tribunal's conduct or conclusions.

The exclusion of the emperor from involvement in war crimes reflects MacArthur's decision to use the imperial institution to support the Occupation's reforms, based on the assumption that to indict Hirohito or force him to abdicate would cause 'a tremendous convulsion' or 'vendetta' among the Japanese people.[5] The British had also argued against the emperor being tried for war crimes. Whether or not the Japanese people would have reacted in this way is debatable, but in any case it was SCAP as much as conservative Japanese leaders who helped wage the massive public relations campaign to transform the emperor into a 'manifest human'. On 1 January 1946 Hirohito issued a New Year's rescript rejecting as a 'false concept that the emperor is divine'.

In February Hirohito embarked on the first of a long series of tours extending to virtually all prefectures in the country to bring him into direct contact with his subjects and, by demonstrating his humanity and oneness with his people, to secularize popular veneration of the throne. These tours were reminiscent of his grandfather's, the Meiji emperor's, calculated as they were to lend the imperial presence in support of a new government's reforming policies. MacArthur believed this worked, and it is true that the institution still evoked remarkable respect, as it does even today. The emperor himself contributed greatly to the transformation of his persona. Shy in personality and inexperienced in mingling with ordinary people, Hirohito appeared so awkward and uncomfortable on his early outings that people felt sorry for him. Others cracked little irreverent jokes about his inability to make conversation, calling him the '"Ah, sō" [Oh, is that so?] emperor'. Conservative leaders worried a great deal about the emperor's fate, but the lack of fanfare about the emperor's announcement of his humanity may indicate that ordinary Japanese had never really thought of him as a god in the Western sense and had other matters to consider closer to home.

Industrial workers and labour reformers, for example, were revelling in their new-found freedom and opportunities to voice complaints and seek improvements in their working and living conditions. They took advantage of the Occupation's early revolutionary zeal and exceeded SCAP's expectations in organizing themselves into unions and pressing their claims. After a new labour law not only made unions for both public and private workers legal, but also laid out procedures under which workers had the right to strike, the number of unions and members sky-rocketed. By the end of 1946 nearly five million workers, including geisha, belonged to a union. On the policy-making side, progressive Japanese bureaucrats, scholars and social workers initiated and drafted legislation to regulate working conditions which SCAP's Labour Division was happy to approve and support. The new Labour Standards Law of 1947 fulfilled prewar workers' demands by declaring that 'working conditions must meet the needs of a worker living a life worthy of a human being'.

During the first two years of the Occupation workers thus succeeded in gaining recognition of their equality as citizens and as employees. While the desperate economic situation put higher wages and job security at the top of their list of priorities, demands for reform of the status system in the factory and participation in management discussion councils reflected the long felt desire for respect. The strength of unions in the early years helped workers achieve these goals. Signs of discrimination between white- and blue-collar workers were the first to go – no more separate dining halls or separate gates, for example. Many unions also achieved the joining of all employees into a single rank system and a unified company-wide pay scale. While few of the management discussion councils became effective decision-making bodies, they brought workers together with managers on an equal basis for the first time, reflected in workers' dispensing with polite forms of language and expressing anger directly.

Prewar farmers' goals also achieved fulfilment with land reform, generally viewed as one of the most successful reforms of the Occupation. By virtually eliminating tenancy, the reform improved the status and income of nearly half the Japanese population. Like labour improvements, work on land reform was initiated by Japanese government leaders immediately after surrender, though in this case SCAP forced an even more comprehensive redistribution of land than the Japanese proposed. Absentee landlords were compelled to sell their lands to the state, and resident landlords were on average limited to owning seven acres provided they cultivated at least two-thirds themselves. By 1950, 90 per cent of the arable land in the country was owned by those who cultivated it, though in many cases the parcels were too small to provide their owners with a living by farming alone. Price supports and other assistance began to close the lifestyle and income gap between country and city, and between strata within the agricultural community itself which had become such a source of complaint in the prewar years.

Another economic reform known as trust-busting or zaibatsu-busting came right out of the New Deal programmes of President Franklin D. Roosevelt's administration and the New Dealers who formed an influential group among early Occupation reformers. The anti-monopoly reforms aimed at dissolving zaibatsu 'holding companies' and eliminating zaibatsu family members as dominant shareholders because the business conglomerates were considered to be one of the pillars of Japanese militarism and feudalism. In practice, delays in implementation of 'economic deconcentration' meant that the 'reverse course' changed economic policies before most of the 325 large enterprises designated for breakup were actually affected.

Nevertheless, the looming threat of breakup for large firms resulted in entrepreneurial initiative being left to small and medium-sized companies. Many that prospered in the postwar economy creatively altered their production lines from meeting wartime to peacetime demands; for example, making rice containers from large artillery casings or pistons for irrigation pumps instead of fighter planes. The optics producers Canon and Nikon became camera manufacturers, while Honda Sōichirō took the first steps towards constructing his motor vehicle empire by manufacturing motorbikes with tiny engines which he had previously made for military communication devices. Catering to consumer demands did not contribute substantially to reconstruction of the nation's economy, however, and it was not until the Cold War shifted American views of Japan's role in its global strategy that Occupation economic policies began to promote recovery of Japanese industry and the people's livelihoods. Until then inflation spiralled and production remained below prewar levels.

Zaibatsu-busting had sceptics among some of the Allies, but no one disagreed with the Occupation's reforms in the education field. The intense campaign to democratize education began in late 1945 with directives to eliminate all nationalist teachers, textbooks and curricula. The directives called for revision of history and geography texts, and for banning of 'moral education' which had centred on the Imperial Rescript on Education. More than 100,000 teachers and school officials resigned or were purged. Remaining teachers formed large, often radical unions. The structure of the school system underwent change as well. Decentralization undermined the pervasive interference of the Ministry of Education, while extension of compulsory education to nine years, promotion of coeducation and expansion of the university sector provided non-elites with more access to opportunities. In the classroom itself new pedagogical techniques were promoted to encourage discussion and exchange among teachers and students.

Radical and far-reaching as all these reforms were, perhaps the most far-reaching was the new constitution promulgated in 1946 which went into effect the following year. According to MacArthur, it was 'probably the single most important accomplishment of the Occupation'. Despite the fact that it was written and imposed by Occupation authorities, its internalization and defence at the popular level has meant that it remains in effect without amendment even today.

On 25 October 1945 the Japanese government established the Constitutional Problem Investigation Committee, but it did not really take MacArthur's statements about the need for constitutional revision seriously. Consequently, it produced a draft in early February 1946 with only cosmetic changes to the Meiji Constitution which MacArthur and his top advisers in Government Section promptly rejected. Exercising his unrestricted authority, MacArthur then ordered Government Section, headed by General Courtney Whitney, to draft the new constitution for Japan. Following principles outlined by MacArthur himself, the committee of twenty-four – sixteen officers and eight civilians – worked around the clock to finish it by a one-week deadline. Although four were lawyers, including Colonel Charles Kades who headed the steering committee, none were specialists in constitutional law, and the only person who had actual knowledge and experience in Japan was Beate Sirota, a 22-year old woman who had lived in Japan since she was 6 years old. The secrecy in which the committee worked is illustrated by Sirota's driving around to many different libraries to collect sample constitutions to avoid arousing suspicion about the committee's assignment.

Although not all the committee members were New Deal Democrats, the resulting Constitution epitomized liberalism and democracy, in some respects surpassing that of the American Constitution. It began with the radical redefinition of the emperor as merely the 'symbol of the state and of the unity of the people', and made clear that sovereignty resided with the people by declaring the Diet 'the highest organ of state power' whose legislative authority could not be limited by executive veto. Following the British parliamentary model, both houses of the Diet were now elected representatives of the people, and the majority party in the lower house provided cabinet members who were responsible to the Diet. Chapter 2 followed with the famous Article 9 renunciation-of-war clause: 'War as a sovereign right of the nation is abolished. The threat or use of force is forever renounced as a means for settling disputes with any other nation.' Chapter 3's list of thirty-one civil and human rights went beyond the American Constitution, for example, in guaranteeing the right of collective bargaining and forbidding discrimination on the basis of race, creed, sex, social status or family origin. State Shinto ended with a guarantee of freedom of religion and separation of religion and the state.

Not surprisingly, the Japanese government officials when presented with the new draft responded with shocked silence. In the garden, just as a B-29 flew overhead, Whitney remarked to the Japanese interpreter, 'We have been enjoying your atomic sunshine', a less than subtle reminder of who was in charge. Over the next few weeks the Japanese tried in vain to obtain substantive revisions to the American draft before submitting it to the Diet. Approval came in June after lengthy discussions, and on 3 November 1946, the ninety-fourth anniversary of the Meiji emperor's birthday, Emperor Hirohito announced promulgation of the new Constitution. By this time it had been warmly embraced by Japanese at all levels. Two years later, even the former minister in charge of constitutional affairs wrote a children's book extolling the Constitution's ideals of peace, popular sovereignty and fundamental human rights. In John Dower's view, this provides an example of how Japanese sincerely embraced the ideas of democracy initially forced upon them.

The democratic revolution below

While radically restructuring the political system, the new constitution also had far-reaching social consequences, since the civil and human rights provisions demanded further reforms of the civil code and other laws. Once freed of legal restrictions, many Japanese people in all spheres of activity took advantage of the opportunities to extend democratization and express themselves.

Soon after surrender, feminists such as Ichikawa Fusae had again taken up the fight to win political and other rights. A new electoral law granted women the right to vote, which women exercised in the 1946 general election in record numbers, and thirty-nine women were elected to the Diet. With the new Constitution declaring equality between men and women, amendments to the civil code followed, significantly improving the legal status of women. Most important was the abolition of the *ie*, the family household system which had institutionalized patriarchal authority since the beginning of the century. This change and other new laws stipulated women's legal equality in marriage, the family, education and the workplace. We will see here and in later chapters that equality for women as well as for minorities has not necessarily been achieved in practice, but in the early Occupation years SCAP's insistence on emancipation of women fostered new portrayals of women in the media and opened up more possibilities for choice in their life aspirations.

In film, for example, promoting women's emancipation was one idea that SCAP film censors would approve. More lead roles for women consequently became available, and women did not appear only as mainstays of the family as in wartime films. In 1946 the studio Shochiku produced a whole series of movies about the 'new woman', including Mizoguchi Kenji's *Women's Victory* (*Josei no shōri*) about professional women in law. The following year Mizoguchi and Kinugasa Teinosuke made biographical films about Matsui Sumako, an early twentieth-century stage actress famous for playing Ibsen heroines, while Kinoshita Keisuke made a film about a young girl who opposes her family to marry the man she loves.

Film-makers also took up other themes that they thought exemplified democracy and freedom. Some themes, notably showing the kiss on screen, aimed more at sensationalism, but nevertheless were defended as freedom and democracy in action. 'Some even went so far as to say that this kind of sensationalism *was* democracy and that democracy *was* license.'[6] Japanese had long regarded kissing as a private act – only foreigners kissed in public – and kissing had been banned from films during the war. Although SCAP actively encouraged the screen kiss, Japanese film studios did not need much encouragement to take it up, for it proved enormously popular with audiences as well as stirring up all kinds of debate over whether it was 'Japanese or not', was motivated 'merely commercially', possessed any sexual meaning, and even whether it was hygienic.

The establishment of 'red-line' districts for prostitution provided another example of practices dubiously justified in the name of human rights. Projecting the behaviour of their own imperial troops abroad on to expectations of the occupying troops' behaviour, the Home Ministry had set up 'comfort facilities' to service the sexual needs of American GIs. Although SCAP initially supported the policy, it reversed its stance in January 1946 and ordered the abolition of all 'public' prostitution on the grounds of its being undemocratic and a violation of women's human rights. The more pragmatic reason was the spread of venereal disease among the troops. Prostitution did not end, though, and the *pan pan* ('woman of the dark') with bright red lipstick and nail polish, cigarette and trendy clothes became a figure associated with characteristic images of postwar Japan. She even became the subject of a popular children's game, *pan pan asobi* (pretending to be a prostitute). The Japanese government responded to SCAP's order by designating 'red-line' districts on police maps of Tokyo where prostitution was allowed, declaring that women had the *right* to become prostitutes. Surveys of *pan pan* discovered that while some had turned to prostitution out of economic desperation, others did so 'out of curiosity', and still others for the gifts that American servicemen showered on them.

The fuss over screen kisses and ambivalence towards the materialistic, Americanized *pan pan* indicates the craze for American ideas and customs that took over popular culture during the Occupation years. This Americanization had already begun in the prewar decades, as described in Chapter 6. Jazz, social dancing and baseball became popular again, for example, as did foreign films. Women's magazines, department stores and advertising again held up American fashions and images of beauty as the ideals for women. Nylon stockings came with the Americans, along with the ideal of long legs and big bosoms. In addition, the popular comic strip and movie *Blondie* presented images of the lifestyle of a 'typical' middle-class American family. Aspects of Americanization were evident in the popular Japanized English words and phrases of the time for things like the jitterbug, the whodunit, the pin-up and the best-seller. On the more political side, publishers also supplied popular handbooks of new terms such as 'open shop/closed shop', 'picket', 'feminism', 'class consciousness' and 'popular sovereignty'.

Left-wing critics imagined a conspiracy by Occupation authorities and Japanese conservative politicians to encourage the 'three Ss' – screen, sex, and sports – to prevent participation in radical politics and protest movements, but some studios and film-makers, such as Kinoshita Keisuke and Kurosawa Akira, made serious films showing that democracy meant more than licence and sensationalism. Kurosawa's *No Regrets for My Youth* (*Waga seishun ni kuinashi*), for example, made academic freedom its subject in 1946. Kurosawa later joined up with two other directors to make *Those Who Make Tomorrow* (*Asu no tsukuru hitobito*), a film which openly promoted the campaign to form a union in the Toho studio and depicted union members' takeover of the film company.

The actual strikes and use of the 'production control' technique in the last of three disputes, which eventually led to Toho's demise, indicates the enthusiasm with which workers participated in labour actions, and the appeal of left-wing radicalism and militancy in the early postwar climate of rights

and freedom. The April 1946 election revealed a new-found political consciousness and the appeal of democracy not only among women as 363
political parties put up 2770 candidates for election, and demonstrations in
May reflected the rising of a democratic revolution below. After being banned
for twenty years, May Day rallies in major cities throughout the country
attracted as many as two million participants according to some estimates.
The leftist American journalist Mark Gayn described Tokyo scenes full of
joyous singing and red flags. Placards calling for food reflected the food crisis,
but others expressed the desire for democracy and equality. Later in the
month a Food May Day attracted participation by about 250,000 people in
a demonstration in front of the imperial palace. Large numbers of housewives, children, female students and teachers were conspicuous among the
demonstrators. Ironically, their appeal to the emperor coincided with the
draft of the new Constitution proclaiming popular sovereignty which had
just been made public.

SCAP's harsh response to these demonstrations presaged the shift in policy that was to come at the end of the following year, but did not stop the
growth of popular movements. MacArthur issued a warning to the Japanese
people 'that the growing tendency towards mass violence and physical processes of intimidation, under organized leadership, present a grave menace
to the future development of Japan', and he threatened to 'take the necessary
steps to control and remedy such a deplorable situation' if it continued.[7] His
condemnation of 'excesses by disorderly minorities' signalled the emerging
association of popular demonstrations and especially the worker movement
with Soviet communism. Despite the warning, students held a 'Student May
Day' later in May, and labour unionists continued their organizing activities and mobilized strikes. The summer of 1946 saw the peak of 'production
control' takeovers and the establishment of two rival labour federations:
the anti-communist, socialist-led Sōdōmei (All Japan General Federation of
Trade Unions) and the communist-dominated Sanbetsu (National Congress
of Industrial Unions). Moreover, although the conservative Yoshida Shigeru
became prime minister in late May 1946, SCAP reforms did not end there.
As mentioned earlier, many reforms followed the approval of the new Constitution which pleased Japanese progressives and disgruntled conservatives.

The 'reverse course' begins

A pivotal point in working-class history and Occupation policy came with
plans for a general strike to take place on 1 February 1947. Rampant inflation was wiping out wage gains, and food distributions remained unreliable,
although American food shipments after the May demonstrations averted
acute shortages. Labour unions representing three million workers planned
to close down government offices and key industries, but assured authorities
that essential telecommunications, food deliveries and railway services to
the Occupation forces would not be interrupted. Nevertheless, on the eve of

the strike MacArthur intervened to prohibit 'the use of so deadly a social weapon'. To strike coordinator Ii Yashirō, this revealed that Occupation authorities were 'deceiving the Japanese people with democracy only at the tip of their tongues'.[8] It proved to be a critical moment which turned the Japanese left wing to anti-Americanism.

In retrospect and certainly in left-wing histories, suppression of the strike symbolized abandonment of reform, although 1947 still witnessed a general election which brought a socialist-led cabinet to power (though very short-lived) and important legislation, including revision of the civil code and enactment of the Labour Standards Law, to implement provisions of the new Constitution which came into effect in May. A new Labour Ministry, including a women's and minors' bureau, was also established. Nevertheless, a vicious cycle had been started as communists and radical labour activists became more militant, which only alienated Occupation authorities further, turning them away from reformism and towards more support for the conservatives. Meanwhile, developments in Europe from early 1948 were reflecting the breakdown of cooperation between the Soviet Union and its wartime Allies. This and the increasing successes of the communist armies in China heightened the Americans' desire to prevent a communist revolution in Japan and, in the emerging Cold War international environment, to turn Japan into an ally standing as a bulwark against communist 'totalitarianism' in Asia. Conservative criticism of SCAP reformism at home at a time when MacArthur was nurturing presidential ambitions may also have contributed to the slowdown in the pace of reform during 1948.

During 1948 the 'reverse course' in Occupation policy became clear. In March SCAP prohibited regional strikes among postal workers, and in the summer MacArthur withdrew the right to strike or bargain collectively from public service workers. Public enterprise workers retained the right to bargain collectively, but not to strike. This happened as a bribery scandal tarnished the reputations of members of the coalition government, which included socialists. In December an injunction halted a coal miners' strike. While the parameters of acceptable labour union activity contracted, substantial American measures for economic recovery and rehabilitation of industry began – an economically weak Japan might be more vulnerable to a communist takeover. The programme of economic deconcentration slowed down to encourage private enterprise, and SCAP turned its attention to ending runaway inflation and black marketeering.

In early 1949 Joseph Dodge arrived in Japan, and like a 'whirlwind' set in motion policies aimed at price stability and a balanced budget. This was intended not only to decrease the likelihood of a communist revolution, but also to reduce the costs of the Occupation and to prepare Japan for a competitive role in the world economy. Aside from insisting on tax restructuring and budget cuts, Dodge had the Japanese government institute a fixed exchange rate of ¥360 to US$1.00 which forced Japanese exporters to cut costs and make their products competitive with foreign goods. As this occurred in the 1950s and 1960s the yen became undervalued, which helped Japanese exports even further. Meanwhile, the Japanese government under Yoshida Shigeru took important steps to stimulate economic activity, including establishment of the Ministry of International Trade and Industry which Chalmers Johnson has called 'the single most powerful instrument for carrying out industrial policy' in Japan.

The so-called Dodge Line had both beneficial and detrimental results. On the positive side it resulted in curbing inflation and reducing consumer prices. It also turned the budget deficit into a surplus in 1950 and encouraged entreprenerial activities. However, the deflationary policies also led to more unemployment, as approximately 160,000 government workers and 330,000 private sector workers lost their jobs in 1949 alone. In addition, wage increases ended, and the number of bankruptcies rose as money became tight. The attack on black marketeering deprived farmers of sales and higher food prices. Although many economists believe that without the Korean War the Dodge Line would have led the Japanese economy into a depression, Japanese conservatives and business leaders admired Dodge and stuck to his balanced budget policies for many years after.

Radical labour unions, in contrast, responded to these policies with work stoppages, sabotage and violent demonstrations throughout the country. These, in turn, provoked a 'red purge' of about 11,000 union members in the public sector between the end of 1949 and the outbreak of the Korean War the following June. After the war began the purge was extended to the private sector, including the media, and at the same time 'depurging' of purged militarists and ultranationalists allowed many individuals to return to public life. Although the Communist Party remained legal, its central committee members were excluded from public service after communist protesters roughed up American soldiers taking photographs during a Memorial Day celebration at the imperial palace plaza. Most of the party's top leaders subsequently left the country or went underground for the duration of the Occupation, and publication of the party's newspaper *Akahata* was suspended until the Occupation ended. The labour movement itself split in reaction to the increased violence and militancy of the communists as well as to the shift in SCAP's policies. Quarrels within the movement resulted in anti-communist forces breaking away and forming a new organization called Sōhyō (General Council of Trade Unions) in July 1950, but while favouring moderate tactics, it did not support the conservative policies of either SCAP or Japanese cabinets. The tough anti-communist actions had alienated socialists and social democrats at the same time as they destroyed the influence of the far left in the labour movement and politics.

Winding down the Occupation

The outbreak of war in Korea accelerated the 'reverse course' in SCAP policies, but also marked the beginning of a new relationship between Japan and the United States as the Occupation moved towards its end. Instead of the poor, unarmed Japan desired in 1945, American foreign policy now required an economically strong and rearmed Japan, though still subordinate and dependent on the United States. American orders for war materials as well as other goods and services, amounting to about US$2.3 billion, created a huge boom for Japanese industry. The procurements pushed industrial and mineral production, such as coal, back to prewar levels, and, contrary to American leaders' vision of Japan as the maker of cheap consumer goods, boosted the shift from light to heavy industry.

The United States did not pressure Japan to make a direct military contribution in Korea, but did order a limited rearmament beginning with strengthening of the police. Prime Minister Yoshida Shigeru initially went along enthusiastically with the plans until it became clear that MacArthur's order to set up a police reserve was actually for the establishment of an 'embryonic army'. Thereafter his enthusiasm receded, and he even secretly asked Socialist Party leaders to hold protest demonstrations to impress John Foster Dulles, who was leading the negotiations for the peace treaty. Yoshida managed to reduce the size of the National Police Reserve from the Americans' initial target of 300,000 to 75,000. Nevertheless, he never publicly acknowledged even in his memoirs that the National Police Reserve meant the beginning of remilitarization. Organized along military lines and developed in close cooperation with US military men, there is little doubt that the new force was 'the disguise of a new Japanese army',[9] but because of the confusion surrounding it, no opposition arose in Japan. It did possess the character of a defence force without 'war-making potential', as prohibited in the Constitution, in that it mainly had ground forces and initially no air forces.

As the war continued into 1951, the Japanese received the shocking news that President Truman had dismissed MacArthur for insubordination as commander of the United Nations forces in Korea. MacArthur nevertheless enjoyed a hero's farewell from Japan in April and was visited at his residence by the emperor himself. Memories of MacArthur as a statesman remained stronger in Japan than in the United States, but they would have been even stronger if not for his remarks to Congress upon his return. When asked if the Japanese would defend the democratic freedoms gained during the Occupation, MacArthur tried to cast the Japanese in a more favourable light than the Germans. In trying to affirm the achievement of the 'great social revolution', however, he likened the Japanese to 'a boy of twelve' who was 'in a very tuitionary condition' and therefore 'still close enough to origin to be elastic and acceptable to new concepts'.[10] Although many Japanese leaders and commentators had referred to themselves as MacArthur's children, they now felt ashamed and insulted. Several large companies even got together to publish an advertisement proclaiming 'We Are Not Twelve-Year-Olds!! – Japanese Manufactures Admired by the World.'[11] This reaction is an indication that by 1951 the Japanese were getting tired of the

Occupation and its paternalistic authoritarianism as well as being on the road to self-sustained economic growth.

It was to be another year before the Occupation officially ended, and even then the American troops did not depart. The peace treaty was signed by forty-nine nations in San Francisco on 8 September 1951, and at the same time the United States and Japan signed a security treaty which put Japan under the American nuclear umbrella in a close relationship known as the San Francisco system. With the treaties, Japan regained its sovereignty except over Okinawa, and the USA obtained the right to maintain bases in Japan and to use its forces to put down internal disturbances if requested by the Japanese government. These provisions did not make the security treaty popular in Japan, as will be discussed further in Chapter 10. The Soviet Union refused to sign the peace treaty, leaving the Kuril Islands north of Hokkaido under its occupation and a source of diplomatic friction in the following decades. But after the signing ceremony Yoshida Shigeru told his advisers that as a loser, Japan had done better at San Francisco than as a victor at Versailles.

The legacy of the Occupation

It is no wonder that the Occupation with all its contradictions and mixed messages has been evaluated in many different ways. Its effects have been both praised and blamed, and opinions have also diverged on its lasting impact. At the Occupation's end MacArthur emphasized how much the country had changed, while Emperor Hirohito rejoiced at Japan's having endured the unendurable unchanged in his poem celebrating the event:

> The winter wind has gone
> and long-awaited spring has arrived
> with double-petalled cherry blossoms.[12]

Later evaluations have differed according to people's assessment of the degree to which the 'reverse course' turned back the democratization of the early Occupation reforms. Ironically, the anti-Americanism of the Japanese left in the decades after the Occupation derived from the perception of Americans' betrayal of early Occupation ideals and promises. As we will see in Chapter 10, conservative Japanese governments accelerated the reverse course during the 1950s, but the popular commitment to peace and democracy had become so deeply entrenched that conservative politicians have been unable to change even one word of the Constitution. In foreign relations there is also no disagreement that the Occupation reversed the wartime relationship of enmity, establishing instead the close economic, social and political relationship between Japan and the United States that continues to the present day, even though not trouble-free. As Yoshida observed, 'The Americans came into our country as our enemies, but after an occupation lasting little less than seven years, an understanding grew up between the two peoples which is remarkable in the history of the modern world.'[13]

Just as American troops did not depart with the official end of the Occupation in April 1952, neither did issues of the war or Occupation. Yoshida also described Japan in 1952 as divided at a 'thirty-eighth parallel' like Korea between a liberal/left opposition defending 'demilitarization and democratization' and a conservative coalition bent on rolling back the 'excesses' of Occupation reforms. These conflicts which dominated the politics of the 1950s are one focus of the next chapter. Their social ramifications are another.

10 Conflict and consensus in the 1950s

Up until 1960 issues raised by the war and the Occupation continued to dominate Japanese politics and society. Until the mid-1950s many Japanese remained preoccupied with survival or, if not destitute, with just making ends meet, but at the same time many thousands involved themselves actively in the political and social issues of the day. The great ideological divide created by the 'reverse course' in SCAP policy and accelerated by Japanese conservative governments made the 1950s a decade of political turmoil. It was marked by violent popular movements and mass demonstrations as well as angry rhetoric between the 'progressive' and 'conservative' political camps, which culminated in the anti-Security Treaty demonstrations and the coinciding Miike coal mine strike in 1960.

Out of this conflict emerged a conservative hegemony centred on the Liberal Democratic Party which consolidated a monopoly on the Diet and ruled in close cooperation with big business and the bureaucracy. The parallel development was marginalization of the left as a perpetual opposition party/ parties, but through their strident protests and success in mobilizing mass demonstrations, the socialists and communists became forces that had to be accommodated, and Marxism became normalized as part of Japanese intel- lectual and political life. In foreign policy too the decade witnessed estab- lishment of the concerns and alignments which have characterized Japanese international relations up to the present day.

While the configuration of political parties and international alignments became stabilized, there also evolved structures and patterns of behaviour in the home and workplace which have come to dominate our images of postwar Japanese society. Militant unionism was repressed or tamed, but workers won a compromise from management. Out of the industrial conflict of the late 1940s and 1950s the so-called Japanese employment system came to maturity, ensuring workers in large corporations of steady wage increases, job security and humane treatment. With these developments in labour rela- tions and spectacular economic growth in the second half of the decade, the lifestyle of the new middle class of 'salarymen' which had become an ideal in the 1920s now became an attainable model for a large fraction of the Japanese population. This model and the demands of the company, combined with increasing suburbanization, extended the prewar trend towards the separation of home and work and accompanying changes in gender roles. Although still unequal in politics and the workplace, for many women, as well as for business managers and conservative bureaucrats and politicians, increased authority of women over family and home was not unwelcome.

Here is one example of the consensus that grew out of the conflicts of the decade, although not all marginalized groups received some compensation for inequality as women did. By the end of the decade, intense confrontations over political and social issues had declined, and stability returned as Japanese throughout society and politics focused on the new national goal of economic growth.

Yoshida Shigeru and consolidation of a conservative hegemony

The key person in setting the domestic and foreign policies of conservative governments for the next three decades was Yoshida Shigeru. According to a public opinion poll in 1984 and to many historians, he was the greatest Japanese figure of the twentieth century. The years he was prime minister from 1948 to 1954 are known as the 'Yoshida era', during which he fixed the structure and operation as well as the policies of the ruling Liberal Democratic Party.

Like many other postwar conservative politicians, Yoshida had already had a long career in the pre-1945 era. Early Occupation reformers called him an 'old liberal', meaning a rather reactionary Taishō liberal type – elitist and paternalistic. But Yoshida was known for being an Anglophile and a wartime peace advocate who had even spent some time in prison for promoting an early surrender. He was more a realist than a staunch pacifist, and in the political environment of the late 1940s he qualified as a conservative, but after 1947 when Occupation authorities were more worried about communism than Japanese remilitarization, they gave him their support. Although nicknamed 'One Man' (*Wan Man*) because of his arrogance and autocratic manner, he got on well with MacArthur and other American leaders, and skilfully negotiated the peace treaty and relations with the United States to support Japan's return to international diplomatic circles and marketplaces.

While Yoshida and other conservatives were pleased with the peace treaty and security pact with the United States, the provisions for American bases and the possibility of American intervention to suppress external aggressors or internal rebellions split the socialists into right and left wings. The right wing supported the peace treaty but not the security treaty, while the left wing and the communists opposed both. Yoshida's Liberal Party had a majority in the Diet, so both were easily ratified, but the split among the socialists continued, undermining protests against further reverse course measures that came after the Occupation ended.

These measures included the transformation of the National Police Reserve into a 'public safety force' in 1952 and into a 'self-defence force' in 1954.

While Yoshida and subsequent conservative leaders in fact resisted American pressure to build up the military, socialists protested against these conversions as steps towards the remilitarization of Japan and made unarmed neutrality the centrepiece of their foreign policy platform. As depurged wartime politicians and government officials returned to political activity, the 'rectification of excesses' multiplied, provoking confrontations in the Diet each time. A subversive activities prevention law smacking of the repressive controls of the 1925 Peace Preservation Law was passed in 1952, and the police were recentralized under the National Police Agency. Recentralization also occurred in educational structures, beginning with replacement of locally elected school boards by boards appointed by the Ministry of Education and with the establishment of a centrally administered teacher rating system. The Ministry also exerted increasing control over curricula and textbooks. The end of trust-busting efforts led to reconcentration of commercial and industrial enterprises into powerful *keiretsu* groupings. These represented reconfigurations of the old zaibatsu, such as Mitsui, Mitsubishi and Sumitomo, though different from them in being more internally competitive and diversified in their stockholders.

Hatoyama Ichirō was one of the depurged officials who returned to political power, forcing Yoshida out of the prime ministership in 1954. By this time, however, Yoshida had constructed a strong faction in the Liberal Party which he passed on to his followers, Ikeda Hayato and Satō Eisaku, both of whom became prime ministers in the 1960s. When the right and left wings of the Socialist Party (JSP) reunited in 1955, the two conservative parties responded with a merger into the Liberal Democratic Party (LDP) which maintained control over the government until 1993. This one-party domination became known as the '1955 system'. By the time of the merger, the LDP's characteristic policies were set: namely, anti-communism at home and abroad and an emphasis on economic growth. It worked closely with big business and the bureaucracy, drawing many of its leaders from these groups, while it attracted voters mainly among rural inhabitants, small businesspeople and middle-class white-collar workers.

Progressives confronted conservative governments over foreign policy as well as domestic issues. Socialist and communist groups, supported by students, intellectuals and labour activists, staged numerous demonstrations against American bases and the visits of American ships. A foreign policy issue provoked demonstrations in 1960 which marked the peak of conflict between the progressive and conservative camps. When the government renegotiated the Japanese–American Security Treaty, progressives mounted a massive campaign to prevent its ratification. This famous anti-Security Treaty or 'Anpo' struggle brought hundreds of thousands of workers, students, white-collar workers, intellectuals and housewives into street demonstrations outside the Diet. Socialist Party representatives jammed the corridor to prevent the Speaker of the Lower House from entering the Diet for the vote on ratification. Prime Minister Kishi Nobusuke called in the police to remove the obstructors and literally to place the Speaker in his chair. When the socialists boycotted the session, the Diet majority of LDP members approved the treaty.

There was so much public criticism against Kishi's autocratic methods and continuing riots that he was forced to resign after US President Dwight D. Eisenhower cancelled his visit to Japan, but the LDP's hold on power remained firm while the socialists split apart again. Reunification of the socialists in 1955 had not overcome differences between the right and left wings, so that, despite their success in mounting mass protests against LDP policies, they were not attracting mainstream voters. Doctrinaire squabbles and an unrealistic foreign policy of non-alignment in the midst of the Cold War alienated voters except among organized workers. The split between the right and left wings became official in 1960 when the right wing broke away and formed the Democratic Socialist Party.

The Anpo demonstrations were seen by some as a sign of the potential for development of participatory democracy at the grassroots level, but their failure in the face of an autocratic government and the redirection of the public's attention away from foreign policy matters and towards achievement of the 'bright life' (*akarui seikatsu*) made 1960 a turning point in Japan's postwar political history. At the same time, while the socialists and communists soon faced the prospect of being perpetual minority parties, their vigorous defence of 'demilitarization and democracy' had blocked conservatives' attempts at constitutional revision and helped to set an informal but publicly acknowledged limit to defence budgets at no more than 1 per cent of the GNP.

Working out a labour–management settlement

A similar outcome resulted from one of the largest and most violent strikes in Japanese history, which also took place in 1960 and occupies with the Anpo struggle one of the most significant places in the history of the Socialist Party's opposition to corporate capitalism. The strike in the Miike coal mines of Kyushu concluded a decade of labour–management battles as management took back the initiative in reworking conditions of employment.

During the first two years of the Occupation, organized workers had achieved not only the right to organize and strike, but even more than what they had demanded in the 1920s and 1930s in relation to job security, wage security and higher status. Management discussion councils gave them a voice in management of factory affairs, while collective contracts gave them regular wage increases and greater job security. The Labour Standards Law of 1947 set minimum standards for working conditions and unemployment benefits for all workers, and a new national commission on labour relations sided with union demands for wages which guaranteed workers' livelihood ('living wages'). Within the new worker-friendly legal and political framework supported by SCAP policies, workers themselves adopted aggressive tactics to win concessions from management.

After SCAP policies turned against communism and radical unionism and the stringent economic policies of the Dodge Line created a need for companies to become more competitive, managers seized the opportunity to regain control of the workplace. Bitter conflict, sometimes violent, characterized the factories of the early 1950s, as it did the floor of the Diet. Management nearly always won these disputes, rolling back many of labour's gains during the 1945 to 1947 period. By the mid-1950s a new labour relationship had evolved in large private firms into what has been called the Japanese employment system. It was slanted to management's benefit, but workers were nevertheless in a better position than they had been either before or during the war.

Management's offensive began in the spring of 1949 with enterprises throughout heavy industry proposing contract revisions aimed at destroying 'old' unions, reducing the 'excessive' powers of management discussion councils, and replacing the requirement for union agreement on personnel decisions with a requirement for simply consultation. As the government's Red Purge moved into the private sector during 1950, managers attacked old unions by firing suspected communists while they encouraged formation of more moderate 'second' unions. In a typical case, Tōshiba concluded a contract with the new union and recognized it as the sole bargaining representative of its workers. These new unions were enterprise-based and only later moved into a loose industrial federation called Dōmei with other moderate unions. They distinguished themselves from the unions making up the militant, though anti-communist Sōhyō federation. Labour bureaucrats in the government supported this type of moderate enterprise unionism in keeping with interwar precedents for 'sound unionism'.

Besides success in destroying radical unions, management in large enterprises took back many of the gains which workers had won in wages and job security. In the tight credit environment of 1949 under the Dodge Line, managers often had no money to grant wage increases even had they wanted to. They worked to eliminate the concept of livelihood wages that were paid without reference to productivity gains or profits. In this economic situation unions could do little more than try to prevent wage cuts, but when the Korean War boom brought inflation, unions pushed again for higher wages on the grounds of livelihood need, demanding fixed, across-the-board increases (a 'base-up' raise) which in effect raised the minimum pay level and benefited younger, often radical workers more than higher level experienced workers. Managers opposed base-up raises since they increased the total wage structure of the firm and offered instead 'regular' raises, that is, a percentage raise for individual workers.

Wage settlements during the early 1950s usually included some mixture of the base-up and regular wage, but overall represented a major victory for management in undermining the livelihood wage concept. These were won at great cost, however, since the unions fought hard. Intense confrontations took place in mines and car factories as well as steel, shipbuilding, machinery and electronics plants. Moreover, as Andrew Gordon points out, the wage system that had matured by the mid-1950s was 'more complex than terms such as *management victory* or *labor defeat* convey'.[1] Rather, it represented an 'amalgam' of prewar, wartime and early postwar wage practices. Entry wages and subsequent raises came to be based on a combination of livelihood factors such as age and evaluation of performance. Seniority was important because it was an indicator of both need and ability. According to Gordon, the most important change over the three periods was the 'shift from an arbitrary, customary wage system to one of greater regularity and, at times, rigidity',[2] though from the union perspective, the 1950s brought back insecurity and the potential for abuse of power by management.

Battles over job security proved to be even more ferocious and lengthy than those over wages, and a settlement over job security did not emerge in most industries until the late 1950s. The Miike coal miners' strike, for example, went on for 313 days and grew in intensity and violence as the struggle continued. Others at Japan Steel and Amagasaki Steel lasted for 173 days and 77 days respectively. Like most of these strikes, the one at Miike arose out of the company's decision to 'rationalize' its workforce. In this specific case, Mitsui's actions followed a government decision to redirect industry's energy source from coal to oil, leading as in many other countries to the closing down of many coal mines. Mitsui, owner of six of the largest colleries in Japan, called for the voluntary retirement of 5000 of its 35,000 workers. At Miike, where there was a strong, militant union of 14,000 members, the call elicited only 1000 instead of the target of 2000 offers to retire. When the company 'nominated' 1200 other workers, including 300 union activists, the union called a strike. In response, the company locked out union workers and, in a move that had become common in large enterprises since the beginning of the decade, formed a second union sympathetic to management. Violence erupted when the company brought in non-union workers and gangster *yakuza* thugs who attacked union leaders, even killing one. Fifteen thousand national police arrived at the same time that the Anpo demonstrations in Tokyo were gathering momentum. Sympathetic unions, in turn, sent 15,000 workers to lend support to the striking coal miners. The situation had reached crisis point with television broadcasts sending out images of a nation apparently on the brink of revolution. The government finally persuaded Mitsui and the union to accept binding arbitration, which ended in defeat for the miners.

However, as in most industries the costs of dismissals had been so great in lost production, bad publicity and low morale that by the end of the 1950s companies tried to avoid large-scale firings and instead to transfer or retrain workers. They also hired more temporary workers to act as a buffer in slow times. At the end of the 1950s the proportion of temporary workers in some industries such as electrical machinery manufacture reached one-third and more. Unions, on their side, could not prevent hiring of temporary workers, and, although they worked to improve the status of these workers, this was mainly related to their upgrading to 'regular' workers who enjoyed a certain degree of job security and regular wage increases. Unions also could not prevent dismissals and therefore supported transfers and retraining of regular workers.

The plight of temporary workers, both male and female, is a reminder that the so-called Japanese employment system which reached maturity in the 1950s encompassed only regular workers in large enterprises (generally over 500 workers). The majority of workers in industry continued to work in non-unionized small and medium-sized firms where they did not enjoy job security or steadily rising wages. Even the regular workers in large companies had no guarantee of 'permanent' employment, so that this common characterization of the Japanese employment system has been overstated. Still, although management in the 1950s succeeded in wresting back control over the workplace in terms of wage structure and personnel decisions and eliminated radical unionism, unions did not disappear altogether, and blue-collar workers did not lose the recognition and respect as 'employees' equal in their status with white-collar employees that had been gained during the early Occupation years. In the next section we will see that blue-collar workers in large enterprises moved closer to equality with white-collar workers in their lifestyles as well.

From just 'managing to get along' to the 'bright new life'

In 1951 Ronald Dore conducted a study of a heterogeneous neighbourhood in central Tokyo.[3] This will give us a picture of urban life and standards of living at the beginning of the decade which we can compare with the picture provided by Ezra Vogel's study of salaryman families in another Tokyo neighbourhood at the end of the decade. Although some sociologists may express doubts about making a comparison between the two dissimilar neighbourhoods, it will help to give a sense of the tremendous changes in lifestyle and standard of living experienced by most Japanese during the 1950s.

The focus here is on changes in urban life and particularly the new middle class, since the 1950s saw a dramatic acceleration in the shift of workers out of agriculture and into industry and the service sector. At the beginning of the decade close to 50 per cent of all workers were employed in the primary sector of the economy. By the middle of the decade it was still over 40 per cent, but by its end the proportion had dropped to about one-third. Although the new middle class of salarymen did not make up the majority of workers at the end of the decade, their pattern of life had become 'a symbol of the desirable life', dominating the mass media, popular literature and 'how-to' books, and thus exerting an important influence on Japanese in the rest of society. Moreover, in contrast to the interwar period when the salaryman's way of life had become an ideal, if unrealistic for even most salarymen, the tremendous economic growth that began in 1955 made attainment of that ideal not a dream, but a real possibility. And not only for most salarymen's families, but also for many families both rural and urban.

In 1951, however, most of the inhabitants of Dore's study were just 'managing to get along'. Housing still remained scarce and primitive. Many families lived in tiny apartments or shared houses. A policeman, for example, lived with his wife and three children in a nine-foot square room with one large cupboard for storing the bedding during the daytime. Their furniture consisted of only a table and two large chests of drawers and cupboards which they had to keep in the corridor. The policeman's wife had one gas ring on which to cook rice (their primary food), accompanied by vegetables, inexpensive fish several times a week and meat on rare occasions. They shared one sink with a cold water tap and one toilet with three other families, and took their baths (but not every day) at the public bathhouse. Heating in winter came only from a brazier burning charcoal or anthracite briquettes.

The family of a widow and two children who worked as clerks in the borough office was representative of many white-collar workers. They lived in an old, small single-storey house made up of three rooms plus a kitchen and a lavatory, but no bath. Their kitchen had a sink and two gas rings, and they possessed a few more pieces of furniture and decorative objects than did the policeman's family. This family owned both a sewing machine and a radio, but no refrigerator, electric iron or electric fan. If they were frugal, they might be able to buy these three items in the future, giving them not only more comfort and convenience, but prestige in their neighbourhood. Families in this neighbourhood often brought out their new gadgets, especially electric fans, to show off to visitors.

Dore's survey of twenty household budgets showed expenditures on food and rent similar to Japanese national averages and to the average distribution of spending in West Germany in 1950. Most of the families were spending almost half or more than half of their incomes on food and about 10 per cent on rent. Less than 5 per cent went on medical expenses and over 5 per cent on insurance and savings, since state social welfare schemes were inadequate in both their coverage and scale of benefits. In keeping with assumptions tracing back to the Tokugawa period, the state extended ongoing public assistance only to those incapable of working. It did not adopt the principle of guaranteeing a subsistence minimum to everyone in society. Even temporary assistance was accompanied by programmes to encourage self-help, thrift and hard work, based on the belief that long-term assistance would engender laziness and dependence. Partly as a consequence of these official attitudes, the receipt of public assistance carried a social stigma.

The Korean War boom and American assistance provided the stimulus and supportive environment for Japan's economic recovery during the early 1950s. American purchases of war materials increased production and provided the capital for significant investment in plant and equipment. Beyond the end of the war, the close relationship established with the United States brought with it American efforts to foster Japanese trade by opening its markets to Japanese products and by supporting reparations treaties with Southeast Asian countries that provided for Japan to furnish goods and services rather than its own industrial plant. Many American firms also made technical cooperation agreements with Japanese companies, enabling Japanese industry to catch up with advanced technology.

At the same time conservative governments' prioritization of economic growth supported the regeneration of Japanese industry. In 1951 the Development Bank replaced the Reconstruction Bank to provide low interest loans for industrial investment, particularly in certain industries such as fertilizers, coal, iron and steel. Tax reforms provided incentives for investment, and a system of foreign exchange allocation allowed officials to channel raw materials to selected companies. The Ministry of International Trade and Industry (MITI) sponsored the reconcentration of companies into conglomerates (*keiretsu*) centred around banks, and supervised their allocation of production quotas and raw materials by what became known as 'administrative guidance'.

All this American assistance and consistent government support occurred in a period of economic expansion worldwide, so that by 1955 the industrial production index had not only returned to the bench-mark level of 1934 to 1936 (100) but risen well beyond it to 181. For ordinary Japanese this meant that their food consumption regained prewar levels, and they could buy inexpensive clothes easily. No one, however, expected the spectacular growth rates which began with the 'Jimmu boom'[4] of 1955. Japan's economy grew by an average rate of nearly 10 per cent during the second half of the decade as production shifted from textiles to consumer goods requiring more advanced technology such as motorcyles, and to steel, shipbuilding, machinery, chemical products and other heavy industrial products. The so-called 'economic miracle' had begun, though Japan's export production did not take off until the following decade.

By the end of the decade over 70 per cent of the Japanese people felt that they were part of the 'middle classes'. This included many blue-collar workers and farmers as well as those employed in occupations which we might usually think of as 'middle class', such as small shopkeepers, white-collar workers and professionals. Such a consciousness as well as the imminent reality of a middle-class standard of living was made possible not only by the rapid economic growth since 1955, but also by the early postwar reforms of land reform, zaibatsu dissolution and labour reform having worked towards a more equal distribution of income among Japanese. Land reform had created a large class of independent farmers in the countryside, though many did not rely exclusively on farming for their income. The introduction of labour-saving machinery and chemical fertilizers and pesticides also helped to lessen the gap between rural and urban standards of living in addition to reducing the need for agricultural labour. In industry, trust-busting had ended and management had taken back some of labour's gains, but workers had not lost everything in the wage settlements of the early 1950s.

According to the Japanese economist Kōsai Yutaka,

> This middle-class consciousness spurred the rapid diffusion of durable consumer goods, a rising rate of children entering universities, a strong desire for home ownership, and a high savings rate, all of which stimulated economic growth.[5]

Whereas only 7.8 per cent of non-agricultural households owned a black and white television in 1957, by 1960 the proportion had gone up to 44.7 per cent. Similarly, while only 20.2 per cent owned a washing machine in 1957, 40.6 per cent owned one in 1960.[6] Ownership of more household appliances became possible as a smaller proportion of income went on food, declining from over 50 per cent in the early 1950s to 42.7 per cent in 1960.[7]

The proportion of income spent on cultural and entertainment expenses also rose dramatically. The economic boom stimulated by the Korean War was evident not only in manufacturing industries, but also in the mushrooming of amusements and entertainments. Although started in the prewar years, *pachinko* (a kind of pin-ball game) now gained widespread popularity, and thousands of coffee shops opened up. Hot spring resorts revived after a period in the doldrums since the end of the war, while race tracks became crowded every day. Films, which had always been popular since the interwar period, profited too – box-office receipts doubled between 1951 and 1953. The 1950s witnessed the full commercialization of film, turning the Japanese film industry into the biggest producer of films in the world by the end of the decade. After the Red Purge in 1950 eliminated communists from the major companies, a number of leftist independent film companies were formed with political aims in mind. Their emphasis on left-wing subjects did not attract sufficient audiences, however, so most had folded by 1955.

The big companies, in contrast, successfully exploited sex and war to attract large audiences, and through cooperation in the late 1950s divided up the market into separate spheres, each with its own audience. A 1950s boom in teenage sex films stepped up the commercialization of sex. Kisses on screen were no longer a novelty by this time, so these and more adult-oriented sex pictures were more explicit in portrayals of sex. The newcomer actress Kyo Machiko launched her career with a series of sex films which were accompanied by an extensive advertising campaign. Besides being one of the few Japanese actresses who became well known to Western audiences,[8] she was the first Japanese actress to receive public attention for her sex appeal. Several years later another boom in so-called *taiyōzoku* (literally, sun tribe) films about the younger generation featured nudity and violence. Critics, housewives and local government agencies protested against the lack of social responsibility in these films, but they were hugely successful at the box office, as were a number of films which capitalized on a growing wartime nostalgia, especially among former soldiers, also during the mid-1950s. These often glorified the *kamikaze* pilots or military leaders such as Admiral Yamamoto Isoroku, commander of the fleet that attacked Pearl Harbor. Significantly, however, popular sentiments against rearmament were too strong for any film about the self-defence forces to be successful at the box office. Meanwhile, period films continued to be very popular, including some of the best films made by the great directors Kurosawa Akira and Mizoguchi Kenji.[9]

The biggest commercial success of the decade, however, was a home drama, *What is Your Name?*, which eulogized traditional family values. This film version of a popular radio serial appeared in three feature-length instalments in 1953 and 1954. Total attendance figures reached over thirty million, and the film's popularity spawned dozens of 'Machiko' (the name of the heroine) products ranging from kimonos and handkerchiefs to toys and china. Special tours took sightseers to the locations where the films were made.

Such success of a film's spin-offs indicates how significant consumption had become to the 'bright life' which many Japanese were beginning to enjoy and to which virtually all aspired by the end of the 1950s. The rapid spread of television during the late 1950s shaped Japanese conceptions of middle-class life, particularly the material objects and possessions associated with it, as seen in American serials such as *I Love Lucy* and *Father Knows Best*. Ezra Vogel's study of the Mamachi neighbourhood of salaryman families between 1958 and 1960 documents the importance attached to acquisition of new consumer goods. As Vogel observed, 'the excitement of the consumer has been enormous'.[10] Families talked about wanting the 'Three Imperial Treasures', giving the three desired pieces of electrical equipment a value comparable to the Imperial family's sacred mirror, sword and jewel. By the late 1950s these included an electric refrigerator or washing machine or perhaps a vacuum cleaner. As Vogel noted, however, most lacked critical judgement in making purchases, going for a big-name maker (*meekaa*) and appearance rather than the features or capacity of the product.

By the time of Vogel's study the acute housing shortages of the late 1940s and early 1950s had ended, but young middle-class couples usually had to live with their parents or in housing provided by the husband's company for a few years while they saved for the down payment on a house. With the down payment saved, they could obtain a loan from a public agency to buy a house in a suburb like Mamachi. As in the past, it would have been constructed of unpainted wood and consist of only three or four rooms plus a kitchen and bathroom. Most families still used traditional *futon* bedding which would be put away during the daytime so that bedrooms could also be used as living rooms. At this time some kitchens still had dirt floors and, except for very modern ones, most were kept closed to guests. Mamachi houses did not yet have flush toilets and sewer connections, although these were common in other parts of Tokyo.

Despite the improvements since Dore's study, Vogel regarded diet as inadequate by Western standards. Rice continued to be the main dish, with other foods used as accompaniments and flavouring, and meat was still eaten in small quantities. Although most families had a small wooden ice-box, wives shopped daily for fresh fish and vegetables. Many families relied on local shops and friends for making large as well as small purchases, but the fixed-price system of department stores and the freedom to shop in an impersonal setting unencumbered with obligations was becoming more and more attractive.

Social aspects of change with the 'bright life'

To obtain the material comforts of the 'bright life' and the social status of a salaryman, it was now necessary to achieve higher levels of education, especially university education, because large enterprises recruited their regular 'permanent' employees from 'good' universities. Even those who wanted to work in a smaller company had an easier time getting a job or changing jobs if they attended a good university. Admission to a good university in turn entailed success in entrance examinations, which led to such stress and long hours of study that examination preparation became known as 'examination hell'. Admission to a good junior and senior high school thus became important not only for the better training they offered for passing the examination of a prestigious university, but often because they acted as feeder schools to the top-ranking universities. Moreover, because the rank of any given university determined the type of job and company one could qualify for, students who did not get into their preferred university often became *rōnin* (the old term for masterless samurai), studying for another year at special preparatory schools to retake the examination.

Consequently, although Japanese society became increasingly a meritocracy based on educational achievement, and the Occupation's educational reforms had made more university places available and accessible to Japanese, the clear hierarchy of universities and company recruitment policies did not work towards greater egalitarianism. It is also important to note that although university education became the goal for all those who aspired to become part of the new middle class, by the end of the 1950s only a small minority of male high school graduates (not quite 14 per cent) and an even smaller minority of female high school graduates (2.5 per cent) entered four-year universities. However, over half of both sexes went on to senior high school, beyond the compulsory nine years of schooling.

Although the figures for actual university attendance remained low, the heightened importance of education for social mobility influenced family life greatly. Once a couple had saved the down payment for a house, they would begin saving for their children's educational expenses. Even if their children did not attend private schools, there would be expenses for music lessons, private tutors and after-school schools (*juku*). Although both parents made choices about the selection of schools, the mother shouldered the main responsibility for the children's education. Reinforced by school expectations of extensive maternal involvement, her child's performance at school and in examinations became a determinant of her status and the family's as well as her child's. Aside from care and management of the home, helping her children to achieve in school occupied a salaryman wife's time. Although the slogan of 'good wife, wise mother' became discredited after 1945, this was the period when more Japanese families could afford not to have the wife/mother in the paid workforce; in other words, for women to be full-time housewives. In contrast to the past, this was also the period when motherly duties became more important than wifely ones in middle-class families.

Motherly duties became concentrated on fewer children from the 1950s onward. In the late 1940s unemployment and food shortages had become severe not only because of wartime destruction and massive repatriation, but due to a postwar baby boom. Faced with 'overpopulation' problems and escalation in the number of illegal abortions, doctors and government officials had responded positively to pressure from a revived birth control movement. In 1948 the Diet passed the Eugenics Protection Law which permitted abortions in cases where the mother's life or health was endangered, and the following year a revision added 'economic' reasons. A further revision in 1952 allowed doctors to perform induced abortions 'at their discretion'. Birth control advocates such as Katō (formerly Ishimoto) Shizue had mixed feelings about the law because it emphasized abortion rather than contraception to prevent unwanted pregnancy and retained traces of the Nazi-based National Eugenics Law in its title. The law reflected state concerns to control population more than to protect women's health or to increase women's control over their reproductive capacities.

Although legalization of abortion eliminated the dangers of backstreet abortions, such reservations about the law were borne out in subsequent years. More than 700,000 abortions were carried out in the first year following the law's passage, and the number rose continuously until 1955. In that year the government worked with the private Family Planning Federation of Japan to promote contraception instead of abortion. However, although the abortion rate subsequently fell rapidly along with the birth rate, abortions remained the main means of birth control because the most common practices of contraception were the comparatively unreliable methods of rhythm and condoms. Doctors licensed to perform abortions had no desire to promote other, more reliable forms of contraception as they became available, and the Family Planning Federation of Japan itself came to rely on income from condom sales which it bought at a heavily discounted price from a large condom manufacturer. In the 1950s Japanese families therefore gained the ability to plan their family size and structure through legal means, but the limitations on choice of means also became set for the next four decades.

This example of family planning developments indicates the limited interest of government officials and conservative politicians in changing traditional gender roles, despite paying some lip-service to constitutional provisions of equality and the Occupation's promotion of women's emancipation. Educational policies during the 1950s revealed the state's desire to keep women's activities centred on the home and local community. In 1958 the Ministry of Education introduced a course entitled 'Industrial arts and homemaking', but industrial arts was to be taught only to boys and homemaking only to girls. Textbooks in other subjects reinforced the secondary role of female characters and their traditional role as homemakers or workers in historically female-dominated occupations, such as nursing, teaching and waitressing.

Company structures and practices for recruitment and promotion also made it virtually impossible for women to pursue careers in large enterprises either as white- or blue-collar workers. By custom and sometimes by contract, women could work for only a few years between the end of schooling and marriage. Even if they subsequently returned to work, it was not as 'regular' workers, so they missed out on job security and regular wage increases.

Consequently, throughout the 1950s the majority of women who worked did so as unpaid workers on the family farm or in a family enterprise, and, even as job opportunities for waged employment expanded with the service and manufacturing sectors, women were generally limited to clerical and low-skilled work and to insecure and low-wage jobs in small or medium enterprises. Their social status and standard of living thus remained dependent on their husband's occupation. To become the wife of a salaryman with a secure job and steady, though not spectacularly high income was the aspiration of most young Japanese women by the end of the 1950s. Small businessmen, craftsmen and farmers complained that they could not compete with salarymen for desirable brides. If her aspiration was achieved, the salaryman's wife could take pride in ruling over her home and children while the company kept her husband away in long hours of work and business socializing.

Minorities in the 'new' Japan

Just as women's equality was not achieved in practice, neither was equality for minority groups in Japan. Okinawans are the largest group of people ethnically distinct from the majority Japanese. In 1945 they had defended their homeland in one of the bloodiest battles of the Second World War. Almost 150,000 Okinawans who died during the war were commemorated on the fiftieth anniversary of the Battle of Okinawa. Nevertheless, following the end of the war, the Ryukyu Islands, of which Okinawa is the largest, were occupied by the United States military, and because of their strategic value in the Cold War remained under American rule even after the peace treaty ended the American Occupation of Japan. The peace treaty stipulated Japan's 'residual sovereignty' over the Ryukyus, leaving no possibility for Okinawa's becoming an independent nation in the future.

During the 1950s the United States governed the islands like a colony, limiting political autonomy and civil liberties and forceably appropriating large tracts of land from Okinawan farmers for military bases. Okinawan land rights were excluded from any form of legal protection, and compensation for the appropriated lands fell below current market values. Many Okinawans attributed the denial of democracy to a perceived racist belief that Okinawans were not capable of self-government, unlike Japanese. Consequently, they responded by claiming they were Japanese. This implied rejection of their own ethnic and cultural identity as Ryukyuans echoed debates over assimilation policies in the pre-1945 period, but, as in the past, claiming to be Japanese did not mean acceptance by Japanese. This added to the difficulties of overcoming the stigma of being Okinawan once the islands reverted to Japan in 1971.

Koreans made up the other large minority which faced ongoing discrimination through the loss of Japanese citizenship. They officially became foreigners when the San Francisco Peace Treaty went into effect in April 1952, but their status hung in limbo when negotiations between Japan and South Korea became deadlocked, and were then suspended in 1953. In addition, the Korean War divided Koreans in Japan between pro-North Koreans and pro-South Koreans. The pro-North Koreans formed close ties with the Japanese Communist Party and were usually part of the core of protestors in demonstrations during the early 1950s, including a bloody clash with police in Tokyo on May Day, 1952. With financial and moral support from North Korea, the pro-North Korean organization focused on educating young Koreans in communism, publishing newspapers and textbooks, and importing North Korean publications as well as being active in left-wing politics. The pro-South Korean organization, in contrast, received little support from South Korea, resulting in its establishing only 50 schools compared to 280 created by the pro-North Koreans by the end of the 1950s. All these schools emphasized teaching of the Korean language, although from 1952 only private Korean schools could teach in Korean, and then only if they taught Japanese as a second language.

Economically, many Koreans in Japan continued to live in poverty as before the war. In December 1955 over 24 per cent of Koreans received financial assistance from the government. Many were unemployed, while the majority of employed worked as unskilled workers. Some ran *pachinko* parlours and dance halls; others turned to criminal activities such as drug-dealing. As in the interwar period, Koreans' impoverished condition reinforced prejudices among Japanese, who in various surveys during the 1950s expressed strong dislike and hostility towards Koreans for being dirty, cunning and culturally inferior. Activism in radical political movements and close contacts with North Korea also provoked Japanese suspicions about Koreans as security risks to the nation. In 1960 over 51,000 Koreans took up Kim Il-sung's invitation to all Koreans in Japan to return to North Korea with its promises of employment, education and decent living conditions. About three-quarters of these people were unemployed. Over 600,000 Koreans remained in Japan, however, leaving their marginalized existence unresolved while the issue of their status complicated the diplomacy between Japan and the two Koreas during the following decade.

Lack of citizenship did not present a problem for Burakumin in the post-war period, but constitutional provisions did not prevent continued social discrimination, especially common in employment and marriage. Soon after the surrender in 1945 former Suiheisha leaders had met to revive the organization, and in 1946 the National Committee for Buraku Liberation (NCBL) was formed, supported by most of the leftist parties. Of nine Burakumin who were elected to the Diet in the first election under the new constitution, seven were members of the JSP. However, little headway against discrimination took place during the Occupation years, partly because most Burakumin were too preoccupied with problems of survival to become involved in political activity, but also because many people expected that the Occupation's democratization reforms would lead to achievement of liberation.

An incident in 1951 revealed that these expectations were too sanguine. The magazine *All Romance* published a story depicting a Buraku community rife with black marketeering, crime, illegal sake-brewing and sex. When the author was discovered to be an employee of the Kyoto city government, the NCBL began a campaign to expose the miserable conditions of Buraku in the city. The campaign succeeded in embarrassing the city government sufficiently to inaugurate a programme of improvements to water supply, sewerage, housing and schools. After the success of similar campaigns against local governments, the liberation movement won more support and reorganized itself as the Buraku Liberation League (BLL) in 1955.

BLL activities attracted more attention and support from the mass media as well as the Socialist and Communist Parties during the late 1950s. The JSP called for a special commission to devise a comprehensive plan for improving the living conditions and opportunities of Burakumin. The LDP resisted the demand for a special commission, but in 1958 it did set up the Dōwa (Assimilation) Policy Committee to consider Buraku problems, and central government funding for Dōwa projects increased.

Political activities of Burakumin and Korean organizations in Japan actually intensified at the start of the 1960s, but the disagreements between the progressive and conservative camps which had caused the turbulance of the 1950s became less serious confrontations after the Anpo riots and Kishi's resignation as prime minister. The new prime minister Ikeda Hayato soon announced a plan to double national income within ten years. Stability and consensus returned as the nation fixed its purpose on economic growth and universal achievement of the 'bright life'. What seemed like an 'economic miracle' will be examined in the next chapter.

11 The 'economic miracle' . . . and its underside

The high growth period from the late 1950s to the early 1970s has been conventionally dubbed the 'economic miracle', since no one predicted that Japan would rise from the ashes of defeat to become an economic power second only to the United States in gross national product (GNP) – ever, much less in such a short time. Prime Minister Ikeda's Income Doubling Plan did succeed in doubling average household incomes within a decade as the rate of growth of the GNP reached double digit figures year after year. With the government's sanction, Japanese people spent their rising incomes on what previously had been considered luxury goods at the same time as they put aside savings at rates that became the envy of other countries. By the early 1970s, according to government opinion polls, 90 per cent of Japanese classified themselves as part of the 'middle' classes. Japanese people at many levels took pride in their nation's economic achievements, which foreigners were heralding in publications with titles like *Asia's New Giant*.[1]

During the 1970s and 1980s both scholars and popular writers focused on finding out the 'secrets' of Japanese economic success, giving the impression that such success resulted from a carefully planned and efficiently executed national economic strategy. The conservative coalition of the LDP, the bureaucracy (especially the Ministry of International Trade and Industry (MITI)) and big business were happy to go along with this image and even to promote it. In 1970, for example, the Vice Minister of MITI modestly expounded on the ministry's prescience:

> The Ministry of International Trade and Industry decided to establish in Japan industries which require intensive employment of capital and technology . . . industries such as steel, oil refining, petro-chemicals, automobiles, aircraft, industrial machinery of all sorts, and electronics including electronic computers. . . . According to Napoleon and Clausewitz, the secret of a successful strategy is the concentration of fighting power on the main battle grounds; fortunately, owing to good luck and wisdom spawned by necessity, Japan has been able to concentrate its scant capital in strategic industries.[2]

Notable in this quotation is not only the credit being taken by the bureaucracy for economic achievements, but the battle imagery. Concentration on 'GNP first' was represented as a new national goal towards which all Japanese could and should aim. The state called upon Japanese people to work hard and sacrifice in the interest of GNP growth much as it prodded them to work selflessly during the war. Ikeda's Income Doubling Plan was intended to deflect the public's attention from the divisive and disruptive political conflicts of the previous decade and to bring peace to the workplace so that production could grow.

During the 1960s this political strategy worked and the standard of living of most Japanese rose substantially. However, by 1970 even as government officials basked in the praise for their wise leadership and ordinary Japanese participated in the 'consumption boom', some Japanese were realizing that GNP growth did not mean economic justice or equality, nor a rich quality of life for most Japanese. The *Asahi shinbun* published a series of articles entitled 'Down with GNP' in 1970 which reflected a new consciousness of the social and environmental costs entailed by the drive towards industrial growth.

This chapter will first describe the economic developments making up the so-called miracle and examine various explanations for the high rates of growth. We will see what improvements in daily life that high growth brought to the majority of Japanese, but we will also consider the costs of economic growth shared by 'middle-class' Japanese as well as those outside the mainstream of Japanese society.

Keys to high-speed growth

According to the Japanese economist Kōsai Yutaka,

> The development of mass-production industries supplying materials needed to make consumer durables increased the demand for labor, accelerated the achievement of full employment, facilitated the movement of the labor force, and stimulated the more equal distribution of income. In turn, these fostered a Japanese-style mass-consumption market economy in which an expanding demand for consumer durables coexisted with a high savings rate. This dynamic logic of industrial society sustained the high growth rate.[3]

This neatly summarizes the chain of developments which characterized the Japanese economy's growth during the 1960s. However, as Laura Hein has pointed out, economists' preoccupation with the mechanisms of growth has obscured aspects of Japanese economic history that did not make direct contributions to growth and 'imparted false prescience to the Japanese', minimizing the importance of luck and international developments which were outside Japanese control but critical to economic success.

To begin with, the labelling of the high growth period as a 'miracle' disregards the transformation of the economy begun in the nineteenth century and the expansion of heavy industry during the 1930s. While many factories had been destroyed and Japanese industry had fallen behind technologically during the war, the Japanese economy was no longer predominantly agricultural. According to Andrew Gordon, the most important prewar and wartime legacy consisted of a cooperative relationship between private firms and government officials, a shared conception of capitalism within certain policy limits set by the state. Wartime demands had also stimulated the shift to heavy industry, and more specifically had encouraged developments which aided postwar growth, for example, in product standardization, subcontracting and seniority-based wages.

Subsequently, defeat in war and the new international context proved to be lucky for the Japanese economy. Loss of the war discredited the former strategy of imperial expansion, oligopoly and tight domestic control. At the same time political power shifts meant that industrial managers and bureaucrats could no longer resist workers' demands for a higher standard of living. Occupation by the United States was decisive in these shifts and began the patronage that was crucial to economic growth. The postwar economic environment of free trade opened up new market opportunities for Japanese products, while the Cold War ensured long-term American assistance. The Korean War has been described as 'a gift from the gods' to Japanese recovery and growth, and American procurements during the Vietnam War provided further demand for Japanese goods which helped sustain the high growth of the 1960s.

As Hein notes, Japanese business and government leaders had no control over these key factors, nor had they defined a clear plan for economic development even by the end of the 1940s. They shared a commitment by then to a 'high-value-added economy with sophisticated export goods', but there was much debate during the next two decades over how to achieve this. Political factors were at least as important as economic ones in shaping official economic strategy. Notably, Ikeda's Income Doubling Plan was explicitly designed to pacify discontent with the government's foreign policy, but doing this represented a major redefinition of economic growth to benefit Japanese consumers as well as producers. The new commitment to raising the standard of living won the cooperation of most Japanese to advance the national goal of economic growth, and the reality of higher personal incomes and consumption during the next decade kept most people satisfied.

Winning the opportunity to host the Olympic Games in 1964 reflected Japan's focus on doubling GNP as well as symbolizing its full re-entry into the international community in areas of peaceful competition. It provided an opportunity to display Japan's industrial and technological achievements and project them to the world through both television and print media. The soaring roof of the main gymnasium represented a triumph of engineering as well as architectural design, for it put the technology of suspension-roof structuring for the first time into practice on a monumental scale. The design of the building evoked a sense of authority by its inspiration from the great tiled roofs of Buddhist temples, combined with stone walls reminiscent of Japanese castles and a curved plan drawn from the Circus Maximus in Rome. Access to the Olympic site was provided by the new, high-speed 'bullet train' system and monorail linking Haneda Airport to the Yamanote city loopline.

While hosting the Olympics was highly symbolic of Japan's national resurrection, it was expansion of manufacturing that drove high growth. As described by Kōsai at the beginning of this section, demand for consumer durables in both foreign and domestic markets expanded the manufacturing sector, ending the high unemployment of the previous decade. Moreover, as full employment was reached and the birth rate declined, a labour shortage developed and wages rose. Higher incomes in turn spurred a 'consumer boom' which kept economic growth going at a dizzying rate. High growth continued until the Nixon 'shocks' of the early 1970s, and the oil embargo in 1973 to 1974 by the Organization of Petroleum Exporting Countries (OPEC) sent the price of oil sky-rocketing.

The state has often been credited with guiding the economy to success. While not denying that it played a major role in the economy and fostered economic growth, the common image of MITI officials and industrialists working in unison to pin-point strategic industries and channel investment into them has been overstated. The wartime experience had legitimated long-term planning and left business with the sense of the government as its ally, but business leaders also felt that they did not want the direct state interference of the wartime period to continue. In the 1950s and 1960s they did not always agree with the policies pushed by economic bureaucrats, and government economic leaders were not always right in selecting the products or industries most likely to prosper. One of the most outstanding examples of this was the difficulty faced by one of Sony's founders, Morita Akio, in obtaining a licence to manufacture transistors. MITI officials failed to see the potential of the new product and suggested that Sony put its resources into other products. Morita went ahead against officials' views and history of course vindicated him.

Worker cooperation and a corporate culture constitute another factor often put forth as an ingredient of Japan's economic success. As seen in Chapter 10, however, the peaceful workplace of the 1960s was the result of intense conflict and industrial strife rather than Confucian values and management's paternalistic benevolence. Moreover, during the 1960s managers appealed to workers' values and to some extent accommodated workers' expectations in order to reconstruct workplace culture as one which envisioned unionized workers' welfare as unified with the welfare of the enterprise. The result was what Japanese critics call 'enterprise society'.

Andrew Gordon points to compromises between management and labour unions in the steel industry during the early 1960s as leading the way to the new workplace culture in the private sector. Managers at Nippon Kōkan and other big steel producers began to emphasize ability and merit as the basis for wages, though also continuing consideration for seniority, age and education. This enabled them to reward loyalty and hold back uncooperative union members. It appealed to workers, especially younger workers impatient with seniority-based wages, who wanted their achievements recognized and rewarded. 'Permanent employment' and wages based exclusively on seniority did not become features of this 'Japanese style' of management, contrary to conventional views, but management did succeed in winning workers' support and devotion to increasing the company's prosperity. Besides rewarding merit while ensuring a degree of security, managers in steel introduced small-group activities (later known as quality control circles) to encourage workers' input into improving productivity. This gave workers a wider range of responsibilities and a sense of solidarity with management. Group competition, as each work group tried to outdo others in meeting productivity goals, spurred even more improvements.

The powerful union-based workplace culture of the late 1940s and 1950s declined much later in public sector industries, including the national railways, the tobacco industry, telecommunications and the postal service. In contrast to the developments outlined above in private sector industries during the 1960s, strong unions in the public sector obtained a place on 'workplace discussion councils', greater control over job assignments and promotion, and a reinstatement of seniority as a major factor in wage increases and promotions. The power of these unions reached its peak in the early 1970s. As we will see in Chapter 12, their power was not destroyed until the late 1970s and early 1980s.

Therefore, by no means a majority of workers became part of the 'enterprise society', and there were many more workers who were neither part of the enterprise nor represented by strong unions. In fact, the small minority of regular workers in private sector enterprise unions owed their relative security to the existence of millions of male and especially female 'temporary' and 'part-time' employees whose labour could be disposed of when demand slowed down. Although the high economic growth and labour shortages of the 1960s and early 1970s led to a drop in the number of temporary workers, the rising rates of return to the workplace of married women were in part-time rather than full-time jobs. These workers received lower wages than regular employees and did not enjoy their benefits and job security. The same was true for the millions of workers in small and medium firms who usually had no unions to represent them. These firms were typically subcontractors or sub-subcontractors for the large enterprises, and provided 'flexibility' for the large enterprises during slow times and destinations for job transfers of 'excess' or less skilled workers.

Consuming and saving in the 1960s

Although the above discussion of workplace cultures shows that wealth accompanying high GNP growth was not distributed equally, even temporary and part-time workers and workers in small and medium-sized companies enjoyed a rising standard of living during the 1960s. Moreover, elimination of the prewar distinctions between blue-collar and white-collar workers in the factories extended to reduced distinctions between their consumption and leisure patterns as well. High growth rates began in 1955 and the middle-class vision of Japanese society was standardized during the late 1950s, but it was Ikeda's Income Doubling Plan that made a mass consumption society a reality.

During the 1960s most households began to be able to afford the electrical appliances that television and advertising codified and disseminated as symbols of membership in the 'middle class'. Electric appliance manufacturers were the biggest advertisers, and their ads aimed to make commodity acquisition a sign of status. Similarly, automobile manufacturers such as Nissan appealed to a 'keeping up with the Joneses' mentality with ads like: 'Our car is the most spacious. It makes your next-door neighbour's look small.'[4] The 'Three Imperial Treasures' desired by the families in Vogel's late 1950s study changed in content as incomes rose and Japanese acquired more and more commodities during the 1960s. In the mid-1960s mass media talked about the 'three Cs or Ks' – *kaa*, *kūrâ* and *karâ terebi* (car, air-conditioner and colour television). By the early 1970s the three treasures had become the 'three Js' – *jūeru*, *jetto* and *jūtaku* (jewels, overseas vacation and house).

The gradual convergence and standardization of lifestyles among blue-collar and white-collar workers, large and small to medium enterprise workers, and rural and urban inhabitants became evident in leisure activities and other consumption patterns as well. A 1970 NHK survey of blue-collar and white-collar workers revealed almost identical uses of time in a 'typical' day for sleeping, meals and personal hygiene. Blue-collar workers spent a half-hour longer at work, but white-collar workers spent twenty minutes more commuting. Some differences were evident in uses of leisure times, for example, blue-collar workers watched more television and listened to more radio than did white-collar workers, who spent more time reading or doing other leisure activities. In dress, however, it was no longer possible to distinguish a white-collar worker from a blue-collar worker when they went to work, though the quality of their suits varied with their incomes. And wives of blue-collar employees, not just white-collar workers, were addressed as *okusan*.

In general, there was a Westernization of consumption among all Japanese as they ate more bread, drank more black tea, beer and whisky, wore Western-style clothing, and enjoyed baseball and soccer, jazz and rock more than judo and traditional forms of popular music. The construction of huge, concrete housing projects helped solve the housing shortage of the 1950s, but standardized domestic space further. Apartments in these projects as well as new detached houses were more Western in their furnishings as well as appliances, as Western-style rooms with wooden floors and carpets replaced Japanese-style rooms with *tatami* straw matting. Nevertheless, Western styles and commodities did not wholly replace Japanese ones. As Vogel noted in a follow-up study at the end of the 1960s, the retention of Japanese styles and commodities often represented a preference for the Japanese, not necessarily an inability to afford the Western.

By the early 1970s most Japanese in both countryside and cities were approaching affluence in terms of their material belongings, but were not quite there. The enthusiasm for acquiring new commodities had not disappeared, and desires and expectations had risen even more rapidly than incomes. In the level of consumption and the proportion of their incomes spent on necessities, Japanese were approaching the patterns in Western developed countries. However, in some areas, particularly housing, Japanese still lagged significantly. As indicated earlier, among Japanese themselves there remained variations in income distribution despite the fact that the vast majority identified themselves as members of the middle class.

An important reason for comparative restraint in consumption was the high proportion of income put into savings. During the high growth period the household savings rate climbed from the already high rate of 12.2 per cent in 1955 to 20.5 per cent in 1973.[5] This contrasts with a personal savings rate of 3 to 9 per cent in the United States during the postwar period. One explanation for the extraordinary savings rate in Japan is that Japanese families wanted to restore household assets that had been destroyed during the war or by postwar hyperinflation. Sheldon Garon has also detailed how progressive organizations as well as conservative governments supported 'New Life' campaigns throughout the 1950s and 1960s which emphasized savings and elimination of wastefulness as well as community-building, patriotism and various 'modernization' projects in daily life and the environment. These campaigns involved many housewives in study groups and as members of community and women's associations. Other factors making it necessary for most Japanese families to save were the lack of consumer credit and the continuing inadequacy of state welfare programmes to provide security in times of illness, unemployment or retirement.

Social costs and inequalities of high growth

The high savings rate and frustration at incomes not keeping up with expectations are indications that more than a decade of high economic growth did not bring affluence or complete satisfaction to many Japanese people. Ezra Vogel also found in his follow-up study of Mamachi in 1969 that success had in fact raised new questions about life goals. Vogel's neighbourhood exemplified a wider shift in the climate of opinion at the end of the 1960s. The media reflected emerging concern about quality of life issues, deterioration of the environment and economic justice.

The aspiration to become a salaryman that had predominated at the beginning of the decade no longer had the same appeal for teenagers and young adults. Although most teenagers of the late 1960s still studied hard to gain admission to a good university and subsequently a good job, they had been born after the war and had not experienced or did not remember the hardships faced by their parents and grandparents before the high growth period. Pushed by their parents to get into a good university, they were often dissatisfied with their experience once they got in. Dissatisfaction with university education and new foreign issues provoked student activism during the late 1960s. Opposition to the Vietnam War and renewal of the Japanese–American Security Treaty in 1970 fuelled student unrest. Radical students occupied university buildings and clashed with police, leading to the closure of some universities, including the prestigious Tokyo University, for months and even up to a year.

Salarymen themselves, who had grown in number and proportion of the workforce, were beginning to question why they had to work so long and hard for the company and why their children had to study so hard to get into a good university. Most did not go so far as to abandon the security and income assured by their jobs, but sought new interests outside their jobs. A wave of 'my home-ism' swept through the late 1960s, emphasizing more attention to family life as well as buying or remodelling a house. One of the 'three Js' of the early 1970s, an overseas vacation, indicates the new interest and affordability of travel, while increasing car-ownership made family travel in Japan more common as well.

The high cost of education, such as *juku* expenses, and aspirations for a house and objects to put in it, reinforced by government policies, pushed an increasing number of married women into the workforce. An 'M curve' began to characterize women's lifetime participation in paid work. The first peak represented their work as full-time regular workers while they were single and in their early twenties, and the second peak represented their return as part-time workers in their early thirties after their children had entered school. Government policies and company structures during the early 1960s shaped this pattern of women's work. Anticipating greater demand for labour arising from high growth, the government encouraged married women to work, but at the same time tried to maintain the family structure by stressing the 'part-time system' for them so that they could meet their 'family responsibilities'. Tax incentives discouraged full-time work for married women, and the 1972 Working Women's Welfare Law assumed that women would need help to 'harmonize' their work and home respons- ibilities. Companies, especially small and medium-sized subcontractors, found part-time married women to be a good source of cheap, disposable labour. The economic and political structure therefore gave women little choice in work opportunities, whether or not they aspired to roles other than housewife. Meanwhile, the education system continued to track girls into a future role centred on home and community; for example, making the homemaking course compulsory for girls in 1969.

Even within these limits, however, women were not simply passive instruments of industrial strategy or compliant followers of official social policies. In the mid-1960s Prime Minister Satō Eisaku appealed to women to have more children, hoping that this would provide a long-term solution to the labour shortage, at the same time as the government was encouraging them to re-enter the workforce after childbearing. The appeal fell flat since no increase in daycare facilities and other childcare support accompanied it. Women continued to have fewer babies, and a growing number of young women went on to post-secondary education, delaying their entry into the workforce. Although only a small minority entered the prestigious four-year universities, experience in the student protest movements of the late 1960s created many leaders of the next decade's wave of feminism.

While Japanese women were exploited for their labour and limited in their life choices, the discrimination they suffered differed from that faced by minority groups. All minority groups had to overcome racism as well as the disadvantages of poverty. This was an important obstacle to achieving equality given both the past and future prevalence of the concept of Japanese uniqueness. Burakumin, although ethnically the same as majority Japanese, were widely viewed as racially different from mainstream Japanese. Correcting this view had been one of the main objectives of Burakumin liberation groups since the 1920s. It finally became part of government programmes established in 1969 to improve the economic and social conditions of Burakumin which had become relatively worse during the period of high growth.

Especially after formation of the Buraku Liberation League (BLL) in 1955, efforts by Burakumin leaders in cooperation with the Socialist and Communist Parties to bring the problems of Burakumin to national attention had helped to put pressure on the LDP to establish a commission of inquiry into Buraku problems. The commission's report in 1965 surveyed the poor conditions in ghetto-like Buraku communities, detailed the lower than average educational and employment achievements of Burakumin, and concluded that the state had a duty to work towards elimination of these problems. The 1969 Law on Special Measures for Dōwa (Assimilation) Projects set out a ten-year plan for improving the physical environment of Buraku, increasing social welfare and public health support, and instituting educational programmes to change public attitudes. Implementation and outcomes of these programmes will be discussed in later chapters, but here we can see that during the 1960s official commitment to eliminating the worst aspects of disadvantaged status and prejudice had begun.

BLL activists became divided over responses to the Special Measures Law. None wanted to be coopted by the state, but most cautiously welcomed the programmes, as did the Japanese Socialist Party. The Japanese Communist Party and its supporters in the BLL, however, opposed the measures because they would separate Burakumin from other workers. This would weaken opposition to the LDP and the capitalist system, which they blamed for the origins of discrimination. These disagreements eventually led to the communist faction splitting off from the BLL in 1979.

The ethnically distinct minority groups of Koreans and Okinawans faced their own peculiar problems in addition to the common one of racial prejudice. Both in a sense were pawns of Japan's diplomatic relations with foreign countries. In the case of Okinawans, the 1960s began with a continuation of colonial-type rule under the United States military, but ended with preparations for reversion to Japan as a prefecture in 1972. Since the San Francisco Peace Treaty had recognized Japan's residual sovereignty over the Ryukyu Islands, reversion was a logical outcome as long as the USA could maintain military bases there. As with the peace treaty, the Okinawans had no input in the reversion negotiations; in fact, the Japanese government opposed their participation. However, because Okinawan opposition to reversion under the terms being negotiated intensified, the Japanese government tried to mollify Okinawans with economic aid and establishment of a cabinet-level Okinawa Development Agency. Its sending of units from the Self-Defence Forces (SDF) upon reversion did not help the public relations efforts, and thousands rallied under the slogan: ' "no" to SDF deployment, "no" to land lease for military use, "no" to *Ryūkyū shobun* [disposal of the Ryukyus], down with the Satō government.' Reversion to Japan thus began in an atmosphere of heightened conflict and hostility as many contentious issues, notably the continued presence of American military bases, remained unresolved.

In the case of Koreans, the complicated and troubled relations among Japan, South Korea and North Korea affected the status of Koreans in Japan. As in the 1950s, competition between North and South Korea divided Koreans in Japan. In the early 1960s this competition intensified after the fall of President Syngman Rhee in 1960 set off a series of political crises and instability in South Korea, providing an opportunity for North Korea to begin a campaign for unification of the country and withdrawal of American military forces. But as the unification movement gathered momentum among Koreans in Japan during early 1960, the military carried out a coup in Seoul and established a strongly anti-communist, nationalist government under General Park Chung-hee. Park's government almost immediately began to take action to aid Koreans in Japan, especially Korean schools and businessmen, which won back support for the pro-South Korean organization.

North–South competition for the allegiance of Koreans in Japan continued during the 1960s and subsequent decades, but a treaty in 1965 establishing diplomatic relations between Japan and South Korea helped to stabilize, though not equalize, the status of Koreans in Japan. Koreans who had lived in Japan continuously since 1945 and their children became permanent residents, and the Japanese government agreed to give 'appropriate consideration' to their education, livelihood protection and national health insurance coverage. This did not solve the economic and social problems faced by Koreans, for they remained legally disadvantaged by their resident alien status. Moreover, although most second-generation Koreans spoke Japanese as their first language and were otherwise assimilated to Japanese culture, officially sanctioned practices continued to discriminate against Koreans in employment and higher education.

Individual Koreans began to challenge discrimination in the courts during the 1970s. In the first case, Park Chonsok sued the large electronic manufacturer Hitachi for employment discrimination in 1970. He had successfully passed a placement examination at Hitachi, using a Japanese alias, and was offered a job, but when the company discovered that he was a Korean it withdrew the offer. After four years of litigation the court ruled that Hitachi had dismissed Park illegally and ordered the company to pay his salary for the time since his dismissal as well as the compensation for which he had sued. Hitachi subsequently reinstated Park, who was still working there in the mid-1990s. Several other lawsuits during the 1970s won favourable judgments for individual Koreans, as will be discussed in Chapter 12, but the struggle against both systemic discrimination and informal prejudice continued.

At the end of the 1960s the courts proved to be an avenue for redress for another marginalized group, the victims of pollution. In their struggles to win compensation these victims brought the human and environmental costs of high-speed growth to national attention. Recognition of these costs contributed to growing expressions of concern about the 'quality' of life even for the self-perceived majority of 'middle-class' Japanese. Victims in four cases of pollution – mercury poisoning in Minamata and Niigata, air pollution in Yokkaichi, and cadmium poisoning in Toyama – filed suits between 1967 and 1969 which they won over the next few years, but the struggle to obtain compensation had started many years before.

In the first and most celebrated case of Minamata disease, the symptoms of mercury poisoning had appeared in the early 1950s:

> Birds seemed to be losing their sense of coordination, often falling from their perches or flying into buildings and trees. Cats, too, were acting oddly. They walked with a strange rolling gait, frequently stumbling over their own legs. Many suddenly went mad. . . . Local fishermen called the derangement 'the disease of dancing cats'. . . .
>
> By the early '50s, a number of Minamata fishermen and their families were experiencing the disquieting symptoms of a previously unknown physical disorder. Robust men and women who had formerly enjoyed good health suddenly found their hands trembling so violently they could no longer strike a match. They soon had difficulty thinking clearly, and it became increasingly difficult for them to operate their boats. Numbness that began in the lips and limbs was followed by disturbances in vision, movement and speech. As the disease progressed, control over

all bodily functions diminished. The victims became bedridden, then fell into unconsciousness. Wild fits of thrashing and senseless shouting comprised a later stage. . . . About forty per cent of those stricken died.[6]

Because of a general attitude of shame and fear towards physical deformities and mental abnormalities, victims were often reluctant to seek treatment or report the disease, and others in the community shunned them. Victims who thought of taking legal action faced threats of ostracism and criticism for being selfish and unpatriotic. The polluting company Chisso was also a major employer in the area, while the victims came from poor fishing villages scattered around the bay.

Nevertheless, the impact of the disease became so widespread that victims formed a Mutual Assistance Society to negotiate with Chisso in 1959. Although a settlement gave them only small amounts of money as 'sympathy' payments rather than compensation, it silenced the victims for a number of years. Although researchers in the Ministry of Health and Welfare and later at Kumamoto University had pin-pointed Chisso effluents as the cause of the disease, the ministry report was kept secret, and the university research team lost its funding and had to disband. MITI and the Ministry of Agriculture and Forestry continued to profess doubt about the cause and source of the disease during the 1960s, and the Ministry of Justice refused to investigate Chisso even after evidence of its role became clear.

Government complicity in covering up industry polluters' responsibility occurred in other cases as well, but in 1967 a Niigata University research team published its finding of a second case of mercury poisoning, and support from leftist lawyers radicalized the victims to take legal action. Their suit was the first of the 'Big Four' pollution cases to be filed in the late 1960s. The victims not only won their suits, but contributed to a change in popular attitudes towards production-first policies of economic growth and environmental protection. Media and public concern was also raised by numerous research reports of environmental deterioration and widespread incidence of white smog, water pollution, contaminated fish and other food (including the staple rice). Both the government and industry felt compelled to support new pollution control laws in the 1970s, which were some of the most stringent in the world, and the establishment of the Environmental Agency in 1971.

The victims' activities also became a model for the citizens' movements that proliferated during the 1970s. These were grassroots organizations which mobilized around local or regional issues, such as highway siting, and utilized litigation, symbolic violence and electoral politics, but not party affiliation, to achieve their aims. Their resort to legal action contradicted the conventional stereotype of Japanese as non-litigious people who preferred informal, non-confrontational methods of dispute resolution.

Despite improvements in their standard of living, Japanese people were also becoming aware of a 'welfare gap' between themselves and people in other advanced industrialized countries – GNP growth had made the nation rich, but not the people. International surveys showed that the Japanese government spent little more on social welfare per person than did governments in developing countries such as Tunisia and Sri Lanka. In addition, Japan lagged behind the United States and Europe in park space, sewerage systems (only 17.1 per cent of dwellings had flush toilets), and public recreational facilities such as indoor sports centres and swimming pools. In Tokyo and Osaka the cost of building a house had doubled between 1950 and 1971, while land prices had multiplied by twenty. To find affordable housing, more and more people moved to the suburbs, which increased commuting times for husbands and isolated housewives in bedroom communities.

Japan as number two

Although the public mood was changing, Japanese felt pride when it was announced that their country's GNP had become the second largest in the world only after the United States. National economic power encouraged neonationalists and conservative politicians to promote an ideology of Japanese uniqueness and to begin to talk about a larger role for Japan in international affairs. As Japanese goods began to rival American products, friction over trade matters also developed with the United States.

But despite emerging dissatisfaction with Japan's subordinate status in its relationship to the USA, no fundamental alteration of the San Francisco system occurred. The LDP realized the benefits of remaining under the American nuclear umbrella, and American military procurements for the Vietnam War helped sustain the high growth rates of the 1960s and early 1970s. With the USA providing Japan's security, Prime Minister Satō could announce 'Three Non-nuclear Principles' in 1967, aligning the LDP with the popular anti-nuclear movement (while turning a blind eye to American ships regularly carrying nuclear weapons in and out of Japan).

The opposition was too weak either to change this foreign policy or to break the LDP's monopoly of power. Leftists opposed the Vietnam War and renewal of the Security Treaty in 1970, but could not mobilize any sizeable protests or undermine the LDP majority in the Diet. The opposition could not take advantage of the LDP's declining electoral support during the 1960s because of its own weaknesses. Creation of a separate Democratic Socialist Party by the right wing in 1960 had split the Socialist Party, and the opposition had fragmented further with establishment of the Komeitō (Clean Government Party) in 1964. The Komeitō was a new kind of party outside the earlier postwar framework of parties based on ideological polarization, although, like the Socialists, it initially supported opposition to rearmament and the American alliance. It extended the influence of the Sōka Gakkai, a 'new' religion founded in the 1930s, into politics. The Komeitō attracted protest voters against the other parties as well as Sōka Gakkai's followers among urban inhabitants who were missing out on the benefits of high growth. Outside the opposition parties some scholars and intellectuals conducted peace research or advocated that Japan use its new position of global economic power to lead the world to peace, but any talk about a wider international role provoked concern about remilitarization both at home and in the Asian region where memories of the war remained strong. Characterization of the Japanese as 'economic animals' reflected wariness of 'economic imperialism' as Japanese trade and investment in Asia grew.

Events in the early 1970s increased the anxiety about Japan's place in the world and created a sense of vulnerability about Japan even as an economic power. These came in the form of the Nixon 'shocks' and the oil crisis of 1973 to 1974. The first 'shock' was US recognition of the People's Republic of China in July 1971. Without even notifying Japan, the USA reversed the Cold War containment policy to which the Japanese government had adhered even though business interests wanted to restore economic relations. One month later, again without consultation, the USA shocked Japan by renouncing fixed exchange rates, which resulted in devaluation of the US dollar against the yen by 17 per cent. Nixon also announced imposition of a 10 per cent surcharge on imports which was directed against Japanese electronic goods and cars. In 1972 the USA put an embargo on soybean exports to Japan, but the worst disruption came the following year when OPEC embargoed oil. This drastically raised the price of oil and pushed the Japanese economy into its deepest recession since the end of the Second World War.

The Japanese were totally unprepared for these developments – no one expected the high growth to end – and suddenly realized the extent of their interdependence with the international economy. Japanese leaders had underestimated the yen's value and had even contemplated its devaluation in the late 1960s. The floating exchange rate suddenly reduced Japan's balance of payments as its exports became relatively more expensive. The soybean embargo exposed a vulnerability in regard to basic food supplies, and the oil crisis drove home recognition of dependence on foreign economies. Oil provided two-thirds of the country's energy supplies and virtually all of it was imported. Many analysts now predicted the collapse of the miracle, and it is certainly true that 1973 ended the period of high growth, ushering in a lengthy recession and forcing adjustments to little or slow growth.

Nevertheless, in the next chapter we will see that adjustments were made. Consequently, while growth slowed down during the rest of the 1970s, it still surpassed growth in other major economies. Defying the mid-1970s pessimists, Japan became touted as 'Number One'.

12 The 'rich country'

Because of the Nixon 'shocks' and the oil crisis of 1973 to 1974, historians as well as economists see the early 1970s as the end of a period in Japan's history since the war. Adjustments in politics and society as well as the economy had to be made with the end to high growth. But while adjustment to slow growth involved new departures in policies and practices, many of the developments in politics, society and the economy during the 1970s and 1980s were extensions or dissemination of patterns established during the 1950s and 1960s. And although Prime Minister Satō Eisaku announced the end of the 'postwar' period in 1969, this was just the first of such pronouncements, since the 'postwar' lingered on in numerous areas, and not only in politics or foreign policy.

In politics the '1955 system' continued in the sense of the LDP's domination of power, although the number of opposition parties had grown. During the 1970s the LDP maintained power through skilful adjustment to demographic changes, while still relying on its rural base and benefiting from weaknesses of the opposition parties. At the same time voter apathy and dissatisfaction with politicians grew during the 1970s and 1980s as corruption scandals became endemic, and a new generation of young urban voters with little sense of party affiliation emerged. LDP governments continued their close ties with the bureaucracy and big business. During this period the image of a monolithic 'Japan Inc' became pervasive in foreign countries, even though the tripartite coalition and state 'administrative guidance' of industry was actually weakening.

During the 1980s the realization of material affluence for the majority of Japanese also helped to keep the LDP in power. The Japanese economy recovered from the early 1970s shocks and a second oil crisis in 1979, achieving growth rates that were no longer miraculous, but higher than those of other advanced industrialized countries. In fact, the economy boomed during the second half of the 1980s. Japan became the largest creditor nation in the world, while Japanese companies spread all over the globe and became household names. Japanese people also became visible as hundreds of thousands travelled as high-spending tourists or bought up prime real estate in foreign countries. No wonder scholars and popular writers sought the 'secrets' of Japanese economic success, exemplified by Ezra Vogel's 1979 book *Japan As Number One*.

The secrets were often found to be in Japanese 'culture', which many Japanese and foreigners regarded as unique and even superior. Social structures and behaviour, such as hierarchy and group orientation, and social values of hard work, loyalty and education were credited not only with economic success, but with preventing social problems found in the advanced industrialized societies of the West. They were considered to be explanations for the cooperative relations between labour and management, notably the commitment of workers to their companies, which contributed to productivity. In the wider society they provided explanations for lower crime rates, especially compared to American ones, and fewer drug problems. The value placed on education accounted for high achievements at tertiary and lower levels and made the Japanese people one of the most literate and highly skilled workforces in the world. Many Japanese writers and commentators as well as conservatives in business and government fostered this image of Japanese social harmony and homogeneity and attributed it to unique Japanese cultural values and traditions. A whole genre of publications known as *Nihonjinron* (theories of Japaneseness) emerged during this period and made best-seller lists.

But alongside these images of an affluent, harmonious society, accompanied by a surge of cultural nationalism, the problems and questions that had become matters of public concern at the end of the 1960s assumed greater seriousness during the 1970s and 1980s. Moreover, new ones emerged and by the end of the 1980s many Japanese were feeling that it might be just a matter of time before Japan suffered social problems similar to those of Western societies. But some of the problems, such as death from overwork (*karōshi*) and high rates of suicide among children, were by-products of the very Japanese values otherwise praised.

In this chapter we will examine more closely the developments of the 1970s and 1980s highlighted in this introductory summary. This is the period when we can rightly say that the Meiji goal of 'rich country' was achieved, but national wealth did not accrue to all Japanese equitably. Many also said that with the death of the Shōwa Emperor Hirohito in 1989 the 'postwar' period had finally ended, but we will see why this pronouncement would still not be the last, since issues raised by the war and the Occupation continued to disturb both domestic and international politics.

Politics and the economy in the 'rich country'

When the foreign-induced shocks of the early 1970s ended high economic growth and caused a recession, the heralding of Japan as 'Asia's new giant' or 'the Japanese superstate' in American best-sellers suddenly appeared premature. Japanese themselves felt the vulnerability of their country's growing prosperity, and foreigners also predicted the sinking of the miracle. During the next fifteen years the Japanese economy defied such pessimistic predictions, but the 1970s did mark a transitional period when Japan as well as other developed countries had to adjust to slower growth.

By 1973 the LDP therefore could no longer expect to stay in power by taking credit for high economic growth rates, even though it tried to revive them. Other domestic developments were also in train to force LDP leaders to rethink the party's policies. The 'economic miracle' had accelerated urbanization and the occupational redistribution of the workforce, eroding the party's original electoral bases in the countryside and the old urban middle class. Even though gerrymandering of electoral districts gave rural areas more weight than urban ones, the LDP began losing votes during the 1960s. As pollution and other quality-of-life issues became prominent in the early 1970s, numerous Socialist and Communist Party candidates succeeded in becoming governors and mayors of large cities, and in the 1972 general election the LDP won fewer seats than ever before. The emergence of progressive party local governments, the spread of citizen movements posing a challenge to the established party system and the rising public demands for state measures to improve the quality of life prompted a significant shift in LDP policies. The adjustments were so successful that despite the recession, followed by a second oil crisis in 1979, and slower growth, the LDP succeeded in maintaining its power into the early 1990s.

The appointment of Tanaka Kakuei as prime minister in 1972 both symbolized and actively inaugurated the shift in policy. Known as the 'computerized bulldozer', Tanaka's public persona departed strikingly from the well-modulated, bland ex-bureaucrats who had dominated the prime ministership during the 1950s and 1960s. With a popularity rating of 62 per cent when he came into office, Tanaka seemed to represent a new kind of politician with support at the grassroots level. His own background reinforced this image, for he was an entrepreneur who had made a fortune in the construction industry after the war rather than a former bureaucrat.

But Tanaka had been a party politician for twenty-five years, so he also represented the more routinized pattern of promotions that had developed in the party by the early 1970s and the emergence of a generation of politicians who developed specialized knowledge on policy issues through their long years of party service. This meant that the LDP was less dominated by the bureaucracy. Tanaka's rise in the party also demonstrates the importance of party factions, which revolved around leaders skilful at fund-raising and advancing their followers' careers more than policy advocacy. Tanaka had built up the largest faction in the party, which he continued to lead even after he became tainted with corruption and was forced out of the prime ministership in 1974.

Tanaka's announcement of a plan to 'remodel the Japanese archipelago', which would 'build a beautiful and pleasant nation to live in', was welcomed by the public as a recognition of the legitimacy of their demands for protection of the environment and improvements to social welfare and social services.

The government subsequently introduced stringent pollution control laws and made 1973 'welfare's birthday' with a broad range of new and expanded social security and health programmes. Tanaka abandoned the commitment to balanced budgets on the assumption that government spending would sustain the high growth of the previous decade while extending industrialization and affluence to the nation's periphery. Consequently, spending on public works projects continued. The most visible example was the extension of railway lines for high-speed 'bullet' trains, notably the line from Tokyo to Niigata built at Tanaka's instigation. However, even before the oil crisis hit in 1973, inflation, land speculation and explosion of the government deficit damaged Tanaka's popularity. Charges of corruption involving the real estate and construction industries forced him out of office in late 1974, and two years later he was arrested (and later convicted) for accepting a ¥500 million bribe from the Lockheed aircraft firm in the United States.

Although Tanaka became a symbol of postwar Japanese political corruption and succeeding tight budget finance ministers tried to rein in government spending, Tanaka's policies had raised public expectations regarding the government's obligation to provide social welfare, so that it became politically impossible to cut such budget items. In the 1974 budget the government for the first time spent more on social welfare programmes than on public works. In subsequent budgets, the most that could be done was to slow down the rate of increase in social welfare expenditures. After a temporary decline in public works spending, these expenditures also increased dramatically during the remainder of the 1970s, since this was the LDP's favourite way of garnering support in regional areas. This stimulated expansion of the building and trades industry in the provinces, creating a new political class of wealthy businessmen as well as more employment opportunities for rural males.

In the early 1980s the LDP instituted new fiscal austerity programmes. Opposition to tax increases and a belief that excessive government spending was responsible for economic decline in Europe and the United States won public support for them. By this time the LDP had succeeded in adjusting its policies to attract voters from new urban constituencies at the same time that it maintained its strength in rural areas. It also benefited from renewed, though slower rates of economic growth after the second oil crisis, and, beginning in December 1986 the third longest expansion period since the end of the war.

Shifts in the structure of the economy and patterns of industrial production and employment helped in the recovery. After the first oil crisis the government had imposed cuts on use of oil, and it introduced further measures to reduce energy consumption and dependence on oil after the second oil crisis. These included construction of nuclear plants over objections from the peace lobby. MITI policy-makers, supported by business, also shifted the emphasis in manufacturing to industries less dependent on imported raw materials and to industries in information technology, such as computers and semi-conductors. Consequently, during the 1980s the old export industries of shipbuilding and machine tools, for example, and heavy energy-users such as steel and petrochemicals began to decline, while automobiles and electronics rose in manufacturing and the service industries grew more quickly. This reduced fields of competition with the newly industrialized countries of Asia, especially South Korea and Taiwan, but opened up others with the United States so that trade friction became characteristic of US–Japan relations. Despite the high value of the yen, exports grew faster than imports, creating huge trade surpluses.

The 1980s was the decade when Japan became an economic superpower. Under Western pressure to share its wealth, Japan greatly increased its aid to underdeveloped nations, especially in Asia, and direct investment overseas expanded rapidly. However, the high value of the yen and labour shortages stimulated Japanese manufacturers to move offshore to low-wage, pollution-tolerant sites in Asia – resulting in what is known as the 'hollowing' of the Japanese economy. Other manufacturers set up plants in the United States and Europe to avoid potential protectionist legislation or to gain tax advantages.

These developments had both positive and negative influences on cross-cultural as well as economic and diplomatic relations with other countries, as reflected in the mass media. In the United States, still Japan's main trading partner, some popular films such as *Gung Ho* (1988) entertained audiences with amusing scenes of cross-cultural misunderstanding and ended happily. *Gung Ho*, starring Michael Keaton, depicted the culture clash when a Japanese company took over an automobile factory. Others such as *Black Rain* (1989) reinforced the 'Japan bashing' going on in newspapers and magazines. In the case of *Black Rain*, the image of Japan was dark, sinister and aggressive. As the American film critic Roger Ebert wrote, '[Osaka is] a vast, dingy, polluted, and cheerless metropolis, with hideous neon advertisements climbing up into the sulphurous skies. Down below where the people live, there are nightclubs like burrows, where evil men plot and scheme.'[1]

Economic issues in international relations remained prominent during the latter half of the decade when there was a boom in consumption and in investment in plant and equipment. In the domestic economy high growth rates in new housing construction and increases in production of consumer durables illustrate the economic expansion. So does the extremely high ratio of investment in plant and equipment to Gross Domestic Product (GDP) exceeding 20 per cent. The unemployment rate dropped to nearly 2 per cent as the expansion created more demand for labour, and a labour shortage became serious in the construction industry. When real disposable income increased during the late 1980s, consumption grew and became noticeable in purchases of luxury goods. Benefiting from a strong yen, Japanese tourists travelled abroad in large groups, spending money on designer goods and *omiyage* (souvenirs to take back to friends and relatives). Purchases of prime real estate in places like Hawaii and Australia and of American icons such as the Rockefeller Center in New York and Columbia Pictures in Hollywood aroused hostility and fears of a Japanese takeover. Japan-bashing in the United States intensified.

Overseas real estate investment paralleled a rise in domestic stock and land prices to extraordinary heights, creating what became known as the 'bubble' economy. In the two-year period between 1986 and 1987, for example, land prices in the Tokyo metropolitan area tripled, and over the next two years land prices in resort areas and other major cities rose sharply too. Meanwhile, stock prices surged, slumping only temporarily with the October 1987 'Black Monday' crash in the American stock-market. There is debate as to whether the increase in asset prices contributed to the consumption and investment boom, but it is clear that the increase was driven by land speculation.

There is also debate about the impact of government policies, but the Hitotsubashi University economist Noguchi Yukio has argued that policies of 'easy money, tight budget' were one of the main causes of the asset price inflation. The loosening of monetary policy resulted largely from strong pressure from the United States to lower interest rates, especially after Black Monday, so that the outflow of capital from Japan would not decline. The tight budget policy came with the Ministry of Finance's desire to cut the large budget deficits run up during the previous decade. A combination of reduced government spending, particularly on public works, and increased revenues from the speculative boom created large budget surpluses in the late 1980s. Instead of then increasing expenditures on public investment, the government used the increased revenues to cut back on the issue of deficit-financing bonds. This meant that financial institutions had to make more loans, fuelling speculation further, since there were fewer bonds in which to invest.

Meanwhile, changes in the raising and use of funds by large corporations, especially in manufacturing, had also made funds available for land speculation. Major companies were raising more funds through the issuance of stocks and bonds rather than loans from banks. Instead of putting all the funds into plant and equipment, they deposited a large proportion into banks and bought other high-yield financial assets. This was called 'zai-tech' or financial engineering. Banks, in turn, shifted their lending to smaller companies and the real estate industry, spurring the land fever.

At the peak of the 'bubble' economy in 1989, a book entitled *The Japan That Can Say 'No'* (*'No' to ieru Nihon*) became a runaway best-seller. Its popularity among millions of Japanese indicates the pride engendered by postwar economic success, accompanied by increasing anger with continued American arrogance despite its economic decline. The early 1970s shocks had worried many Japanese about Japan's weakness in the world economy, but Japan had overcome the crisis and soared to new heights in the 1980s which some even called the 'second economic miracle'. The shocks, along with environmental concerns, had also turned Japanese inward and towards their past, which commercial interests capitalized upon and reinforced. The national railways, for example, hired Japan's largest advertising agency to conduct an ad campaign to lure new customers during the early 1970s. The resulting 'Discover Japan' campaign drew on Japanese desires for a more simple rural past, but, being a product of the culture or information industries, contributed to making the past yet another commodity in the Japanese marketplace.

Nationalist political leaders encouraged the view of trade disputes being anti-Japanese attacks and blamed American economic decline on laziness and ethnic diversity, not structural factors common to all capitalist economies. Prime ministers believed that the public mood had sufficiently changed so that in the mid-1970s they began to make visits to Yasukuni Shrine which is dedicated to the war dead, and even the Christian prime minister Ohira Masayoshi made visits to the Shinto shrines at Ise at New Year. The emergence of a sense of cultural strength and superiority underlay establishment of the Japan Foundation in 1972 to promote knowledge of Japanese language and culture abroad.

It was not only LDP politicians and old right-wing nationalists who promoted the new nationalism. By the early 1980s many academics, intellectuals, social commentators and popular writers found millions of readers for the new genre of *Nihonjinron*. These writings portrayed Japanese culture, people and society as harmonious and homogeneous, bound together by a long history of racial purity, common language and identity with the islands of Japan. In defining who and what was Japanese, these writings differentiated Japan and the Japanese from other peoples and cultures. They asserted Japanese uniqueness and, implicitly or explicitly, its superiority.

Diversification and marginalization in the midst of affluence

As must be clear from preceding chapters, this portrayal of homogeneity and consensus contradicted the reality, both past and present. At the same time that *Nihonjinron* publications were so popular, inequalities among Japanese were becoming greater, and Japanese society was in the process of becoming more diverse. Consequences of economic growth and expanding involvement in global culture and the global economy stimulated these changes. Marginalized groups, both old and new, were exploited and/or left behind, but, supported by international pressure, voiced their complaints and demands more publicly than in the past.

The largest marginalized group was made up of women workers. The changes in industrial organization of the 1970s and 1980s, notably expansion of service industries, provided more work opportunities for women, as did passage of the Equal Employment Opportunity Law (EEOL) in 1985. Corporations adjusted to slower growth by relying more and more heavily on part-time workers, who were mostly middle-aged women. High consumer prices and ferocious competition for their children's educational achievement forced more married women to re-enter the workforce, at an earlier age and for longer in their lives. The peaks in the 'M curve' pattern of women's workforce participation therefore became more pronounced and closer together, although the tail of the second peak declined less sharply as more women continued to work into their fifties and sixties. By the end of the 1980s about half of all women aged 15 and over were in the labour force, making up almost 40 per cent of all workers. Among working women, approximately half were married.

The EEOL theoretically opened up more opportunities for careers in management for the increasing number of women graduates of four-year universities. Its consequences will be discussed in Chapter 13, but the circumstances of its passage already presaged its lack of effectiveness. Although women's organizations had lobbied for such a law, it was mainly international pressure which prompted the government to pass it, namely signing the International Convention on Elimination of All Forms of Discrimination Against Women during the United Nations' Decade for Women (1975 to 1985). According to the Ministry of Labour, it was primarily intended 'to improve working women's welfare and to promote measures to enable them to harmonize work and family roles' (in other words, not primarily to recognize women's fundamental right to work without discrimination and unfair treatment). Consequently, the law represented a compromise with various conservative interests and, lacking enforcement provisions, depended on the goodwill of businesses.

Considering the assumptions about women's proper role held by government politicians and officials and the desire of companies for cheap, disposable labour in a period of slow growth, it is not surprising that married women were given little choice in job opportunities when they re-entered the workforce. They were increasingly forced into part-time jobs, especially in small and medium-sized firms. In 1990, 69 per cent of part-timers were women, which was close to 30 per cent of all women workers. Women also made up the majority of temporary and casual workers. Part-time work was not defined primarily by number of hours worked, since the number increased during the 1980s, and in many cases approached the same as full-time workers' hours; nor did it indicate different kinds of work from that of full-time employees. Part-time was a status, meaning the worker had no benefits such as sick leave, vacations or a pension in addition to receiving lower wages and smaller bonuses.

Not only were most jobs for married women part-time, they were also in small and medium-sized companies. The dual structure of the economy remained in place throughout the 1970s and 1980s, and small and medium-sized firms employed a growing number and proportion of the workforce. The dominance of small and medium-sized firms was particularly striking in manufacturing, the core of Japan's export economy. In manufacturing 99.5 per cent were small or medium-sized firms which employed 74.3 per cent of workers in the industry in 1981. As Norma Chalmers has argued, size of firm is a key factor in determining wages and benefits in Japan. In the 1980s starting wages were similar in all firms, but the wage/benefit gap between 'core' workers in large firms and 'peripheral' workers in small/medium-sized firms grew with age. In addition, according to Chalmers' findings, 'the smaller the firm by the number of regular employees, the greater the tendency for its workers to be in older age brackets, for the proportion of female workers to increase, and for education levels to be lower'.[2]

The smaller the firm, the longer the number of working hours. In the 1980s the government put pressure on companies to 'internationalize' working hours, i.e. to shorten them to bring them into line with conditions in other advanced industrial countries. Large firms generally complied by introducing a five-day week, but the smaller the firm, the less likely it was to shorten the week.

Women workers suffered from lower wages not only because of part-time status and working in small/medium-sized firms, but because they were women. The wage gap between male and female workers barely changed during the 1970s and 1980s; women's hourly earnings remained a little over 60 per cent of men's. Even in jobs where men and women did the same work, women were paid less.

Like women, members of minority groups were relegated to lower paid and lower status jobs in the peripheral workforce. But although discrimination continued, some improvements were discernible for Burakumin and Koreans. The Dōwa programmes begun in 1969 brought about a cleaner environment, better schools and community facilities, and improved housing in Buraku communities. Buraku families also directly received various allowances, subsidies and scholarships, and indirectly benefited from subsidized rent, favourable loan schemes and preferential treatment for childcare. Perhaps because of increased loans and grants to Buraku families, more Burakumin moved out of Buraku communities, so that the percentage of Burakumin in such areas fell from almost 72 per cent in 1971 to 41.4 per cent in 1993, when a major survey of Buraku communities was conducted. However, there was much regional variation, with some Buraku areas such as in Osaka still having about 87 per cent Burakumin.

Income levels and educational achievements showed some improvement, but averages still lagged behind those of non-Burakumin. The percentage of Burakumin receiving 'livelihood security support', for example, dropped from 76 per cent in 1975 to 52 per cent in 1993, but this was almost twice as high as non-Burakumin in the same areas. Similarly, while Burakumin entered senior high school in the same proportion as non-Burakumin, their rate of absenteeism in primary and middle schools was almost twice the mainstream average. And while entry into higher education increased, it lagged behind national figures.

Partly because of lower tertiary educational achievement, few Burakumin found jobs in large enterprises, but discrimination also continued to force them into lower wage, lower status employment. The Special Measures Law did not make discrimination illegal, so that employers could continue to discriminate against Burakumin without penalty. Large corporations used family registration records (*koseki*) to determine who was a Burakumin. Responding to pressure from the Buraku Liberation League (BLL), the Ministry of Justice restricted access to family registries in the mid-1970s, but companies then bought lists of Buraku communities compiled by private detectives.

Families also used the lists to block marriage of their children to Burakumin, but there were some signs of declining prejudice in the 1980s. Although the vast majority of older Burakumin had married fellow Burakumin, less than a quarter of under-25s did. Surveys showed that opposition among non-Burakumin to their children marrying a Burakumin also declined significantly.

In the early 1980s when the Special Measures Law was due to expire, debate over the continuation of its approach arose. Both the government and BLL were satisfied with physical and educational improvements, and individual Burakumin would have lost benefits if the emphasis had shifted from group programmes to personal initiative. The government wanted to cut back on programmes because of its new tight budget goals and was also hearing complaints against preferential treatment of Burakumin from non-Burakumin. The Special Measures Law was extended through compromise, but its focus narrowed to improvements of the physical environment, meaning that little effort would go towards eliminating discrimination.

The BLL then lobbied for a 'basic law' which would establish a more comprehensive approach to ending discrimination and symbolize a national commitment to equality for Burakumin. However, the response was mixed. The JCP as well as the LDP and some policy-makers in the bureaucracy believed that new legislation was unnecessary because Buraku problems were already being resolved. Others in the government believed that legislation against discrimination would violate constitutional freedoms of marriage and contract and simply 'drive discriminatory consciousness underground and harden it'.[3]

The situation of Koreans also presented a picture of slow improvement, but through a combination of different factors. An external factor was diplomatic agreements between Japan and South Korea, which worked to resolve the legal status of the increasing number of third-generation Koreans born in Japan after 1970. Like earlier generations, they were aliens, but were granted permanent residency. Following Park Chonsuk's victory in the courts (discussed in Chapter 11), several other Koreans successfully filed suits against discriminatory practices. One of the most significant cases arose in 1979 when Kim Hyonjo filed a suit to receive a pension for which he had paid the premiums but been denied on grounds of his Korean nationality. Kim won his pension on an appeal in 1982. Although his victory helped other individual foreign residents to receive their pensions, the nationality restriction was removed only under external pressure. Japan's signing of the International Agreement on Human Rights in 1979 and the International Treaty on Refugees in 1982 led to revisions in domestic laws, including laws on public housing as well as the National Health Insurance Law.

Job opportunities for Koreans expanded but only to a certain extent. Local governments began to hire resident Koreans as schoolteachers even though the Ministry of Education reiterated in 1982 that education boards were not permitted to hire foreigners for permanent positions in public schools. Given this official position, it is no surprise that the national civil service remained closed to Koreans.

Socially, there were some signs that prejudice was finally beginning to break down. Certainly there were few cultural differences between Japanese and third-generation Koreans. This generation spoke Japanese as their first language and in other ways had become assimilated to Japanese culture. Declining prejudice may be reflected in the rise in marriages between Koreans and Japanese during the 1970s and 1980s. In 1970, 42.7 per cent of Korean marriages were with Japanese, but by 1985 this percentage rose to 71.6.

Ironically, self-assertion and revival of Korean identity among younger Koreans paralleled these trends and countered further assimilation. In 1980 Han Jonsok started what became a widespread movement among Koreans refusing to be fingerprinted as required in the Alien Registration Law. This became one of the most important political and social issues of the decade for Koreans in Japan and, as in the past, affected political relations between Japan and South Korea. The Japanese government responded by reducing the requirement for fingerprinting to first-time only registration. Koreans could have avoided the various disadvantages of their alien status by applying for naturalization, but only a minority did so. A growing number of younger Koreans began to assert their identity as 'Koreans living in Japan', forgoing the use of Japanese names which would hide their Korean identity and actively participating in Korean cultural activities.

A cultural revival and new activism characterized developments among Ainus too. Assimilation had been encouraged, if not forced, since the nineteenth century, and as stated in a 1980 report to the United Nations, the Japanese government maintained that 'ethnic minority groups do not exist in Japan'.[4] However, the 1970s and 1980s saw increasing criticism of assimilation policies and the official denial of Ainu as an indigenous people. Moreover, criticism mounted against discriminatory treatment, for, despite the long history of assimilation policies, the Japanese image of Ainus as 'hairy, dirty, *shōchū*-drinking natives' was still widespread. Increased tourism to Hokkaido in the 1970s only refined the image of a racially different Other, as in ads promoting visits to a 'real Ainu village' with 'the ancient customs and culture of the famed hairy Ainu'.[5]

Ainu activists in the Hokkaido Utari Association increasingly voiced complaints against such stereotypes while working to recover and convey

Ainu cultural heritage to the younger generation. In 1986, for example, the Association protested against Prime Minister Nakasone Yasuhiro's statements that Japan comprised a single ethnic group, asserting that the Ainu had been thoroughly assimilated with the Japanese majority. Using himself as an example, he referred to his own bushy eyebrows to suggest that he must have Ainu blood, which provoked even more anger among Ainus.

In the 1980s Ainus used the courts and sought new legislation to fight discrimination and inaccurate portrayals of the Ainu. Mieko Chikapp successfully sued a publisher and authors of *Ethnography of the Ainu* for unauthorized use of her photograph. Chikapp also criticized the book for misleadingly describing the Ainu as a near-extinct ethnic group. Meanwhile, the Association began to work for the abolition of the Hokkaido Former Aborigines Protection Act and the enactment of a new law which would recognize the Ainu as an independent ethnic group with its own culture and guarantee Ainu rights as indigenous people of Hokkaido. In 1989 the national government set up a body to examine the 'New Law'.

As in the case of eliminating nationality restrictions on receiving pensions, international pressure supported the Association's efforts, and in the 1990s would contribute at last to recognition and legitimation of Ainu claims to rights as an indigenous people. The United Nations' Year of Indigenous People in 1993 put pressure on the Japanese government to reverse its long-standing position and finally to recognize the Ainu as an ethnic minority, and Japan's ratification of the International Convention on the Elimination of All Forms of Racial Discrimination provided Ainu groups further recourse for protecting their human rights. In addition, the Sapporo District Court's 1997 decision in what was popularly known as the Nibutani Dam case found that the Japanese government is bound by obligations under Article 27 of the International Covenant on Civil and Political Rights and Article 13 of the Japanese Constitution to guarantee the right of minorities to enjoy their own culture. Significantly, the court was the first government body to recognize the Ainu both as a minority and as an indigenous people. The decision not only signalled a turning point in the Japanese legal system's attitude towards Ainu rights and culture, but also presaged new legislation to promote and disseminate Ainu language and culture. The Diet repealed the old Protection Act, as desired by the Utari Association, and passed a new law that went some, though not all, of the way towards meeting the Association's demands.

While these 'old' minorities made mixed progress, some new ethnic/cultural groups began to migrate to Japan during the 1980s, diversifying Japanese society in an unprecedented way. Vietnamese were the first new group to arrive during the 1970s, admitted reluctantly as refugees by the Japanese government under international pressure. During the 1980s other groups entered Japan to fill the growing labour shortages created not only by the constantly declining birth rate since the 1960s, but to do 'dirty, dangerous or difficult' jobs that Japanese no longer wanted to do. Migrant

workers came from the Middle East and Southeast Asia on temporary contracts, but many stayed longer both legally and illegally. These new workers
differed greatly from Japanese not only in their language and ethnicity, but
in their religious beliefs and practices and social customs. Consequently, like
the old minorities, they encountered prejudice and discrimination.

Still another group recruited by Japanese companies were women from
Asian countries, especially the Philippines, to fill jobs in the entertainment/
sex industry or to become brides for rural men. Filipino women were often
recruited under false pretences, however. Lured by promises to make them
singers or actresses, they often ended up being virtual prisoners and forced
to be prostitutes. Those who arrived as mail-order brides for rural men did
not usually suffer such oppressive treatment, but stories of difficulties arising
from cultural differences often appeared in the media.

During the 1970s and 1980s Japan and the Japanese people thus became
increasingly involved with people of different cultures and ethnicities, not
only through brief experiences of travel abroad, but through exposure in the
media and personal contact in their daily lives. *Nihonjinron* writers asserted
Japanese purity and homogeneity against a reality of increasing diversification. The obstacles to overcoming discrimination for both new and old
minorities were great, and, as indicated above, it was often external pressure
from the international community that provided the necessary impetus for
change. In the next section we will examine other social developments
which were influenced by movements abroad, but which also had their own
indigenous origins.

Catching up with the West

Ever since the Meiji Restoration Japan had been trying to 'catch up' with
the West. In the 1970s and 1980s it accomplished this. Both foreigners and
Japanese often pointed out that economic success had been achieved without destroying Japanese 'traditions', and in fact had been achieved because
of Japanese traditions. It was thought that Confucian values of hard work,
frugality, loyalty and learning had worked as the Japanese counterpart of
the West's Protestant ethic. Their resilience in the process of industrialization
was also used to explain avoidance of the West's social problems – high
rates of crime, drug usage, divorce and poverty.

However, by the end of the 1980s Japanese society was 'catching up' with
the West in more than economic ways. Besides increasing activism and
litigation by minority groups, women emerged as a new force in politics.
New kinds of less submissive heroines emerged as role models in popular
culture, while the younger generation in general expressed less commitment
to study, work and company than did their parents and grandparents. While
the economy 'bubbled' the future was rosy, and young people could afford
to go from job to job if they pleased. But the government and economic
leaders were already concerned about how to keep Japan at the forefront

of economic and technological development now that the advantages of followership were gone. The government was also worried about the problems of a society ageing more rapidly than others in the world.

As pointed out in Chapter 11, many middle-class salarymen and their families were beginning to question the sacrifices being made for the country's high-speed economic growth even in the early 1970s, but most Japanese males still aspired to the job security and comfortable lifestyle of the large enterprise worker and most Japanese females hoped to become salarymen's wives. Moreover, the competition for educational achievement grew more intense, and the 'education mama' became a stock figure, devoted to getting her one or two children over the series of exam hurdles into a successful career.

At the same time, however, some women sought more choices as a new wave of feminism washed over Japan. At a 1970 demonstration a banner asking 'Mother, is marriage really bliss?' announced the movement's rejection of domesticity as women's fate and indicated its demands for equal employment opportunities. A new emphasis on reproductive rights and sexual liberation reflected the movement's stimulus from the women's liberation movement in the United States. Nevertheless, the movement also grew out of indigenous Japanese conditions. Many leaders came out of the radical movements of the late 1960s, dissatisfied with sexist treatment from male activists who relegated them to traditional female jobs like typing. The new feminists also criticized the cultural values of the economic miracle that undervalued women because their reproductive roles made them less productive than men.

From the mid-1970s women's groups became more diverse and focused on separate issues, but they actively contributed to attitudinal changes. United Nations sponsorship of the International Women's Year in 1975 and inauguration of the UN Decade for Women also reinforced their pressure on the Japanese government to initiate policies to end sex discrimination. The Equal Employment Opportunity Law of 1985 was one concrete result.

In the 1980s increased activism in many different community causes and the emergence of the charismatic Doi Takako as the first woman leader of the main opposition party, the Social Democratic Party of Japan, seemed to promise a new era of political participation for women too. In addition to the peace movement, women were especially active in movements related to the environment, consumer interests, welfare of children and the elderly, and cultural projects. When in 1989 there were 22 women elected to the House of Councillors, up from 10 or fewer in previous elections, the media dubbed this 'the Madonna phenomenon'. Women's votes were also responsible for the LDP's loss of its majority in the upper house. At the time many commentators explained this as women voters' outrage against a sex scandal involving Prime Minister Uno Sōsuke, but it was more likely opposition to a new consumption tax and dissatisfaction with the handling of another major political corruption scandal involving the Recruit conglomerate.

Meanwhile, girls as well as boys went on to higher levels of education, and upon completion the majority took full-time jobs until marriage. These were mainly clerical jobs as 'office ladies' ('OLs') or service positions, but gave young women large disposable incomes, since most continued to live with their parents. Free of responsibilities and living expenses, they became both big spenders and big savers. During the 1980s consumption expenditure of single women under the age of 30 increased by 15.8 per cent while that of single men increased by only 2 per cent.

The retailing, entertainment and travel industries understandably targeted this market, while new women's magazines sprouted up to reach the growing readership of young, educated working women. These magazines featured articles on travel and food as well as fashion and soon became a major advertising medium. Both the consumer industries and young women consumers flourished because of the continuing expectation that women would eventually become good wives and wise mothers.

Young women were the main generators of the 'cute' style that began in the mid-1970s, dominated popular culture in the 1980s, and continued to flourish in the 1990s. The word '*kawaii*' (cute) emerged in the early 1970s along with a craze among teenagers and young women for a new 'cute' handwriting style and a fashion for acting and dressing in a childish manner. Educators did not take kindly to the new handwriting style, and some schools even banned it. However, business, beginning with the company Sanrio, capitalized on this fashion by first producing cute-decorated stationery, then all sorts of 'fancy goods', such as *Hello Kitty*, with cute cartoon characters and other sweet, cheerful, childlike motifs. By the 1980s the cute style spread to clothes, food, celebrities, and house designs and décor. Even police boxes were designed as gingerbread houses, and love hotels were incongruously named after *Anne of Green Gables* and Laura of *Little House on the Prairie*. Both conservative critics and radicals from the protest movements of the 1960s deplored the values of sensual abandon and play that they associated with the consumption of expensive cute things. Other interpretations saw the fascination with cute culture as an escape from the restrictions and hard work of adulthood. One researcher noted that it was young women in the period immediately before marriage who became most immersed in cute culture, anticipating their loss of freedom and personal consumption. Certainly once they married, women's spending habits changed drastically, directed at household and children's education expenses rather than personal items or recreation.

We have seen in a previous section of this chapter that the number and proportion of married women returning to the workforce when their children reached school age rose steadily during the 1970s and 1980s. This was motivated largely by rising lifestyle expectations shaped by the consumer industries and by high education expenses. Consumer prices also remained high as protectionist policies for domestic agriculture and industry did not significantly break down even under international pressure. Because of these costs, women stubbornly refused to have more babies despite government pleas. In 1989 newspaper headlines announced the '1.57 shock', referring to a new low in the birth rate. Threats to legalized abortion emerged as one issue on which diverse women's groups managed to unite and fight successfully more than once during the 1970s and 1980s. They were less united in lobbying for legalization of the contraceptive pill, but in any case, opposition to the pill by conservative government officials and medical practitioners' organizations was too strong to overcome.

Another reason for women's reluctance to have more children was the all-encompassing nature of childrearing, but this, in turn, is an indication of the intensified focus on education for children during these decades. During the 1980s children's behaviour reflected the stresses of such pressure and the long hours of study in 'examination hell'. Absenteeism, juvenile crimes, bullying and high suicide rates became concerns in the 1980s. Educational approaches continued to emphasize rote learning, even though Prime Minister Nakasone and education commentators recommended changes to encourage creativity and initiative to keep Japan at the technological forefront. School practices and textbooks also encouraged group work and conformity. The old saying 'If the nail stands up, hammer it down' applied throughout life once a child reached school age.

The primary importance placed on formal educational achievement for determining career possibilities created greater income and lifestyle disparities during the 1980s. Most Japanese lived longer (the longest in the world), and led more comfortable lives as beneficiaries of improved diet and medical treatment. However, differences in housing, clothing and leisure patterns between, for example, a graduate of a vocational high school who could only become a factory worker and a graduate of an elite university who could join a large company became much greater during the 1980s. In addition, a class of super rich emerged at the top of the income pyramid as a result of the boom in real estate prices at the end of the decade, while there appeared a visible class of homeless people at the bottom for the first time. The myth of all Japanese being middle class became exposed as a myth. National surveys revealed widespread consciousness of the inequalities in distribution of wealth and income at the end of the 1980s.

The shift to tight budget policies in the early 1980s also meant that social welfare and health programmes did not keep expanding sufficiently to provide an adequate cushion for those at the bottom of the socioeconomic pyramid. Nor did national pension programmes assure sufficient income for retirement. Besides eliminating free healthcare for the elderly, the government introduced new policies which clearly placed care of the elderly on families, more specifically on women, as it faced the prospect of rising welfare expenditures in a rapidly ageing society. Even in the early 1970s demographers predicted that by the first decade of the twenty-first century people over the age of 65 would make up 20 per cent of the population. If birth rates continued below replacement level, the proportion of working, tax-paying age groups would decline in parallel to this development. Bureaucrats and politicians therefore encouraged women to have more children and to work part-time not only to fill the labour shortage, but also to care for the elderly. Cultural norms also favoured such home care.

When the 1980s ended with the 'Madonna phenomenon', it appeared that women might revolt against these increased but unequally rewarded demands for both of their roles in the home and the workplace. Women voters appeared to be a new political force representing widespread dissatisfaction with the corruption which pervaded all the political parties, socialists and LDP alike. Other disadvantaged groups also engaged in more activism. Emerging problems of youth and the elderly began to come to national attention.

The end of 'the postwar'?

The year 1989 was also the year when Emperor Hirohito died after reigning for 64 years. Political factors had saved him from trial and execution as a war criminal in 1945, but as long as he lived, memories of the war could not be forgotten and despite his 'humanization', the question of his war responsibility remained a matter of debate. Did his death finally mean the end of 'the postwar'? Many hoped so, but as we will see in Chapter 13, postwar issues refused to go away.

During the 1980s repercussions of Japan's wartime atrocities periodically disturbed its foreign relations and became domestic issues. Treatment of the war in Japanese textbooks for schoolchildren drew attention because of Professor Ienaga Saburō's long-running suit against the Ministry of Education which had forced him to revise the wording and depiction of Japanese actions in order to receive the Ministry's approval for his textbook. The Ministry, for example, required him to change 'Japan invaded China' to the less pejorative 'Japan advanced into China'. Ienaga's suit not only rallied supporters in Japan, but also official criticism of Japanese history education from the Chinese government. Japanese bureaucrats and politicians also provoked Chinese anger by denying wartime atrocities such as the 'rape of Nanking'.

More generally throughout Asia there were repeated demands for the Japanese government to make an official 'apology' for the war, and, while welcoming increasing Japanese investment, at the same time viewing it as potential economic imperialism. While reporting of Asian criticism in the Japanese media kept war issues alive, younger Japanese still studied little about the war (or the twentieth century more generally) at school, and school excursions to Hiroshima reinforced the image of the Japanese as the war's victims.

Other Asians also warily viewed the gradual buildup of Japanese military forces. The buildup occurred despite the end of the Cold War in the late 1980s when the Soviet Union collapsed. As the United States contemplated

Plate 12.1 The past in the present: the Peace Dome in the Peace Park, Hiroshima
Source: Elise K. Tipton

scaling down its military presence in the Asia-Pacific, it encouraged Japan to take more responsibility for its own defence. New pressures also came from the United States and Europe to carry more of the burden for international security as the outbreak of regional conflicts replaced the threat of an East–West nuclear war.

When Hirohito died in 1989, Japan's economy was still riding the bubble. Representatives from 163 foreign countries attended his funeral, including American President George Bush, in recognition of Japan's high status in the world. Security measures described by television stations as making Tokyo 'like a city under martial law' ensured that there were only two minor disruptions by left-wing groups which did not interrupt the funeral cortege. Several groups around the country displayed placards accusing Hirohito of war responsibility, and others criticized the government's decision to include Shinto rites in the state funeral. Despite such political debate surrounding the emperor's funeral, equally remarkable was the lack of interest among ordinary Japanese. Just over 200,000 people lined the streets compared to the anticipated 850,000, and in contrast to the 1.5 million who had pressed to watch the far from charismatic Taishō emperor's procession in 1927. Many used the national holiday to go skiing or to watch videos at home.

The 1980s thus ended with a mixture of emotions surrounding economic, political and social debate. The economy still bubbled, and the new nationalism of the 1980s reflected pride in Japan's achievement as a 'rich country'. However, its assertion of Japanese homogeneity and continuities with the past at the same time represented efforts to deny social change and to overcome insecurities derived from the drive to national wealth, since, in fact, continued economic success in the 1970s and 1980s had brought increasing involvement in global politics and culture and diversification of Japanese society and culture which undermined the values and institutions of the conservative elites.

As we will see in the next chapter, after the bubble burst in 1991, the anxieties about social change and dissatisfaction with Japanese politics that surfaced during the 1970s and 1980s came to dominate headlines. A weary sense of pessimism was to set in exacerbated by a decade of low growth and recurrent recessions.

13 The 'lost decade'

> The Japanese, with their low level of social capital, may be compared to a family living in a dilapidated house who have worked hard and scrimped to save money and have then used it not to improve their own home but to lend to others.[1]

This is the way the economist Noguchi Yukio summed up the situation of the Japanese at the beginning of the 1990s. One would expect that the Japanese people would have benefited from the high yen in the form of lower prices of imported goods and from budget surpluses going into more social capital. However, corporations did not pass on profits to consumers. As pointed out in the previous chapter, they channelled profits into 'zai-tech' investment activities instead. In addition, the government preferred to reduce bond issues and did not direct domestic savings into improvement of domestic infrastructure but into acquisition of assets abroad. Consequently, when the bubble economy collapsed in 1991, Japanese people were left with a lot of luxury goods, but woefully inferior social security programmes compared to other economically developed countries.

Slow economic recovery, a low birth rate and a rapidly ageing population meant that most Japanese had to turn away from high consumption and conserve their yen for retirement. Those who were employed did not feel the pinch so much, but as 'restructuring' became a word in everyday vocabulary, the famed 'Japanese employment system' with its pillars of 'lifetime' employment and seniority-based wages and promotion gradually disappeared. Unemployment rates reached new highs since the 1950s, especially hitting new university graduates and middle managers in their forties.

In contrast to the years of miracle growth, the government, including both politicians and bureaucrats, seemed too mired in corruption and conservative values to lead the country out of the economic slump. Moreover, political confusion and unstable leadership set in with the collapse of the '1955 system' in 1993. The splintering of the LDP gave birth to a welter of new, but often ephemeral parties, so that the rump of the LDP remained the largest party in the Diet and the core of a succession of coalition governments. The need for structural reform of politics and the economy was voiced everywhere, but little progress was made in practice. As a leading newspaper editorialized at the lead-up to the first general election of the twenty-first century, 'the 1990s is often referred to as a "lost decade". Much of the blame for this lost time falls on political parties for their inability to fulfill their primary obligations.'[2]

But what were their 'primary obligations' and to whom? Constantly shifting party membership of individual politicians, the frequent emergence and disappearance of new parties, and the continuing exposure of political corruption suggested the answer was individual self-interest. Japanese people's distrust of political parties was reflected in declining identification with any party. In addition, during the 1990s even the bureaucrats, who had traditionally been arrogant but honest, became involved in corruption scandals.

Political corruption was but one aspect of social and cultural decline. As we look at various social groups in this chapter, we will see little improvement, if not decline, in their economic and social situations. The old minorities of Koreans and Burakumin perhaps continued to experience slow improvement, but the working conditions and social position of women, Okinawans and new minorities remained the same if not worse. Calls for educational reform heightened as children and youth displayed growing problems, and once privileged middle-class salarymen emerged as a new troubled social group.

The mass media, popular culture and consumer industries were often blamed for spreading materialist values and encouraging violence and decadence. We will see that they also offered some new role models and lifestyle choices. But at the beginning of the twenty-first century there were still no prospects of a major transformation in Japanese politics or society, and many ordinary Japanese as well as opinion-leaders were wondering where the country was heading.

Politicians and bureaucrats

In party politics the most dramatic development of the decade was the collapse of the '1955 system' in 1993. In hindsight, the LDP's loss of its majority in the 1989 Upper House election even while the economy still bubbled indicated the fragility of its hold on power during the 1980s and foreshadowed its decline in the 1990s. Voters, especially in urban areas, were sick of the corrupt practices of politicians, agricultural subsidies, and the wasteful public works spending which aimed at maintaining the loyalty of the LDP's rural constituencies but kept consumer prices high and social welfare programmes inadequate.

In 1993 the nearly four decades-old one-party system came to an end when the LDP split. This ushered in a confusing period characterized by the establishment of new parties, often short-lived, and changing party affiliation by individual Diet members. Although one socialist, Maruyama Tomiichi, headed a coalition government (in an unlikely partnership with the LDP), the socialists proved unable to capitalize on the breakup of the LDP and win the electorate despite having moderated their unpopular foreign policy platform of unarmed neutrality during the late 1980s. Socialists, it was revealed in recurring corruption scandals, were no more honest than LDP politicians. In 1989, for example, a leading Socialist Party Diet member, Ueda Takuzō, was forced to resign after being implicated in the Recruit Cosmos bribe scandal. Three prominent leaders of other opposition parties, the Kōmeitō and Democratic Socialist Party, were also accused of involvement in 'money politics' scandals. Consequently, the remainder of the LDP endured as the core of a series of coalition governments which characterized the rest of the decade.

A new electoral system was introduced by the first Cabinet after the 1993 collapse under LDP breakaway Hosokawa Morihiro, but by the end of the decade it had not yet led to clear realignments of parties offering voters real choices in either domestic or foreign policies. The new system of 60 per cent of Lower House members chosen from single-member districts and 40 per cent by proportional representation has actually enhanced the localist bias in Japanese electoral politics because those elected by proportional representation are from regional districts. Since local economic interests have become increasingly diverse since the 1980s, this means that it will be very difficult for any government to generate a political consensus for bold national policies. Moreover, since many Diet members have 'inherited' their seats from their fathers or other relatives, there is little expectation of change being introduced by 'new blood'. Continuities with the past often pre-date even formation of the '1955 system'. Hosokawa, for example, is the grandson of one of the feudal lords of Tokugawa times.

With party fragmentation and instability, conservatives of the LDP have therefore continued in power, but the dependence on coalition partners to get legislation through the Diet has given certain small parties disproportionate influence. The Kōmeitō in particular gained more leverage. Voters, however, remained wary of its connections with the lay Buddhist organization Sōka Gakkai, as evidenced by the party's decreased number of seats in the House of Representatives election in June 2000.

In that election the coalition of the LDP, Kōmeitō and New Conservative Party (Hoshutō) managed to put together a majority of seats, but all three lost seats, and the LDP won only 233 out of 480 seats. An extremely low voter turnout of 63 per cent (the second lowest on record) saved the LDP from an even greater loss, while also showing voters' lack of confidence in any of the parties' abilities to steer the nation forward. The LDP's decline from its previous holding of 271 seats reflected an inability to win the support of urban voters, who gave more of their votes to the Democratic Party. Following the election, one foreign journalist pointed out the downward spiral that the LDP had put itself in. Pork barrelling to maintain its rural base of support led to the loss of urban votes which, in turn, made the LDP even more dependent on country voters.

Continuing revelations of bribery and corruption during the 1990s also turned voters against party politicians. In late 1992 Kanemaru Shin, 'long-time political godfather' as head of the faction originally led by Tanaka Kakuei in the 1970s, was arrested for taking a bribe from the parcel delivery service Sagawa Kyūbin. Public outrage forced his resignation from the LDP after investigating police also discovered a cache of gold bullion and currency in his office. Kanemaru was only one of many politicians tainted by accusations of graft. During the first half of the 1990s three prime ministers, including one representative of a new opposition party, were implicated in corruption scandals. What dismayed voters was the huge sums of money now involved in these cases.

Another shocking and depressing development was revelation of the involvement of bureaucrats and police in corrupt practices and cover-ups of negligence and incompetence. Bureaucrats and police officials had enjoyed a reputation for honesty and competence in the postwar period. However, investigations of bribery cases in the 1990s revealed active participation by a number of top-level bureaucrats. Particularly damaging to the bureaucracy's reputation was the arrest in 1996 of the administrative vice minister of the Ministry of Health and Welfare, Okamitsu Nobuharu, on charges that he had accepted expensive favours, including membership in a golf club, from a company seeking Ministry subsidies for its homes for the elderly. Ironically, Okamitsu had been appointed to clean up the Ministry's tarnished reputation after officials had endangered lives by covering up the distribution of HIV-contaminated blood.

Police officials also became implicated in a spate of corruption scandals, made more damaging by attempts to cover up the corruption when detected. In addition, several cases of negligence or slow response called into question the efficiency of the police, for example, in the cases of the sarin gas attack and a teenage bus hijacking which will be discussed later in this chapter. Although these cases did not undermine all confidence in the overall moral standards and effectiveness of the police, they did lead to the establishment of a Council on Police Reform in 2000 which was concerned with improved procedures for disclosing information and stronger mechanisms for maintaining internal discipline and reviewing police work.

Questions about government competence in emergency situations also arose with its clumsy response to the severe earthquake in the city of Kobe in 1995. For decades Japanese in the Tokyo area have been anticipating an earthquake of major proportions such as that in 1923, so all were taken by surprise when the disaster hit Kobe, an area not previously prone to earthquakes. The various responsible agencies failed to collaborate effectively in dealing with the disaster. Moreover, in the aftermath another aspect of Japan's cherished self-image as a classless society was undermined when it was evident that more houses in less affluent areas were damaged than in wealthier areas because of their poor construction.

Economic recession and its impact on workers

The area of incompetence which most affected Japanese people's lives as well as the climate of opinion was that of economic policy. The longest and deepest recession since the end of the war set in with the bursting of the bubble economy. Stock and land prices began to fall in January 1990 and plunged precipitously over the next thirty months. Most specialists estimate that the decline in the total value of stocks and land amounted to about five trillion US dollars by 1995, equivalent to almost one year of Japan's GNP.[3] Japan's real growth rate fell from 3.1 per cent in 1991 to 0.4 per cent in 1992. Bankruptcies multiplied, and financial institutions faced huge non-performing loans. As manufacturing firms cut back investment and slashed payrolls, the official unemployment rate, which seriously underestimates the real rate because it does not include part-time workers, had risen to more than 3 per cent by 1994 and to further unprecedented heights during the rest of the decade.

Ten years later, at the beginning of the twenty-first century, economic indicators pointed tentatively to recovery, but a year later to another recession, and economists remained divided over the future shape and direction of the Japanese economy. Pre-election polls in 2000 showed that economic recovery was the primary concern of voters. Japan remained the second largest economy in the world, but the recessions of the 1990s undermined many assumptions and practices which had been associated with Japan's postwar economic success.

One assumption that went was the view of Japanese economic policy-makers as perspicacious, far-sighted planners and leaders. There was constant talk about the need for economic reform, meaning deregulation of the economy, to get it going again. Nevertheless, neither party governments nor bureaucrats introduced significant new measures for accomplishing this aim. In an analysis of economic developments of the decade, Kozo Yamamura stressed that

> the appearance of deregulation all too often does not mean deregulation in substance, and . . . the seemingly large number of deregulation measures adopted and proposed cannot be equated in substance to a similarly large *amount* of deregulation, implemented or proposed – that is, Japan's economy is still heavily regulated compared to other industrialized economies and is likely to remain so in the coming decades.[4]

Even the number of deregulation measures adopted (674) was still small since there were over 10,000 regulations, such as licences and permits, enforced by the bureaucracy. Yamamura went on to note that the number of regulations should not be given too much weight since the United States has even more. However, it is also notable that the areas of greater regulation in the USA that Yamamura mentioned – workplace safety, manufactured consumer products and public health – were areas where Japanese people have felt relative deprivation.

The United States and other Western countries pressured the Japanese government to pump more money into the economy by keeping interest rates low, in fact close to zero. While loath to increase its budget deficit further, the government continued to spend on public works projects which ensured the rural vote, but did not stimulate economic recovery. Neither old nor new businesses responded with developments in new technology or products.

To existing firms, 'restructuring' simply meant slashing jobs to cut costs. In manufacturing, some factories closed, and large parent firms reduced their orders to subcontractors. Even the privileged core salarymen and blue-collar workers in large enterprises were not immune to payroll-cutting measures. Fringe benefits such as bar entertainment shrank or disappeared, wage increases and bonuses became smaller, and more weight was placed on performance criteria for wage payments. Redundant employees who were not fired often became so-called 'window' employees, given a desk by a window with no work to do and ostracized by fellow workers in the hope of their voluntary resignation. By the mid-1990s, however, even some of the largest enterprises, such as National Panasonic and Toyota, began to let core staff go. This particularly hit middle managers in their forties, as was the case in other advanced industrial countries. Unemployment for this generation meant not only loss of income, but social and psychological humiliation. Restructuring also affected another age cohort, since sacked middle-aged workers were not replaced with young people. Recruitment of new university graduates was curtailed, and while the job market for male graduates thus became very tight, female graduates were virtually shut out, since companies filled the few available places first with males.

While experienced white-collar workers and young, well-educated males and females were hurt by restructuring, the much larger number of workers in small and medium-sized firms suffered even more as their firms lost sub-contracting orders from large firms. As pointed out in Chapter 12, there was already a large gap in wages and benefits between these 'peripheral' workers and 'core' workers in large firms. During the 1990s the proportion of small and medium-sized firms reached 90 per cent of all firms and employed a growing proportion of the workforce. Most of the workers continued to be women in part-time or temporary status. When the recessions hit, such workers were the first to have their hours cut or lost their jobs.

At the same time more and more married women sought to re-enter the workforce in order to maintain their families' lifestyle and to meet educational expenses. Although work opportunities increased with the expansion of service industries as well as access to previously male-dominated occupations, most married women had to take part-time jobs since companies were shedding full-time workers. In the decade between 1986 and 1996 the percentage of regular female employees decreased from 67 per cent to 58 per cent. Although working, married women still retained primary responsibility for household tasks and childrearing, and government surveys showed that this perception actually strengthened during the 1990s. Rather than reducing the time they spent on housework, many working women tried to 'prove' that their working would not inconvenience the household. 'Once I decided to continue working I didn't want to cause my family any inconvenience so I decided not to slacken on housework.'[5] Consequently, according to a 1998 government White Paper, Japanese men spent only twenty minutes a day on housework even when their wives worked. In addition, working women often sought to avoid neighbours' as well their family's criticism for failure to perform wifely duties.

As a result of employers' cost-cutting efforts and the persistent view of women as supplementary labour, the inequalities between men and women actually worsened during the 1990s. Whereas the wage gap between men and women narrowed in other advanced economies, it widened in Japan. Even excluding part-timers and considering many women's interrupted employment pattern due to marriage and childrearing, the wages of women who worked continuously were lower than men's doing the same or equivalent work. In fact, the gap widened as the number of years of continuous service rose. The Equal Employment Opportunity Law (EEOL) thus did nothing to reduce the earnings gap between men and women.

Neither did the law contribute to an increase in the number or proportion of women in managerial positions. Large companies were able to continue to discriminate against women by further development of a two-track recruitment and promotion system. In this system a recruit must choose to apply for either the managerial or clerical track, with only the former leading to top-level positions in the company. Theoretically the managerial track was and is open to both sexes, but in practice male full-time employees automatically enter it whereas most women enter the clerical track. Companies also continued to discriminate against women in informal ways, including interviewing women only after all qualified male applicants were placed and encouraging women to resign upon marriage or childbirth. Consequently, even ten years after the passage of the EEOL, only 1.2 per cent of women workers were at department head level, and the majority of these worked in small or medium-sized firms. A revision of the law went into effect in 1999, stiffening its previous exhortations to employers to 'endeavour' to avoid discrimination by making these endeavour categories 'prohibitions'. It is still too early to see the effects of this revision, but a government White Paper on gender equality in 2000 stated that women made up only 16.1 per cent of central government employees recruited as 'career track' bureaucrats in 1999. Only 1 per cent of section chiefs and assistant section chiefs in government ministries and agencies were women in fiscal 1998. Consequently, gender equality in the workplace will take a long time to be achieved.

It is also unlikely that the number of women applying for the managerial track will rise rapidly because of the unattractiveness of a corporate career. Its requirements of long hours and job transfers more or less preclude marriage and motherhood. Even in the department store industry which promotes more women to managerial levels than other industries, Millie Creighton found that most department store managers had never been married. Moreover, the corporate management practice of entertaining middle- and upper-level executives in hostess clubs at night makes it difficult for women with families to develop the networks necessary for promotion, and the masculine orientation of such corporation-sponsored recreation sends the message to women that careers are for men.

Moreover, while company practices continued to favour men, the recessions' transformation of the corporate workplace made such careers even more undesirable than before. Since promises of lifetime employment faded even in large firms, men had to work longer and harder for the same income even to keep their jobs. In opposition to the policies of the 1980s which had encouraged shortening of working hours and days, salarymen took less vacation time and worked more unpaid overtime since there was a reduced number of employees after restructuring to do the same volume of work.

As in advanced industrial countries elsewhere, stress became the number one topic in Japan during the 1990s. In a 1998 survey by a Tokyo think-tank, 68 per cent of respondents stated that they often felt worried or anxious, almost double the percentage in a comparable 1990 survey. Another question revealed a similar increase in feelings of irritation and anger. Perhaps even more telling of increasing depression levels was the rise in suicide rates of middle-aged men. As one stress researcher commented, 'so many commuter trains were stopped because of suicides that we were really made aware of how often it happened'. Hospitals also reported significant increases in the number of male patients suffering depression due to overwork, anxiety and suppressed anger at corporate restructuring.

'*Karōshi*' ('death from overwork') was a word coined in the 1970s which revealed the high toll on salarymen exacted by the drive for high economic growth. During the 1990s *karōshi* became such a widespread concern that the Labour Ministry launched *karōshi* hotlines in 1994 in an attempt to reduce such deaths. Many doctors and social critics pointed to the sudden death of Prime Minister Obuchi Keizō from a stroke in 2000 as an example of *karōshi*. Obuchi was known as a workaholic who took only a few days off from work in his twenty months in office. Critics used his death to attack the attitudes internalized by Japanese which contributed to *karōshi*. In short, working to the point of exhaustion is regarded as a virtue, and proof of one's indispensability. Sleeping more than absolutely necessary and taking vacations is viewed as self-indulgent – for foreigners, slackers or the unsuccessful.

The 1990s as 'the era of women'?

With relatively privileged core male employees suffering from overwork even before the recession began, the 1990s initially at least looked promising for women. After the EEOL's passage in 1985 and the spectacular performance of women candidates and voters in the 1989 election, 'the era of women' (*'onna no jidai'*) became a catchphrase in the early 1990s. It connoted freedom, affluence, independence and power. However, as the previous discussion of women's position in the workplace has revealed, although in some ways their job opportunities had expanded, women still faced inequality and discrimination in employment at the beginning of the twenty-first century. The underlying reason for this was the continued expectation of women's role as domestic-oriented, making their paid labour outside the home merely 'auxiliary'.

The patriarchal underpinnings of institutions and practices remained firmly established to perpetuate the sexual division of labour and to constrain women's choices, but the media and even the state did not always send out consistent or uniform messages. Consequently, women could respond in different ways to the varied and sometimes contradictory conceptions of their proper role, especially with growing diversity in attitudes due to class, age, ethnicity and education. Popular culture and broadening opportunities to interact with foreign people and ideas offered some alternatives to the 'traditional' image of women's proper role as passive and submissive. For example, *manga* (comics and anime, their animated video and film versions) written for young women began to feature young fantasy heroines with supernatural powers in the mid-1970s and 1980s, and in the 1990s these heroines became more aggressive and violent (e.g. the schoolgirl heroines of *Sailor Moon*). In science fiction and fantasy the image of the adult 'cyborg woman' rose to prominence at the same time.

The state itself sent out mixed images through television. The government-funded NHK emphasized self-improvement content in its programmes aimed at women. Its extremely popular 'morning drama' serials explicitly and implicitly promoted the ideal of women working outside the home, but simultaneously reinforced traditional values of self-sacrifice and loyalty to the family. This was certainly evident in one of the most popular morning dramas of all times, *Oshin*, which aired in 1983 and was subsequently broadcast in over forty countries. Like all the heroines in morning dramas, Oshin, born into an impoverished family in rural northern Honshu, overcomes all kinds of obstacles, and achieves her dream of success both inside and outside the family. The story fulfilled its educational objective by situating Oshin's struggles in the historical events of the twentieth century. Although the dramas were primarily aimed at a housewife audience, they tied into current interests to attract younger women viewers as well. For example, stories during the 1990s concentrated on relationships between mothers and daughters, or elder and younger sisters, or on divorce, and theme songs and graphics featured in those popular among teenagers.

While differing from the NHK in their commercial goals, women's magazines similarly provided models of behaviour as well as fashion and style for women. Using highly prescriptive language and tone, their articles and advertising were intended to instil traditional feminine traits now epitomized in the appearance, manners and behaviour of the JAL (Japan Airlines) flight attendant. 'Intelligence' sometimes seemed to have more to do with appearance than with mental ability, as in an article noting that the Crown Princess Masako was 'intelligent indeed' because she wore grey eye shadow contrasting with a deep raspberry-pink lipstick.

Nevertheless, as Laura Miller has suggested from her study of two magazines for young working women in the mid- to late 1990s, discussions of 'bad girls' who were strong-willed, nonconformist and sexually active may have inadvertently presented them as 'anti-models' and conveyed 'a type of covert admiration'. In any case, the advice and images presented in women's magazines were often contradictory, making it very difficult to be the perfect woman. For example, there was a fine line between being praised for expressing opinions and holding convictions, and being criticized for self-centredness and aggressiveness. Conflicting images thus offered women some space to accommodate individual needs and desires, but it was still within the framework of male-dominated institutional structures and expectations.

Socialization and internalization of establishment expectations remained effective among most Japanese women, but there were some indications of changing life goals and behaviour, especially among younger women. One indicator of growing dissatisfaction with the strictures of Japan's male-dominated society was a report that in 2000 the number of Japanese women living and working abroad for more than six months had for the first time exceeded that of men. This reinforced observations of the enthusiasm for the foreign (especially Western) demonstrated by young women in their choice of hobbies, education, travel destinations and so forth, but at a deeper, longer term level.

In a turnaround from the 1980s, beauty contests and contestants began to disappear during the late 1990s, including the Miss Tokyo pageant in 2000 after a forty-three-year history as the country's most acknowledged regional beauty pageant. The 1999 revision to the EEOL and lack of sponsorship money due to the recessions help to explain the decline of the contests, but more fundamental and far-reaching is the lack of interest among women themselves, and reportedly among men too. For example, applications in Tokyo's Hachioji contest used to number more than 120 per year, but suddenly decreased to seventy in 1998. Other contest organizers also reported significant declines in candidates. Sensitivity to sexual harassment issues may also have contributed to the trend, as suggested by changes in some application requirements, such as no longer asking for the women's body measurements.

The rising age of marriage for women was another indicator of women's changing hopes, not a rejection of marriage itself but of notions of marriage based on the sexual division of labour. Surveys and studies of young university and working women found that they still wanted to marry, but were seeking romantic love and a husband who would be a partner and companion with shared interests. They rejected loveless marriages and those which would confine them to the home and housework. Consequently, in order to find the ideal husband, more and more women postponed marriage beyond the age of 25 even though it might mean being labelled 'Christmas cakes' (i.e. stale after the 25th).

The rising age of women's marriages and their idealization of the foreign revealed the gap which had developed between young men's and young women's expectations of marriage and priorities in life. In general, young men still sought a wife who was obedient and would 'make a bright and happy home'. They still envisioned marriage in which the husband and wife lived and worked in separate spheres with separate duties. They resented the reversal of positions in marriage negotiations which saw young women becoming the 'choosers' rather than the 'chosen'.

The male-dominated media sensationalized transgressive behaviour, notably the sexual activities of young women, but many feminists criticized it too. Young women who picked up Western men for sex were dubbed 'yellow cabs' after the phenomenon was observed first in New York, and later more commonly in Hawaii and Bali. Equally shocking were stories of high school girls participating in phone sex and prostitution to earn money to buy designer clothes and other expensive products. Others sold their school uniforms and underwear to stores catering to certain men's fetishes. To some, this behaviour constituted women's sexual liberation and empowerment, but although equality may have been achieved in the bedroom, it was offset by the lack of equality in the workplace.

Sex, violence and consumerism

Even sexual liberation was questionable in light of the increasing commercialization of sex and spread of pornographic images in visual media which came under greater attack by feminists in the 1990s. Commercial television channels chased high ratings more crassly by exploiting women's sexuality to an even greater extent than in previous decades. So did *manga*, advertisements, magazines and video programmes. And often in tandem with sex came more aggressive and violent images for selling all kinds of commodities.

Sexual sadism and treatment of women as sexual objects in *manga* for men was not new, but from the late 1980s a new genre of sexually oriented *manga* called 'Lolita eros' emerged. These comics emphasized sex with young girls. They often featured rape and other violence against girls, but depicted the victims not as traumatized but as grateful for the ecstasy stimulated by the violence. *Manga* for female readers, especially girls, did not feature sadistic sex like male-oriented *manga*, but there was less emphasis placed on virginity than previously. Sex between loving partners was condoned, while marriage remained the ideal. As mentioned earlier, though, the young fantasy heroines and cyborg women of 1990s *manga* and anime were far more physically aggressive and violent than their predecessors of the 1980s.

Plate 13.1 Role-playing in Harajuku, Tokyo, 2000
Source: Elise K. Tipton

Women's groups and a small minority of men became more vocal from the late 1980s in protests against advertisements and other media which used women's bodies in an exploitative or discriminatory way. In 1991, for example, they succeeded in getting posters promoting AIDS awareness withdrawn from train stations and other public places. One poster was considered offensive to women because it condoned Japanese men's engagement in prostitution when on business trips abroad. It showed a businessman hiding his face with his passport, with the copy: 'Have a nice trip! But be careful of AIDS.' Stimulated by a lecture by Filipina women denouncing prostitution tours to Asian countries, some fifty men formed The Association of Men Opposed to Prostitution in Asia at the end of the 1980s. Its representative, Taniguchi Kazunori, published a book on the problem in 1993. But while some men began to question concepts of masculinity and femininity in Japanese society, they remained a small minority. Moreover, although protests attracted more media coverage and thus raised awareness of discrimination against women, the mass media and the leisure and consumer industries remained primarily under male control.

At the same time, the main group of consumers being targeted by these industries were young, educated, unmarried working women, including 'office ladies' who opted for the clerical track. This is because traditional expectations themselves gave these women large disposable incomes and freedom from responsibilities. Consequently, they had more leisure time and money to spend on entertainment, travel and personal development than their single male counterparts. And while the advertising and consumer industries limited and shaped their choices in pursuing this lifestyle, their tastes in turn shaped or reshaped fashions, foods and entertainment. The transformation of horse-racing and soccer during the 1990s is an example of successful marketing to this group of women consumers. Promoters updated and repackaged the sports to appeal to the tastes of these women, offering new merchandise, logos and advertising images of fun and excitement. Young women's participation, in turn, made them popular, and in the case of horse-racing, transformed it into a respectable leisure pursuit.

The recessions affected the purchasing power of even young working women, however, and many economists blamed the slowness of recovery on the lack of domestic demand. With job security threatened even for regular, core workers and little assurance of any safety net being provided by government programmes, consumers did not feel confident enough to increase their spending. The big, elegant department stores which had been catering to the designer tastes of the affluent in the 1980s suffered significantly. Instead, discount stores began to proliferate as Japanese consumers looked for bargains, and for the first time since the 1950s bought secondhand goods and automobiles. Top-class hostess bars, such as those in Ginza, lost business as large firms cut back on entertainment spending. Former favourite travel destinations of Japanese tourists, such as Hawaii and Australia, also suffered as overseas travel shrank and the remaining tourists were less free-spending.

Social *malaise* at the turn of the century

As the twenty-first century began, there were faint signs of economic recovery, but the public mood was hardly optimistic. Against the background of continuing economic uncertainty and lack of trust in government and politics, the manifestation of social problems in a wide range of fields dampened the outlook for the future.

For children brought up in the affluent, consumption-oriented years of the bubble, the recession years must have been a rude shock to their lifestyle expectations. This was one possible explanation for the disturbing series of violent crimes committed by teenage males at the beginning of the twenty-first century. A 17-year-old boy shocked the nation by hijacking a bus and killing one passenger in the middle of the 'Golden Week' holiday season. He said he wanted to get back at his parents and society. A few days later another 17-year-old murdered a woman in her own home and later told police that he 'wanted to have an experience of murdering someone'. Aside from teenage violence, bullying, lack of commitment to study and absenteeism continued to be problems in the schools. In addition, violence against teachers and disruptive classroom behaviour became new concerns which intensified calls for educational reform.

Some educational experts blamed rigid schools with their strict rules, uniform curricula and authoritarian classrooms for children's feelings of oppression, which then manifested themselves in bullying and truancy. The social and economic system's emphasis on examination performance for career success forced children to focus on academic studies. If they did not perform well in their studies they were considered failures by both their parents and society, and indeed their options for work and hopes for status were limited. In addition, since the entrance examinations to prestigious schools and universities tested rote learning, students learned to memorize in school and after-school cram schools.

The teenage hijacker reportedly performed well but was bullied in junior high school. After he failed to gain entrance into the high school of his choice, he lost confidence and left high school. He joined online chat rooms, but became the target of bullying there as well. According to the psychiatrist who treated the boy before the hijacking, the boy represented the problems of present-day youth, 'trapped between their parent's [sic] overprotection and high expectations'. 'It's an all-or-nothing society. . . . Once they drop out of the ideal category and feel they've lost people's attention, some kids get very depressed and life loses meaning to them.'[6]

The psychiatrist joined with many other commentators in blaming adults and the social system more generally for problems of juvenile delinquency. According to these criticisms, parents during the booming 1980s had spoiled their children with material things, but not taught them responsibility and discipline. In addition, they overprotected their children, and by treating them 'like kings at home' did not give them the skills for communicating and relating to other people outside the home where they were not the centre of attention. They also put too much value on results and not process, so that academic failure led to loss of self-esteem and confidence.

Lack of ability to communicate in other ways also became a concern of educators during the 1990s. One high school in Fukuoka on the island of Kyushu tried to encourage students to talk more in class by introducing a new compulsory subject called 'Japanese communication'. Meanwhile, there arose much debate about the position of English in the school curriculum and Japanese society more generally. Various Ministry of Education panels investigated English-language education during the decade, leading to re-commendations for greater emphasis on English starting in primary school. The apparent lack of ability of Japanese to speak English, even though it is a compulsory subject from middle school onwards, worried many business and government leaders as English increasingly became a *lingua franca* in international economic and political dealings, especially with the spread of the Internet.

Renewed interest in educational reform thus resulted from a desire to ensure Japan's position as a leading economic power as well as to resolve social problems of youth which were spilling out of the home and schools and endangering the wider society. More emphasis on problem-solving than rote learning was proposed by many educational experts and social psychologists to make school more interesting. Industry and government also hoped that this would promote the creativity that Japan required for technological development. It even planned to establish a new university named

Monozukuri Daigaku (literally, 'creating things university') which would aim at enhancing technological education for rejuvenating manufacturing. But this attempt to revive manufacturing instead of information technology in the present information age indicates the outdated assumptions of Japanese business and government leaders. At the same time, calls for more emphasis on morals from conservative politicians suggested the desire for a revival of pre-1945 Confucian-based ethics courses and illustrated their clinging to an idealized past.

It was not only children and teenagers who seemed to lack a sense of morals and values, which then manifested itself in criminal behaviour. The sarin gas attack in major subway stations in Tokyo in 1995 not only shocked Japanese out of their sense of public safety, but also suggested the spiritual and social alienation of some of society's elite. Members of Aum Shinrikyō had perpetrated the attacks which left twelve dead and hundreds injured. The Aum sect was just one of dozens of new religions which had flourished since the 1970s, in itself an indicator of a widespread search for psychological comfort and new values. In earlier times of economic, social and political uncertainty, such as the late Tokugawa decades and the 1930s, various new religions had also emerged. The people whom Aum had attracted, however, were not those who had missed out on the benefits of high economic growth, but rather its beneficiaries – university graduates in various scientific and technological fields.

Prospects for the older generation who had lived and worked according to the values of hard work, frugality and sacrifice for the family were not necessarily brighter. Considering demographic trends, the prospect of a younger generation uncommitted to work, society or the nation augured badly for the twenty-first century. The proportion of working, tax-paying adults was rapidly shrinking as the proportion of retirees grew. In the 1980s the government had already made clear its policy of making families shoulder the main burden of caring for the elderly. This responsibility fell primarily to middle-aged women. Nevertheless, attitudinal surveys revealed that fewer Japanese remained committed to the responsibility of caring for their elderly parents, and middle-aged and elderly people themselves did not want to be a burden on their children. In addition, labour shortages and the greater desire of the younger generation of women to work indicate that there will be a future shortage of unpaid domestic labour to care for the elderly.

Issues of health and care for the elderly, particularly those no longer capable of independent living, occupied more and more attention during the 1990s. Various programmes relying on volunteers (including many middle-aged housewives) were featured in the media, but these did not seem to be an adequate solution for the long term. Some have suggested that the existing gendered division of labour may need to be scrapped, and care of the elderly put in the hands of people and institutions outside the family. However, there were still no signs of such a shift in government policy at the beginning of the twenty-first century.

Besides heightened awareness of concerns related to different age groups, attention increased as to the needs and demands of still disadvantaged social groups during the 1990s. Discrimination against the 'old' minorities remained, although improvements to their physical environments continued. This posed a dilemma for some activists, such as Buraku Liberation League leaders, as to what policies should now be pursued. Issues related to new immigrants became more prominent as more stayed on in Japan, married Japanese and established families. Educational questions arose as their children entered school, and classrooms were no longer homogeneous in culture, ethnicity or even language. In addition, questions of citizenship arose for these children with only one Japanese parent. At least efforts to abolish gender-biased citizenship qualifications succeeded – children born of a Japanese mother were granted citizenship.

A diversity of needs and demands from other groups also emerged during the 1990s. Some groups, such as the disabled, were not new, but only now felt willing and confident enough to demand an end to their invisibility and access to opportunities to participate in mainstream public life. Two other groups might be called Japanese returnees from abroad, but from very different circumstances. Third- and fourth-generation descendants of Japanese immigrants to South America comprised one of these groups. They came to Japan in hopes of bettering their living, but like other new immigrants, faced difficulties because of their lack of Japanese language skills and cultural knowledge. In their case, however, they looked Japanese.

The other group of returnees also faced some problems of language, especially in schools, but possessed advantages other minorities did not have. These were children of Japanese businessmen who had worked abroad. Their proficiency in English made them a valuable asset to companies whose international dealings were steadily expanding. Their relatively elite social backgrounds also made them a group not to be ignored. But they raised problems of reintegration into Japanese society and particularly the educational system, not just related to language but cultural values.

Internationalization and globalization

The new dilemmas posed by immigrants and returnees derived from Japan's increased involvement with the outside world with ideas, values and practices not always compatible with those of the conservative elites who dominated Japanese society and politics. 'Internationalization' had become a catchword during the 1980s, but many commentators expressed cynicism about its realization. Many Japanese showed an enthusiasm for foreign cultures and foreign travel. Young Japanese in particular followed trends in American fashion and popular culture, and some Japanese popular culture products, including *manga*, video games, karaoke and toys, enjoyed similar success in the USA and other Western societies. Japanese popular culture proved even more successful in a wider range of products, such as popular songs and singers, in Asian countries. However, despite the requirement of English in the middle school curriculum and its promotion in primary schools, Japanese education remained insular and conservative in important areas such as history. Furthermore, the debates over handling of 'problems' raised by new immigrants' children in the schools revealed a reluctance to make education multicultural. This both reflected and contributed to the continuing difficulties Japan faced in negotiating a new role in international politics commensurate with its economic power.

The decade began with a foreign policy issue which challenged Japan to take a wider role in international politics, but in so doing raised the previously taboo subject of constitutional revision. The issue arose after US congressional leaders criticized Japan for failing to commit human as well as material resources in the Gulf War. Under pressure from key LDP leaders who favoured a more assertive role in world affairs, Prime Minister Kaifu Toshiki's government introduced what became known as the PKO (peace-keeping operations) bill. The bill proposed that Japanese armed military personnel, ships and warplanes be allowed, for the first time since 1945, to operate outside Japan's 1000 nautical mile 'self-defence perimeter' in UN peace-keeping operations. The opposition parties vehemently opposed the bill as a step towards Japan's return to military power. So great was popular as well as parliamentary resistance to this perceived undermining of the peace constitution that the bill was passed only after two years of heated debate and in revised form.

The debate removed the taboo on discussion of constitutional revision, although no proposals for amendment were put forward. Under American pressure, budgets for military expenditures continued to creep up, but still remained less than those of some European nations. The USA scaled down some of its military bases in Japan, but the alliance remained intact despite the efforts of protest groups, especially in Okinawa. Central government interests prevailed over those of Okinawa, which remained one of the poorest prefectures in the country. Although Japanese governments sought international recognition by campaigning for a permanent seat on the UN Security Council, Japan's role in international conferences and agencies continued to be rather passive. In these settings Japan usually followed the lead of the United States or that of the majority.

Strong pacifism among the Japanese people made Japanese 'hawks' proceed carefully, but, in addition, other Asian nations would not forget the war and continued to be wary of a revival of Japanese military power. Demands for redress for crimes of the past commanded national and international attention when in 1991 Kim Hak Sun overcame her shame and expressed her willingness to testify publicly about having been forced into prostitution with Japanese soldiers during the Second World War. Joined by others, she demanded compensation from the Japanese government in the courts. More Korean and other Asian women numbering in their thousands came forth with similar stories, exposing official government

establishment of brothels at the war fronts throughout Asia, forced recruitment of the so-called 'comfort women' to service them, and the terrible conditions amounting to what many label 'sexual slavery'. The government
initially denied sponsorship of the brothels, but Chūō University professor
Yoshiaki Yoshimi discovered documents verifying it. The government still
refused to pay compensation, saying its peace treaty with South Korea had
ended further reparations. It only encouraged formation of a private organization to raise compensation funds.

Demands from Asian nations for an apology for wartime aggression peaked
in 1995 with the fiftieth anniversary of the end of the war, but the apology
resolution proposed in the Diet was watered down to an expression of 'self-
reflection' which more than half the MPs still did not vote for. Instead the
LDP published a history book denying any aggression or war crimes, such
as the 'rape of Nanking'. Two of the LDP Diet members who worked on
the book later became prime ministers – Hashimoto Ryūtarō and Mori
Yoshiro. Mori created a scandal in May 2000 when he referred to Japan as
a 'country of the gods with the emperor as its core', words reminiscent
of prewar and wartime rhetoric. Japanese politicians and bureaucrats consequently continued to anger other Asians with their refusal to acknowledge
and repent Japan's imperialist past.

Aside from unrepentant party politicians, there emerged a group of well-
known academics who formed the Society for Writing New History Textbooks. Centred on Professors Fujioka Nobukatsu and Sakamoto Takao,
the Society's central demand was removal of discussion of 'comfort women'
from school history textbooks. They argued that this discussion was one
example of history education about the Second World War which was too
self-criticizing. In their view, history education should instil pride in Japan's
past, telling a 'proper story of the nation' which focuses on Japan's achievements and uniqueness.

The Society's campaign generated debate about Japan's national identity
as other historians and history educators began to criticize the group's
picture of Japanese history and its basis on a static, monolithic view of
Japan and the Japanese. While the emergence of a movement of nationalist
historians was disturbing, the debate it provoked indicated rejuvenation of
the Japanese intellectual scene. Critical re-examination of Japan's national
identity will have important implications for Japan's position and role in
the Asia-Pacific region as well as for the diverse non-Japanese groups now
making up Japanese society.

Japan at the beginning of the twenty-first century

It has become almost a cliché to say that at the beginning of the twenty-first
century Japan stands at a turning point in its modern history. Having
achieved the Meiji goal of a rich country, the question is now about ways to
maintain affluence and distribute it more equitably among all Japanese.

Unlike earlier periods of economic downturn, this will require innovations and creativity of a different kind since Japan no longer stands in the advantageous position of being able to borrow and adapt more advanced technology. Japanese themselves must now make the scientific and technological breakthroughs. Considering the comparatively low level of investment in basic scientific research and the conformist orientation of education, few Japanese or foreigners have expressed confidence in this happening. Nevertheless, Japan has defied pessimistic forecasts many times in the past, so it is wise for historians not to make gloomy predictions shaped by the present mood.

Whether or not affluence will be spread more equitably is also uncertain. As discussions of minorities have shown, the Japan where all were homogeneous or middle class never really existed even in the 1960s and 1970s, but inequalities in the distribution of income were not as great as in Western industrialized countries. Moreover, even as inequalities grew during the 1980s bubble, disadvantaged groups also became more vocal in their protests. Often supported by international pressure, they made some gains. There is little doubt that people in Japan enjoy much longer, healthier and more comfortable lives than they did forty years ago. In fact, their life expectancies are the longest in the world.

Nevertheless, there is still some truth in the saying common among Japanese that 'the country is rich but the people are not'. Compared to other OECD countries, expenditures on social security and welfare remain embarrassingly low for the second largest economy in the world. Consumer prices continue to be high, housing woefully crowded and pollution levels unhealthily high. Meanwhile, during the 1980s and 1990s Japanese social developments began to catch up with Western ones in undesirable ways. Juvenile delinquency and other crimes increased, suicide rates of male youths and the elderly rose, disparities in income grew, and more marriages and families broke down.

Consciousness about the necessity of reforms in a wide range of areas was acute, even though there was not yet any consensus about the way forward, and little evidence of any fundamental transformation of institutions and structures being undertaken in politics, the economy or society. Male-dominated conservative elites continued in power in party politics, the bureaucracy and business, although the Japanese public displayed little trust in any of them. About all we can say is that uncertainty characterized the outlook for the future. Still, the Japanese people have weathered worse situations than this. Perhaps there is less reason for pessimism than the latest newspaper headline or television newsbite would indicate.

Glossary of Japanese terms

Bakufu Shogunal government.

Bakuhan Tokugawa political system comprising the shogunate (*bakufu*) and feudal domains (*han*).

Bakumatsu Period of the end of the Bakufu or shogunate, 1853 to 1868.

Bunka Culture.

Bunmei kaika Civilization and enlightenment.

Burakumin Descendants of Tokugawa outcasts, literally 'hamlet people'.

Bushidō The way of the warrior.

Chōnin Townspeople of the mercantile class during the Tokugawa period.

Daimyō Feudal lord.

Ee ja nai ka 'What the hell!' chant of crowds in disturbances during 1867.

Ero-guro nansensu 'Erotic, grotesque nonsense'.

Eta Outcasts of pre-Meiji times, literally 'great filth'.

Fudai daimyō Feudal lords who had been allies of Tokugawa Ieyasu.

Fukoku kyōhei 'A rich country, strong army'.

Genrō Elder statesmen, oligarchs of the early Meiji government.

Gōshi Nominal 'rural' samurai.

Han Feudal domain.

Heimin Commoners, a class designated during the Meiji period.

Hibakusha Atomic bomb victims.

Hinin Outcasts of pre-Meiji times, literally 'non-human' or 'non-persons'.

Ie Household.

Jōi Expel the barbarians.

Juku After-school schools.

Kaikoku 'Open the country'.

Kamikaze Divine wind.

Karōshi Death from overwork.

Kawaii Cute.

Ken Prefecture.

Koku Measurement used for tax assessment and samurai incomes during the Tokugawa period, equivalent to 4.96 American bushels of rice or rice equivalents.

Kokutai National polity, national essence.

Koseki   Family registration records.
Kōtō chūgakkō   Higher middle schools.
Manga   Comics.
Minponshugi   Yoshino Sakuzō's concept of democracy, literally 'people-as-the-base-ism'.
Minzokugaku   Folklore studies.
Modan boi, mobo   Modern boy.
Modan gāru, moga   Modern girl.
Modan raifu   Modern life.
Modanizumu   Modernism.
Monpe   Pantaloon-like trousers worn by peasant women, recommended for all women during the Second World War.
'Onna no jidai'   'Era of women'.
Ōsei fukko   Restoration of imperial rule.
Oyakata   Labour recruiter, supervisor, literally, 'parent-like person'.
Pan pan   'Woman of the dark', Americanized prostitute of the Occupation period.
Risshin shusse   Success, self-advancement.
Rōnin   Masterless samurai.
Ryōsai kenbo   'Good wife, wise mother'.
Sakoku   Closed country.
Sankin kōtai   Alternate attendance system.
Shinheimin   'New commoners', former Tokugawa outcasts.
Shishi   'Men of spirit', terrorists who advocated 'Revere the emperor, expel the barbarians' during the Bakumatsu period.
Shizoku   Former samurai.
Sonnō jōi   'Revere the emperor, expel the barbarians'.
Taiyōzoku   'Sun tribe' films about the younger generation during the 1950s.
Takenoko seikatsu   'Bamboo-shoot living'.
Tayū   Highest class of licensed prostitutes during the seventeenth century.
Tennōsei   Emperor system.
Terakoya   Temple schools for commoners during the Tokugawa period.
Tokumi-donya   Semi-official shipping syndicates of the late Tokugawa period.
Tozama daimyō   'Outside' feudal lords, former enemies of Tokugawa Ieyasu.
Ukiyo   'Floating world'.
Ukiyo zōshi   *Chōnin* fiction.
Ukiyoe   Woodblock prints depicting *chōnin* life.
'Ume yo, fuyase yo'   'Give birth and multiply'.
Watakushi shōsetsu   I-novel.
Zaibatsu   Large financial combine or company.

Further reading

General works and anthologies

Bernstein, Gail L. (ed.), *Recreating Japanese Women, 1600–1945*, Berkeley: University of California Press, 1991.

Denoon, D., M. Hudson, G. McCormack and T. Morris-Suzuki (eds), *Multicultural Japan: From Paleolithic to Postmodern*, Cambridge: Cambridge University Press, 1996.

Dore, R.P., *Aspects of Social Change in Modern Japan*, Princeton, NJ: Princeton University Press, 1967.

Duus, Peter (ed.), *The Cambridge History of Japan*, Vol. 6, *The Twentieth Century*, Cambridge: Cambridge University Press, 1988.

Francks, Penelope, *Japanese Economic Development*, London and New York: Routledge, 1992.

Gluck, Carol and Stephen R. Graubard (eds), *Showa: The Japan of Hirohito*, New York and London: W.W. Norton, 1992.

Harootunian, Harry D., *History's Disquiet: Modernity, Cultural Practice, and the Question of Everyday Life*, New York: Columbia University Press, 2000.

Iriye, Akira (ed.), *Mutual Images: Essays in American–Japanese Relations*, Cambridge, MA, and London: Harvard University Press, 1975.

Jansen, Marius (ed.), *Changing Japanese Attitudes to Modernization*, Princeton, NJ: Princeton University Press, 1965.

—— (ed.), *The Cambridge History of Japan*, Vol. 5, *The Nineteenth Century*, Cambridge and New York: Cambridge University Press, 1989.

Kodansha Encyclopedia of Japan, 9 volumes, Tokyo and New York: Kodansha, 1983.

Koschmann, J. Victor (ed.), *Authority and the Individual in Japan*, Tokyo: University of Tokyo Press, 1974.

Livingston, Jon, Joe Moore and Felicia Oldfather (eds), *The Japan Reader*, 2 volumes, New York: Pantheon Books, 1973.

Lockwood, William, *The Economic Development of Japan*, Princeton, NJ: Princeton University Press, 1968.

Lu, David J. (ed.), *Japan: A Documentary History*, 2 volumes, Armonk, NY: M.E. Sharpe, 1996–7.

Miyoshi, Masao and H.D. Harootunian (eds), *Japan in the World*, Durham, NC, and London: Duke University Press, 1993.

Morris-Suzuki, Tessa, *The Technological Transformation of Japan from the Seventeenth to the Twenty-First Century*, Cambridge: Cambridge University Press, 1994.

Najita, Tetsuo and J. Victor Koschmann (eds), *Conflict in Modern Japanese History: The Neglected Tradition*, Princeton, NJ: Princeton University Press, 1982.

Patrick, Hugh (ed.), *Japanese Industrialization and Its Social Consequences*, Berkeley and Los Angeles: University of California Press, 1976.

Shively, Donald (ed.), *Tradition and Modernization in Japanese Culture*, Princeton, NJ: Princeton University Press, 1971.

Tsunoda, Ryusaku, William Theodore de Bary and Donald Keene (comps), *Sources of Japanese Tradition*, Vol. 2, New York and London: Columbia University Press, 1964.

Vlastos, Stephen (ed.), *Mirror of Modernity: Invented Traditions of Modern Japan*, Berkeley, Los Angeles and London: University of California Press, 1998.

Wakabayashi, Bob Tadashi (ed.), *Modern Japanese Thought*, Cambridge and New York: Cambridge University Press, 1998.

Wray, Harry and Hilary Conroy (eds), *Japan Examined: Perspectives on Modern Japanese History*, Honolulu: University of Hawaii Press, 1983.

Journals

Japan Forum
Japan Quarterly
Japanese Studies
Journal of Asian Studies
Journal of Japanese Studies
Monumenta Nipponica
U.S-Japan Women's Journal: English Supplement

Tokugawa Japan

Beasley, William G., *The Meiji Restoration*, Stanford, CA: Stanford University Press, 1972.

Bix, Herbert P., *Peasant Protest in Japan, 1590–1884*, New Haven, CT: Yale University Press, 1986.

Craig, Albert, *Chōshū in the Meiji Restoration*, Cambridge, MA: Harvard University Press, 1961.

Gerstle, C. Andrew (ed.), *18th Century Japan: Culture & Society*, Sydney: Allen & Unwin, 1989.

Goodman, Grant K., *The Dutch Impact on Japan (1648–1853)*, Leiden: Brill, 1967.

Hanley, Susan, *Everyday Things in Premodern Japan: The Hidden Legacy of Material Culture*, Berkeley: University of California Press, 1997.

—— and Kozo Yamamura, *Economic and Demographic Change in Preindustrial Japan, 1600–1868*, Princeton, NJ: Princeton University Press, 1977.

Harootunian, H.D., *Things Seen and Unseen: Discourse and Ideology in Tokugawa Nativism*, Chicago, IL, and London: University of Chicago Press, 1988.

——, *Toward Restoration: The Growth of Political Consciousness in Tokugawa Japan*, Berkeley and Los Angeles: University of California Press, 1970.

Hibbett, Howard, *The Floating World in Japanese Fiction*, Rutland, VT, and Tokyo: Tuttle, 1959.

Huber, Thomas, *The Revolutionary Origins of Modern Japan*, Stanford, CA: Stanford University Press, 1981.

Jansen, Marius B., *Sakamoto Ryōma and the Meiji Restoration*, Princeton, NJ: Princeton University Press, 1961.

Jenkins, Donald, *The Floating World Revisited*, Portland, OR: Portland Art Museum, 1993.

Jones, Sumie (ed.), *Imaging/Reading Eros: Sexuality and Edo Culture, 1750–1850*, Bloomington: University of Indiana Press, 1995.

Kang, Etsuko Hae-Jin, *Diplomacy and Ideology in Japanese–Korean Relations, From the Fifteenth to the Eighteenth Century*, Basingstoke, London and New York: Macmillan and St Martin's Press, 1997.

Keene, Donald, *Anthology of Japanese Literature to the Nineteenth Century*, Harmondsworth: Penguin, 1978.

——, *The Japanese Discovery of Europe, 1720–1830*, Stanford, CA: Stanford University Press, 1969.

——, *World Within Walls: Japanese Literature of the Pre-Modern Era, 1600–1867*, New York: Holt, Rinehart & Winston, 1976.

Koschmann, J. Victor, *The Mito Ideology: Discourse, Reform, Insurrection in Late Tokugawa Japan, 1790–1864*, Berkeley: University of California Press, 1987.

Leupp, Gary P., *Male Colors: The Construction of Homosexuality in Tokugawa Japan*, Berkeley, Los Angeles and London: University of California Press, 1995.

McClain, James, *Kanazawa: A Seventeenth Century Castle Town*, New Haven, CT, and London: Yale University Press, 1982.

Nakane, Chie and Shinzaburō Ōishi (eds), *Tokugawa Japan: The Social and Economic Antecedents of Modern Japan*, Tokyo: University of Tokyo Press, 1990.

Nishiyama Matsunosuke, *Edo Culture: Daily Life & Diversions in Urban Japan, 1600–1868*, Honolulu: University of Hawaii Press, 1997.

Ooms, Herman, *Tokugawa Ideology: Early Constructs, 1570–1680*, Princeton, NJ: Princeton University Press, 1985.

——, *Tokugawa Village Practice: Class, Status, Power, Law*, Berkeley: University of California Press, 1996.

Seigle, Cecilia, *Yoshiwara: The Glittering World of the Japanese Courtesan*, Honolulu: University of Hawaii Press, 1993.

Shively, Donald H., 'Sumptuary Regulation and Status in Early Tokugawa Japan', *Harvard Journal of Asiatic Studies*, 25, 1964–5, pp. 123–64.

Smith, Thomas, *The Agrarian Origins of Modern Japan*, Stanford, CA: Stanford University Press, 1959.

Toby, Ronald, *State and Diplomacy in Early Modern Japan: Asia in the Development of the Tokugawa Bakufu*, Princeton, NJ; Princeton University Press, 1984.

Totman, Conrad, *Japan Before Perry: A Short History*, Berkeley: University of California Press, 1981.

——, *The Collapse of the Tokugawa Bakufu, 1862–1868*, Honolulu: University of Hawaii Press, 1980.

Vaporis, Constantine, 'To Edo and Back: Alternate Attendance and Japanese Culture in the Early Modern Period', *Journal of Japanese Studies*, 23 (1), winter 1997, pp. 25–67.

Vlastos, Stephen, *Peasant Protests and Uprisings in Tokugawa Japan*, Berkeley: University of California Press, 1986.

Walthall, Anne (ed. and trans.), *Peasant Uprisings in Japan, A Critical Anthology of Peasant Histories*, Chicago, IL: University of Chicago Press, 1991.

White, James, *Ikki: Social Conflict and Political Protest in Early Modern Japan*, Ithaca, NY: Cornell University Press, 1995.

Wilson, George M., *Patriots and Redeemers in Japan: Motives in the Meiji Restoration*, Chicago, IL: University of Chicago Press, 1992.

Yamakawa, Kikue, *Women of the Mito Domain: Recollections of Samurai Family Life*, trans. Kate Wildman Nakai, Tokyo: University of Tokyo Press, 1992.

Yamamura, Kozo, *A Study of Samurai Income and Entrepreneurship: Quantitative Analyses of Economic and Social Aspects of the Samurai in Tokugawa and Meiji Japan*, Cambridge, MA: Harvard University Press, 1974.

Meiji Japan

Blacker, Carmen, *The Japanese Enlightenment: A Study of the Writings of Fukuzawa Yukichi*, Cambridge: Cambridge University Press, 1964.

Bowen, Roger W., *Rebellion and Democracy in Meiji Japan: A Study of Commoners in the Popular Rights Movement*, Berkeley: University of California Press, 1980.

Bowring, Richard, *Mori Ōgai and the Modernization of Japanese Culture*, Cambridge: Cambridge University Press, 1979.

Burks, Ardath W. (ed.), *The Modernizers: Overseas Students, Foreign Employees and Meiji Japan*, Boulder, CO: Westview Press, 1985.

Coaldrake, William H., *Architecture and Authority in Japan*, London and New York: Routledge, 1996.

Dower, John W. (ed.), *Origins of the Modern Japanese State: Selected Writings of E.H. Norman*, New York: Pantheon Books, 1975.

Duus, Peter, *The Abacus and the Sword: The Japanese Penetration of Korea, 1895–1910*, Berkeley: University of California Press, 1995.

Fujitani, Tadashi, *Splendid Monarchy: Power and Pageantry in Modern Japan*, Berkeley: University of California Press, 1996.

Gluck, Carol, *Japan's Modern Myths: Ideology in the Late Meiji Period*, Princeton, NJ: Princeton University Press, 1985.

Hardacre, Helen, *Shinto and the State, 1868–1988*, Princeton, NJ: Princeton University Press, 1989.

—— with Adam L. Kern (eds), *New Directions in the Study of Meiji Japan*, Leiden and New York: Brill, 1997.

Huffman, James L., *Creating a Public: People and Press in Meiji Japan*, Honolulu: University of Hawaii Press, 1997.

Iriye, Akira, *Pacific Estrangement: Japanese and American Expansion, 1897–1911*, Cambridge, MA: Harvard University Press, 1972.

Irokawa, Daikichi, *The Culture of the Meiji Period*, trans. and ed. Marius Jansen, Princeton, NJ: Princeton University Press, 1985.

Jansen, Marius B. (ed.), *The Cambridge History of Japan*, Vol. 5, *The Nineteenth Century*, Cambridge and New York: Cambridge University Press, 1988–9.

—— and Gilbert Rozman (eds), *Japan in Transition, From Tokugawa to Meiji*, Princeton, NJ: Princeton University Press, 1986.

Keene, Donald, *Dawn to the West: Japanese Literature of the Modern Era*, 2 volumes, New York: Holt, Rinehart & Winston, 1984.

—— (ed.), *Modern Japanese Literature: An Anthology*, New York: Grove Press, 1960.

Kelly, William, *Deference and Defiance in Nineteenth Century Japan*, Princeton: Princeton University Press, 1985.

Kinmonth, Earl H., *The Self-Made Man in Meiji Japanese Thought: From Samurai to Salary Man*, Berkeley: University of California Press, 1981.

Nagai, Michio and Miguel Irrutia (eds), *Meiji ishin: Restoration and Revolution*, Tokyo: United Nations University, 1985.

Neumann, William, *America Encounters Japan: From Perry to MacArthur*, Baltimore, MD, and London: The Johns Hopkins University Press, 1963.

Pittau, Joseph, *Political Thought in Early Meiji Japan, 1868–1889*, Cambridge, MA: Harvard University Press, 1967.

Pyle, Kenneth B., *The New Generation in Meiji Japan*, Stanford, CA: Stanford University Press, 1969.

Rubin, Jay, *Injurious to Public Health: Writers and the Meiji State*, Seattle: University of Washington Press, 1984.

Scheiner, Irwin, *Christian Converts and Social Protest in Meiji Japan*, Berkeley and Los Angeles: University of California Press, 1970.

Seidensticker, Edward, *Low City, High City*, Cambridge, MA: Harvard University Press, 1991.

Siddle, Richard, 'Colonialism and Identity in Okinawa before 1945', *Japanese Studies*, 18 (2), September 1998, pp. 117–33.

Wigen, Kären, *The Making of a Japanese Periphery, 1750–1920*, Berkeley: University of California Press, 1995.

Yates, Charles L., *Saigō Takamori: The Man Behind the Myth*, London: Kegan Paul International, 1995.

Social and political developments, 1912–1945

Anderson, Joseph and Donald Richie, *The Japanese Film: Art and Industry* (expanded edn), Princeton, NJ: Princeton University Press, 1982.

Arima, Tatsuo, *The Failure of Freedom*, Cambridge, MA: Harvard University Press, 1969.

Barshay, Andrew E., *State and Intellectual in Imperial Japan: The Public Man in Crisis*, Berkeley, Los Angeles and Oxford: University of California Press, 1988.

Beckmann, George and Okubo Genji, *The Japanese Communist Party, 1922–1945*, Stanford, CA: Stanford University Press, 1969.

Berger, Gordon, *Parties Out of Power in Japan, 1931–1941*, Princeton, NJ: Princeton University Press, 1977.

Bix, Herbert, *Hirohito and the Making of Modern Japan*, New York: HarperCollins, 2000.

Doak, Kevin M., *Dreams of Difference: The Japan Romantic School and the Crisis of Modernity*, Berkeley and Los Angeles: University of California Press, 1994.

Duus, Peter, *Party Rivalry and Political Change in Taishō Japan*, Cambridge, MA: Harvard University Press, 1968.

Fletcher, Miles, *The Search for a New Order: Intellectuals and Fascism in Prewar Japan*, Chapel Hill: University of North Carolina Press, 1982.

Garon, Sheldon, *Molding Japanese Minds: The State in Everday Life*, Princeton, NJ: Princeton University Press, 1997.

——, *The State and Labor in Modern Japan*, Berkeley, Los Angeles and London: University of California Press, 1987.

Gordon, Andrew, *Labor and Imperial Democracy in Prewar Japan*, Berkeley, Los Angeles and Oxford: University of California Press, 1991.

——, *The Evolution of Labor Relations in Japan: Heavy Industry, 1853–1955*, Cambridge, MA: Council on East Asian Studies, Harvard University, 1988.

Hane, Mikiso, *Peasants, Rebels, and Outcastes: The Underside of Modern Japan*, New York: Pantheon Books, 1982.

Harootunian, Harry D., *Overcome by Modernity: History, Culture, and Community in Interwar Japan*, Princeton, NJ, and Oxford: Princeton University Press, 2000.

Hastings, Sally Ann, *Neighborhood and Nation in Tokyo, 1905–1937*, Pittsburgh and London: University of Pittsburgh Press, 1995.

Havens, Thomas, *Farm and Nation in Modern Japan: Agrarian Nationalism, 1870–1940*, Princeton, NJ: Princeton University Press, 1974.

Ishimoto, Shidzue, *Facing Two Ways: The Story of My Life*, Stanford, CA: Stanford University Press, 1984.

Kasza, Gregory, *The State and Mass Media in Japan, 1918–1945*, Berkeley and Los Angeles: University of California Press, 1988.

Large, Stephen S., *Emperor Hirohito and Shōwa Japan: A Political Biography*, London and New York: Routledge, 1992.

Marshall, Byron, *Capitalism and Nationalism in Prewar Japan: The Ideology of the Business Elite, 1868–1941*, Stanford, CA: Stanford University Press, 1967.

Maruyama, Masao, *Thought and Behaviour in Modern Japanese Politics*, New York: Oxford University Press, 1969.

Miller, Frank O., *Minobe Tatsukichi, Interpreter of Constitutionalism in Japan*, Berkeley and Los Angeles: University of California Press, 1965.

Minichiello, Sharon (ed.), *Japan's Competing Modernities: Issues in Culture and Democracy, 1900–1930*, Honolulu: University of Hawaii Press, 1998.

——, *Retreat from Reform*, Honolulu: University of Hawaii Press, 1984.

Mitchell, Richard, *Censorship in Imperial Japan*, Princeton, NJ: Princeton University Press, 1983.

——, *Janus-Faced Justice: Political Criminals in Imperial Japan*, Honolulu: University of Hawaii Press, 1992.

——, *Political Bribery in Japan*, Honolulu: University of Hawaii Press, 1996.

——, *Thought Control in Prewar Japan*, Ithaca, NY: Cornell University Press, 1976.

Morley, James (ed.), *Dilemmas of Growth in Prewar Japan*, Princeton, NJ: Princeton University Press, 1971.

Najita, Tetsuo, *Hara Kei in the Politics of Compromise*, Cambridge, MA: Harvard University Press, 1967.

Rimer, J. Thomas (ed.), *Culture and Identity: Japanese Intellectuals During the Interwar Years*, Princeton, NJ: Princeton University Press, 1990.

Seidensticker, Edward, *Tokyo Rising: The City Since the Great Earthquake*, Cambridge, MA: Harvard University Press, 1991.

Shirane, Haruo and Tomi Suzuki (eds), *Inventing the Classics: Modernity, National Identity, and Japanese Literature*, Stanford, CA: Stanford University Press, 2000.

Silberman, Bernard and H.D. Harootunian (eds), *Japan in Crisis: Essays on Taishō Democracy*, Princeton, NJ: Princeton University Press, 1974.

Smethurst, Richard, *A Social Basis for Prewar Japanese Militarism*, Berkeley and Los Angeles: University of California Press, 1974.

——, *Agricultural Development and Tenancy Disputes in Japan, 1870–1940*, Princeton, NJ: Princeton University Press, 1986.

Smith, Henry D. II, *Japan's First Student Radicals,* Cambridge, MA: Harvard University Press, 1972.

Smith, Robert and Ella Lury Wiswell, *The Women of Suye Mura*, Chicago, IL: University of Chicago Press, 1982.

Smith, Thomas C., 'The Right to Benevolence: Dignity and Japanese Workers, 1890–1920', *Comparative Studies in Society and History*, 26 (October 1984), pp. 587–613.

Tamanoi, Mariko, *Under the Shadow of Nationalism: Politics and Poetics of Rural Japanese Women*, Honolulu: University of Hawaii Press, 1999.

Tanaka, Stefan, *Japan's Orient: Rendering Pasts into History*, Berkeley, Los Angeles and London: University of California Press, 1993.

Tipton, Elise K. (ed.), *Society and the State in Interwar Japan*, London and New York: Routledge, 1997.

——, *The Japanese Police State: The Tokkō in Interwar Japan*, Sydney and Honolulu: Allen and Unwin and the University of Hawaii Press, 1991.

—— and John Clark (eds), *Being Modern in Japan: Culture and Society from the 1910s to the 1930s*, Honolulu and Sydney: University of Hawaii Press and Australian Humanities Research Foundation, 2000.

Titus, David, *Palace and Politics in Prewar Japan*, New York and London: Columbia University Press, 1974.

Tsutsui, William M., *Manufacturing Ideology: Scientific Management in Twentieth-Century Japan*, Princeton, NJ: Princeton University Press, 1999.

Uno, Kathleen S., *Passages to Modernity: Motherhood, Childhood, and Social Reform in Early Twentieth Century Japan*, Honolulu: University of Hawaii Press, 1999.

Waswo, Ann, *Japanese Landlords: The Decline of a Rural Elite*, Berkeley and Los Angeles: University of California Press, 1977.

Weiner, Michael, *Race and Migration in Imperial Japan,* London and New York: Routledge, 1994.

Nationalism, imperialism and the Second World War

Barnhart, Michael, *Japan Prepares For Total War: The Search For Economic Security, 1919–1941*, Ithaca, NY: Cornell University Press, 1987.

Beasley, William G., *Japanese Imperialism, 1894–1945*, Oxford: Clarendon Press, 1987.

Ching, Leo, *Becoming 'Japanese': Colonial Taiwan and the Politics of Identity Formation*, Berkeley: University of California Press, 2001.

Cook, Haruko Taya and Theodore F. Cook, *Japan at War: An Oral History*, New York: The New Press, 1992.

Crowley, James, *Japan's Quest for Autonomy: National Security and Foreign Policy, 1930–1938*, Princeton, NJ: Princeton University Press, 1966.

Dower, John, *War Without Mercy: Race and Power in the Pacific War*, London and Boston, MA: Faber and Faber, 1986.

Duus, Peter (ed.), *The Cambridge History of Japan*, Vol. 6, *The Twentieth Century*, Cambridge: Cambridge University Press, 1988.

——, Ramon Myers and Mark Peattie (eds), *The Japanese Informal Empire in China, 1895–1937*, Princeton, NJ: Princeton University Press, 1989.

——, Ramon Myers and Mark Peattie (eds), *The Japanese Wartime Empire*, Princeton, NJ: Princeton University Press, 1996.

Fogel, Joshua (ed.), *The Nanjing Massacre in History and Historiography*, Berkeley and London: University of California, 2000.

Havens, Thomas, *Valley of Darkness: The Japanese People and World War Two*, Lanham, MD and London: University Press of America, 1986.

Heisig, J. and John Maraldo (eds), *Rude Awakenings: Zen, the Kyoto School and the Question of Nationalism*, Honolulu: University of Hawaii Press, 1994.

Hicks, George, *The Comfort Women*, Sydney: Allen & Unwin, 1995.

Hogan, Michael (ed.), *Hiroshima in History and Memory*, Cambridge: Cambridge University Press, 1996.

Igarashi, Yoshikuni, *Bodies of Memory: Narratives of War in Postwar Japanese Culture, 1945–1970*, Princeton, NJ: Princeton University Press, 2000.

Iriye, Akira, *After Imperialism: The Search for a New Order in the Far East, 1921–1931*, Cambridge, MA: Harvard University Press, 1965.

——, *Pacific Estrangement: Japanese and American Expansion, 1897–1911*, Cambridge, MA: Harvard University Press, 1972.

——, *Power and Culture: The Japanese–American War, 1941–1945*, Cambridge, MA: Harvard University Press, 1981.

Lebra, Joyce (ed.), *Japan's Greater East Asia Co-Prosperity Sphere in World War II, Selected Readings and Documents*, Kuala Lumpur: Oxford University Press, 1975.

——, *Japanese-Trained Armies in Southeast Asia: Independence and Volunteer Forces in World War II*, New York: Columbia University Press, 1977.

Morris-Suzuki, Tessa, *Shōwa: An Inside History of Hirohito's Japan*, Sydney: Methuen, 1984.

Myers, Ramon and Mark Peattie (eds), *The Japanese Colonial Empire, 1895–1945*, Princeton, NJ: Princeton University Press, 1984.

Shillony, Ben-Ami, *Politics and Culture in Wartime Japan*, Oxford: Clarendon Press, 1981.

——, *Revolt in Japan: The Young Officers and the February 26 1936 Incident*, Princeton, NJ: Princeton University Press, 1973.

Thomas, Julia, 'Photography, National Identity, and the "Cataract of Times": Wartime Images and the Case of Japan', *American Historical Review*, 103 (5), 1998, pp. 1475–501.

Treat, John Whittier, *Writing Ground Zero: Japanese Literature and the Atomic Bomb*, Chicago, IL: University of Chicago Press, 1995.

Tsurumi, Kazuko, *Social Change and the Individual: Japan Before and After Defeat in World War II*, Princeton: Princeton University Press, 1970.

Wetzler, Peter, *Hirohito and War: Imperial Tradition and Military Decision Making in Prewar Japan*, Honolulu: University of Hawaii Press, 1998.

White, James (ed.), *The Ambivalence of Nationalism: Modern Japan between East and West*, Lanham, MD, and London: University Press of America, 1990.

Wilson, Sandra (ed.), *Nation and Nationalism in Modern Japan*, London: Routledge-Curzon, 2002.

Yamanouchi, Yasushi, J., Victor Koschmann and Ryūichi Narita (eds), *Total War and Mobilization*, Ithaca, NY: East Asia Program, Cornell University, 1998.

Young, Louise, *Japan's Total Empire: Manchuria and the Culture of Wartime Imperialism*, Berkeley: University of California Press, 1998.

The Occupation

Burkman, Thomas W. (ed.), *The Occupation of Japan: Arts and Culture*, Norfolk, VA: General Douglas MacArthur Foundation, 1988.

Cohen, Theodore, *Remaking Japan: The American Occupation as New Deal*, New York: Free Press, 1987.

Dower, John, *Embracing Defeat: Japan in the Wake of World War II*, New York and London: W.W. Norton and The New Press, 1999.

——, *Empire and Aftermath: Yoshida Shigeru and the Japanese Experience, 1878–1954*, Cambridge, MA: Council on East Asian Studies, Harvard University, 1979.

——, *Japan in War and Peace: Selected Essays*, New York: The New Press, 1993.

Finn, Richard B., *Winners in Peace: MacArthur, Yoshida and Postwar Japan*, Berkeley, Los Angeles and Oxford: University of California Press, 1992.

Hirano, Kyoko, *Mr. Smith Goes to Tokyo: The Japanese Cinema under the American Occupation, 1945–1952*, Washington, DC: Smithsonian Institution Press, 1992.

Hosoya, C., N. Andō, Y. Ōnuma and R. Minear, *The Tokyo War Crimes Trial: An International Symposium*, New York: Kodansha International, 1986.

Kawai, Kazuo, *Japan's American Interlude*, Chicago, IL: University of Chicago Press, 1960.

Minear, Richard, *Victor's Justice: The Tokyo War Crimes Trial*, Princeton, NJ: Princeton University Press, 1971.

Molasky, Michael S., *The American Occupation of Japan and Okinawa*, London: Routledge, 1999.

Moore, Joe, *Japanese Workers and the Struggle for Power, 1945–1947*, Madison: University of Wisconsin Press, 1983.

Schaller, Michael, *The American Occupation of Japan: The Origins of the Cold War in Asia*, New York: Oxford University Press, 1985.

Schonberger, Howard B., *Aftermath of War: The Americans and the Remaking of Japan, 1945–1952*, Kent, OH: Kent State University Press, 1989.

Ward, Robert and Yoshikazu Sakamoto (eds), *Democratizing Japan: The Allied Occupation*, Honolulu: University of Hawaii Press, 1987.

Wildes, Harry Emerson, *Typhoon in Tokyo: The Occupation and Its Aftermath*, New York: Macmillan, 1954.

Political developments since 1945

Allinson, Gary D. and Yasunori Sone (eds), *Political Dynamics in Contemporary Japan*, Ithaca, NY: Cornell University Press, 1993.

Apter, David E. and Sawa Nagayo, *Against the State: Politics and Social Protest in Japan*, Cambridge, MA: Harvard University Press, 1984.

Curtis, Gerald (ed.), *Japan's Foreign Policy After the Cold War: Coping with Change*, Armonk, NY: M.E. Sharpe, 1993.

——, *The Japanese Way of Politics*, New York: Columbia University Press, 1988.

Gordon, Andrew (ed.), *Postwar Japan as History*, Berkeley and Los Angeles: University of California Press, 1993.

Hein, Laura, *Fueling Growth: The Energy Revolution and Economic Policy in Postwar Japan*, Cambridge, MA: The Council on East Asian Studies, Harvard University, 1990.

—— and Mark Seldon (eds), *Censoring History: Citizenship and Memory in Japan, Germany, and the United States*, New York: M.E. Sharpe, 2000.

Ishida, Takeshi and Ellis Krauss (eds), *Democracy in Japan*, Pittsburgh, PA: University of Pittsburgh Press, 1989.

Jain, Purnendra and Takashi Inoguchi (eds), *Japanese Politics Today: Beyond Karaoke Democracy?*, South Melbourne: Macmillan Education Australia, 1997.

Johnson, Chalmers, *MITI and the Japanese Miracle: The Growth of Industrial Policy, 1925–1975*, Stanford, CA: Stanford University Press, 1982.

Koschmann, J. Victor, *Revolution and Subjectivity in Postwar Japan*, Chicago, IL: University of Chicago Press, 1996.

Large, Stephen S., *Emperor Hirohito and Shōwa Japan: A Political Biography*, London and New York: Routledge, 1992.

McCormack, Gavan and Yoshio Sugimoto (eds), *Democracy in Contemporary Japan*, Armonk, NY: M.E. Sharpe, 1986.

—— (eds), *The Japanese Trajectory: Modernization and Beyond*, New York: Cambridge University Press, 1988.

McKean, Margaret, *Environmental Protest and Citizen Politics in Japan*, Berkeley: University of California Press, 1981.

Packard, George R., *Protest in Tokyo: The Security Treaty Crisis of 1960*, Princeton, NJ: Princeton University Press, 1966.

Stockwin, J.A.A., *Governing Japan: Divided Politics in a Major Economy*, Oxford: Blackwell, 1999.

Stronach, Bruce, *Beyond the Rising Sun: Nationalism in Contemporary Japan*, Westport, RI: Praeger, 1995.

Yoshino, Kosaku, *Cultural Nationalism in Contemporary Japan: A Sociological Enquiry*, London: Routledge, 1992.

Social and cultural developments since 1945

Allison, Anne, *Permitted and Prohibited Desires: Mothers, Comics, and Censorship in Japan*, Boulder, CO: Westview Press, 1996.

Anderson, Joseph and Donald Richie, *The Japanese Film: Art and Industry* (expanded edn), Princeton, NJ: Princeton University Press, 1982.

Bestor, Theodore, *Neighborhood Tokyo*, Stanford, CA: Stanford University Press, 1989.

Cole, Robert, *Japanese Blue Collar*, Berkeley and Los Angeles: University of California Press, 1971.

Coleman, Samuel, *Family Planning in Japanese Society: Traditional Birth Control in Modern Urban Culture*, Princeton, NJ: Princeton University Press, 1983.

DeVos, George and William Witherall, *Japan's Minorities: Burakumin, Koreans, Ainus, and Okinawans*, Claremont, NY: Minority Rights Group, 1983.

Dore, Ronald, *City Life in Japan: A Study of a Tokyo Ward*, Berkeley and Los Angeles: University of California Press, 1967.

Edwards, Walter, *Modern Japan Through its Weddings: Gender, Person, and Society in Ritual Portrayal*, Stanford, CA: Stanford University Press, 1989.

Gessel, Van C. and Tomone Matsumoto (eds), *The Showa Anthology: Modern Japanese Short Stories*, 2 volumes, Tokyo: Kodansha, 1985.

Gordon, Andrew (ed.), *Postwar Japan as History*, Berkeley and Los Angeles: University of California Press, 1993.

——, *The Wages of Affluence: Labor and Management in Postwar Japan*, Cambridge, MA: Harvard University Press, 1998.

Hendry, Joy, *Marriage in Changing Japan: Community and Society*, New York and Rutland, VT: St Martin's Press and Tuttle, 1981 and 1986.

—— and Massimo Raveri (eds), *Japan at Play*, London: Routledge, 2001.

Hibbett, Howard (ed.), *Contemporary Japanese Literature: An Anthology of Fiction, Film, and Other Writing Since 1945*, New York: Alfred A. Knopf, 1977.

Ivy, Marilyn, *Discourses of the Vanishing: Modernity, Phantasm, Japan*, Chicago, IL: University of Chicago Press, 1995.

Krauss, Ellis, Thomas Rohlen and Patricia Steinhoff (eds), *Conflict in Japan*, Honolulu: University of Hawaii Press, 1984.

Lie, John, *Multiethnic Japan*, Cambridge, MA: Harvard University Press, 2001.

Linhart, Sepp and Sabine Frühstück (eds), *The Culture of Japan as Seen Through its Leisure*, Albany, NY: State University of New York Press, 1998.

Low, Morris, Shigeru Nakayama and Hitoshi Yoshioka, *Science, Technology and Society in Contemporary Japan*, Cambridge: Cambridge University Press, 1999.

McCormack, Gavan, *The Emptiness of Japanese Affluence*, New York and Sydney: M.E. Sharpe and Allen & Unwin, 1996.

Maher, John and Gaynor Macdonald (eds), *Diversity in Japanese Culture and Language*, London and New York: Kegan Paul International, 1995.

Martinez, D.P. (ed.), *The Worlds of Japanese Popular Culture: Gender, Shifting Boundaries and Global Cultures*, Cambridge: Cambridge University Press, 1998.

Mitchell, Richard, *The Korean Minority in Japan*, Berkeley and Los Angeles: University of California Press, 1967.

Miyoshi, Masao and H.D. Harootunian (eds), *Postmodernism and Japan*, Durham, NC, and London: Duke University Press, 1989.

Napier, Susan, *Animé from Akira to Mononoke: Experiencing Contemporary Japanese Animation*, London: Palgrave, 2001.

Partner, Simon, *Assembled in Japan: Electrical Goods and the Making of the Japanese Consumer*, Berkeley: University of California Press, 2000.

Robertson, Jennifer, *Native and Newcomer*, Berkeley and Los Angeles: University of California Press, 1991.

Rohlen, Thomas, *Japan's High Schools*, Berkeley and Los Angeles: University of California Press, 1983.

Ryang, Sonia (ed.), *Koreans in Japan: Critical Voices from the Margin*, London: Routledge, 2000.

Schoppa, L., *Education Reform in Japan: A Case of Immobilist Politics*, London: Routledge, 1991.

Siddle, Richard, *Race, Resistance and the Ainu in Japan*, London and New York: Routledge, 1996.

Tobin, J., *Remade in Japan: Everyday Life and Consumer Taste in a Changing Society*, New Haven, CT: Yale University Press, 1992.

Treat, John Whittier (ed.), *Contemporary Japan and Popular Culture*, London: Curzon Press, 1995.

Tsurumi, Shunsuke, *A Cultural History of Postwar Japan*, London and New York: Kegan Paul International, 1984.

Upham, Frank, *Law and Social Change in Postwar Japan*, Cambridge, MA: Harvard University Press, 1987.

Vogel, Ezra, *Japan as Number One: Lessons for America*, Cambridge, MA: Harvard University Press, 1979.
——, *Japan's New Middle Class* (2nd edn), Berkeley, Los Angeles and London: University of California Press, 1971.
Wagatsuma, Hiroshi and George DeVos, *Japan's Invisible Race: Caste in Culture and Personality*, Berkeley: University of California Press, 1966.

Women since 1945

Allison, Anne, *Nightwork*, Chicago, IL: University of Chicago Press, 1994.
AMPO – *Japan Asia Quarterly Review* (ed.), *Voices from the Japanese Women's Movement*, Armonk, NY, and London: M.E. Sharpe, 1996.
Brinton, Mary C., *Women and the Economic Miracle*, Berkeley and Los Angeles: University of California Press, 1993.
Diggs, Nancy, *Steel Butterflies: Japanese Women and the American Experience*, Albany: State University of New York Press, 1998.
Fujimura-Fanselow, Kumiko and Atsuko Kameda (eds), *Japanese Women: New Feminist Perspectives on the Past, Present, and Future*, New York: The Feminist Press, 1995.
Gelb, Joyce and Marian Palley (eds), *Women of Japan and Korea*, Philadelphia, PA: Temple University Press, 1994.
Hunter, Janet (ed.), *Japanese Women Working*, London and New York: Routledge, 1994.
Imamura, Anne E. (ed.), *Re-Imaging Japanese Women*, Berkeley, Los Angeles and London: University of California Press, 1996.
——, *Urban Japanese Housewives: At Home and in the Community*, Honolulu: University of Hawaii Press, 1987.
Iwao, Sumiko, *The Japanese Woman: Traditional Image and Changing Reality*, New York: The Free Press, 1993.
Kondo, Dorinne, *Crafting Selves: Power, Gender, and Discourses of Identity in a Japanese Workplace*, Chicago, IL: University of Chicago Press, 1990.
Lebra, Takie Sugiyama, *Japanese Women: Constraint and Fulfillment*, Honolulu: University of Hawaii Press, 1984.
Lippit, Noriko M. and Kyoko I. Selden (eds), *Japanese Women Writers: Twentieth Century Short Fiction*, New York: M.E. Sharpe, 1991.
Pharr, Susan, *Political Women in Japan: The Search for a Place in Political Life*, Berkeley and London: University of California Press, 1981.
Roberts, Glenda S., *Staying on the Line: Blue Collar Women in Contemporary Japan*, Honolulu: University of Hawaii Press, 1994.
Skov, Lise and Brian Moeran (eds), *Women, Media and Consumption in Japan*, Honolulu: University of Hawaii Press, 1995.
Tanaka, Yukiko and Elizabeth Hanson (eds), *This Kind of Woman: Ten Stories by Japanese Women Writers, 1960–1976*, Ann Arbor: University of Michigan, Center for Japanese Studies, 1995.

Notes

1 Tokugawa background: the ideal and the real

1 Quoted in Donald H. Shively, 'Sumptuary Regulation and Status in Early Tokugawa Japan', *Harvard Journal of Asiatic Studies*, 25, 1964–5, p. 158.
2 For reproductions of the series, see Ichitaro Kondo (ed.), *The Fifty-three Stages of the Tokaido by Hiroshige*, English adaptation by Charles S. Terry, Honolulu: East–West Center Press, 1965; *Hokusai and Hiroshige: Great Japanese Prints from the James A. Michener Collection, Honolulu Academy of Arts*, San Francisco: The Asian Art Museum of San Francisco, 1998.
3 Constantine Vaporis, 'To Edo and Back: Alternate Attendance and Japanese Culture in the Early Modern Period', *Journal of Japanese Studies*, v. 23(1), winter 1997, p. 31.
4 Quoted in Teruoka Yasutaka, 'The Pleasure Quarters and Tokugawa Culture' in C. Andrew Gerstle (ed.), *18th Century Japan, Culture and Society*, Sydney: Allen & Unwin, 1989, p. 9.
5 Quoted in ibid., p. 27.
6 Quoted in Thomas C. Smith, *The Agrarian Origins of Modern Japan*, New York: Atheneum, 1966, p. 75.
7 See Stephen Vlastos, *Peasants Protests and Uprisings in Tokugawa Japan*, Berkeley: University of California Press, Table 1, 'Principal Types of Peasant Protests, Japan, 1601–1867'.
8 Taxes were assessed in terms of *koku*. One *koku* equalled 4.96 American bushels of rice or rice equivalents, which in theory was the amount an adult could live on for one year.
9 Quoted in Yamakawa Kikue, *Women of the Mito Domain: Recollections of Samurai Family Life*, trans. Kate Wildman Nakai, Tokyo: University of Tokyo Press, 1992, p. 158. Interestingly, high-quality bamboo skewers characteristically made by poor samurai during the Tokugawa period became a Mito speciality which continued into the twentieth century.
10 Quoted in Shively, 'Sumptuary Regulation', pp. 124–5.
11 Quoted in ibid., p. 125.

2 The mid-century crisis

1 Quoted in John W. Hall, *Japan, From Prehistory to Modern Times*, New York: Dell Publishing, 1970, p. 236.
2 This point as well as much of the preceding analysis of the Tempō reforms derives from Harold Bolitho, 'The Tempō Crisis' in Marius B. Jansen (ed.), *The Cambridge History of Japan*, Vol. 5, Cambridge: Cambridge University Press, 1989, pp. 116–67.

3 Quoted in ibid., p. 129.
4 Quoted in ibid., pp. 165–6.
5 Quoted in William Neumann, *America Encounters Japan: From Perry to MacArthur*, Baltimore, MD, and London: The Johns Hopkins University Press, 1963, p. 23.
6 Quoted in W.G. Beasley, 'The Foreign Threat and the Opening of the Ports' in Jansen (ed.), *Cambridge History*, Vol. 5, p. 269.
7 M. William Steele and Robert Eskildsen (trans.), 'Edo Commoners on the Eve of the Restoration – The Coming of the Black Ships', *Working Papers in Japan Studies*, No. 2, Tokyo: Japan Studies Program, International Christian University, 1989, p. 9.
8 Ibid., p. 10.
9 *The Complete Journal of Townsend Harris*, Rutland and Tokyo: Charles E. Tuttle, 1959, revised edn, p. 357.
10 Keiki is an alternate reading of his given name.
11 George Wilson, 'Pursuing the Millennium in the Meiji Restoration' in Tetsuo Najita and J. Victor Koschmann (eds), *Conflict in Modern Japanese History*, Princeton, NJ: Princeton University Press, 1982, p. 186.
12 Tōyama Shigeki notes that 1070 men later received awards for their loyalist activities. About two-thirds of these were samurai. Tōyama Shigeki, *Meiji ishin*, Tokyo: Iwanami Shoten, 1954, p. 43 n. 8.
13 H.D. Harootunian's characterization in his 'From Principle to Principal: Restoration and Emperorship in Japan' in Hayden White (ed.), *The Uses of History: Essays in Intellectual and Social History*, Detroit, MI: Wayne State University Press, 1968.
14 W.G. Beasley, *The Meiji Restoration*, Stanford, CA: Stanford University Press, 1972, p. 170. Although attributing more revolutionary motives to the *shishi* than Beasley, Thomas Huber delineates a similar division between 'romantics' and 'pragmatists' among the loyalists. Thomas Huber, ' "Men of High Purpose" and the Politics of Direct Action, 1862–1864' in Najita and Koschmann (eds), *Conflict*, pp. 124–5.
15 Huber, ' "Men of High Purpose" ', p. 111.
16 Quoted in Beasley, *Meiji Restoration*, p. 211.
17 See Yamakawa Kikue, *Women of the Mito Domain: Recollections of Samurai Family Life*, trans. Kate Wildman Nakai, Tokyo: University of Tokyo Press, 1992.
18 Quoted in Beasley, *Meiji Restoration*, p. 293.
19 For the various possible translations and connotations of '*ee ja nai ka*', see George M. Wilson, *Patriots and Redeemers in Japan: Motives in the Meiji Restoration*, Chicago, IL: University of Chicago Press, 1992, pp. 98–9.
20 Ibid., p. 100.
21 Albert Craig, *Chōshū in the Meiji Restoration*, Cambridge, MA: Harvard University Press, 1961, pp. 6–7, 352, 360.
22 Thomas Huber, *The Revolutionary Origins of Modern Japan*, Stanford, CA: Stanford University Press, 1981.

3 The early Meiji Revolution

1 Quoted in Albert Craig, 'Kido Kōin and Ōkubo Toshimichi: A Psychohistorical Analysis' in Albert Craig and Donald Shively (eds), *Personality in Japanese History*, Berkeley, Los Angeles, and London: University of California Press, 1970, p. 292.
2 Ibid., p. 293.
3 Ivan Morris, *The Nobility of Failure: Tragic Heroes in the History of Japan*, New York and Ontario: New American Library, 1975, p. 220.

4 Quoted in Ernst Presseisen, *Before Aggression: Europeans Train the Japanese Army*, Tucson: University of Arizona Press, 1965, p. 39, and in D. Eleanor Westney, 'The Military' in Marius Jansen and Gilbert Rozman (eds), *Japan in Transition from Tokugawa to Meiji*, Princeton, NJ: Princeton University Press, 1986, p. 177.
5 Virginia Spate and David Bromfield, 'A New and Strange Beauty: Monet and Japanese Art' in *Monet and Japan*, Canberra: National Gallery of Australia, 2001, p. 2.
6 *The Complete Journal of Townsend Harris*, Rutland and Tokyo: Charles E. Tuttle, 1959, revised edn, p. 344.
7 Quoted in Edward Seidensticker, *Low City, High City*, Cambridge, MA: Harvard University Press, 1991, p. 91.
8 Translated in Donald Keene (ed.), *Modern Japanese Literature*, New York: Grove Press, 1956, pp. 31–3.
9 Quoted in Sharon Sievers, *Flowers in Salt: The Beginnings of Feminist Consciousness in Modern Japan*, Stanford, CA: Stanford University Press, 1983, p. 59.
10 Quoted in E. Patricia Tsurumi, *Factory Girls: Women in the Thread Mills of Meiji Japan*, Princeton, NJ: Princeton University Press, 1990, p. 90.

4 The 1880s and 1890s: defining a Japanese national identity

1 David Lu, *Japan, A Documentary History*, Armonk, NY, and London: M.E. Sharpe, 1997, p. 309.
2 Ibid., p. 344.
3 Joseph Pittau, SJ, *Political Thought in Early Meiji Japan, 1868–1889*, Cambridge, MA: Harvard University Press, 1967, p. 80.
4 Takashi Fujitani, *Splendid Monarchy: Power and Pageantry in Modern Japan*, Berkeley, Los Angeles and London: University of California Press, 1996, p. 107.
5 Ibid., p. 223.
6 Ryusaku Tsunoda, William Theodore de Bary and Donald Keene (comps), *Sources of Japanese Tradition*, Vol. 2, New York and London: Columbia University Press, 1964, pp. 139–401.
7 Sharon Nolte and Sally Hastings, 'The Meiji State's Policy Toward Women, 1890–1910' in Gail Bernstein (ed.), *Recreating Japanese Women, 1600–1945*, Berkeley, Los Angeles and Oxford: University of California Press, 1991, p. 172.
8 Ibid., p. 156.
9 Richard Siddle, 'Colonialism and Identity in Okinawa before 1945', *Japanese Studies*, 18(2) (September 1998), p. 121.
10 William Coaldrake, *Architecture and Authority in Japan*, London and New York: Routledge, 1996, p. 223.
11 Quoted in Helen Hardacre, *Shinto and the State, 1868–1988*, Princeton, NJ: Princeton University Press, 1989, p. 119.
12 Taken from a quote in ibid., p. 66.
13 Quoted in Neil Harris, 'All the World a Melting Pot? Japan at American Fairs, 1876–1904' in Akira Iriye (ed.), *Mutual Images: Essays in American–Japanese Relations*, Cambridge, MA, and London: Harvard University Press, 1975, pp. 44–5.

5 Late Meiji: an end and a beginning

1 Quoted in Kenneth Pyle, *The New Generation in Meiji Japan: Problems of Cultural Identity, 1885–1985*, Stanford, CA: Stanford University Press, 1969, p. 198.
2 Quoted in Stewart Lone, *Japan's First Modern War*, London: St Martin's Press, 1994, p. 180.
3 Quoted in ibid., p. 18.

4 Howard Martin quoted in William Neumann, *America Encounters Japan, From Perry to MacArthur*, Baltimore, MD, and London: The Johns Hopkins University Press, 1963, p. 105.
5 Quote from *The Illustrated London News* in Donald Keene, 'The Sino-Japanese War of 1894–1895 and Its Cultural Effects in Japan' in Donald Shively (ed.), *Tradition and Modernization in Japanese Culture*, Princeton, NJ: Princeton University Press, 1971, p. 132.
6 Quoted in Lone, *First Modern War*, p. 60.
7 Helen Hardacre, *Shintō and the State, 1868–1988*, Princeton, NJ: Princeton University Press, 1989, p. 113.
8 For a fascinating account of the ill-fated Baltic fleet, see Richard Hough, *The Fleet That Had to Die*, London: Severn House, 1958.
9 Quoted in Akira Iriye, 'Japan as a Competitor, 1895–1917' in Akira Iriye (ed.), *Mutual Images*, Cambridge, MA, and London: Harvard University Press, 1975, pp. 76–7.
10 Ibid., p. 77.
11 For a translation, see Donald Keene (ed.), *Modern Japanese Literature*, New York: Grove Press, 1956, pp. 142–58.
12 Robert Cole and Ken'ichi Tominaga, 'Japan's Changing Occupational Structure and Its Significance' in Hugh Patrick (ed.), *Japanese Industrialization and Its Social Consequences*, Berkeley and Los Angeles: University of California Press, 1976, p. 58.
13 Gary Saxonhouse, 'Country Girls and Communication Among Competitors in the Japanese Cotton-Spinning Industry' in Patrick (ed.), *Japanese Industrialization*, p. 100.
14 Stephen Large, *Organized Workers and Socialist Politics in Interwar Japan*, Cambridge: Cambridge University Press, p. 12.
15 Repetition of the *nembutsu* was in certain Buddhist sects a reflection of one's devotion and a means to acquire grace, perhaps like reciting 'Hail, Mary's. The factory director is quoted in Andrew Gordon, *The Evolution of Labor Relations in Japan*, Cambridge, MA: Council on East Asian Studies, Harvard University, 1988, p. 83.
16 Quoted in ibid., p. 65.
17 Quoted in Earl Kinmonth, *The Self-Made Man in Meiji Japanese Thought*, Berkeley: University of California Press, 1981, p. 68.
18 Ibid., pp. 123–4.
19 Ibid., p. 157.
20 Ishikawa Takuboku, 'The Romaji Diary' in Keene (ed.), *Modern Japanese Literature*, p. 217.
21 Quoted in Oka Yoshitake, 'Generational Conflict after the Russo-Japanese War' in Tetsuo Najita and Victor Koschmann (eds), *Conflict in Modern Japanese History*, Princeton, NJ: Princeton University Press, 1982, p. 197.
22 Translation in ibid., p. 217.

6 An emerging mass society: demands for equity and the dilemmas of choice

1 Translation in Sharon Sievers, *Flowers in Salt*, Stanford, CA: Stanford University Press, 1983, p. 163.
2 Ibid., p. 176.
3 George Beckman and Okubo Genji, *The Japanese Communist Party, 1922–1945*, Stanford, CA: Stanford University Press, 1969, p. 270.
4 A Diet opponent of the Peace Preservation Law, quoted in Elise K. Tipton, *The Japanese Police State: The Tokkō in Interwar Japan*, Sydney and Honolulu: Allen & Unwin and the University of Hawaii Press, 1990/1991, p. 151.

5 Quoted in Mikiso Hane, *Peasants, Rebels, and Outcastes: The Underside of Modern Japan*, New York: Pantheon Books, 1982, p. 152.
6 Young-Soo Chung and Elise K. Tipton, 'Problems of Assimilation: The Koreans' in Elise K. Tipton (ed.), *Society and the State in Interwar Japan*, London and New York: Routledge, 1997, p. 171.
7 Sheldon Garon, *The State and Labor in Modern Japan*, Berkeley, Los Angeles and London: University of California Press, 1987, pp. 249–50.
8 Andrew Gordon represents the former view, while Thomas C. Smith argues the latter. Gordon, *The Evolution of Labor Relations in Japan: Heavy Industry, 1853–1955*, Cambridge, MA: Council on East Asian Studies, Harvard University, 1988; Smith, 'The Right to Benevolence: Dignity and Japanese Workers, 1890–1920', *Comparative Studies in Society and History*, 26 (October 1984), pp. 587–613.
9 Quoted in H.D. Harootunian, 'Introduction: A Sense of an Ending and the Problem of Taishō' in Bernard Silberman and H.D. Harootunian (eds), *Japan in Crisis: Essays on Taishō Democracy*, Princeton, NJ: Princeton University Press, 1974, p. 10.
10 A prominent example in English is Tatsuo Arima, *The Failure of Freedom*, Cambridge, MA: Harvard University Press, 1969.
11 Roy Starrs, 'Writing the National Narrative: Changing Attitudes toward Nation-Building among Japanese Writers, 1900–1930' in Sharon Minichello (ed.), *Japan's Competing Modernities: Issues in Culture and Democracy, 1900–1930*, Honolulu: University of Hawaii Press, 1998, p. 223.
12 Quoted in Edward Seidensticker, *Kafū the Scribbler: The Life and Writings of Nagai Kafū, 1879–1959*, Stanford, CA: Stanford University Press, 1965, p. 46.

7 Contesting the modern in the 1930s

1 *Tōkyō hyakunenshi*, Vol. 5, Tokyo: 1979, p. 271.
2 Quoted in Mikiso Hane, *Peasants, Rebels, and Outcastes: The Underside of Modern Japan*, New York: Pantheon Books, 1982, p. 36.
3 Ibid., p. 115.
4 Quoted in Ann Waswo, 'In Search of Equity: Japanese Tenant Unions in the 1920s' in Tetsuo Najita and J. Victor Koschmann (eds), *Conflict in Modern Japanese History*, Princeton, NJ: Princeton University Press, 1982, p. 396.
5 Ann Waswo, 'The Origins of Tenant Unrest' in Bernard Silberman and Harry Harootunian (eds), *Japan in Crisis: Essays on Taishō Democracy*, Princeton, NJ: Princeton University Press, 1974, p. 381.
6 Quoted in Sandra Wilson, 'Angry Young Men and the Japanese State' in Elise K. Tipton (ed.), *Society and the State in Interwar Japan*, London and New York: Routledge, 1997, p. 112.
7 Quoted in Ryusaku Tsunoda *et al.* (eds), *Sources of Japanese Tradition*, Vol. 2, New York and London: Columbia University Press, 1958, p. 263.
8 Quoted in Hane, *Peasants*, p. 118.
9 Tsunoda *et al.*, *Sources of Japanese Tradition*, Vol. 2, p. 263.
10 Ibid., p. 275.
11 Quoted in Norman Graebner, 'Hoover, Roosevelt, and the Japanese' in Dorothy Borg and Shumpei Okamoto, *Pearl Harbor as History: Japanese–American Relations, 1931–1941*, New York and London: Columbia University Press, 1973, p. 45.
12 Ibid., p. 46.
13 Sandra Wilson, 'The Past in the Present: War in Narratives of Modernity in the 1920s and 1930s' in Elise K. Tipton and John Clark (eds), *Being Modern in Japan: Culture and Society from the 1910s to the 1930s*, Honolulu and Sydney: University of Hawaii Press and the Australian Humanities Research Foundation, 2000, p. 183.

14 H.D. Harootunian, 'Figuring the Folk: History, Poetics, and Representation' in Stephen Vlastos (ed.), *Mirror of Modernity: Invented Traditions of Modern Japan*, Berkeley, Los Angeles and London: University of California Press, 1998, p. 158.

8 The dark valley

1 Thomas Havens, *Valley of Darkness: The Japanese People and World War Two*, Lanham, MD, and London: University Press of America, 1986, p. 12.

2 Gordon Berger, 'Politics and Mobilization in Japan, 1931–1945' in Peter Duus (ed.), *The Cambridge History of Japan, Vol. 6, The Twentieth Century*, Cambridge: Cambridge University Press, 1988, p. 133.

3 Peter Duus, *The Rise of Modern Japan*, Boston, MA: Houghton Mifflin, 1976, p. 222.

4 Quoted in Yoshiko Miyake, 'Doubling Expectations: Motherhood and Women's Factory Work Under State Management in Japan in the 1930s and 1940s' in Gail Bernstein (ed.), *Recreating Japanese Women, 1600–1945*, Berkeley, Los Angeles and Oxford: University of California Press, 1991, p. 274.

5 Saguchi Kazurō, 'The Historical Significance of the Industrial Patriotic Association: Labor Relations in the Total-War State' in Yasushi Yamanouchi, J. Victor Koschmann and Ryūichi Narita, *Total War and Mobilization*, Ithaca, NY: East Asia Program, Cornell University, 1998, p. 283.

6 Quoted in Havens, *Valley of Darkness*, p. 72.

7 Ibid., p. 88.

8 John Dower, *War Without Mercy: Race and Power in the Pacific War*, London, and Boston, MA: Faber and Faber, 1986, p. 213.

9 Ibid., p. 43.

10 Quoted in Joyce Lebra (ed.), *Japan's Greater East Asia Co-Prosperity Sphere in World War II, Selected Readings and Documents*, Kuala Lumpur: Oxford University Press, 1975, p. 159.

11 Quoted in Louis Allen, *Singapore, 1941–1942*, London: Davis-Poynter, 1977, p. 259.

12 Quoted in Lebra (ed.), *Japan's Greater East Asia Co-Prosperity Sphere*, pp. 127–8.

13 Joyce Lebra, *Japanese-Trained Armies in Southeast Asia: Independence and Volunteer Forces in World War II*, New York: Columbia University Press, 1977, p. 157.

14 Ibid., p. 107.

15 Michael Weiner, *Race and Migration in Imperial Japan*, London and New York: Routledge, 1994, p. 198.

16 Tessa Morris-Suzuki, *Shōwa: An Inside History of Hirohito's Japan*, Sydney: Methuen, 1984, p. 98.

17 Haruko Taya Cook and Theodore F. Cook, *Japan at War: An Oral History*, New York: The New Press, 1992, p. 239.

18 Morris-Suzuki, *Shōwa*, p. 105.

19 Ibid., p. 186.

9 'Enduring the unendurable' and starting over in the 'new' Japan

1 John Dower, *Embracing Defeat: Japan in the Wake of World War II*, New York: W.W. Norton, 1999, p. 27.

2 Haruko Taya Cook and Theodore Cook, *Japan at War: An Oral History*, New York: The New Press, 1992, p. 478.

3 Quoted in ibid., p. 41.

4 Richard B. Finn, *Winners in Peace: MacArthur, Yoshida and Postwar Japan*, Berkeley, Los Angeles and Oxford: University of California Press, 1992, p. 11.
5 Dower, *Embracing Defeat*, p. 324.
6 Joseph Anderson and Donald Richie, *The Japanese Film: Art and Industry* (expanded edition), Princeton, NJ: Princeton University Press, 1982, p. 177.
7 Quoted in Dower, *Embracing Defeat*, p. 265, and Finn, *Winners in Peace*, p. 114.
8 Quoted in Dower, *Embracing Defeat*, p. 270.
9 The words of Frank Kowalski, a SCAP army colonel who worked with Japanese on formation of the National Police Reserve. Finn, *Winners in Peace*, p. 266.
10 Quoted in Dower, *Embracing Defeat*, p. 550.
11 Ibid., p. 551.
12 Translated in ibid., p. 553.
13 Yoshida Shigeru, *The Yoshida Memoirs*, trans. Yoshida Kenichi, Boston, MA: Houghton Mifflin, 1962, p. 60.

10 Conflict and consensus in the 1950s

1 Andrew Gordon, *The Evolution of Labor Relations in Japan: Heavy Industry, 1853–1955*, Cambridge, MA: Council on East Asian Studies, Harvard University, 1988, p. 383.
2 Ibid., p. 384.
3 Ronald Dore, *City Life in Japan: A Study of a Tokyo Ward*, Berkeley and Los Angeles: University of California Press, 1967.
4 Emperor Jimmu was the mythical first emperor of Japan, descendant of the Sun Goddess Amaterasu.
5 Yutaka Kōsai, 'The Postwar Japanese Economy, 1945–1973' in Peter Duus (ed.), *The Cambridge History of Japan, Vol. 6, The Twentieth Century*, Cambridge: Cambridge University Press, p. 512.
6 Ibid., p. 515.
7 The 1960 figure compares with 34.9 per cent spent on food in the United States and 39.8 per cent in West Germany. Hiroshi Hazama, 'Historical Changes in the Life Style of Industrial Workers' in Hugh Patrick (ed.), *Japanese Industrialization and Its Social Consequences*, Berkeley, Los Angeles and London: University of California Press, p. 43.
8 For example, for her role in *Teahouse of the August Moon* as well as in the critically acclaimed *Rashomon*, directed by Kurosawa Akira, which won the 1951 Venice Festival prize.
9 For example, Kurosawa's *Seven Samurai* and Mizoguchi's *A Story from Chikamatsu* came out in 1954.
10 Ezra Vogel, *Japan's New Middle Class*, Berkeley, Los Angeles and London: University of California Press, 1971 (2nd edn), p. 71.

11 The 'economic miracle' . . . and its underside

1 Hugh Patrick and Henry Rosovsky, *Asia's New Giant: How the Japanese Economy Works*, Washington, DC: Brookings Institution, 1976.
2 Quoted in Laura Hein, 'Growth Versus Success: Japan's Economic Policy in Historical Perspective' in Andrew Gordon (ed.), *Postwar Japan as History*, Berkeley, Los Angeles and Oxford: University of California Press, 1993, p. 100.
3 Yutaka Kōsai, 'The Postwar Japanese Economy, 1945–1973' in Peter Duus (ed.), *The Cambridge History of Japan, Vol. 6, The Twentieth Century*, Cambridge: Cambridge University Press, p. 512.
4 Marilyn Ivy, 'Formations of Mass Culture' in Gordon (ed.), *Postwar Japan as History*, p. 250.

5 These percentages were derived from the new system of national accounts begun in 1955. According to the old system, the figures were 13.4 per cent for 1955 and 25.1 per cent for 1973. Charles Horioka, 'Consuming and Saving' in Gordon (ed.), *Postwar Japan as History*, p. 283.
6 Quoted in Frank Upham, 'Unplaced Persons and Movements for Place' in Gordon (ed.), *Postwar Japan as History*, p. 338.

12 The 'rich country'

1 One wonders whether Ridley Scott deliberately named his film after Ibuse Masuji's famous postwar novel about the survivors of the Hiroshima atomic bombing. It is also coincidental that the well-regarded Japanese director Imamura Shōhei made a film from Ibuse's novel in 1989 too, which was a critique of Japanese social traditions and discrimination against survivors of the bomb. Imamura's film was held up for release in the United States so that it would not be confused with Scott's movie. Quote from Ebert's review in *Cinemania 96*, CD-Rom.
2 Norma Chalmers, *Industrial Relations in Japan: The Peripheral Workforce*, London and New York: Routledge, 1989, p. 53.
3 Quoted in Frank Upham, 'Unplaced Persons and Movements for Place' in Andrew Gordon (ed.), *Postwar Japan as History*, Berkeley, Los Angeles and Oxford: University of California Press, 1993, p. 331.
4 Quoted in Georgina Stevens, 'The Ainu and Human Rights: Domestic and International Legal Protections', *Japanese Studies*, 21 (2) (September 2001), p. 187.
5 Quote from *The Japan Times* in Richard Siddle, 'The Ainu: Construction of an Image' in John Maher and Gaynor Macdonald (eds), *Diversity in Japanese Culture and Language*, London and New York: Kegan Paul International, 1995, p. 90.

13 The 'lost decade'

1 Yukio Noguchi, 'The "Bubble" and Economic Policies in the 1980s', *Journal of Japanese Studies*, 20 (2) (summer 1994), p. 300.
2 'Editorial', *The Daily Yomiuri*, 3 June 2000, p. 6; also in *Yomiuri shinbun*, 3 June 2000.
3 Kozo Yamamura, 'The Japanese Political Economy after the "Bubble": Plus Ça Change?', *Journal of Japanese Studies*, 23 (2) (summer 1997), p. 291 n. 1.
4 Ibid., p. 318.
5 Kaye Broadbent and Tessa Morris-Suzuki, 'Women and Industrialisation in Japan', paper presented at 'Costed, Not Valued: Women Workers in Industrialising Asia' Conference, University of New England, Armidale, Australia, 1998.
6 Kamiya Setsuko, 'Spoiled Kids Reared on Expectations, not Values', *The Japan Times*, 30 May 2000, p. 3. This was the sixth article in a series on the 'rising generation'.

Index

Abe Nobuyuki 130
Adachi Ginkō 66
agrarian economy 6, 8, 10–13, 20, 111–15,
116, 117, 150
Ainus 63, 64, 65, 201–2
Aizawa Seishisai 30
Aizu 33, 40
Akutagawa Ryūnosuke 105
anarchists 81–2, 95, 97, 98, 106
Andō Shōeki 20
Araki Sadao 117, 118
arms limitation 90, 119, 120
art works 6–7, 8, 44–5, 69, 70, 75
Ashio 81
assassinations 29, 31, 41, 43, 116
atrocities 122, 126, 136–7, 134, 207, 227
Aum Shinrikyō 224
Aung San 136, 137
Axis alliance (1940) 122, 130

Baltzer, Franz 67
Beasley, William G. 14, 30
Beate Sirota 152
Beckmann, George 96
Berger, Gordon 130
Besshi 81
Black Monday (1987) 196
Bolitho, Harold 22
bright life (*akarui seikatsu*) 164, 167–74
Buck, Pearl 122
Buddhism 38, 46, 67–8, 98, 180, 212
Burakumin 44, 65, 88, 97–8, 176, 185–6,
199–200
Burma 136, 137, 138
Bush, George 208

Carnegie, Andrew 84
censorship 52, 95, 114, 127, 128, 137, 147,
148, 153
Chalmers, Norma 198–9
Chamberlain, Basil 64, 69

Chiang Kai-Shek 121, 122, 130
Chichibu uprising (1884) 51
Chikamatsu Monzaemon 10
China: Arrow War 26; Boxer Rebellion
(1900) 77; communism 156; German
territories (Shandong) 89, 90, 120;
Incident (1937) 122, 125; Japanese
atrocities 122, 134, 207, 227; Japanese
victory (1895) 48, 55, 63; Korea 73, 74;
Manchu dynasty overthrown (1911)
121; Manchuria *see* Manchuria; May
Fourth Movement (1919) 90; Opium
War (1839–41) 22, 25; reunification
121; Shanghai 114, 122; Sino-Japanese
War *see* Sino-Japanese War; territorial
losses 76; trade 3, 76, 89, 91; Treaty of
Shimonoseki (1895) 76; Twenty-One
Demands 89, 92, 119; United States 23,
122, 190
Chisso 188
Chōshū 15, 22, 30, 31, 32, 33, 34, 39, 40,
42, 43, 51, 58, 74, 91
Christianity 3, 48, 80, 81
civil service 84, 85, 201
Coaldrake, William 66
Cold War 151, 156, 164, 174, 179, 190
comfort women 126, 135, 226–7
communism 37, 96, 97, 98, 106, 114, 142,
148, 156, 157, 176, 185, 193
Conder, Josiah 46
conflict and consensus: 1950s 161–76
Confucianism 5, 15, 20, 38, 55, 59, 60, 83,
180, 203
conservative hegemony 162–4
Constitution (1889) 56–9, 65, 68, 94, 96,
129, 151
Constitution (1946) 144, 151–3, 155, 156,
158, 159
consumerism 102–4, 182–90, 220–2
Coolidge, Archibald Cary 77–8
cotton industry 50, 80, 95